ALSO BY BARNEY FRANK

Speaking Frankly: What's Wrong with the Democrats and How to Fix It

FRANK

FRANK

A LIFE IN POLITICS
FROM THE GREAT SOCIETY
TO SAME-SEX MARRIAGE

BARNEY FRANK

PICADOR   FARRAR, STRAUS AND GIROUX   NEW YORK

FRANK. Copyright © 2015 by Barney Frank. All rights reserved. Printed in the United States of America. For information, address Picador, 175 Fifth Avenue, New York, N.Y. 10010.

picadorusa.com • picadorbookroom.tumblr.com
twitter.com/picadorusa • facebook.com/picadorusa

Picador® is a U.S. registered trademark and is used by Farrar, Straus and Giroux under license from Pan Books Limited.

For book club information, please visit facebook.com/picadorbookclub or e-mail marketing@picadorusa.com.

Designed by Jonathan D. Lippincott

The Library of Congress has cataloged the Farrar, Straus and Giroux edition as follows:

Frank, Barney, 1940–
    Frank : a life in politics from the Great Society to same-sex marriage / Barney Frank.
        p.   cm.
    Includes index.
    ISBN 978-0-374-28030-7 (hardcover)
    ISBN 978-0-374-71142-9 (e-book)
    1. Frank, Barney, 1940–   2. Legislators—United States—Biography.   3. United States. Congress. House—Biography.   4. Gay legislators—United States—Biography.   5. Politicians—Massachusetts—Biography.   6. United States—Politics and government—1945–1989.   7. United States—Politics and government—1989–   I. Title.   II. Title: A life in politics from the Great Society to same-sex marriage.
    E840.8.F72 A3 1990
    328.73'092—dc23
    [B]

                                                                        2014040383

Picador Paperback ISBN 978-1-250-08326-5

Our books may be purchased in bulk for promotional, educational, or business use. Please contact your local bookseller or the Macmillan Corporate and Premium Sales Department at 1-800-221-7945, extension 5442, or by e-mail at MacmillanSpecialMarkets@macmillan.com.

First published by Farrar, Straus and Giroux

First Picador Edition: March 2016

10   9   8   7   6   5   4   3   2   1

To Jim, who made "better late than never"
my all-time favorite cliché

Contents

FRANK

FROM BAYONNE TO BOSTON

In 1954, I was a fairly normal fourteen-year-old, enjoying sports, unhealthy food, and loud music. But even then I realized that there were two ways in which I was different from the other guys: I was attracted to the idea of serving in government and I was attracted to the other guys.

I also realized that these two attractions would not mix well. At the time, public officials were highly regarded. The president, Dwight Eisenhower, was one of America's most admired and respected military heroes. I was a homosexual, an involuntary member of one of America's most despised groups. I knew that achieving success in any area where popularity was required would be impossible, given the unpopularity of my sexual orientation.

If this were fiction, a spoiler alert would now be appropriate, because the story ends with a dramatic turnabout. When I retired from Congress in January 2013, the divergent reputations of elected officials and homosexuality persisted, but with one major difference: The order was reversed. Legal protections for lesbian, gay, bisexual, and transgender people were more popular than elected officials as a class. Congress was held in particularly low esteem. While I did not do any polling on the subject myself, I was told that my marriage to my husband, Jim Ready, scored better than my service in the House.

When I first entered public life in 1968, I had to figure out how to keep the public's negative feelings about my sexual orientation from interfering with my political effectiveness. By the time I'd overcome that obstacle, a larger one appeared: the growing unpopularity of government itself, and the consequent diminution of its capacity to assist the unfortunate. My influence over the political system grew even as the system's influence diminished. This was good for my self-esteem but bad for my public policy agenda.

This book is a personal history of two seismic shifts in American life: the sharp drop in prejudice against LGBT people and the equally sharp increase in antigovernment opinion. During my six decades in the public realm, Americans have become more accepting of once-despised minorities but also more resistant to coming together through government to improve the quality of our lives. How did this happen and what can be done to further the victories and reverse the defeats?

The many years I've spent advocating unpopular causes have taught me that it's important to begin with your best case, not in the hope of making instant converts but to persuade your audience that there is room for debate about a subject. Fortunately, when it comes to attitudes toward government, that case is even better than a no-brainer—it is a pro-brainer: the story of the millions of children who have been protected from brain damage by federal rules that were adopted over the vehement objections and dire predictions of affected industries.

Before 1970, lead was a major component of paint and gasoline. Its corrosive effects, which are uncontested today, had their worst impact on the very young, impairing in particular the development of the brain cells known as neuroglia. All young people were exposed to lead, and poorer children were the most exposed, since the paint in their homes was more likely to contain lead and to chip, and because they often lived in crowded urban areas adjacent to heavy traffic flows.

Over the objections of private industry, many public health advocates, especially those focused on children, pressed for action. They were successful. The process began in 1970 with the Clean Air Act, which was followed by the Lead-Based Poisoning Prevention Act a year later. A series of amendments and implementing regulations steadily increased the restrictions, culminating in 1978 with a ban on lead in paint, and a statute enacted in 1990 and effective in 1995 prohibiting lead in gasoline.

Critics of government regulation should heed all of this carefully. As the prohibitions came into effect, the incidence of death and illness from lead ingestion dropped drastically. Between 1975 and 1980 and 2007 and 2008, lead levels in children's blood dropped 90 percent. In 1990, the FDA estimated there were already seventy thousand fewer children with IQs below seventy because of the rules.

The paint and gasoline industries denied that lead was harmful in the amounts present in their products and predicted severe economic harm if they had to remove it. They were never able to explain why banning lead in fact coincided not just with fewer brain-damaged children but also with their own continued prosperity. Lead-damaged brains still exist, sadly, and there is more to be done to reduce the number. But the undeniable fact is that millions of Americans have healthy brains today in large part because, contrary to the old joke, some people from the government did come to help them.

•

In 1954, the government was still popular, but homosexuals were held in universal contempt. This had been made explicit the previous year when President Eisenhower issued an executive order decreeing that people like me could never receive security clearances. We were too inherently untrustworthy to help protect our country from its enemies.

I do not remember being specifically aware of the order at the time, but as an avid newspaper reader growing up in Bayonne, New Jersey, I must have seen the *New York Times* headline that referred to us as "perverts," and I was fully aware of what awaited me if my true nature was known. (I say "true nature" for the edification of that dwindling set of bigots who justify mistreating us because we "chose an alternative lifestyle." Being hated is rarely an experience sought by teenagers.)

At fourteen, I decided I would keep my sexual identity a secret forever, although I didn't give much thought to how that was going to work. Terrified by the obloquy that would come with being found out, I regarded total concealment as my only option. The recognition that there could be no role for a "queer" in public life had an additional and deep emotional impact: It is very probably the reason that I later approached every tough election campaign with the assumption I would lose.

A televised Senate hearing first inspired my fascination with government. My father was what we now call an "early adopter." When I was born in 1940, he celebrated by buying a television set—before almost everybody else and before there was much to watch. I have early memories of Western movies, the second Billy Conn–Joe Louis fight, *Howdy Doody*, and Senator Estes Kefauver's investigation into organized crime. I enjoyed all the programs, but I never wanted to be a cowboy, a boxer, or a puppeteer. I preferred the idea of sitting behind an impressive dais grilling colorful Mafiosi. At ten, I was more intrigued than instructed, but when another set of hearings came on the TV four years later, I was hooked by both the spectacle and the subject matter. This was the Army-McCarthy brawl.

In 1954, Senator Joseph McCarthy turned his demagogic attention to the U.S. Army. The army had just finished fighting two Communist regimes in Korea—but this did not stop McCarthy from deeming it soft on communism. The army hired the Boston lawyer Joseph Welch as its lead counsel in the Senate hearings that were held on McCarthy's accusations.

Welch became a hero to Americans in general, and liberals in particular, for the deftness of his anti-McCarthy thrusts. One of the deftest was his sly allusion to the sexual orientation of McCarthy's chief aide, Roy Cohn. A closeted gay man, Cohn would angrily denounce any attempt to "out" him until the day he died of AIDS-related illnesses decades later.

In questioning one of McCarthy's assistants, Welch asked him if he was contending that a certain photograph had come from "a pixie." Unwisely trying to turn Welch's sarcasm against him, McCarthy intervened and asked Welch to define "pixie." Welch pounced. "A pixie," he gleefully explained, "is a close relative of a fairy." This devastating use of anti-gay prejudice to demean Cohn added greatly to Welch's reputation and went wholly unrebuked even by those liberals who rightly considered themselves America's staunchest opponents of bigotry.

I was among the nonrebukers. I was glad to see Welch score heavily against the McCarthy side. I accepted the widespread contempt for homosexuals as an indelible fact of life. It never occurred to me to fault Welch for expressing it. Indeed, those hearings—in which an anti-gay slur played such a highly praised part—made a very favorable impression on me and kindled my interest in public life.

That interest was greatly intensified by the murder of Emmett Till. Till, an African American from Chicago, was about my age. While he was visiting relatives in Mississippi, some men thought he had been disrespectful to a white woman. No one alleged that he had done more than whistle at her, and even that was disputed, but the price he paid was to be brutally murdered. It was clear that local law enforcement knew who had killed him. They had no objection to his death, and certainly no intention of doing anything to the killers. I was outraged. I soon learned that the federal government could do little to prevent such horrors because Southern senators had successfully filibustered antilynching laws passed by the House. I took from this an enduring belief in the need for a strong federal government. After all, Southern racists were able to protect murderers only because their legislators exploited fears of centralized power. Changing this reality would be an important goal for me.

Civil liberties and civil rights were not the only causes that inspired strong convictions. My parents were not involved in politics, but they were staunch liberals. In our very Jewish but largely secular household, the nearest thing we had to a Bible was the then very liberal *New York Post*. I supported the Franklin Roosevelt–Harry Truman tradition of active government intervention to make our society a fair one. My interests did not become wholly political, but they broadened. By the 1954 midterm elections, I was rooting equally for the Democrats and the Yankees.

I was also thinking more often about how much I would like to take part in governing. The fast-paced verbal combat I'd seen on TV appealed to me. I was good at talking in class, arguing politics and sports with my peers, and making people laugh, often at the expense of my debate adversaries. After the Till murder, I also wanted to make America conform more closely to my ideals.

But I was a Jewish homosexual. While I planned to keep my sexual orientation a secret, it was too late to conceal my Jewishness—I had already outed myself with a bar mitzvah. In 1954, anti-Semitism was still a significant problem facing Jews in our choice of careers. We were rarities in elected office and held congressional seats almost entirely in areas with large Jewish populations—a few neighborhoods in a handful of big cities. The one exception—Senator Richard Neuberger of Oregon—was widely known because he was so unusual. But Jews were not hindered when it came to achieving appointed office—"Jew Deal" was one of the epithets thrown at FDR's administration. Knowing this, I figured that I could work as someone's aide—as long as I kept my sexuality hidden.

•

In 1956, I volunteered to work on Adlai Stevenson's second presidential campaign. It wasn't fun, but it was the beginning of my education in political reality. Bayonne is a blue-collar community in New Jersey's Hudson County, very close to New York City. The population was overwhelmingly ethnic—Polish, Irish, and Italian—and Catholic. Politically, it was the domain of one of America's most ruthless and corrupt political machines. (Hoboken, a few miles from Bayonne and very much like it, was accurately portrayed in the 1954 movie *On the Waterfront*.) I naïvely expected to be a small cog in a well-oiled campaign on behalf of our Democratic nominee. In fact, the Democrats who controlled the county had no great sympathy for Stevenson and even less for the idea of liberals getting involved in politics. The Volunteers for Stevenson effort I joined had been set up by the machine under the leadership of a reliable political lieutenant and was given little to do. It soon dawned on me that not all Democrats shared my passion for advancing the liberal agenda—protecting its fiefdom was far more important for the county organization.

The organization's concerns turned out to be well founded. Across the bay in New York, Stevenson campaign alumni led by Eleanor Roosevelt would stick together and eventually overthrow the Tammany Hall machine. In 1961, Carmine DeSapio, the legendary Tammany Hall boss and Greenwich Village district leader, lost a primary to a leader of the new "reformers." When DeSapio attempted a comeback two years later, he lost to another political newcomer, Edward Koch.

The Hudson County machine proved less vulnerable. But its leaders could see that a cultural chasm was opening between the college-educated progressives who were Stevenson's most devoted fans and the white working-class voters who were their mainstays. After one of Stevenson's eloquent, intellectually sophisticated speeches, a supporter told him he would "get the votes of all the thinking people." "Thank you, madam," he replied, "but I need a majority." As with Joseph Welch, a widely admired and oft-quoted remark was more than a clever quip—it was an expression of a deeper political reality. The condescension in Stevenson's comment did not bother his admirers, but it did not help him with the wider public.

Such tensions would remain submerged for the next few years. In 1960, John F. Kennedy's charisma and ethnoreligious appeal kept them at bay, and in 1964, Barry Goldwater's self-acknowledged conservative extremism rendered them irrelevant. But by 1966, the alienation of the white working class had become a serious problem for Democrats, as it remains. Today, most white men vote for Republican presidential candidates even in races that Democrats win. The only identifiable groups of white men who vote reliably for Democrats are Jews and gays.

In 1956, the same year I worked for Stevenson, the Soviet Union brutally suppressed the revolt against tyranny in Hungary. It confirmed my conviction that America, with all of its faults, was morally superior to the Soviet system, and that helping nations resist Communist domination was a valid objective. At the time, my revulsion did not seem to me controversial. It struck me as entirely consistent with my liberal views—Hungary, after all, was Emmett Till multiplied by tens of thousands. Given its earlier suppression of dissent in East Germany, and its crackdown in Poland, I believed—then and subsequently—that the Soviet Union was indeed the head of an evil empire, and I was never one of the liberals who mocked Ronald Reagan for saying so. It was not until I entered Harvard, in September 1957, that I learned that my judgment was not universally shared by others on the left side of the political divide.

•

This was not the only difference between my version of liberalism and the views I encountered in Cambridge. In Bayonne, I saw the political world divided neatly into liberals—mostly Democrats—and conservatives—mostly Republicans, with the large exception of the Southern defenders of racism. Now, for the first time, I encountered people who were to my left—not only in their attitude toward the Soviet Union but also in their view of America's cultural and economic situation.

My relationship to ideologues on my left is well illustrated by my reaction to the folk singer Pete Seeger. Though I disagreed with the political message of his lyrics, like most of my schoolmates, I was appalled when Harvard president Nathan Pusey inexplicably banned him from performing a concert in 1961 because Seeger had refused to answer questions from the House Un-American Activities Committee about any Communist affiliation. This act of censorship struck us as particularly strange because Pusey had come to Harvard from Wisconsin, where he had distinguished himself by standing up to Senator McCarthy at the height of his strength. In the face of the widespread opposition, Pusey compromised, announcing that Seeger would be allowed to sing from a Harvard stage but not make a speech. Since Seeger communicated his views most effectively in his songs, Pusey was alone in thinking that he had saved face, and the concert proceeded with little further controversy.

A year later, when I heard Seeger sing "Little Boxes," I recognized the gulf that divided me from many others on the left. The song was a mockery of the postwar housing that had been built for working-class and lower-middle-class Americans. "Little boxes on the hillside," the lyrics went. "And they're all made out of ticky-tacky and they all look just the same." At one concert I attended at Harvard, most of the audience—filling Harvard's largest venue—appeared to find this a hilariously accurate critique. They were oblivious of the fact that these "little boxes" had been built on a large scale to be affordable by families who would not otherwise have been able to be homeowners. The aesthetic disdain Seeger and many of my fellow students felt for these units was not, I knew, shared by the occupants, most of whom were happy—and proud—to own them. These occupants were, after all, the kinds of people I had grown up with in Bayonne and whom I had dealt with pumping gas at my father's Jersey City truck stop. And I knew they disagreed completely with Seeger's critique. The mass production of homes for working families was an example of our capitalist system's efficiency. But Seeger, and many of his listeners, preferred to think that the capitalist profit-making system was depriving people with limited incomes of the chance to live in large, individually designed houses—which they of course could not afford. When I insisted that the inhabitants of this "ticky-tacky" were very satisfied with their "little boxes," I was often told that they did not have the knowledge—or the sensibility—to know they were being mistreated.

In fact, as I later came to understand, few of those homes were built by the private sector alone. A large number of the occupants were returning World War II veterans, and they were able to afford even moderately priced homes only because of one of the great triumphs of U.S. government social policy—the package of veterans' benefits enacted after the war. Unfortunately, this positive example of how government can improve the quality of our lives was soon to be ignored, even by many of its beneficiaries. Years later, Tip O'Neill would lament that government policies helped create a solid middle class, only for many members of that class to become the government's staunchest critics.

During my undergraduate years—1957 to 1962—the existence of people to my left was more interesting to me intellectually than it was relevant politically. Even so, debates with the campus left sharpened my beliefs. Why, I was asked, if I so strongly desired a more equal distribution of wealth, was I not a Socialist?

I knew that embracing socialism—even the most democratic form of it—would end any chance I had for a government position, but I was not prepared to let expediency be my only answer. Fortunately, my academic work came to my rescue. I entered my freshman year ready to concentrate—Harvard's word for major—in government. Given my interest in public policy, I also enrolled in the basic economics course, and I was pleasantly surprised to find that I had both an intellectual fascination with the discipline and an affinity for it. If I had not been skeptical of my mathematical skills (justifiably—calculus scared me off), I would probably have switched to that field. As it was, I took as many nonmathematical economics courses as I could fit into my schedule. Those classes made it clear to me that the best system was one where the creation of wealth relied primarily on market mechanisms—with a strong government providing appropriate regulation, lessening inequality without destroying incentives, and playing an active role when necessary to keep the economy functioning at high levels of employment.

My academic work affected more than my political ideology—it also shaped my career plans. During my first two years in college, I'd aspired to become a lawyer. As a solo practitioner, I figured I could readily hide my sexuality, while remaining available for government appointments if any were offered.

But in my junior year, an alternative arose. One of my instructors in the Government Department, Douglas Hobbs, flatteringly told me he thought I should seriously consider pursuing a Ph.D. and becoming a college professor. I hadn't previously considered this, but the idea had a great deal of appeal. I greatly enjoyed reading, thinking, and talking about politics, and the notion of doing this for a living was very tempting. This was, incidentally, the beginning of a pattern: Until my retirement, all of my major career choices were originally proposed by someone else.

In April 1960, at the end of my junior year, my father died suddenly of a heart attack. I finished the last month of the semester and returned home. Taking a leave from school, I spent much of the ensuing six months helping my mother settle my father's estate. At the time, my sister Ann was married and beginning to raise her young family, my sister Doris was seventeen and just about to start college, and my brother, David, was ten.

My task was to get a fair price from my father's old business partner for our share of the truck stop and also for a piece of property they had been developing together. Unfortunately, relations between my father and his partner had soured, and we believed the partner was trying to take advantage of us. As a result, I turned to friends of my father who had Mafia connections to improve our negotiating position. By the fall we were able to work things out. With a little additional help from my father's friends, we realized enough money from the settlement that I was able to return to college in September, and my siblings were able to continue their educations. We also benefited from the Social Security payments that were available to dependents of an eligible parent who had died. Together these funds helped my family stay solvent until my brother entered high school and my mother was able to return to her work as a legal secretary. She had been an excellent one before her marriage and became a reasonably well-compensated, first-rate legal secretary again.

I returned to Harvard in September 1961. By that time, the Kennedy administration was employing a conspicuous number of the university's professors. One joke at the time asked, "What is the best way to get to Washington?" The answer was, "Go to Harvard Square and turn left." Here was the path I hoped to follow. I would become a professor of political science with a serious interest in public policy economics, and would from time to time emulate John Kenneth Galbraith, Arthur Schlesinger, Jr., and others by taking academic leaves to serve elected officials whom I supported. As to my personal life, the university, with its semi-isolation from the rest of the world and its tolerance for differences, was the closest thing I could find to a cloister where my privacy would be safeguarded. I assumed my forays into the outside world would not last long enough for the discrepancies between my life situation and that of most heterosexuals to become apparent. As I was to learn later, many men went to Washington for temporary service without bringing their families with them. As a result, those of us with no spouse were much less conspicuous there than we would have been in other cities.

If I needed any further evidence that my sexual orientation and elected office were incompatible, I received it from one of the most popular political novels of the time: Allen Drury's *Advise and Consent*, which I read during my year off from school. It dramatically demonstrated that the six years since 1954 had seen no change in the respective popularity ratings of government and homosexuality. The plot involved an effort by a devious FDR-like figure to press the Senate into confirming his nominee for secretary of state. One target of the administration's pressure was a bright, conscientious young senator who was highly regarded by his elders. The senator was inclined to vote against the nominee. Then a man came forward who told the president's people that he and the senator—by now happily married with a young daughter—had had a homosexual encounter during World War II. The man produced a photograph supporting his story. Confronted with a choice between voting for a nominee he strongly distrusted and being exposed, the senator killed himself.

Advise and Consent was a major bestseller. In 1962 it was made into a movie with Charles Laughton and Walter Pidgeon playing paragons of public virtue. John F. Kennedy's brother-in-law, Peter Lawford, also appeared as a very appealing senator. The contrast between the movie's manly ethos of public service and the shame of homosexuality was clear.

Fiction and reality were in complete accord. Following Eisenhower's example, the Kennedy administration took its own explicit anti-gay steps. The civil service director John Macy stated that homosexuals were not welcome in federal jobs. And the administration took rapid action to avert the possibility that foreign homosexuals might be allowed into the country.

The prevailing immigration laws excluded several categories of people from even visiting as tourists because of their undesirability. Since the word "homosexual" was too shocking to use when the laws were adopted, the phrase used for our exclusion was "afflicted with a psychopathic personality." Everyone knew that meant us. Even so, this linguistic delicacy suggested an opportunity to a Canadian citizen, Clive Michael Boutilier. After having lived legally in the United States, he was denied citizenship. He challenged the ruling, claiming that the exclusionary language simply did not apply to him. He acknowledged that he was homosexual but denied that this made him a psychopath.

Federal immigration officials feared that the Supreme Court would agree with Boutilier and invalidate the antihomosexual clause. This was the famously liberal Warren Court that included Hugo Black,

William O. Douglas, and William Brennan, and would include Abe Fortas by the time the case reached it in 1967. To forestall the terrible possibility of LGBT people coming freely to the United States, Congress, with the support of the Kennedy and later Johnson administrations, moved successfully to replace the sixty-year-old language with a more explicit ban on "aliens afflicted . . . with sexual deviation." Their fears turned out to have been unjustified: The most liberal Supreme Court in U.S. history ended up ruling that excluding people like me under a denigrating, nonspecific rubric was perfectly acceptable.

In the familiar legal expression, those determined to exclude us wound up with both a belt and suspenders—the new "sexual deviation" language was also included in the Immigration and Nationality Act of 1965. This vaunted legislation was strongly supported by every liberal group in the country. When, more than twenty years later, I succeeded in repealing the exclusion outright, I checked to see if anyone in Congress had opposed it at the time. Nobody had said a word.

It is important to stress that this renewed assault on gay people began in one activist, liberal administration and was carried out by its successor. My sexual orientation remained highly unpopular even while government as a force for societal improvement was at a high point in its approval ratings. It was in this frame of mind that I enrolled in graduate school in Harvard's Government Department. In the prevailing circumstances, I believed an advanced degree would give me the best chance to pursue the kind of career I wanted.

I would later discover a flaw in this plan: I was good at every aspect of scholarship except writing it down. But in the early years that was not a problem. I started teaching undergraduates and was gratified to find that I enjoyed it. Besides teaching, I stepped up my political activity. I participated in Harvard's understated student government and became an active member of the Young Democrats.

It was through my student government work that I met Allard Lowenstein, who would become an essential figure in my political development. Lowenstein was eleven years older; by his late twenties he had already become an activist for all seasons. With the powerful support of Eleanor Roosevelt, the moral leader of post–World

War II liberalism, he was engaged in practical agitation on behalf of a number of causes, including racial justice in the United States and South Africa. We met in 1959 when he came to Cambridge calling for an end to South Africa's brutality toward what was then Southwest Africa (now Namibia). I spent time with him as his appointed driver—the Harvard Student Council was his sponsor—and I found his blend of passionate advocacy and strategic savvy immensely appealing.

I apparently succeeded in convincing him that I was a kindred spirit, and we stayed in touch. In the summer of 1960, I saw him at a National Student Association congress. As a past president of that organization, he remained an inspiration for reform-minded students. In late 1963, during my second year in graduate school, he asked me to take a leadership role in what was to be the Mississippi Summer project of 1964. The prototype for that effort was a campaign to help Aaron Henry, the NAACP's state president, run for governor. At that time—nearly one hundred years after the adoption of the post–Civil War amendments—the great majority of African Americans in Mississippi were disenfranchised. They were kept from the polls by the law and, when necessary, by force.

Violence against black people seeking to register or vote was not news, but assaults on white Yale and Stanford students were. The publicity generated by the Henry campaign inspired Lowenstein and black leaders to try again in 1964 on a larger scale. Since there was no gubernatorial election that year, the effort would have a broader focus: It would contest the near-total disenfranchisement of black Mississippians by challenging the state's delegation to the upcoming Democratic presidential convention, which would be chosen by an all-white electorate.

When Lowenstein withdrew from the campaign after a dispute with more radical activists, my leadership role disappeared, but I was happy to go anyway as a volunteer. My group left our training center in Ohio for Mississippi on the same Sunday that three fellow Freedom Summer participants—local CORE field-workers James Chaney and Michael Schwerner, and volunteer Andrew Goodman—were murdered by a mob that included the local sheriff. When we arrived in Mississippi, we heard that the three had disappeared, and we assumed, correctly, that they were dead.

In order to replace Mississippi's all-white convention delegation with an integrated slate, we planned to create a new organization—the Freedom Democratic Party. I went to obtain the official forms for starting a new party and was pleasantly surprised when the white official I encountered smiled when I said I was working on a third party, and said Governor George Wallace would do well. I felt no need to correct his assumption that I was there to help the Alabama racist who had challenged Lyndon Johnson in some primaries, with distressingly good results.

My work that summer consisted mostly of organizing the presentation of our case. When we feared a local office might be attacked, I spent the night there, although our pledge of nonviolent resistance made me wonder what good we could do. I also made a run to northern Mississippi with another volunteer—Richard Beymer, who played Tony in the movie *West Side Story*—to deliver leaflets. But my direct organizing of Mississippi voters was limited by the fact that my accent (to this day more New Jersey than New England), my poor diction, and my rapid speech, especially when I got excited, rendered me largely incomprehensible to rural Mississippians of both races.

Harking back to my Pete Seeger reaction, I sharply disagreed with much of the Freedom Summer leadership on the larger purpose of our enterprise. They were critics of what they saw as a materialistic, mind-numbing middle-class America. Their goal was not for African Americans to live in ticky-tacky little boxes but to guide them into new forms of economic and social organization, where cooperation replaced competitiveness, and creativity was freed from the deadening bourgeois mind-set. In friendly debates—the threat of violence bound us together—I argued that most black Mississippians wanted to be like most white Americans, though without the vicious racial prejudice. William McCord, who wrote *Mississippi: The Long, Hot Summer* about our experiences, accurately summarized—and quoted—my view:

> While he worked hard for the Negro cause in Mississippi, Frank did not fall prey to utopian illusions: "This ideology of nonviolence is fine, but when it comes to defending my

home, I side with those who keep a rifle by the door." As for
the future, he did not believe that Negro progress would
usher in a millennium. "As conditions improve—and they
will—the Negro will seek his spot in suburbia, drink his
beer, and watch TV. That's fine! Some of these people think
that they are going to reform our entire civilization and that
the Negro will be the spearhead of this new age. Not me. I'm
not here to build a perfect society, just to insure that the
Negro gets a chance to live his life in his own way. If these liberals have the same illusions about the Negro that they used
to hold about unions, they are bound for the same disappointment they had in the thirties."

Meanwhile, I was learning the tactical importance of remaining realistic. We hoped to present a vivid contrast between the segregated Mississippi convention delegation and our own integrated
one. But that required asking courageous delegates to risk certain
ostracism, probable economic retaliation, and possible violence
from the Mississippi establishment and its less savory allies—the
bodies of our three missing comrades had been found. This was
difficult work.

Seeking to gain support from wary politicians, our Washington
office boasted prematurely that we would have a dozen or so whites
on our integrated slate. Since part of my job was to help secure these
people, I knew we would not come close to that number. I urged the
Washington contingent not to make promises we could not keep
that could then be used to discredit us. "Hold your fire until we
hear the ayes of our whites" was my exact message. I was pleased that
the boasts stopped.

For all my disagreements, I was impressed by the movement's
discipline. That summer, most of the country was focused on the
passage of the great national civil rights bill outlawing segregation in
employment and public accommodations. Even so, the Council of
Federated Organizations—which included the NAACP, the Student
Nonviolent Coordinating Committee, the Southern Christian Leadership Conference, and CORE—decided to put the even more funda-

mental right to vote first. This meant asking black Mississippians to temporarily accept the segregation of restaurants and theaters they had earlier braved violence to enter. Setting aside important goals to pursue others more effectively is hard for emotionally committed advocates to accept. Years later, I would strenuously argue the point with LGBT activists.

With my Ph.D. orals scheduled for that September, I had to return to Cambridge to study. I did not try hard to find a way around this scheduling conflict. I had the strong suspicion—which turned out to be valid—that I would disagree with the Freedom Democrats' next steps, and I was not emotionally prepared to argue face-to-face with colleagues I admired so greatly.

On my way north, I stopped in Washington, D.C., to meet with Joseph Rauh. One of the heroic figures of postwar liberalism, Rauh combined excellent legal skills with equally good political judgment. As a lawyer for the United Auto Workers and a longtime ally of Senator—and soon to be vice presidential nominee—Hubert Humphrey, he would find himself in a stressful position at the Democratic convention. When I arrived at his office, he asked me if I was a lawyer. I said "no." He said "good."

My job was to help Rauh compose a brief on behalf of the Freedom Democrats, drawing on information I'd compiled during the summer. By documenting the Mississippi Democratic Party's suppression of black voters, we hoped to bolster the Freedom Democrats' case to be seated at the convention.

Although we had tried to be scrupulously accurate, the ad hoc, underfunded nature of our work, which relied on volunteer fact gatherers who were as unsophisticated as they were brave, made it highly likely that there were some errors. Rauh feared that conservatives, who were strongly entrenched in the organized bar, would go over his brief in great detail, and if they found *any* inaccuracy, exaggeration, or distortion of the facts, would pursue disciplinary proceedings against him. Since the brief was being submitted to the Democratic Party and not to a legal tribunal, no criminal penalties could attach, which meant that a nonlawyer—me—was safe from retribution. Rauh's submission identified me in a footnote as a major source for the information it contained. There are few documents I've ever been prouder to appear in.

The logistical arrangements for my one-day stopover in Washington also brought me into contact with a national political leader whom I had read about and admired but never met. Through my work with the National Student Association, I had become very friendly with two sisters, Barbara and Cokie Boggs (later Barbara Sigmund, mayor of Princeton, and Cokie Roberts of journalistic repute). I knew their family home was a large one in the D.C. suburbs, and I asked if I could spend the night there.

Cokie showed me to a very comfortable room in the basement. The next morning, I went upstairs to the dining room, where her father, Congressman Hale Boggs, was having breakfast. Boggs was an important leader in the House and a close ally of Lyndon Johnson. He was in a potentially dangerous situation because Johnson's embrace of civil rights was not popular in his New Orleans district. His district was also adjacent to Mississippi, and our delegation was seeking to unseat his colleagues there. That fall, his wife, Lindy, would be Lady Bird Johnson's traveling companion on a whistle-stop tour through the South that was intended to counteract the appeal of Barry Goldwater and his vote against the civil rights bill.

I soon realized that Cokie and Barbara had not warned their father I would be visiting. As he later told them, when I came up from the basement, blinking in the light, he assumed at first that I was the exterminator or some other such workman, and he was taken aback when I sat down and poured myself a cup of coffee. After I explained to him who I was and what I was doing there, he asked me, with the graciousness of a Southern gentleman and the concern of a liberal Southern politician, if the accommodations had been comfortable, if the coffee was good, if I needed anything else, and in general if his family's hospitality had been satisfactory. When I enthusiastically answered yes to each question, he said, "Son, in that case I'm going to ask you a favor. Please don't ever tell anybody that you were here."

After I left, Cokie later told me, her father remonstrated with her. Didn't she think he was in enough trouble for seeming too liberal for Louisiana without his daughters turning his house into a stop on the

Underground Railroad? To his enormous credit, in 1965 he became one of the first white Southerners to support a civil rights bill. And with my discretion a minor contributing factor, he became House majority leader a few years later. He would have been the Speaker of the House had he not been lost in a 1972 plane crash in Alaska, where he was campaigning for another member.

At the Atlantic City convention, the Freedom Democrats' demand to supplant the all-white Mississippi delegation was rejected. Given the magnitude of the challenge we were presenting to the status quo, and the fear of Goldwater's already potent appeal to the South, I was not surprised. As a consolation, the party—acting on Johnson's orders, with some influence exerted by Humphrey—offered to seat two Freedom Democrats alongside the official racist group. This was much less than we had pushed for but far more than would have been conceivable only two years before—when John F. Kennedy was accommodating political reality by appointing as a federal judge William Harold Cox, who used the word "nigger" from the bench.

At the time, I expressed the view that the Freedom Democrats should accept the seating offer but state that it left a great deal more to be achieved. If they had done that, it is likely the official delegation would have bolted the convention—and the party—rather than accept the indignity of sharing the spotlight. But the civil rights coalition never tested that possibility: Its response was total rejection and a denunciation of the party's immorality. My mentor Al Lowenstein, more than incidentally, was prepared to support the two-seat offer with one change—allowing the Freedom Democrats to decide who would occupy those seats, rather than acquiesce in the national party's choices. But there was no opportunity to negotiate such a deal in the face of the Freedom Democrats' anger at the very idea of compromise.

As I would argue again and again throughout my career, there is a price to pay for rejecting the partial victories that are typically achieved through political activity. When you do so, you discourage your own foot soldiers, whose continued activity is needed for future victories. You also alienate the legislative partners you need. A very imperfect understanding of game theory is at work here. Advocates often tell me that if they give elected officials credit for incremental successes, they will encounter complacency and lose the ability to push for more. But if you constantly raise your demands without acknowledging that some of them have been satisfied, you will price yourself out of the political marketplace. When members of Congress defy political pressure at home and vote for a part of what you want, they are still taking a risk. Telling them you will accept only 100 percent support is likely to leave you with nothing.

The Mississippi campaign focused on winning the right to vote. In later years, many of its leaders would become disillusioned with the democratic process and turn toward various forms of direct action. When the Vietnam War and civil rights militancy tore the left apart, I remained a staunch advocate of conventional political activity.

●

Well before the summer of 1964, I'd begun working on electoral campaigns. My 1956 Stevenson debacle did not dissuade me from participating in a string of Massachusetts Democrats' bids for office. In those efforts, I met a great number of people who would shape my career. The first of these was a law student named Michael Dukakis. In 1958, he persuaded the Harvard Young Democrats to support a liberal Democratic challenger to an incumbent Republican congressman. I spent Election Day 1958 outside a temple in Brookline handing out literature for our candidate, John Saltonstall, who lost. (Twenty-two years later, that same polling place gave me one of my best margins in my first election to Congress. Nothing could have seemed less likely to me at the time.)

In the 1960 presidential race, I once again supported the intellectuals' hero, Adlai Stevenson, and helped organize Harvard for his campaign. Like many liberals, I was skeptical of his rival, John F. Kennedy. But as the presidential convention neared, I began to have doubts about my choice. Kennedy's main opponent for the nomination that spring was Senator Hubert Humphrey. He was unquestionably the most effective liberal leader in the Congress, but he had lost to Kennedy in several primaries. I remember being impressed by Arthur Schlesinger's summary of the situation: "I am nostalgically for

Stevenson, ideologically for Humphrey, and realistically for Kennedy." By that summer, I was a convert to Schlesinger's view. At the time, many disenchanted leftists claimed that Kennedy and Nixon were virtually indistinguishable. Once again Schlesinger emerged as the spokesman for those of us on the realistic side, quickly writing *Kennedy or Nixon: Does It Make Any Difference?*, which made the case for Kennedy from the left. I have often reminded friends who lament the passing of the good old days when we had inspiring leaders like President Kennedy that people with attitudes similar to theirs were usually critics of Kennedy at the time.

I ended up campaigning for Kennedy in New Jersey, since the election coincided with the time I spent at home following my father's death. When I returned to Harvard in 1961, I joined the primary campaign of Attorney General Edward McCormack, who was running for the president's former Senate seat against Ted Kennedy. McCormack was a courageous liberal, and I believed the president needed to be pressured by the left. I have never, retrospectively, been so happy that someone I admired so much was defeated, but I still believe that supporting McCormack was the right decision at the time. In his forty-seven years in office, Ted Kennedy would become the most effective advocate of racial justice, economic fairness, and the protection of various groups against discrimination ever to serve in Congress. How could I have voted against him in his first race? On this point, my only defense is the one I have heard attributed to Samuel Bernstein, who was chided for not letting his son put more time into music: "Who knew he would turn into Leonard Bernstein?"

Over the next several years, the choice between conventional political activity and direct action became sharper. Riots in African American neighborhoods and antiwar demonstrations inside and outside universities increased the tensions within the old Democratic coalition. In 1964, I'd amiably debated strategy with my comrades in Mississippi. Only one year later, the amiability was replaced by anger. The militant left was contemptuous of liberals, whom they saw as morally corrupt, spineless, or both. In fact, progress was speeding up on the racial front: The stated goal of the Mississippi Summer was significantly advanced by passage of the Voting Rights Act in 1965.

Of course, vigorous demonstrations, which were met with brutal violence, played a role in winning national political support for the act. But once national legislation was passed, and African Americans got the vote, they most often recognized that the ballot was a superior means of fighting for what they needed.

In 1966, I was appointed director of student affairs at the Institute of Politics at the John F. Kennedy School, which Harvard had recently established in the wake of the president's death. (Despite my work for his political adversary McCormack, Ted Kennedy made no objection.) The new position elevated the role of politics in my life—to the further detriment of my putative scholarly work. It also raised my profile in the political world, not always for the better.

One of my major institute responsibilities was to run the Visiting Fellows program, which brought important people—usually high government officials—to Harvard for meetings with students. To facilitate genuine conversation, and to give students a chance to see major public figures in an intimate setting, we organized private sessions that were closed to the media. Even two years earlier this would have been a popular approach. But by the fall of 1966, the government's conduct of the Vietnam War had become emblematic of antidemocratic secrecy and a lack of public accountability. In a decision that I count, in hindsight, among the stupidest in which I ever participated, we invited Defense Secretary Robert McNamara to Cambridge. In another, which comes close on the stupidity scale, I decided I could handle the logistics myself, giving little thought to the depth of antiwar anger. During his visit, McNamara's car was mobbed by irate students as we tried to get him to his next appointment—note of historical interest: It was to a seminar run by Henry Kissinger. He was rescued by a flying squad of Harvard and Cambridge policemen, and with a composure that I greatly admired, he proceeded to carry out the rest of his program. But the spectacle of the U.S. secretary of defense being temporarily captured by a mob of Harvard students reverberated around the world. That it happened just before the midterm congressional elections magnified the embarrassment—to the Johnson administration, Harvard, the institute, and me.

In response to this episode, some undergraduates circulated a petition among their fellow students that apologized to McNamara, while making clear that this apology in no way indicated support for the war. Two of the leading organizers, James Segel and Richard Morningstar, were students of mine. They became friends and would be close political confederates throughout my career.

The most enduring impact of the McNamara incident was on me. Here was the most important responsibility I had ever been given, and I had conspicuously failed to carry it out. I was furious at the personal criticism leveled at me—especially from the leaders of a new organization, Students for a Democratic Society. And I deeply regretted any political damage inflicted on the Democrats, whose losses in the 1966 election did nothing to retard the war effort but did put an end to hopes for further progress on the social and economic fronts. Most profoundly, I feared that the growing prevalence of angry, uncivil disobedience would deepen the socioeconomic split in the coalition for stronger government action. Of course, the temporary capture of McNamara did not do this by itself, but as a visible symbol of successful disruption, it enhanced the tactic's appeal to many on the left, particularly younger people. In a political application of Newtonian physics, the growing popularity of such rhetoric and behavior provoked an equal and opposite reaction from older whites, for whom patriotism was an important value. (Remember that in the late 1960s, World War II veterans were a significant part of the population.)

•

In November 1966, not long after the McNamara fracas, I received a phone call from Michael Dukakis. The young law student I'd met as an undergraduate was now serving in the Massachusetts legislature. He asked me to become the unpaid staff member for a group of mostly young liberal state legislators who had just formed what they called the Democratic Study Group, inspired by a similar congressional organization. Reasoning that this work would benefit both the world at large and my Ph.D. thesis on the legislative process, I eagerly said yes.

The group met every Monday when the House was in session at the home of Representative Katherine Kane, which was around the corner from the Statehouse. I sat in on their discussions of strategy, kept records of the decisions, researched the issues, and helped the members coordinate with each other.

I began 1967 following the career path I had anticipated when I opted for academia. I was a scholar—albeit an embryonic one—and I also served as an assistant to elected officials I admired. That June, when my stint as an undergraduate instructor at the Institute of Politics ended, I moved out of Harvard housing and into an apartment in Cambridge, ready to pursue my dual line of work.

Then, in September, I received another life-altering phone call with a job offer, another unpaid one. The caller was Christopher Lydon, then a political reporter for *The Boston Globe*, later the creator of *The Connection*, one of our best political talk radio shows. He asked if I was interested in joining the campaign team of Kevin White, who was running for mayor of Boston. White had been elected Massachusetts secretary of state in 1960 but had not made a strong impression in that position. He'd also led a group of liberals who had taken control of the Democratic Party organization in Boston's Ward Five, where I would later run for office.

White had unexpectedly survived a tough multicandidate primary election and now faced a single opponent in the final election. That opponent, Louise Day Hicks, was the potent symbol of white Bostonians' resistance to demands for school desegregation. The political, economic, and educational establishments in the city were horrified at the prospect of her victory, but the divisive primary campaign had dissipated their power and alienated many of White's potential supporters.

When a runoff election takes place soon after a first-round vote, the hard feelings inevitably kindled by any campaign do not have time to soften. Few political statements are as often uttered and infrequently meant as "We ran against each other, but we're still good friends." Supporters of a failed candidate have little love for the person who defeated their champion. And the feeling is usually mutual. Good winners exist in politics as in other areas, but it sometimes takes a while for magnanimity to replace anger—especially when the anger is directed at those who've spent the past few months demeaning you.

That is where I came in. Like most people at Harvard at the time, I had been engaged in national and state politics but had paid little attention to Boston's intra-Democratic battles. Since I hadn't supported White or his rivals, I was acceptable to all of Hicks's foes, if only by process of elimination. I agreed to work for White, not out of any great support for him (I knew little about him then) but because I shared the dread of seeing Boston elect a mayor whose sole qualification was her willingness to demagogically defend a racially unfair status quo.

So I went to see White at his home on Beacon Hill. He was detained and kept me waiting for two hours. But I later learned he was favorably impressed that I spent those hours in his study reading a great novel about Boston politics, Joseph Dinneen's *Ward Eight*, which I had found on his bookshelf. He was even more impressed when I asked if I could borrow the book so I could finish it. What might have seemed a bit forward in a more polite setting apparently struck him as just the kind of pushiness he wanted in a campaign aide.

I spent the next month working as his scheduler. My friend the process of elimination enabled me to play several other roles as well. Many of White's top advisers had full-time jobs, which left them free to campaign only after five. I had finished my teaching and administrative duties for the semester, the better to write that elusive thesis, so I was one of the few people he trusted who was available all day.

This was my first experience of full-time campaigning. My short attention span and disinclination to plan ahead turned out to be great assets in this atmosphere. In fact, my impatience in face-to-face dealings, which can be a handicap, suited White perfectly. We could communicate rapidly with little small talk. The campaign succeeded. White beat Hicks, decisively but not overwhelmingly. I prepared at long last to write what I was beginning to fear was a phantom thesis.

Then came another phone call. This time it was the mayor-elect, who asked me to meet him. The Saturday after the election I was attending a National Young Democrats convention at a hotel in Boston. We were discussing a project initiated by Al Lowenstein to "Dump Johnson" and nominate someone else for president in 1968. White picked me up at the hotel and drove me out to suburban Wellesley, where we talked while his son played hockey. He surprised me by insisting that I come to work in the new administration in January.

I remember my precise reaction: "Wow!" That is "wow" as opposed to "hooray" or "damn." The mayor-elect wanted me to be his chief of staff. The good news was that this was not the kind of political job I had hoped to have—it was a much bigger one. The bad news was that I still had a Ph.D. to complete, and I was scared.

I had never considered what it would be like to hold a job that was the focus of so much day-to-day media attention. There were no instances anywhere in America—or in the world, for that matter—of known homosexuals occupying prominent positions in public life. The closest I could think of was Walter Jenkins, one of President Johnson's most important aides, who had been caught by the police in a homosexual act in a Washington, D.C., YMCA during the 1964 campaign. He was not only fired but also immediately became a nonperson. President Johnson's first public response featured his volunteered assurance that he had spent the previous night in bed with Lady Bird.

The risk of exposure was not the only intimidating factor. More important was my worry that the job White sketched out was beyond my capabilities. I had never administered anything more complicated than the Institute of Politics programs, and, as noted, the McNamara debacle had not built up my self-confidence.

So I told White that I would not accept the offer, citing my dissertation as the primary reason. Serendipitously for the mayor-elect, the chair of the Harvard Government Department, Samuel Huntington, was his friend, neighbor, and political ally. "We'll get Sam to give you a deadline extension of a few years," he confidently and accurately predicted. He added, "You can then write a great thesis on your experiences at the highest level of city government."

White had taken advantage of my negotiating mistake—a type of mistake I would learn to avoid committing in the future. Whenever you give someone a reason for a decision that is not your real reason, you leave yourself vulnerable. If your ostensible objection is resolved, you have no recourse to your true but hidden objections.

Thus deprived of my dissertation argument, I had to confess that

I was afraid of failure—perhaps I was not the skillful, high-level political operative I seemed. White's response was irrefutable.

"You want me to be an effective liberal mayor," he said, "making a lot of changes in a conservative city and a conservative government. The people I've had with me in the secretary of state's office are good guys, but not many of them share your agenda, and without some new blood, I won't be able to be the kind of mayor you want me to be. If you walk away to be a professor, and because you're too nervous about how you'll do, don't come complaining to me in six months when I haven't been able to move the way you want me to."

Case closed. If I was truly committed to racial, economic, and social progress, how could I justify—to myself—ducking this challenge for personal reasons? So I said yes, on the condition that Sam Huntington deliver my extension. He did—an unlimited one. I understand this to mean that I am still entitled to submit a thesis and receive a doctorate. Whether that's truly the case is a question that is in no danger of ever being answered.

2

CITY HALL

My work for Mayor White began immediately, and to my great relief, I soon came to believe that I would not disgrace myself on the job. White's closest political friend was the state treasurer, Robert Crane, a shrewd, insightful man whose amiability led people to underestimate him. When I was late to a meeting, Crane had said, "Wait. Where's the fat Jewish kid?" Not even a wholly complimentary comment could have been more welcome.

At the same time, I was under no illusion that anyone's solicitude would extend to my sexuality. Bob Crane became a close friend, before and after I came out of the closet, but in those days, there is no chance he would have insisted on the participation of "the fat Jewish gay kid." Just a few months later, I heard White and Crane mock Truman Capote, whom one of them had seen on a talk show, for being such a screaming fag. My consolation prize was my recognition that they would not have spoken that way in my presence had they any suspicion about me.

By January, White had outlined my responsibilities. As his executive assistant, I would sit just outside his office and serve as his agent in dealing with the problems, complaints, and crises that arose from the basic functioning of city government. This would be emotionally draining work. I was in the grief business. If there was no problem, I was not needed. When problems arose, I had to find solutions—or at least ameliorations. Harry Truman's description of the presidency actually applied to my work as the mayor's surrogate: "The president,"

Truman said, "is a glorified public relations man who spends his time kissing and kicking people to get them to do what they are supposed to do anyway."

As I saw it, I had made an implicit deal with the mayor. I would deflect flak for him and help him provide basic city services, and in return I would have more leverage to promote liberal policies. But I soon came to value the first part of the bargain for its own sake. Winning arguments and achieving great social advances were important parts of the job. At least as important were a range of everyday tasks that were essential for the quality of our lives but that the private sector at its most productive and efficient would not undertake.

From the time I was seventeen, I realized, I had lived in the sheltered atmosphere of the university, where snow removal, police protection, and sanitation work were automatically carried out by a reasonably efficient bureaucracy, with no need for debate. I had taken these services entirely for granted. Now I was partially responsible for seeing that they got done.

To my pleasant surprise, I was good at it. I ran political interference for administrators, refereed disputes among them, listened to public grievances, pushed the bureaucracy to respond and, not least, helped the press secretary explain all of this to the media.

As it turned out, there was a close connection between this work and my interest in making society less unequal. While even the city's richest residents needed well-paved streets and an efficient fire department, it is also true that the less money people have, the more they depend on publicly provided services. Improving those services improves their quality of life. Moreover, wealth and political influence are inevitably correlated, and when resources for public services are scarce, the lower-income areas usually suffer first—especially those largely populated by minorities. In working to overcome such disparities, I was also working to pull the mayor toward the left. The progressive mission was not just about advancing certain policies on racial integration, income distribution, and other issues. It was also about making sure basic public services were supplied as they should be.

At the time, urban liberalism was at its zenith. Two other mayors had been elected with great national publicity on the same day that

White won. Carl Stokes of Cleveland was very close in age to White. He was also the first African American mayor of a large city. Joseph Alioto in San Francisco did not share their youth—he was fifty-one— but he was one of America's best, and best-known, trial lawyers. Not surprisingly, Alioto and Stokes were both very much on the progressive side. It was less clear that the mayor of the more socially conservative Boston would share their views. But he did. The three were frequently featured as harbingers of a new, pragmatic liberal approach to urban government. White would soon join several other big-city mayors in traveling road shows that pressed the national government for greater support for cities and the low-income people who lived in them. (By that time, New York City's liberal mayor John Lindsay had gotten into political trouble, and we spent some time trying to differentiate ourselves from him. I was quoted as saying he had given good intentions a bad name.)

Given White's victory over an outspokenly bigoted opponent, race would inevitably top his agenda. But the murder of Martin Luther King, Jr., three months into the administration elevated the issue even higher, both morally and politically. The mayor received word of King's death while he was watching *Gone With the Wind* at a local theater. That night, a riot broke out in the predominantly black neighborhood of Roxbury, and the very next night, James Brown was scheduled to perform at the Boston Garden, which raised the prospect of further rioting.

Discussing the concert, White initially expressed puzzlement that a football player—he was thinking of the fullback Jim Brown—would have that kind of appeal. I must acknowledge that I was not one of those in a position to correct him. The mayor also said he wanted to cancel the concert. But Boston's one black city councillor, Thomas Atkins, later general counsel of the NAACP, and members of the mayor's staff advised that it should go on. White immediately accepted Atkins's opinion and then persuaded the local public television station to broadcast the show. As a result, the city did not need to worry about thousands of black and white young people streaming into and out of the Garden. Instead, most of those young people stayed home to watch. To help keep people indoors, the broadcast was repeated immediately after it concluded.

Soon after, White convened Boston's business establishment to formulate a program that would direct housing, jobs, and other services to the city's African American population. The business leaders also agreed to provide $100,000 that White could use to address immediate needs. Due to my troubleshooting responsibilities, and the good relations I had with the city's black leadership, I was put in charge of the checkbook.

The money soon came in handy. When a black family was attacked by whites in the mostly white area of Dorchester, they called the local Black Panthers for protection, and the police responded by confiscating the Panthers' weapons and filing charges against a member of the group. The city's lawyers persuaded the police to drop the charges, but on the day of the Panthers' scheduled court appearance, I received an anguished phone call. It was from Jeep Jones, a youth worker greatly admired by young black men whom White had hired to head up the city's Youth Activities Commission. He explained that the Panthers would not agree to the settlement unless their rifles were returned to them. Police officials drew the line at this, and White's testy relations with the police commissioner—whom he had tried unsuccessfully to fire—kept him from overruling them. My solution was to tell Jones that we would provide funds to buy the Panthers replacement guns—although I did ask him to price the weapons himself, lest we be overcharged. Even back then, $100,000 was not a huge amount. I am relieved to add that there was never any sign that the rifles were used to shoot anybody.

White showed his liberal bona fides in other realms as well. The city boycotted grapes in solidarity with Cesar Chavez and the Farm Workers and took early pro-environmental steps (the first Earth Day was held during White's third year in office). On his own initiative, White pioneered the appointment of women to high office. Among these was my sister Ann Lewis. Following the King assassination, Ann had volunteered to help organize our response to the flood of incoming mail and phone calls. Impressed by her positive effect on my work, White decided to make Ann my deputy. Sensitive to the charge of nepotism, which was considered a bad thing in the circles I'd previously traveled, I started to explain to City Councillor Fred Langone that it had been entirely White's decision. "Don't you dare apologize," he interrupted me. "If you can't take care of your own in this business, what good are you?" Ann did not remain my assistant long. As White began contemplating a role in national politics, he soon promoted her to be one of his top political aides.

In 1969, the Stonewall upheaval shook New York as gays protested police harassment, marking the unofficial beginning of the "gay rights movement." But sexual minorities remained largely peripheral to Boston's politics. So I was somewhat surprised that year when a self-identified gay man—at the time, one of the few I had ever met—came to my office to complain of police brutality at a gay bar. I was eager to follow up, both because I wanted very much to respond to the complaint as a public official and because this struck me as an opportunity to meet other gay men, which up until that point I had not been able to do. I asked him to set up a meeting with the victims so I could get the information I needed. Unfortunately, the man never called me back, and no other complaints from the gay and lesbian community came to my attention.

I was disappointed. My experience was that if I presented a plausible case of police misconduct, especially if I could identify the officers involved, the department would investigate, report back to me that nothing untoward had occurred, but privately reprimand those involved and order them not to repeat the behavior. (I learned this from friendly sources—some police officials wanted good relations with the mayor's office.)

With our large concentration of colleges and universities, Boston was a center of antiwar activity. One of my main responsibilities was to work with law enforcement to maintain the right to demonstrate peacefully and keep the police from overreacting when protesters were unruly. This was not as difficult as many thought. The police supervisors I worked with, Warren Blair and Charles Barry, were fully willing to show flexibility. Their greatest difficulty, they told me, was imposing restraint on police officers when demonstrators viciously insulted their wives and mothers. We successfully avoided the police violence that had marred the Chicago Democratic convention and the student occupation of Columbia University without ceding control of the city's public places to disrupters.

My work with the police confirmed one belief and taught me another. I saw once again that the ideologically and emotionally driven choice of direct action over less dramatic political activity is often counterproductive. When demonstrations became disruptive, the mayor had to use his scarcest resource, his political capital, to resist the popular demand for a harsher police response. This made it harder for us to adopt progressive policies in other areas where there was political opposition to overcome.

Even more damaging was the cumulative impact of the angry tactics adopted by some on the left. Police officers and other city workers who had been unable to afford college educations were infuriated by young people whom they considered privileged causing trouble as they tried to go about their work. The prevalent anti-American rhetoric added literal insult to injury. The Nixon-Agnew ticket benefited from the rift within the Democratic coalition between working people and the children of middle- and upper-income professionals.

Democratic leaders didn't help matters any when they responded ambivalently to radical protest. This ambivalence had two causes. Many liberals who were themselves committed to electoral politics shared the demonstrators' strong opposition to the Vietnam War and to lingering racism, and were to some degree morally intimidated by their passion. At the same time, some Democratic office holders and candidates feared that criticizing the radicals' tactics would cost them votes from their base that they needed to win. The requirement to choose between the most radical, angry people who are on your side and the general population that fears and dislikes them wounded the Democrats for the next decade and after. Our historic consolation is that Republicans now confront the same dilemma in the form of the Tea Party.

Watching my allies struggle with this problem led me to an insight I found crucial. We politicians frequently praise ourselves for bravely defying our enemies. But in most cases this is not so hard. Indeed, excoriating—and even more usefully, being excoriated by—one's opponents is the optimal way to harvest campaign contributions. Every time AIDS activists tried to embarrass Jesse Helms, they enriched his war chest; his supporters immediately sent money.

Criticizing allies is something else altogether. True political courage involves standing up to one's friends.

In the late 1960s and early '70s, quite fortunately, the disaffection of white working class voters from liberal Democrats mainly involved personalities and not policy. The notion of government as a positive force in our lives retained much of its strength. This proved useful to me as I delved into the issue that would absorb more of my time than any other in my public life: housing for low-income people, particularly rental housing for those who could not afford to own homes.

Boston had an unusually high concentration of public housing—rental units built entirely with public funds and administered by a public agency that gave tenant eligibility to people with very low incomes. One day, John Connolly, a young white public housing tenant from South Boston—the bastion of Louise Day Hicks's political strength—came to see me. He proposed that tenants like him be allowed to fill the sixty temporary groundskeeping jobs at the projects that were doled out every summer.

Inquiring into the situation, I learned that these jobs, which paid well for such work, were traditionally given to the sons and daughters of the political elite and their friends. Thirty of the jobs were dispensed by the mayor, and the five Boston Housing Authority commissioners handed out the rest. Here was a great opportunity to demonstrate the new values of city government. A workforce of public housing residents would be more racially integrated and economically deserving than the old elite workforce.

Mayor White enthusiastically approved the idea and told me to tell Jacob Brier, chairman of the BHA, to implement it. Brier, a holdover from the previous administration, responded with outrage. "Is the mayor crazy?" he angrily asked me. "These are the best patronage jobs around. He can do what he wants with his half, but I'm not giving up mine and neither are the other members." Trying to persuade him—I was still in the early stages of my education—I responded that residents of the various developments would do a better job of keeping up the grounds, because it was where they and their families lived. Diligence in lawn mowing and litter removal were not the hallmarks of summer patronage workers. This suggestion drove Brier into even higher dudgeon. "Barney, Barney," he expostulated, "if these fucking people were any good they wouldn't live in public housing."

White did turn his patronage jobs over to the housing tenants' council to fill, and his first appointee to the board did the same. He was careful to appoint subsequent board members who did not think that living in public housing was a sign of great moral deficiency.

My next effort to improve housing conditions for low-income people was far less successful. I was a strong advocate of "infill housing": using various federal subsidies to build affordable units in existing vacant lots throughout the city—literally filling in the unoccupied spaces. The rationale was to avoid placing massive concentrations of the poor in a few high-rises. Far better to build scattered units that would not have a heavy impact on any one area.

At the time, I was not familiar with what would come to be known as NIMBY—Not in My Back Yard. This is the unfortunate universal reaction to efforts to build low-income housing, or halfway houses for the mentally ill, or any other socially purposeful edifice, anywhere near anybody. Although Boston had many poor whites who would have been eligible for such housing, the program was inevitably seen as a sneak attack by "Mayor Black"—as White had come to be called—on the racial integrity (in other words, purity) of white neighborhoods. While my work on summer jobs was a success, the infill program was a debacle. It created a few housing units—and a lot of anger.

I had a stronger impact on the city's streets than on its buildings—though I learned an all-important and chastening lesson in the process. The interstate highway system had long seemed to me one of the country's greatest achievements—a shining example of what a strong federal government could accomplish if it was willing to mobilize national resources for the public good. Interstate 95, which traveled in a fairly straight line from southern Florida to northern Maine, was a crucial component of the system, but its Boston leg had not yet been built. I soon learned that highway planners intended to route that leg through predominantly low- and lower-middle-income neighborhoods, including one of the city's few racially and economically integrated areas, the South End. When I met with local activists opposed to the route, I was instinctively skeptical of their arguments. Severing the link that carried commerce up and down the entire East Coast for the sake of a few Boston neighborhoods seemed both excessively provincial and unthinkably radical.

In response, my interlocutors insisted that the proposed route was not dictated by geography. Rather, it typified a disturbing pattern: Improvements to public infrastructure always tore up the poorest residential neighborhoods.

My first—fortunately unspoken—reaction was that this was absurd. It sounded like the same paranoia I had encountered in Mississippi and afterward in my disputes with the angry left. Shortly thereafter, I sought out William McGrath, the chief transportation planner for the city, whose work I regarded highly. I recounted the complaint that highway projects and other improvements were deliberately sited to affect the poorest people in the target area, expecting him to reassure me that this was not true. Instead, to my dismay, he affirmed it.

It's simple economics, he explained. Your job is to build the road as cheaply as possible, consistent with the necessary quality standards. One major expense is acquisition of the land on which the road will be built. When no existing vacant land is available—almost always the case in a city—housing occupied by lower-income people costs less than any alternative. All else being equal, low-income neighborhoods are the path of least resistance for the highway engineers.

This meant that I did not have the option of advocating a less socially destructive route through the city. Even if Boston wanted to spend the extra money to preserve affordable housing, the funds were controlled by unsympathetic federal and state officials who would not have agreed.

The question then became how we could justify a major breach in the interstate highway system to save the homes of several thousand vulnerable Bostonians. Fortunately, all of this was happening in 1970, when concern for the environment was becoming a powerful force. Cars and trucks were high on the environmental movement's list of villains.

Working with two gifted city officials, Fred Salvucci and John Lynch, I urged White to do what he wanted to do instinctively. He came out in opposition to the I-95 project and to another proposed highway, and in favor of more public transportation. Frank Sargent, the liberal Republican governor, originally sided with the conventional wisdom of the time and criticized White. But we won the ensuing public debate, helped by the rising popularity of environmentalism and the enthusiasm of the affected neighborhoods, and Sargent reversed himself and joined the opposition, killing the two roads. This early victory of the antihighway forces was to be followed by others, and transportation policy, especially in urban areas, was never the same. (The integrity of the interstate system was not entirely forsaken. At Salvucci's urging, all parties agreed to rename a large part of Route 128, the state highway that circles Boston, Interstate 95. Drivers confused by an exit numbering sequence perverse even by Massachusetts standards will, on reading this, at least know why the system exists, even if they cannot figure out the system itself.)

•

In the fall of 1970, White ran for governor and lost decisively to Sargent, the incumbent. By that time, I was emotionally and physically exhausted after three years of full-time work in politics and governing. It showed.

I do not drink much—my taste buds have not changed since I first became a teenager. Instead, I deal with tension through food—using the Yiddish for overeating, I needed only two words to answer a reporter who asked why as my campaigns got tougher, I got bigger: "stress fress." (Cokie Roberts later observed that as one of my hardest campaigns went on, I got fatter and my opponent got crazier.)

In December 1970, I told White that I could no longer do the job. His response was very flattering—he offered me other positions, including running the Housing Authority, given my interest in good rental housing for the poor. Relishing how much that would have agitated Jacob Brier, I considered it. But then I got another one of those phone calls that would alter my fate.

My former boss at the Institute of Politics, Richard Neustadt, told me that a fellowship was available beginning in January 1971. This would provide two things: a badly needed respite from responsibility, and the chance to get serious about my degree, since the fellowship meant a year back at Harvard with few duties.

I had yet to do any work on my thesis besides pick a topic. In theory, my three years working with Kevin White amounted to a massive research effort that I could draw on to produce a case study of how city government worked. But I was much more interested in changing reality than in describing it, and my dissertation remained mostly notional. I did write one lengthy piece during my stay at the institute—an article for *The Boston Globe Magazine* on how I lost one hundred pounds. (Not having to do any serious work for six months played a major role.)

As I contrasted my success as a political and administrative troubleshooter with my failure as a scholar, I realized that a key aspect of my makeup helped explain both results: I have a very short attention span. In my city job, I had to deal with three or four big issues and a handful of smaller ones every day. I can shift gears and juggle multiple concerns better than most people. Given the need to respond quickly to a new problem, I do very well. But when something requires long periods of concentration, not so much. With any task, my competitive advantage over other people diminishes in direct proportion to the time we have to spend on it. Understanding this, I was ready to say yes when I received the next phone call that shaped my career.

It came from Michael Harrington, a state legislator I had worked with when I was executive secretary of the Democratic Study Group. He had won a special election to Congress in 1969, taking a seat that had been held by Republicans since the nineteenth century. Most significantly, he was one of the earliest candidates to run on an anti–Vietnam War platform and win a tough race. This had particular appeal, because I felt somewhat guilty that I had not done very much against the war. So I agreed to go to Washington as his chief of staff—I would be his administrative assistant, in congressional terminology.

In Washington, I hoped to utilize the hard-earned political knowledge I had acquired working for White. One of the most important lessons I'd learned was cautionary in nature. The most committed activists on the left and the right are convinced that the majority of voters agree with them but that institutional flaws in our democracy prevent popular sentiment from prevailing. They are usually wrong. Today conservatives are more profoundly damaged by this state of mind than liberals, but in the late 1960s and early '70s it was primarily a problem for liberal Democratic officeholders. Their allies were certain that the great mass of voters were ready for a sharp shift to the left, and they excoriated those in power for failing—or maybe refusing—to take advantage of this opportunity.

In recent years, this tension between committed activists and political reality has worsened significantly, exacerbated by changes in how people—especially the most ideologically driven—get their information. Thirty years ago, people watched, read, and listened to the same relatively few outlets, albeit with varying degrees of skepticism. Over the past decade, America's political community has come to live in two parallel media universes. Each wing ingests information and opinion that reinforces its own policy preferences *and* its own conviction that those preferences reflect majority opinion.

Given my own policy preferences, I would have been very happy if the liberals had been right about majority opinion. But after three years working with an electorate consisting mostly of working- and middle-class citizens, I knew they weren't. Yes, people wanted more and better government services. But they did not support the significant reallocation of society's resources necessary to bring this about. My appreciation of the point was strengthened by the wisdom of two tough-minded Boston politicians.

In a meeting with Fred Langone, the city councillor who had rebuked me for seeking to justify the hiring of my sister, I criticized the residents of the city's Hyde Park section. They had pressed the mayor to build a public swimming pool in the area, and he had agreed. When work began, we received complaints about the construction noise and the flow of trucks removing excavated material and bringing in concrete. "What do people expect?" I asked Langone in an injured voice. "How do they expect us to build a pool without doing the things they are upset about?"

He was unsympathetic. "Hey, kid," he lectured me, "ain't you heard the news? Everybody wants to go to heaven, but nobody wants to die."

State representative John Melia's lesson came when I asked him to support a bill that would allow the city to tax some of the tax-exempt property within its borders; there were many such properties and they benefited from city services without being assessed any property taxes. Melia declined. "Pal, you know I'm a great friend of the mayor," he explained, "and I help him whenever I can. But I have a rule for staying alive in this business. Vote for every program, and vote against every tax increase, and the people will love you."

In those years, incident after incident revealed to me that broad programs for social and economic transformation had little appeal to most voters, black, white, or Hispanic. Two days after the murder of Dr. King, I was entering city hall for a morning meeting with leaders of the black community when I was confronted by a dozen or so picketers. They were protesting the city's response to the assassination and insisting that the police presence in black neighborhoods be removed. As I argued with them, Dan Richardson, who had been elected to chair the community board of Boston's Model Cities program, heard me, leaned out the window—this was the old city hall, which had windows that opened—and told me to get upstairs for our meeting and stop wasting time with those people. The agenda of the community representatives had little in common with their self-appointed advocates downstairs.

At the time, I often heard echoes of the argument I had resisted in Mississippi—that African Americans did not want integration into white middle-class society; they wanted to create and run their own institutions. The issue was now discussed in terms of "community control" of the organs of city government in minority neighborhoods. For a small number of the most militant, the call for community control was in fact a demand for a form of separatism: They wanted a semiautonomous black-run operation to perform city services, with funding provided from general city revenues. But it soon became clear that the majority of the "community" had no great interest in taking over snow removal, street paving, park maintenance, or most other activities. What they did want—understandably—was greater influence over those government activities where they felt victimized by racially driven mistreatment. In the case of public housing, for example, black tenants and their allies believed that drastic action was necessary to break the plantation mentality manifested by the Housing Authority chairman I quoted earlier. When White agreed to give tenants a bigger role in running their housing developments, the offer was voted down by white residents of the city's largest project, Columbia Point, but eagerly accepted by the black tenant population of the Bromley Heath project.

The best illustration of the distinction between "community control" as a utopian endeavor and as a defense against mistreatment lies in the concept's application to two major agencies. Overwhelmingly, African Americans wanted much more involvement in running the police department, especially in their neighborhoods. But no one ever demanded similar control over the fire department, because no one saw a discriminatory pattern in its operation. (There was unhappiness over the dearth of black firefighters, but no one asserted that this meant less attention was given to fires in buildings inhabited by minorities.)

What the radicals failed to appreciate was that most voters would support change only if they could be persuaded it was very much in their self-interest—and as *they* perceived their self-interest, not as it appeared in some idealist's model. Even those at the lower end of the scale were often afraid that they would lose what little they had in a radical shift in societal arrangements. Two hundred years ago, Jeremy Bentham explained why his advocacy of "the greatest good for the greatest number" did not call for socialism—leveling, as it was then known. A person's pain in losing something, he asserted, is usually greater than the pleasure someone else experiences in benefiting from that loss. This principle helps explain why both Bill Clinton and Barack Obama faced so much popular opposition to their plans to extend health care coverage, and why efforts to redistribute income by raising taxes rarely gain sufficient support from those who would benefit from them.

While I was confirmed in my belief that left-wing theorists had overestimated the appeal of radical change, I had to acknowledge as well that I had overestimated the beneficence of government as it existed. In many realms, official action has disproportionately negative effects on those bereft of income and political influence. The revelation did not come from the vitriolic denunciation of poor people by officials at the Housing Authority. It was William McGrath, the respected, well-meaning transportation planner, who shocked me into recognizing the long reach of "institutional racism," which should more accurately, if awkwardly, be designated "institutional classism."

The government decisions in question were not motivated by animus against blacks, Hispanics, or poor people. The victims of such decisions whom I would later represent in Fall River and New Bedford were overwhelmingly white and working-class. Rather, the decisions were the consequence of public officials following the path of least resistance in issuing waste disposal permits, installing infrastructure, zoning for industrial use, siting high-rise commercial buildings, or locating facilities for people in need of treatment or confinement. But the absence of bad motives in no way alleviates the bad effects. Trying to educate well-meaning people—including many of my fellow liberals—about the need to correct this harmful tendency has been a part of my self-appointed mission ever since.

Even though the White years demonstrated that creating a fairer society would be harder than I expected, they did not lead me to despair. White's successful effort to avert rioting after the King assassination and our subsequent steps toward racial fairness earned him the support and gratitude of African Americans. This support could not be explained solely in terms of solid accomplishments. Given the limited jurisdiction and resources of city government, there was only so much we could do about African Americans' economic disadvantages. The city bureaucracy also proved difficult to change. Entrenched officials and employees often resisted the mayor's efforts to provide basic services more fairly and efficiently. But the mayor still deserved praise. His forthright acknowledgment that racial discrimination was common, his appointment of African Americans to important city positions, and his visibility in black neighborhoods—a first for a Boston mayor—counted for a lot.

Although these actions came at little if any cost to the white majority, they nonetheless generated angry criticism. When white voters wielded the "Mayor Black" epithet, they were expressing a perception of neglect. White himself, a superb politician, recognized this early on and sought to show equal concern for the sensibilities of whites as well as blacks and Hispanics, who were receiving recognition from city government for the first time. But too many of Boston's whites regarded mayoral respect as a zero-sum game pitting themselves against the black population.

•

When I moved to Washington in 1971, I recognized that I was giving up my planned scholarly career. If I'd been forced to admit I was not very good at scholarship before I had served Kevin White, I would have been unhappy. But now I had an alternative line of work that I valued and enjoyed.

As I've mentioned, Harrington's strong opposition to the Vietnam War was especially gratifying. When the war began, I was skeptical of its supporters' domino theory, the idea that if South Vietnam fell, so would its neighbors. But I fully supported keeping the 1960s version of communism from extending its hold over an additional tens of millions of people. We had done that in Korea, and while the South Korean government was repressive, it was never as bad as its northern neighbor, and it was on the way toward democracy. As time passed and the moral and pragmatic cases for the war in Vietnam became harder to make, I had to keep my anger at antiwar militants' tactics from affecting my view of their cause. My view of the war was also affected by my continued support for President Johnson's domestic agenda, and by my close association with Mayor White, whose need for federal assistance argued against vehement denunciation of the administration's major foreign policy effort. After Nixon was elected in 1968, antiwar sentiment became easier for many Democrats. Partisanship was now boosting antiwar feelings rather than retarding them.

In Washington, I found that while Nixon and Agnew preached social conservatism to great political advantage, their administration was an activist one in economic affairs. At the time, support for a larger public sector remained very strong. It's frequently noted that Nixon proposed policy changes in health care and welfare that congressional Democrats rejected as too conservative, only to settle for less years later. The administration's use of wage and price controls to steer the economy was perhaps even more notable. These measures accompanied Nixon's decision to take the United States off the gold standard. He engineered this major shift in the management of our currency with the help of his secretary of the treasury, John Connally, himself a champion of vigorous governmental action.

In one area of public policy that is central to liberal concerns today, the Nixon administration was the first to play a significant role. Under the auspices of Interior Secretary Harold Ickes, Franklin Roosevelt's administration did pick up where his cousin Theodore had left off in promoting conservation. But to contemporary environmentalists, some of the proudest New Deal successes—the Tennessee Valley Authority and several large dams—are mistakes to be corrected. It was only under Nixon that the government took on the new missions embodied in the Clean Air and Clean Water Acts. These were most fervently pushed by congressional Democrats, but with considerable Republican support. Nixon not only acquiesced in these efforts but also appointed enthusiastic advocates to run newly established agencies.

One critical aspect of the Clean Air Act was the restrictions on lead, which I cited earlier as one of the best examples of effective government policy we have seen. Its partner, the Lead-Based Poisoning Prevention Act, was also signed into law by Nixon.

For all of his unexpected actions that we applauded, we were still eager to see Nixon go. Happily for me, I agreed with Harrington's decision to support Maine senator Ed Muskie for the Democratic nomination in 1972. Muskie was one of the most effective liberals in the Senate. He and Senator Gaylord Nelson of Wisconsin were considered Congress's best environmental advocates, and even before arriving in Washington, I had volunteered to help his campaign. The first of these efforts involved representing Muskie's interests at an Al Lowenstein–inspired Dump Nixon rally in Providence, Rhode Island. Before the rally, I met separately with its fervent antiwar organizers, some of whom still resented Muskie for running on Hubert Humphrey's ticket in 1968, and with the leaders of the much more conservative Rhode Island Democratic establishment. That meeting took place in the hotel suite maintained by Providence's mayor, Joseph Doorley.

"This is a great layout, Joe," one of the statewide officeholders noted. "What's the price?"

"Price?" the mayor responded with a wolfish grin (a phrase I had previously encountered in novels and until then thought was an example of excessively melodramatic writing). "To he who assesses?" Rarely has a question been so conclusively answered by another question.

In January 1972, Harrington gave me an unpaid leave to go to Ohio and help Governor John Gilligan pick the delegates for the Muskie slate to the Democratic convention that summer. By the time I returned to Washington, it was clear that a deep disenchantment with the war and those held responsible for it was sweeping Democratic ranks. Muskie's once-inevitable nomination was rapidly falling victim to George McGovern's moral crusade.

The passionate McGovernites were suspicious of Muskie supporters such as Mayor White. Indeed, when McGovern decided to anoint White his vice presidential candidate at the upcoming party convention, the Massachusetts McGovern delegation, which had beaten the Muskie slate in our primary, rebelled against its own native son. As a result, McGovern had to make another choice: the ill-fated Senator Thomas Eagleton.

Harrington's strong antiwar stand immunized him from rising antiestablishment sentiment, and his reelection seemed assured. But his district had been Republican for close to a century. He also had a penchant for controversy—he once voted present on a Happy Birthday resolution for Harry Truman to protest the waste of congressional time. As a result, we couldn't take anything for granted.

When I accepted Harrington's job offer, I promised to stay with him through his reelection campaign. But my promise to remain at his side became awkward when I got another career-changing phone call. It was from Steve and Shelley Cohen, two then-married friends with whom I had worked in the White administration. They urged me to return to Massachusetts and run for state representative in the seat about to be vacated by the moderate Republican Maurice Frye.

I was initially dismissive. I had spent all of my adult life, as well as part of my teens, convinced that I was unelectable. At the time, the only Boston Jews in public office represented heavily Jewish neighborhoods. I spoke too fast (my poor diction had not been improved by the elocution classes my mother had insisted I take twenty-five years earlier), and I had lived in Boston—albeit in the proper district—for only four years. Boston voters were not then in the habit of conferring elected office on people who were, by Boston standards, barely more than visitors. (Shelley and Steve were not, to my knowledge, aware of my sexual orientation at the time, though as close friends who knew my life well they would not have been surprised by the news. In fact, just a few years later, Shelley was the first friend to tell me—very supportively—that she had figured it out.)

Steve and Shelley effectively countered my objections to running. They did not deny that I would be an atypical candidate, but they pointed out that I would be running in an equally atypical district. Boston's Ward Five covered Beacon Hill, the Back Bay, and small pieces of the South End and Fenway areas. By every demographic indicator, it differed from the rest of the city in ways that were favorable to me—or, more precisely, that minimized my electoral disadvantages. The median length of residency in the city was near the bottom, which meant that voters in the area were less likely than voters elsewhere in the city to hold my own recent move to Boston against me. The heavy dose of Harvard on my résumé would have been at best a mixed blessing elsewhere; it was a great credential in a district with the city's highest level of educational attainment. The ward also had a low percentage of families with children. There were not yet identifiably "gay" areas, but there were more single people on the census rolls than in any other constituency. The district also included a large subsidized-housing development and one of the few genuinely racially integrated areas in Boston.

As the Cohens observed, the prominence I had gained working for White was an overwhelmingly positive electoral asset, not just with these voters but also across the ward, in which the White administration was very popular. Moreover, many more of the district's thousands of college students were now able to vote (the voting age had been lowered to eighteen a year earlier). With McGovern running for president, they were clearly going to be very helpful to any Democratic candidate.

I was still far from optimistic about my chances—ingrained self-doubt is a powerful force. But I accepted my friends' argument that I could win, and I realized that I was now closer to achieving my impossible dream—elected office—than I had ever expected to be. And given the partisan history of the ward, if I ran and lost as a Democrat, it would not be seen as my personal failure. Losing would leave me no worse off than if I had never run at all. The district as it was then constituted had only once in the twentieth century voted Democratic—in 1941, when a solidly Republican city council seat was won by a Democrat only because the twenty-one-year-old Republican candidate was undeniably brilliant but insufferably arrogant. He was McGeorge Bundy, later in a more likable guise to become John F. Kennedy's national security adviser. The winner, A. Frank Foster, was one of the rare Jews to win a non-Jewish seat, probably aided by the use of the initial instead of his first name, Abraham. He lost to a better-mannered Republican in the next round, and moved south to the Jewish neighborhood of Mattapan to launch a second, more successful electoral career.

So I told the Cohens that I would run—with one big if: I was morally bound to ask Harrington to release me from my pledge to stay with him through his reelection. He had every right to refuse. Only six months remained before Election Day, and I'd been given a big role in his organizational structure. Most important, not just for my relationship with him but also for my own future reputation, I had given him my word, and he had relied on it.

Keeping commitments that are not legally binding is beneficial to most human activity, but it is essential in the unstructured world of politics. After all, politicians have no legally enforceable ties to each other, but they must collaborate to achieve their goals. Political figures who are known to abandon a promise whenever it is momentarily expedient find it increasingly hard to form partnerships, which must be built on mutual trust. In politics, you learn to be careful before giving your word, but once you have given it, you pay a high reputational price for breaking it.

Not for the last time, I was the beneficiary of a more senior politician's generosity, which I had no right to expect. Harrington was surprised to learn that I had the candidate itch, but he said that in his experience, it had to be scratched, and he released me from my pledge with no resentment.

And so in May 1972, I returned to Boston. I was ready to run. Of course, I now had to deal with what would be my major preoccupation for the next fifteen years: what I came to think of—constantly—as "the gay thing."

Three years after Stonewall, the country was beginning to confront the question of how to treat those of us who were lesbian, gay, and bisexual (transgender was not yet on the agenda). More stressfully, we were deciding what roles we would play in that process. Attempting to become the first openly gay elected official was not the role I chose for myself. Indeed, my candidacy reinforced my already firm determination to keep my secret. I was sure that the electorate was no more ready to receive the news than I was to deliver it.

The next question I faced was how I would respond to legislation that sought to make us legally equal. The answer was easy. I would be an active supporter of every proposal to fight anti-LGBT discrimination. I was prepared to be something of a coward when it came to acknowledging who I really was, but I was even more determined not to be a hypocrite.

I would not water down the public expression of my profound private anger. I recognized that vigorously advocating gay rights might increase the likelihood that some people would conclude I was in the closet. I also noted the contrary position that people might assume that if I were gay, I would be afraid to take that stance. I rejected the relevance of the debate. There was no way I could live with myself—a dominant consideration, since at that point I didn't foresee being able to live with anybody else—unless I helped wage an all-out war on homophobia. I promised myself that I would.

I soon got the chance to act on my promise. Massachusetts gay rights activity had just begun, with the founding of two organizations. Women belonged to the Daughters of Bilitis. (I have never learned who or what Bilitis was.) Men made up the Homophile Union of Boston (HUB), linking gay and civic pride in one acronym. With others they had staged Boston's first Gay Pride Parade in June 1971, in honor of the Stonewall events in June 1969. I was introduced to both groups, and to the most prominent uncloseted lesbian in the city, Elaine Noble, who was an articulate member of the faculty of Emerson College and one of a small handful of out professionals. I had met Noble through my sister, Ann Lewis, who cochaired the Massachusetts chapter of the newly formed National Women's Political Caucus with her and a third woman, Lena Saunders, an African American leader of a public housing tenants' group. A married straight woman, a lesbian, and an African American represented the coalition that the women's caucus was seeking to build.

In June 1972, I rode in a car in the city's second Gay Pride Parade. It was my first step into the world of gay politics. My next step was to help HUB form a cooperative relationship with the Boston Police Department. To my surprise, the organization was concerned not about too much police activity but too little, a problem they acknowledged was not the department's fault. The problem was that when a gay man was the victim of a crime in circumstances that would reveal his homosexuality, he had no way to seek help without going on the public record. The police, I was pleased to discover, were happy to take information about crimes discreetly and do all they could to move against criminals without requiring victims to appear publicly in court.

As I expected, running for office required me to take a stand on LGBT-related issues. HUB sent every candidate for the state House and state Senate legislative questionnaires, asking them to sponsor gay rights legislation and support the bills when they came up for votes.

I happily committed myself to sponsoring a package of bills. One would abolish the law criminalizing some sexual acts between consenting adults (the so-called sodomy law). Another would outlaw discrimination based on sexual orientation in public and private employment. I assumed that as a freshman in a chamber where seniority counted for something, I would be following the lead of more senior liberal members in the ensuing debates. This would be the ideal situation: I would take the stand I wanted to take but without the excessive prominence that I was not yet ready to enjoy.

From the outset, my focus was on the November election. There were three other candidates in the Democratic primary, but they were not well-known in the district, and I ended up receiving 80 percent of the vote.

In the general election, my most important mission was to persuade voters that I would be an effective advocate for their local, neighborhood-based problems. Living in residential enclaves of the downtown core, the inhabitants of Beacon Hill and Back Bay worried constantly about the incursion of commercial activity into their lives. They also worried about high-rise buildings and other commercial construction impinging on their eighteenth-, nineteenth-, and early twentieth-century homes, which were tenuously protected by special architectural zoning. They were concerned as well by competition for scarce parking spaces from shoppers and commuters and overuse of the Boston Common, the Public Garden, the Charles River Esplanade, and the Commonwealth Avenue Mall—great public parks that were visited by tens of thousands every day.

My naïveté and arrogance led me to presume that voters would enthusiastically welcome my candidacy. It didn't take long for a dangerously large number of opinion leaders in the ward to let me know that they thought I was overqualified for the job. They worried that I had a broader political agenda in mind and, most tellingly, that I would spend my time on big ideological issues at the expense of the more mundane matters on which they wanted their only locally elected representative to focus. (Seats on the city council were no longer distributed geographically.) Perhaps they recalled John F. Kennedy's remark that he would never run for governor because he didn't want to spend his time parceling out sewer contracts.

I did all I could to alleviate these anxieties. I began with a campaign slogan that sought to turn an obstacle into an advantage: PUT BARNEY FRANK TO WORK FOR WARD FIVE.

Trying to dispel strongly held perceptions in the course of a campaign is extremely difficult. The time is too short and the atmosphere too highly charged. Instead, I hoped to persuade my target audience that my unusual background would lead me not to neglect nuts-and-bolts local issues but rather to address them with more clout. Skeptics had no idea of the intensity of my attraction to the governing process. I was fascinated by it intellectually and was a firm believer in its moral worth at every level. I had learned in my city job that delivering good results for my boss in the realm of the mundane was essential to advancing the ideological goals that had motivated me since the days of Joseph McCarthy and Emmett Till.

My appeal to the nonideological segment of the electorate was enhanced by another decision that joined good electoral politicking with moral rectitude: I publicly endorsed Republican senator Edward Brooke for reelection to a second term. Brooke was the only African American in the Senate, and the first to serve there since the Reconstruction era. He was a moderate liberal and a leader on housing policy. His opponent was a more conservative Democratic district attorney, John Droney, whose only claim to historical notice is that he later lost his ability to speak and was very ably represented in public by his eloquent first assistant, John Kerry.

I endorsed Brooke because I believed his defeat would be disastrous to the cause of racial progress. Serendipitously for me, doing the right thing was also helpful in a district with many Republicans and Independents. Crossing party lines to support Brooke allowed me to emulate the "Old Dope Peddler" in the popular song by comedian-lyricist-musician Tom Lehrer. I was "doing well by doing good."

Nationally, the McGovern campaign was becoming a disaster for Democrats. His securing the nomination as the articulate champion of the angry left resulted in a demonstration of how Newtonian physics works in the political sphere: While the reaction in the electorate at large was opposite, it was also, sadly for the liberal side, unequal.

But not in my district. Thousands of newly enfranchised teenage college students lived in Boston. They had never before been a factor in the ward's elections and represented a potential increase of 20 percent or more in its total vote. But given their lack of interest in local politics—after all, most of their homes were elsewhere—the assumption of most political experts was that they would pull the McGovern lever and skip the rest of the ballot.

My task was to change this by identifying with McGovern and by stressing my support for issues that would attract their interest. Fortunately, none of this gave me pause. Although I had supported Muskie, and was pessimistic about McGovern's chances, I was in full agreement with his platform and knew many of those engaged in his campaign. In particular, my sister Ann was playing a major role in his Massachusetts effort at White's request. She arranged for McGovern to have his picture taken with me—and to endorse my candidacy.

With his campaign's permission, I then created a poster with a headline borrowed from an old Jewish joke I had first heard in the Catskills. An obnoxious name-dropping man called Goldberg claimed friendship with an unlikely range of world figures. Finally, one exasperated colleague challenged his assertion that he was very close to the pope. "Come with me to Rome and I'll show you," Goldberg replied. At the Vatican, Goldberg leaves his skeptic in St. Peter's Square and goes inside. Minutes later, two figures appear on the balcony, and one Italian is heard to ask another, "Who's that guy up there with Goldberg?"

In my version, McGovern plays the pope, and the poster asks, "WHO'S THAT GUY WITH BARNEY FRANK?" We hung the poster in every place we could where students would see it. It was a great success. Apparently few if any of those who saw the poster had heard the joke before, so my own Goldberg variation not only drew attention to my candidacy—and McGovern's endorsement of it—it also gained us a reputation for wit. The first printing became a collector's item and disappeared into dorm rooms; we had to reprint the poster several times.

The text on the poster noted my support for the legalization of marijuana, gay rights, strong environmental laws, and the cause of the United Farm Workers—Cesar Chavez was another of my endorsers, following the city's decision to boycott nonunion grapes in its purchases for jails and hospitals. My stands on these issues won the approval of *The Phoenix* and *The Real Paper*, two widely read underground newspapers that had recently appeared in the Boston area. I also benefited from the civility of my opponent, Virgil Aiello. He was a moderate Republican, of the sort that sadly has disappeared almost entirely even in Massachusetts. He didn't join in supporting my social agenda, but neither did he fight it with demagogy.

I won by a greater margin than I had hoped for at the campaign's outset, when I doubted that I could win at all. But I gladly acknowledged the good luck that was involved. Even though I trailed George McGovern in my district, I still won my race. This led me to state publicly that I was one of the very few Democrats in America to have ridden in on George McGovern's coattails.

A few days after the election, I saw McGovern at a function at the Institute of Politics. On the chance that meeting me had not been the most memorable event of his previous year, I reintroduced myself and thanked him for helping me win my race. He did not seem happy, and I realized that he thought I was being sarcastic, so I reassured him that I was serious. A day or two later, I received a call from Bob Shrum, an old political friend who had been a senior McGovern staffer. "Did you meet George the other night?" he asked me. When I told him that I had, he responded, "George told some of us that he had finally met a Democrat who told him that his presidential race had been helpful. We figured it must have been you." I was glad not to be one of the many sheriffs, county commissioners, state legislators, and others who blamed him for ending their careers. Forty years later, I had the wonderful opportunity to thank McGovern again for helping launch my electoral life. At a celebration of his great life's work, I stood with him alongside my "Who's that guy?" poster.

•

After an intense but brief rush of postelection euphoria, I set about becoming a legislator. In Massachusetts, legislators must file proposed bills for the coming year in the first week of December. When that week passed, it was clear that no one else was going to sponsor the gay rights bills I'd supported. And so, even before I took office, I knew that I was not a sponsor of the package, but *the* sponsor. Once again I was the survivor of a process of elimination, but this time it did not seem an unmixed blessing.

What would I do if I was asked "the question"? I came up with a plan. With mild indignation, I would reject the view that a legislator's support for the right to do something automatically meant that he or she indulged in the activity in question. I was a white man who strongly supported ending racial bias. I was a male advocate of a woman's right to choose. I did not smoke marijuana, but I defended the right of others to do so without criminal penalty.

I realized this was hardly a bulletproof defense. After all, if I was asked whether I did in fact smoke marijuana, I was ready to answer honestly—that I had tried it once, but wasn't very good at it and didn't repeat the effort. (I had to stop giving that truthful answer when Bill Clinton ruined the "I didn't inhale" defense for all time. I discovered the edible form much later.) And no one was going to ask me if I was a closeted woman or an African American.

Contrary to my apprehensions, no one asked me the question. Even more surprisingly, there did not appear to be any public comment on the fact that an unmarried thirty-two-year-old man was the state's most ardent advocate of gay rights. I was sure that there was some private discussion of what this said about me. Even so, it was seemingly unacceptable to raise what would still have been an accusation. The prevailing attitude, I believe—certainly in respectable circles in the Northeast—was that homosexuality was an unfortunate condition. Those of us who suffered from it deserved some sympathy, but not blame.

The most obvious question was why the press was also silent. As I came to understand it, journalists regarded homosexuality as a serious handicap for a public official but not as a trait they would be justified in bringing to light. For the next several decades—until very recently—this was a rare and probably unique example of the media putting personal privacy over newsworthiness. Ironically, while this approach protected individual gay or lesbian public figures, it worked to the disadvantage of our cause. Since the media's respect for sexual privacy ended when someone was entangled in a scandal, the list of known gay, lesbian, or bisexual public figures was composed disproportionately of people in that category. This did not improve our reputation.

In January 1973, I filed my first package of legislation, which included my bill repealing the state's sodomy law. When that bill later came to the floor, the reaction was unprecedented. Members of the Massachusetts House cast their votes by pushing Yes or No buttons on their desks, and these votes are tallied on two scoreboards in the front of the chamber. When the roll call on the sodomy bill was held, by a prearrangement of which I was unaware, almost everybody voted yes. To the great surprise of spectators, the board lit up solidly green. And then, amid raucous laughter on the floor, 90 percent of the members promptly switched to red. The bill lost overwhelmingly, by a vote of 208 to 16. Much to my chagrin—which I tried to hide but probably didn't—the legislators regarded my first bill as a joke.

That laughter dissipated two days later. Rachelle Patterson, a political columnist for *The Boston Globe*, wrote a searing column angrily rebuking my colleagues for mocking a serious effort to help victims of prejudice. Her words resonated profoundly. The day her essay appeared, several representatives apologized to me, and there was never a repetition of the prank. In fact, I was somewhat relieved by the experience. I had gotten more votes than I had expected. And that my colleagues responded somewhat humorously rather than angrily was a good sign—they were playing a joke on someone they regarded as a colleague rather than an outsider.

Early in my first term, I spoke out on gay rights for the first time. The occasion was a public hearing on my bill to ban discrimination in private employment on grounds of sexual orientation. (This was no sign of any support for it. Unlike many legislatures, including Congress, Massachusetts's rules require a hearing on every bill filed.) As I rose to speak, I thought I might be asked to explain my particular interest in the bill. When no one asked, I assumed—correctly—that I would have a few more years to decide how I'd answer.

As it turned out, I was asked only one question in the hearing, and it too gave me relief. My fellow freshman Royal Bolling, Jr., was one of five African Americans newly present in the House that year, giving the state's black community significant representation for the first time. "Representative," he began, "I've been dealing with job discrimination based on prejudice for a long time"—at this point I braced mentally for his objection to any effort to link the two causes—"and

I agree with you that it's just as wrong here as it is in my case, so I support your bill."

At the time, many black leaders, especially among the clergy, rejected any linkage between our causes. They believed that homosexuality was immoral or they worried that gay civil rights harmed their own cause by raising the specter of guilt by association with less popular victims. Bolling's words flatly repudiated those objections. His statement affected me greatly because revulsion at racism was one of the initial reasons I wanted to serve in government, and I still regarded combating it as my single highest priority. After Stonewall, I hoped that I could add gay rights to my agenda at no cost to my work in the racial fight, but I was prepared to put race first if I had to choose. The warm personal and political support I got from Bolling and from my other black colleagues—especially Representatives Doris Bunte and Mel King—gave me the best gift I could receive: one less moral dilemma in a career that already had too many.

3

BEACON HILL

I did not have to sit in the Massachusetts legislature very long before I realized that the most important divide was not between Republicans and Democrats but between loyal followers of the House leadership and the dissidents. If I was going to be both principled and effective, I would need to have good relations with both sides.

The Speaker in Massachusetts was extremely powerful. Most Democrats voted with him almost all the time, and there was a significant number of Republican members willing to give him the votes he needed in return for political favors. He selected all the committee chairs. He also doled out membership on committees, good office space, and legislative staff.

I realized early on that I could go my own way on policy matters as long as I refrained from impugning the motives of the leaders and from joining in frontal assaults on their prerogatives. My role as a "leadership liberal" reprised the deal I had made with White and, more implicitly, with my constituents. I would use whatever talents for governance I had to be useful to them on nuts-and-bolts matters— and in so doing I would also maximize my ability to achieve my ideological objectives.

This was easier than it might have been due to the personality of the Speaker, David Bartley. He was more liberal than his predecessor or his successor, and politically more flexible. He was young—having become Speaker four years before, at age thirty-four—and had the time and inclination for a post-Speakership career. This gave him the incentive to govern the House with a lighter touch and to seek accommodation with the liberals—especially those who had, as I did, good media relations. And because his ego was secure, he did not equate dissent with personal attack—as long as it wasn't phrased that way.

Happily for my relationship with Bartley, I was immediately useful to him. Boston's public transportation system—the fabled MTA on which Charlie made the second most famous ride in our history— was in crisis. Its deficit—the large amount it still owed after fares were collected—was funded almost entirely by the communities in the region, whose only revenue source was the property tax. Federal money was available for buying equipment but not for running it. There was a broad consensus among serious students that unless the state, with its broader revenue streams, assumed half the cost, the system could not continue to operate on the scale needed to sustain the metropolitan region's economy. But funding the MTA with state money required a two-thirds vote in each house, and for many legislators around the state, taxing their constituents to pay for the city's subways was politically toxic. Bartley appointed me to the Transportation Committee, where I helped bypass the committee's chairman and get the necessary legislation through the panel.

The help I gave Bartley with the MTA allowed me to challenge him on a matter of deep principle. For many years, ethnicity had defined Massachusetts's political geography, especially in greater Boston. A plurality of the area's State Senate seats belonged to the Irish. There were two seats dominated by Italians, two suburban seats where Jews had the advantage, at least one seat where it helped enormously to be Polish, and another where the Portuguese usually won. By 1972, there were more than enough African American voters to form a majority-black district, but they were parceled out into adjoining districts so as not to jeopardize any predominantly white district.

The deeply rooted tradition was that each legislative chamber did its own redistricting and then concurred unquestioningly in the other's. Race was no longer an issue for us in the House. But when the Senate produced a plan that maintained that body's racial purity, the five black House members objected. They won the support of

Republican governor Frank Sargent, who promised to veto any all-white plan the Senate passed. His vow was the necessary condition for blocking the Senate's plan. But it was not sufficient. The Democrats had more than enough seats to override Sargent's veto.

That is where we came in. Building on my work for Mayor White, I had formed close personal and political relationships with the two leading black legislators, King and Bunte. When we learned of Sargent's inclination to veto the Senate plan, we met with other liberals who had demonstrated a willingness to defy the leadership in the past and we were able to secure the votes to uphold Sargent's veto.

The main beneficiary of the status quo was Senator William "Billy" Bulger, who was working his way up the leadership ladder and soon would become the longest-serving and most powerful Senate leader in the state's history. His South Boston–based district had a large share of black voters—an ideal balance for him and others seeking to maintain Irish dominance of the seat. There were too few blacks for an African American to win a primary—the only election that mattered—but enough to threaten a South Boston candidate if the Irish vote was split by multiple candidacies. Bulger was thus able to play the race card to discourage competition from his base, guaranteeing him easy, continuous reelection. He was—not surprisingly—furious with us for threatening the comfortable alignment of his Senate seat.

His anger was only increased by the fact that the city was on the verge of a racial crisis prompted by court-ordered efforts to desegregate the schools. South Boston was Louise Day Hicks's political base, and the neighborhood vehemently—and soon violently—opposed the busing of students across district lines. Even worse, the assault on this bastion of Irish ethnic and cultural pride was being waged on behalf of the city's black population with the eager participation of suburban liberals—whom the people of South Boston accused, with some justification, of being biased against them.

Our coalition of Republicans, liberals, and mavericks held together in the face of heavy pressure, and Sargent's veto was sustained. Two significant consequences ensued. First, the state's Democratic leaders chose to establish the state's first black Senate district at the

expense of suburban liberals—especially, and not entirely incidentally, Jewish suburban liberals. The city of Newton and the town of
Brookline, with heavy populations of Jews, were merged into one
district. As the leadership viewed it, if we liberals were so eager to
give the blacks a Senate seat, we could give them one of ours. The
newly configured districts also left Bulger in strong shape. He lost the
black voters in his district and gained white liberal voters from my
own part of the city. This suited him perfectly well. As before, he
could keep Irish voters in South Boston unified behind him by warning of the danger that a non-Southie candidate could win the seat.

A future consequence of the redistricting was also a form of liberal punishing, aimed entirely at me. Eight years later, Bulger's fury
at my role had not diminished. When the Massachusetts congressional delegation was reduced by one after the 1980 census, he was by
then Senate president. He used his powers to dismantle my district
in the U.S. House of Representatives—in a manner that left most
people, myself included, convinced that I would not survive.

Although my defiance of Bulger and the other entrenched Democratic leaders would cost me later on, it required no great political
courage at the time. Neither did my advocacy of other political positions that were in varying degrees unpopular and unconventional. I
was in a unique political situation. Given the unusual nature of the
district I represented, I was very unlikely to lose my seat. Given my
own unusual nature, I was equally unlikely to win any other. Being
unbeatable where I was, and unelectable anywhere else, gave me that
rare political commodity: the freedom that comes from having nothing left to lose. I took full advantage of my wholly secure electoral
position in my first reelection campaign. We turned a photo in which
I appeared somewhat disheveled into a poster that read NEATNESS
ISN'T EVERYTHING. I was learning the political benefits of humorous
self-denigration when it came to unimportant parts of my persona.

As I hoped, I was able to enhance my electoral strength with constituent service. Grateful for my help with the city's subway finances,
Kevin White invited me to pick a project that would benefit my
constituents—and, of course, myself in turn. That is why Commonwealth Avenue, one of America's most beautiful avenues, is lit at

night by elegant and expensive electric lights that combine modern illumination with an architecturally appropriate nineteenth-century appearance.

At year's end, Bartley confirmed my status as a liberal trusted by the leadership when he named me to the Ways and Means Committee. This was largely symbolic. Although the committee was very important, it had no real decision-making power because the leadership tightly controlled everything. But joining it was an important symbol of my acceptance. Among other things, it was proof that "the gay thing" was on no one's radar screen but mine.

It was now time for another career decision. I was still convinced that I was holding the only elected office I could ever hope to win. I also knew that as much as I enjoyed that job, ten years in it would be enough. For one thing, it paid barely enough to live on—most members had other sources of income. And although the jurisdiction was interesting, state governments in America operate within tight constraints. It is at the federal level—then and now—that the major economic questions are addressed. I was pretty sure that after ten years in the Statehouse, I would be ready to move on.

But only if I had something else to do. Once again, I made a career choice under the influence of someone else. Alexander Cella was an ethnic street pol with a first-rate mind and a profound commitment to liberalism. He had been a state representative from blue-collar Medford but had lost a primary to a bus driver whose popularity, rumor went, was based in part on his willingness to depart from his route and drop passengers at their doors. Cella was promptly hired as a policy aide to the Speaker and became a lawyer. One evening in December 1973, when I ran into him as I was leaving the office, he volunteered that I ought to follow his example.

After very little thought, I agreed. I do not necessarily concur with the oft-given advice that aspiring policy makers should go to law school. In Congress, I found economics far more useful, and I also wish I had forced myself to take more courses in accounting—the language in which political debates about both taxation and spending are most often conducted. But while economic thinking was most relevant to both city and national governing, lawyering is at the core of state government. It is at the state level that most of the laws governing personal and economic conduct are adopted. Crime, domestic relations, property ownership, retail transactions—these are all largely state matters.

In addition, I knew that becoming a lawyer would help me cope with one persistent form of obfuscation I encountered in my dealings with defenders of various status quos. "Why don't we do it this way?" I would propose on some issue. "You can't do that," somebody's counsel would tell me. "Why can't we?" I would ask. "Are you a lawyer?" was the frequent response. When I answered that I wasn't, there followed the condescending debate stopper: "Then you wouldn't understand."

With these thoughts in mind, I entered Harvard Law School in the fall of 1974. Three years later, when I was asked if I was a lawyer and I replied that I was, I found that "You can't do that" quickly became, "Well, you *could* do that, but it wouldn't be a good idea." (At that point, economics often became relevant.)

I continued my legislative work and constituency service without any crises, even after Bartley was replaced as Speaker by Tom Mc-Gee, a much more conservative politician who was much less tolerant of dissent. Unexpectedly—and unsettlingly—my next major political struggle was not with the House leadership, nor the Republicans, but with a man I greatly admired: Michael Dukakis.

Over the previous decade, he had emerged as the most effective progressive in Massachusetts politics, and in 1974 he was elected governor. As he prepared to take office, he'd asked me to be his secretary of transportation. I was torn. This was a very attractive offer. I expected that Dukakis would lead a successful and progressive administration. And the time was ripe. Democrats, especially liberals, had done very well in the post-Watergate elections. If Richard Nixon's finely tuned political instincts led him to push for an expanded government role in health care, some form of national minimum income, and our first serious environmental policy, while, to top it all off, telling a reporter that he was "now a Keynesian," the odds were overwhelming that the newly reempowered Democratic majorities could make major advances on our policy agenda. I foresaw the coming of a liberal version of the Era of Good Feeling.

But two considerations led me to turn down the offer. Most important, I had just been reelected to a second term, and I wasn't ready to give up my seat. Second, taking a full-time job would have meant leaving law school after only one semester. I was not happy at the prospect of adding another busted academic effort to my phantom pursuit of a Ph.D. Fortunately, Dukakis ended up giving the position to our intellectual leader in the antihighway fight, Fred Salvucci. Technical mastery of transportation issues and a level of political skill not always present in great engineers allowed him to do the job much better than I would have.

Another beneficial result of my decision became clear a few months into Dukakis's term: I would not have to resign from his administration. It turned out that my reading of the political mood, both nationally and in our state, could not have been more wrong. Analysts have given a number of reasons for the popular turn against government, including the distrust brought on by Vietnam, the violent expression of African American disappointment at the lingering impact of racism and the angry white reaction to it, the spectacle of a vice president forced out of office for tawdry corruption, and the disregard of democratic rules by a president. While all of these factors contributed to the growing rejection of collective action, I believe the single biggest cause was the one later summed up by the Clinton campaign: "It's the economy, stupid."

By the mid-1970s, the enormous advantage America had enjoyed over every other economy in the world since World War II was eroding rapidly. This decline had two major components—the reindustrialization of the developed economies and the growing assertiveness of the oil-producing nations.

While the former was to have more profound long-term effects, the latter was felt with greater immediacy. Indeed, the recession that followed the OPEC oil embargo of 1973 hit Massachusetts particularly hard. I broke with Dukakis over how the state government should react to that recession. With our economy slumping, we did not have enough revenue to support the current level of public expenditure. I publicly and privately insisted that Dukakis seek a tax increase, not to avoid any cutbacks but at least to minimize them. But he had campaigned on what he called "a lead pipe guarantee" not to raise taxes.

Instead, he proposed significant reductions in various state-funded welfare payments. He also proposed cuts that I supported, involving government waste and patronage. But in the absence of increased tax revenue, it was clear that the poorest people in the state would bear much of the burden.

Pushing for higher taxes instead of cutting welfare payments is rarely a preferred platform for elected officials. Given the socioeconomic composition of those who regularly go to the polls, it essentially means asking those who do vote to give some of their money to those who don't. This usually does not win elections (although Mitt Romney did demonstrate in 2012 that a candidate can define the recipient class so broadly, and make the political point so crudely, that the electoral math reverses).

By the late spring of 1975, I had become known as the leading liberal in the budget fight. My African American colleagues advanced the same position, but the language of political analysts—then and now—curiously treats "blacks" and "liberals" as separate, albeit usually allied, factions. My best guess is that this reflects the implicit assumption that blacks are supposed to support civil rights and aid for the poor, so that referring to them as "liberals" would be redundant.

I failed to defeat Dukakis's cuts to the state's General Relief fund and failed as well to protect the mostly elderly recipients of Supplemental Security Income. I had expected to win that last fight but lost it, 112 to 123. This was an early, powerful indication that my post-Watergate hopes for a new Great Society had been unrealistic.

Dukakis ultimately accepted the need for tax increases, and to his credit he did so knowing he would pay a political price. I joined in the effort to pass the increases, but my disaffection with him remained. Perhaps ironically, his commitment to intellectual integrity exacerbated my feeling. Like another leader I greatly respected, Al Lowenstein, he had a deep-seated reluctance to do anything important for largely political reasons.

I can think of only one elected official in our history who showed a total, unflinching immunity to the attractions of reelection. Montana's Jeannette Rankin was the first woman elected to the U.S. House—in 1916, two years after Montana established woman suffrage and three years before the nation followed suit. On firm principle, she voted against declaring World War I (as it was not then called) and lost the next election. Twenty-two years later, with distaste for European entanglements at a peak, she won a second term. After the Japanese attacked Pearl Harbor, she was the only member of Congress to vote against declaring World War II, and promptly lost the next time around. She was a woman of complete integrity and rotten luck—a pacifist who could not win an election without the country almost immediately going to war.

Compared to most elected officials, Dukakis and Lowenstein only rarely seemed to take positions because those positions conformed to public opinion. The problem was that neither man could admit any fallibility even to himself. Consequently, they would proudly defend their ill-chosen views on the merits. Given their great persuasive power, and the respect they'd earned from ideological allies, the regrettable result was increased support for the proposition in question. And so Dukakis did not simply propose welfare cuts as an unfortunate political necessity. He also went on to explain why benefit cuts were not so bad—which would only make it harder to undo them later!

Even as I championed government spending, I did recognize the need to improve how the money was spent. All those dollars wasted by the fabled three horsemen of the fiscal apocalypse—fraud, waste, and abuse—meant less money to run a good transit system or provide an adequate minimum income for the truly needy. And in two areas I took the lead in achieving reform. There was undeniable evidence that some recipients of income transfer programs were double-dipping, so I proposed legislation mandating the computerization of recipient lists. This would allow cross matching to catch those who were illegally benefiting from participating in multiple programs. To my annoyance, several of my allies on the left objected, confirming the unfortunate correlation between deep compassion and political obtuseness that afflicts some of the advocacy community. But they had no votes, and the system became law, with both political and substantive benefits.

The fight for better spending practices in the transit system was much tougher. The law governing compensation for union members mandated binding arbitration for all contracts, in practice ruling out any way to take fiscal constraints into account. When the power to set expenditures is separated from the responsibility to pay for them, all kinds of mischief are likely to ensue.

In 1978, I sponsored a bill that repealed compulsory arbitration. After a long, bitter struggle with the politically sophisticated and well-organized transit workers' union, the bill passed. The reforms worked, and they set the stage for the expansion of the system rather than its shrinkage. But the workers were furious, and I bore much of the brunt of their anger.

•

While I remained slow to recognize how unpopular government was becoming, I was happily aware that we were making real progress on the LGBT front. Even so, I was not ready to respond forthrightly when I took up another gay-related issue and was at last asked "the question."

On the border of my ward's Bay Village neighborhood, there were two gay bars that were frequent trouble spots. They attracted rowdy, sometimes violent patrons, and the owners made no effort to keep the disruption out of the adjacent residential area. After the owners derisively rejected the neighborhood association's requests for cooperation, requests that I strongly supported, I joined the residents in petitioning the Liquor Licensing Authority to close the bars or, at the very least, cut back their hours of operation at night. The bars tried to rally support in the LBGT community, but their justifiably shady reputation, and the fact that the neighborhood included more LGBT residents than most others, undercut that effort. The owners did ask me to a very private meeting to see if we could come to some arrangement that would allow them to continue to operate without restriction. In an episode out of a B movie from the 1940s, Henry Vara, the principal owner, began by telling me in injured tones how aggrieved he was that I had said he had some form of Mafia connection. I acknowledged that I had passed along a rumor to that effect but added that I had never claimed to know if it was true. "Well, it's not true," he answered. "I don't know those people and I have no dealings with them." At that point, his bar manager–bouncer interjected indignantly, "Besides, we hear you were connected yourself back in

New Jersey." This was an accurate reference to some of my father's associates when he ran his truck stop, and to the dealings my mother and I had with them in winding up his estate. But it did not help Vara's disavowal of mob ties, which he acknowledged by snarling at his aide, "Shut up!"

Once I declined to be his ally, I became Vara's target. He knew exactly what to do. When we took up the neighborhood's request for relief at a hearing, his lawyer, Frank DiMento, suddenly asked me—under oath—if I was gay.

The hearing was presided over by the chairman of the Liquor Licensing Authority, a very decent former police officer named Charlie Byrne. He immediately volunteered that I did not have to answer. That was the good news—evidently, using anti-gay prejudice to discredit an opponent no longer worked as well as it had for the great civil libertarian Joseph Welch twenty-five years earlier. But the bad news is that I answered anyway—by denying it. I report this with a lingering sense of shame—though not with fear of criminal liability since the statute of limitations for perjury has long since elapsed. I answered as I did because I feared the inference that would be drawn from my silence. (The number of times heterosexual public figures decline to discuss their sexuality on privacy grounds is very small.) Clearly, I was still struggling personally with how to deal with "the gay thing."

And I stress *personally*. Had my resistance to honesty been based wholly on fear of the electoral consequences, I would have had more courage. That was because Elaine Noble had just become the first openly gay winner of a partisan election for public office in the country—in a newly created district that consisted largely of areas that had previously belonged to my own district. While San Francisco city supervisor Harvey Milk's forceful style, passionate eloquence, and martyrdom make him the best known of our early openly gay elected officials, Noble herself was the first person with the courage and skill to break the barrier.

If she could do it, why couldn't I? That was the question I faced—from myself and, I learned a few years later, from others in the LGBT community whose "gaydar" had worked. I rationalized that it was easier for a woman than for a man to come out—a partial truth—and also that she had been elected by the most left-wing, countercultural constituency in Massachusetts. Most important, though, I simply was not ready to expose my previous masquerade and to share the deep secret I had kept for twenty years.

In the public realm, I perceived some progress on LGBT issues. My bill to ban employment discrimination was losing by smaller margins, after debates conducted respectfully. I continued to intervene on behalf of gay men with the police department. And for the first time in my life, I felt free to joke about it all.

When one of my pet causes was being debated on the floor of the House, a socially conservative Democrat from New Bedford challenged me angrily and accurately: "If it's not prostitution, if it's not fornication, if it's not support of rights for homosexuals . . . it's this bill. Mr. Speaker, I want to know when the gentleman from the Back Bay is going to stop."

I responded: "Mr. Speaker, it is true that I have introduced bills relating to pornography, gambling, prostitution, adultery, marijuana, and homosexuality. But I am going to make a commitment to my colleague from New Bedford. I will keep on trying until I find something he likes to do."

Meanwhile, my support for LGBT goals was evolving quickly into friendships with leaders of the community. I regularly attended functions that combined political and social purposes—and regretted that my self-imposed silence kept me from fully sharing in the comradeship.

Beyond Massachusetts, I met the movement's rising national leaders. I was delighted when the activist Steve Endean was elected to the board of one of the leading liberal organizations in the country, Americans for Democratic Action, as its first openly gay member in 1974. Endean shared my preference for political organizing over public theatrics, and my eagerness to collaborate with him, combined with a need to break out of my total personal isolation, led me to confide to him that I was also gay—one of the very first times I admitted this to anyone. His reaction at first disappointed me, though it confirmed my confidence in his political judgment. "Shit," he said, "you're the third lead sponsor of a state gay rights bill to come out to me this year. Here I've been bragging about all this straight support

we have, but it turns out to be mostly from closet cases!" His preference for electoral coalitions over sexual solidarity was complete—and
one of our earliest assets.

My next trial as a gay advocate came in November 1974, when a
public referendum mandated that the Massachusetts House shrink
from 240 seats to 160. Eighty seats had to be abolished. I was not on
the target list—my relationship with the House leadership was still
characterized by mutual tolerance. But geography compelled reunit-
ing Ward Five. This meant that Elaine Noble's district and my own
would be merged into one.

This was the kind of crisis over "the gay thing" that I had dreaded.
I would win against Noble in a primary. Many more of the new Ward
Five's voters hailed from my district than hers, and while I had once
represented many of her constituents, she had never represented any
of mine.

And, candidly, I had a better reputation as an effective liberal legislator. I had by then realized that while there were many things I could
do barely, if at all—such as writing my dissertation—I had a combination of talents that made me successful at the unique job of legislating.

•

Three aspects of legislative work define it. The first, which it shares
with the work of chief executives, is that it has an all-encompassing
jurisdiction. Even though representatives and senators specialize in
various subjects, every one of them has to vote on everything. Second, unlike presidents and governors, legislators rarely control the
timing of the issues before them, which gives their work an improvi-
sational quality, especially as they have significantly less staff.

Finally, and most crucially, legislatures operate in a uniquely unstructured forum. Generally when people engage in legally binding
transactions, one or both of two principles apply. One is money: I will
pay you so much if you will do this in return—sell me your car, paint
my house, work in my store. The second is hierarchy. In every formal
organization, there is a person at the top who is legally empowered to
give binding instructions to others, who may in turn have that power
over workers below them.

Except in legislatures. Legislators do not pay each other for votes,

and every member of a parliament in a democratic society is legally
equal to every other member. Some are of course more influential
than others, but not even a long-serving Speaker of the U.S. House
can order any other member to do anything. (With one exception: A
presiding officer facing the lack of a quorum can send the sergeant at
arms to physically compel absent members to attend a session. As the
formal parliamentary expression goes, good luck with that. When boy-
cotting members do show up to a session, it is public opinion, not
armed officials, that is the cause.)

This formal legal equality among legislators puts a premium on
personal relations as the basis for legislative influence. Indeed, the
similarities between gaining respect in a legislature and becoming
popular in high school deserve serious attention from sociologists.
For example, it is very helpful in both situations to be good at what
you do but not to seem overly impressed with yourself when you do
it. Exhibiting any sense of superiority invites debunking. Sociability
is highly prized—loners are suspect, and an inclination to nonconfor-
mity is a serious handicap to the goodwill of your peers. And as I've
mentioned, reliability in your personal dealings is essential.

This last point is even more essential in the legislative context
than anywhere else. Because parliamentary bodies have to arrive at
binding decisions on the full range of human activity in an atmosphere lacking the structure provided by either money or hierarchy,
members have to find ways to bring some order out of what could be
chaos. And so once you have promised another member that you will
do something—vote a certain way, sponsor a particular bill, or conduct
a hearing—you are committed to do it. You have, in the most solemn
of obligations, "given your word." It is permissible later to ask that
member to "release" you if you can plausibly plead some unforeseen
change in circumstances, and the convention is for that colleague to
do so if your reason is good enough—usually political necessity; breaking your word because you changed your mind rarely qualifies.

The need to minimize instability accounts for another highly valued parliamentary norm: the strong bias against relitigating an issue
that has been legitimately decided. If every issue is always on the
active agenda, if an issue that was already disposed of by a majority

can be reopened whenever the side that lost regains an advantage, instability infects not just the body that made that decision but also the society that it is governed by. It is the explicit rejection of that principle by the Tea Party Republicans that contributes heavily to political gridlock.

A representative or senator's effectiveness thus is based on his or her ability to deal with a very wide range of issues, with never enough time, and with little guidance from others. You do this in a forum where personal ties are as important as substance, and where you and the people you seek to influence are continuously filtering decisions through the screen of public opinion. For many highly intelligent people, working on important issues in this fluid atmosphere is distracting at best and deeply frustrating at worst. Having to vote yes or no on a politically conceived response to a complex economic or scientific matter, with little opportunity to study it and no chance to improve it, is a source of constant dissatisfaction. The opportunity to shape that response yourself may only make things worse. Accepting the compromises arrived at by others is bad enough; deliberately omitting important ideas and intentionally inserting undesirable provisions yourself is much worse. But you will not be an effective legislator if you cannot tolerate a steady diet of this. I could. After a few years of legislating, I came to adopt as my guiding principle the wisdom expressed by a great twentieth-century student of human affairs, Henny Youngman, in an immortal two-liner: "How's your wife?" "Compared to what?"

Better than some other liberals, I was fortunately able to maintain the personal relationships essential to legislative influence. My experience working at my father's Jersey City truck stop, negotiating with Mafia figures to settle his estate, and campaigning in Mississippi left me more comfortable than some of my high-minded allies in dealing with a broad cross section of people. I also possessed other useful gifts: I was able to shift intellectual gears rapidly, assimilate information quickly, and speak with little preparation.

Legislative skill is not transferable to other lines of work, and I acknowledge that some of my assets would be drawbacks in other occupations. My short attention span, and my ability—and, consequently, predilection—to make snap decisions with incomplete information can be defects in more structured institutional settings. And even in legislating, one trait that is usually helpful—a willingness to settle for the best achievable outcome in a given set of circumstances—poses a danger. It diminishes the chance to achieve a better result by altering those limiting circumstances. I kept this danger in mind but was not always successful in avoiding it. Henny Youngman was a good guide, but not a perfect one.

•

Fortunately for my career, a group of lesbian political leaders in Boston applied the "compared to what?" standard when they met with me to discuss the Elaine Noble situation. When Noble's district was combined with mine, my original, agonized decision was to step aside in her favor. That was based on a single factor: She was out of the closet and I was in it. Eight years after Stonewall, it was clear that being honest about our sexuality was the best political tool we had. As much as I wanted to continue being a representative, I could not single-handedly eliminate the only openly gay elected official in the state. After explaining this to some friends in the LGBT community, I was summoned to meet with the state's lesbian leadership at the home of Byrd Swift, a respected activist. (It was a very nice home on Commonwealth Ave., reflecting her membership in both of the prominent families whose names she bore.)

To paraphrase their words, they instructed me to cut the crap and get reelected. They took turns arguing that I was the more able legislator and that my value to the cause of equality outweighed the advantage of Noble's openness. I do not know if any of them were influenced by the presumption that I was gay and could not stay closeted forever.

I received their message with mixed emotions. Their assurance that I could run without betraying our cause meant a lot to me. But I also had lingering feelings of guilt, which I assuaged by pledging to myself that I would come out too at some point.

Once I made the decision to run, my own electoral concerns disappeared. Noble decided not to contest our race and instead entered the party's Senate primary, which she lost to Paul Tsongas. I won re-election easily. My district was immune to the increasing conservatism that was elsewhere sweeping the electorate, and my constituent services had been productive and well received.

But 1978 was to be a very rough year for me. Over the course of it, I angered every element in the leadership of the Massachusetts Democratic Party. In a grave error that I regret to this day, I endorsed Barbara Ackermann, the liberal former mayor of Cambridge, when she entered the Democratic gubernatorial primary against Dukakis. The problem was that Dukakis had another challenger as well, Edward King, representing the conservative wing of the Democratic establishment. Because of our close and long-standing collaboration, I allowed my disagreement with Dukakis's welfare policies to harden into a sense of betrayal. This was compounded by my seller's remorse. In Dukakis's 1974 race, I had energetically rebutted his critics on the left. Two contributors to the alternative press who later became important mainstream journalistic voices, Paul Solman of PBS and Joe Klein of *Time*, saw what I didn't—that Dukakis's liberalism was at its strongest when it came to "reform" issues like cleaning up elections. It was not as pronounced in areas of economic policy or the regulation of personal behavior (for example, he later opposed the adoption of children by gay men and lesbians).

When the 1978 campaign began, it was widely believed that Dukakis would win decisively. He had done an excellent job of guiding the state through a devastating snowstorm earlier in the year, and King was not highly regarded. But King's blunt repetition of conservative themes resonated with the voters' mood. He won by a large margin—large enough, in fact, that we Ackermann supporters could not be held mathematically responsible for the outcome. Even so, we did bear a substantial part of the blame. Our criticisms made Dukakis less popular and distracted him from battling his main opponent.

In the general election, I endorsed King's opponent, Frank Hatch. It was an easy choice. Hatch was a moderate to liberal Republican, of the sort who have of course largely disappeared from that party's leadership. (Hatch quit the Republican Party years later on ideological grounds.) Unfortunately, he lost to King by five points.

My third break with normal political behavior that year was to endorse Republican senator Ed Brooke for reelection. When I endorsed Brooke the first time, his opponent was a Democratic district attorney—a party regular whose candidacy excited very few people and whom no one expected to win. But in 1978, Brooke's opponent was one of the most promising younger Democrats to emerge in years: Congressman Paul Tsongas. He had come from behind in a tough Democratic primary, building on an outstanding record in two terms in Congress. To most Democrats, he was an exciting new face with a great future ahead of him.

I agreed with all of this. But I also continued to believe that coping with the legacy of racism was our single greatest moral responsibility as a nation. Although many white liberals voiced their agreement with that position, I learned to my dismay that few of them understood the depth of feeling within the black community on the matter. I experienced a particularly vivid example of that when a distinguished Harvard professor who was also one of the leading liberal voices in the country told a group in my presence that he had turned down the suggestion that he run against Brooke because he did not wish to go to the Senate, although, he said, "I would even outpoll him in Roxbury" (at the time the center of Boston's African American population). I thought of that comment and the lack of understanding it demonstrated as I observed the anguish of Boston's black leaders—almost all Democrats—in the campaign's closing days when it became clear that Brooke would lose. His defeat, I believe, struck them as proof that even the liberals in the white majority were prepared to disregard their deepest feelings when they wanted to.

Initially, I encountered more resentment from my friends for opposing Tsongas than for rejecting Dukakis. Despite this, my stance in the governor's race had the longer-lasting negative impact on my standing, for a basic, albeit often neglected, principle of political life: Losers hold grudges longer and more deeply than winners remain grateful. Almost every day of King's governorship brought a new reason for my friends to blame me.

By the end of 1978, I had fought to defeat the outgoing and incoming Democratic governors as well as the incoming Democratic senator. But I wasn't through alienating allies. I had strongly backed Kevin White in 1975 when he ran for his third term as mayor. He remained relatively liberal in his orientation, and he was being unfairly pilloried by the anti–school busing forces, even though his role was primarily to maintain order as the federal judiciary's mandate was carried out.

But by 1979, I was in profound disagreement with his determination to create a citywide political machine focused less on good governance than on power. So I endorsed Mel King, my close colleague and the leader of the Legislative Black Caucus, in the primary election. When he was eliminated, I then surprised almost everybody—myself included—by endorsing White's 1975 opponent and nemesis, Joseph Timilty, in the final. Timilty was an old-school politician, but he had matured substantially in my judgment. He had become a force for conciliation, refusing to demagogue the racial issue, and he was becoming a leader on affordable housing. In other words, I found him to be an ideologically acceptable replacement for White. I am opposed to term limits as a general principle, but I felt strongly that White had stayed too long.

White won without me—which by then was becoming a discouragingly familiar pattern.

Surprisingly, this serial alienation of the major figures in the Massachusetts Democratic Party did not damage my political standing as much as it might have and, as I look back on it now, as much as it probably should have. By 1979 it was becoming clearer that the rise of conservatism was not a temporary event but a genuine swing to the right. In retrospect, the 1976 presidential nominations were clear early signs of this. President Gerald Ford, a mainstream conservative Republican who not long before had sought to impeach the most liberal member of the Supreme Court, William O. Douglas, barely survived a challenge for the nomination from his right by Ronald Reagan. The Democrats nominated Jimmy Carter, who articulated an ethic of austerity and mixed support for some government initiatives with a harsh critique of government in general. (The contrast between Carter and McGovern was telling: You'd have to go back to 1904, when the Wall Street lawyer Alton Parker succeeded the militantly populist William Jennings Bryan, to find two adjacent Democratic nominees who were so far apart on the political spectrum.) In 1978, the antigovernment mood intensified. Californians passed the tax-limiting Proposition 13, providing a model for similar referenda restricting government activity elsewhere, including Proposition 2 ½ in Massachusetts in 1980, which limited property taxes.

Politicians took notice of this move in public opinion and adjusted their behavior accordingly. After forty years as an elected representative, I am still struck by how often people underestimate the impact of popular opinion on elected officials, and by how odd their assessment of that impact can be. Legislators who accommodate voter sentiment are denounced as cowardly, and those who defy it are just as fiercely accused of rejecting democratic norms. Both of these opposing views of a representative's obligations are wholly defensible. Less so is the tendency of most voters to alternate between them, depending entirely on whether or not they agree with the official's substantive position.

In any case, my own safe district allowed me to become one of the few white politicians who still loudly advocated traditional liberalism in the late 1970s. In 1976, I had strongly supported Congressman Morris Udall for the Democratic nomination. Even though I was happy to see Carter defeat Ford, I was not enthusiastic about his presidency. He did begin to move forward on LGBT issues, expressing opposition to discrimination and meeting with LGBT leaders. These important steps were facilitated by Midge Costanza, a highly placed and closeted White House adviser who resolved the question of how to handle "the gay thing" the same way I had: pro-LGBT advocacy coupled with personal radio silence. Carter's presidency also marked the transformation of LGBT rights into a partisan issue. In 1976, Carter and Ford both sent us positive signals. But by 1980, the rise of Ronald Reagan turned the GOP into a strongly anti-LGBT party—even though in 1978, Reagan had successfully opposed an effort to ban gay schoolteachers via the longest-playing combination of high melodrama and low farce in American politics—the California referendum process.

My decision to persist in advocating the politically unpopular did not reflect any extraordinary moral courage on my part. What I was exhibiting was not a hunger for martyrdom but the political freedom that comes from having nothing left to lose, greatly strengthened by my having nothing left to win, either. My effectiveness in defending the neighborhoods I represented and the disproportionate number of liberals who lived in them guaranteed my reelection to the House. I was free to fight for liberalism from my safe seat, unencumbered by electoral worries. But I was also restless. By my seventh year in the House, with a conservative Democratic governor allied to conservative Democratic leaders in the legislature, the thrill of legislative work had diminished considerably.

I did see one beacon on the horizon. I was then writing occasional columns for *The New Republic*, and in one of them I supported the case that Ted Kennedy, the most prominent and articulate champion of unapologetic liberalism, should challenge Carter for the Democratic nomination in 1980. Perhaps I would one day leave Boston for Washington and work for him. While I never discussed the column with Kennedy, I did hear from some of his aides, and when he decided to run in late 1979, I was asked to go to New York to help run his campaign in that state. Outsiders have two advantages in this kind of work. As nonresidents, there is no chance they will put their own electoral interests ahead of the candidate's. And they are also less likely to have personal enemies in their state of temporary residence, or to be seen as rivals by the host state's political figures.

Unfortunately, my first experience with the Kennedy campaign was a fiasco. New York's Kennedy supporters resented the idea that they needed a non–New Yorker, and I was sent ignominiously back to Massachusetts in a few days, with both my career plans and my ego in serious disrepair.

By late 1979, it was increasingly uncertain that there would ever be another Kennedy administration, especially after Kennedy performed uncharacteristically badly in an interview with CBS's Roger Mudd. I decided it was time to adopt career plan B. I would publicly acknowledge my homosexuality and combine the private practice of law with a role in the national movement for lesbian and gay rights, drawing on my experience as a prominent elected official in both pursuits.

Only as I think about this now—thirty-five years later—do I recognize how profound a shift this represented. Instead of advocating a bigger role for government across the board, I would strive to achieve progress in one specific area. This was not because gay rights was intrinsically more important to me. It was because, for the first time in my life, the prospects for rolling back legally sanctioned homophobia seemed better than the prospects for advancing economic fairness.

I soon took the first step down my new career path: telling my closest friends and relatives the truth (some of them suspected it already). The reactions were wholly supportive but varied in other ways. My lesbian and gay sisters and brothers were happy for our cause— even Endean, whose sense of solidarity overcame his regret at losing a putative straight ally. And knowing the personal stress of living in the closet, they celebrated my liberation from it. My siblings were comforting. They assured me that the love and mutual support we had always shown each other would be undiminished.

Meanwhile, my political allies coupled personal affirmation with political caution. They reminded me—unnecessarily but caringly— that coming out would greatly complicate any possible political future. My response was that publicly affirming my sexuality was part of my plan for advancing social change in an unelected capacity.

I wasn't ready to leap immediately from being a closeted elected official to being an openly gay activist, so I decided to run for reelection to the House one last time, and spend the next two years preparing for my new life. I was confident that with my Harvard law degree and what would be a ten-year record of legislative and electoral success, I could make plenty of money practicing law and play a leading role in the emerging national gay rights movement.

And then on a Sunday afternoon in May 1980, the phone rang again.

This time the life-altering call came from Margie Segel, who was then the wife of Jim Segel, my former aide and a legislative ally and close friend. She had just received a call from a liberal state representative looking for her husband. When she said that her husband was not at home, the caller asked if he knew that Pope John Paul II had just ordered Father Robert Drinan, the nationally prominent Catholic priest and liberal congressman from Massachusetts, not to run for re-election. She told the caller that she was sure her husband did not know, since it was something he would certainly have mentioned to her. The caller's reply was, "Oh! If Jimmy doesn't know, that means that Barney doesn't know." And so she called me immediately to tell me the news. Since the caller seemed glad I didn't know, she explained, it was obviously important that I should know, and quickly.

She was right. Timing was critical. Drinan had shared the bad news with his close circle the day before. Nomination petitions bearing the signatures of two thousand registered voters from the congressional district had to be filed by 5:00 p.m. on Tuesday.

If I chose to run, I would have fifty-two hours to gather those signatures. The decision I made turned out to be one of the two most important in my life. Coming out of the closet would be the second. Ironically, the first decision postponed the second.

I had come to terms emotionally with going public about my sexuality. I had finally found a way to free myself from the constant fear of exposure and the consequent need for self-denial that life in the closet had required. But becoming a candidate for Congress put me right back where I had been at fourteen: confronting the irreconcilability between my sexuality and my political ambition.

We had made a great deal of progress in reducing homophobia, but I did not believe I could possibly win a seat in the U.S. Congress—in a district of more than four hundred thousand people—as an openly gay man. This was especially the case because I did not actually live in that district. Legally, according to the Supreme Court's interpretation of the Constitution, that was not necessary. But politically, according to the prevailing rules of the game, it was all but essential.

Yet I chose to run anyway. My logic was simple: I couldn't imagine a better chance to win an important office, and if I did win that office, I believed I could exert more influence on public policy than I could in any other conceivable role.

Of course, I wasn't ready to make my decision on the spur of the moment, and without consultation. Fortunately, Jim Segel returned home shortly after my conversation with his wife, and we arranged to meet immediately. I told him that I was thinking seriously about running. He gave me the excellent direct advice you get only from a very good friend: "Fuck think! If you want to run, start now and I'll help. If you're going to piss this away by agonizing, let me know now so I can take my kids to the movies like I promised." Rebecca and Jennifer never got to the movies that day.

Throughout this book, I have attempted to rebut a popular misconception about politics: that public offices are filled with ambitious, driven men—women are rarely included in this stereotype—whose electoral success is the result of a carefully plotted pursuit of political victory. What this omits is the crucial role that luck plays in this process. In America, you get to run for office only when the right vacancy arises. This means that even the most determined would-be state senator or mayor or congressman is not the master of his fate. During my first campaign, *The Boston Globe* Statehouse reporter, Bob Turner, wrote a very helpful and gratifying column about me titled "Born to Be a Congressman." Similar things were said about me when I retired.

But I did not owe my career in Congress solely to my talent or driving ambition. I owed it first and foremost to a man over whom I had no influence: Pope John Paul II. (After I took over his seat, Drinan regretted never getting the chance to ask the pope if he was happy with the way that decision worked out.)

The fact that successful politicians owe so much to luck was summed up best by Tip O'Neill. When Edward Markey, who is now a senator from Massachusetts, expressed regret that he had won a seat in Congress at the age of thirty only because of the early death of O'Neill's friend Torbert Macdonald, O'Neill assuaged Markey's guilty feelings. "Eddie," he said, "don't you realize that we are in a business where you only get ahead because of the death, defeat, or disgrace of one of your friends?" O'Neill understood this well. He'd become Speaker of the House only after Congressman Hale Boggs, my involuntary post-Mississippi host, was lost in a plane crash while campaigning for a colleague in Alaska.

•

My decision to run for Congress had immediate consequences. First, I began telephoning my relatives, friends, and political allies to solicit their help. Second, I put aside all thoughts of making my homosexuality public. One of my first calls was to my sister Doris and her husband, Jim Breay. When Jim answered the phone, I told him I was now a congressional candidate and asked him a question: Did you just hear a closet door slam?

Jim immediately offered their house—which was in the district—as a temporary headquarters, and he and Doris were from then on indispensable sources of personal and political support. Doris was my campaign treasurer for my entire thirty-two-year tenure in Congress, and in that capacity handled well over $25 million in complex financial transactions with great skill. And she consistently refused any payment for her work.

Simultaneously, I began organizing my petition drive and courting Drinan's political committee. I was greatly aided by my brother, David, who had worked as Drinan's press secretary a few years earlier and was now an aide to the liberal New York congressman Stephen Solarz.

My legislative record—in substance and, to be candid, in stridency—was close to Drinan's. And with all of my quirks—known and suspected—I was not on the face of it a more controversial choice than a Catholic priest with his own distinctive personality.

There was one other aspirant who had as strong a claim as I did to be Drinan's liberal heir. He was a charismatic antiwar activist who had served in Vietnam. When Drinan had first run for Congress in 1970, this man was the peace caucus's second choice. After losing narrowly to Drinan, he campaigned strenuously and effectively for him. Two years later he lost a Congressional race to a right-wing smear campaign orchestrated by the Nixon hit man Charles Colson, but he continued to be an active leader of Massachusetts progressives. He had the enduring gratitude of the Drinan people for his grace in defeat in 1970, and by then he was living in the district.

Because we did not want to split the liberal vote, he and I needed to decide which one of us would run. Game theory helps explain why I became the candidate. Simply put, he had other electoral options, given his broader political appeal, and I did not. That is, he had much more to lose than I did if we couldn't work things out. There was an added factor in my favor. One of his closest friends—a fellow antiwar veteran—was positioned to win my seat in the state house if I ran for

Congress. Given all that, and his willingness to put personal ambition aside for the sake of his political convictions, he endorsed me.

Our view that he had many more options than I did soon proved correct, as John Kerry went on to be a lieutenant governor, senator, Democratic presidential nominee, and secretary of state. With Kerry's gracious support, I won the backing of the Drinan Committee, and the primary race was on.

The four of us who won ballot positions neatly exemplified the Democratic Party's divides at the time. State Representative David Mofenson and I were liberals. Arthur Clark, mayor of Waltham, the second-largest city in the district, and Robert Shaffer were more conservative, though in national terms, only Shaffer was genuinely on the right. Clark was opposed to abortion, no fan of gay rights, and far more supportive of a large military budget than I was. He also enjoyed backing from the AFL-CIO (my efforts to restrain Boston transit workers' wages did not help me with the union leadership, though I did receive support from the more liberal United Auto Workers). With the backing of the Drinan Committee, which voted 25 to 5 in my favor, the subsequent public endorsement of Drinan himself, and my legislative record, I was the leading liberal candidate. Clark, as the candidate with the largest electoral base, was the dominant conservative.

I could not have achieved my status in the race without the willingness of two leading liberals to put aside legitimate personal grievances. Though I'd backed his Republican opponent, Senator Paul Tsongas made no objection when his twin sister, Thaleia Schlesinger, signed on as my press secretary (and, as she realized was necessary, my fashion adviser). Meanwhile, Michael Dukakis remained benevolently neutral. I would learn from Tsongas and Dukakis the importance of disciplining my own emotional responses in the course of political battles.

•

I campaigned vigorously from early May through November, disliking almost every minute of it. I went from store to store to introduce myself, accompanied where possible by a popular local figure. I marched in July 4th parades and attended fairs, picnics, and any public gathering at which I was at least marginally welcome—my entourage and I were loudly chased away from one outdoor wedding. We concentrated our activity in those parts of the district where I lacked support. Our hope was that by introducing myself in person, I would dispel the presumption that I was a radical interloper. After all, my campaign faced a number of obstacles. Even though I'd moved into the district, I was coming there from Boston, and the shady life of a big city conjured up fears and distrust. (It is an axiom in most states that mayors of the largest city rarely become governors.) Even more problematic was my legislative record of aggressively championing gay rights, legal abortion, gun control, racial integration, legalized prostitution within certain areas, and the right of adults to consume marijuana and pornography (not necessarily at the same time). I was also unmarried—meaning at best that I had no appreciation of family life. And I was Jewish. By itself, my religious background might not have loomed large, but it reinforced the likelihood that I would be viewed as something of an alien. (As a point of historical interest, I am still the only Jewish congressman to represent Massachusetts since Leopold Morse retired in 1888. In his case a contributing factor was that he did get married—to a Christian, alienating both sides of the divide.)

My biggest liability, as usual, was that I hated campaigning. I know that politicians often tell a crowd how much they like the trail. Later in my career, after I felt secure in my seat, I shared with audiences my conviction that whenever they hear that, they are almost certainly listening to a liar or a sociopath. Candidates for elected office are always under tremendous pressure. On Election Day, they know they will be either winners or losers. No other profession confronts its members with such a stark result. Lawyers who lose cases may feel sorry for their clients, but they do not go to prison or lose significant amounts of money. Doctors whose patients die may grieve, but they will continue to practice medicine. For candidates who lose, that enterprise is over. And the loss is not just complete, it also is very public. There may be people in my former line of work who enjoy living with this prospect, but I haven't met any of them.

While you are contemplating the possibility of utter failure, you are also expected to pretend that you enjoy twelve- to fourteen-hour stints cheerfully introducing yourself to strangers, many of whom wish you would leave them alone. You repeat yourself eight or ten times a day to audiences, an ordeal alleviated only by encounters with journalists whose objective is to expose, embarrass, or confound you. From time to time these ordeals will be set aside for a debate, which will be judged significant only if you or your opponent says something stupid, clearly erroneous, or politically damaging.

Campaigning for state rep in my small, friendly legislative district had not been unpleasant. But running for Congress, especially in the hostile sections of the district where I had to spend most of my time, was awful. Moreover, the more I dislike something, the worse I am at doing it—and the worse I perform, the unhappier I get. I regret this aspect of my personality but have been unable to change it.

Despite my many defects as a candidate, my campaign was well run. The political strategist John Marttila, the pollster Tom Kiley, and the media specialist Dan Payne crafted a winning strategy. They focused on maximizing my appeal—ideological, if not personal—in the southern parts of the district, which included the liberal (and disproportionately Jewish) cities of Brookline and Newton.

My lifelong ally Jim Segel and my brother, David, who took a leave from his work for Solarz, executed this strategy well. And Thaleia Schlesinger successfully persuaded the media to report the substance of what I said, rather than dwell on the occasionally ungracious way I said it. Mary Beth Cahill, a young woman from the politically critical town of Framingham, signed on to help direct our field operation—including the critical get-out-the-vote drive. As the Irish daughter of a worker at the local GM plant and a committed liberal, she bridged the ethnic/ideological gap, and turned out to be enormously good at politics—a fact recognized later by several other politicians, including John Kerry, whose presidential campaign she managed (and managed well). The two finance cochairs, Richard Morningstar and my longtime ally from Massachusetts liberal politics, Nancy Korman, drew heavily on the liberal and Jewish communities—overlapping but not identical—to make my campaign the best funded in the race.

Finally, Dorothy Reichard—who'd been Drinan's chief Massa-

chusetts administrative and political aide—provided continuity between the past and present. She mobilized support for my campaign
and would remain indispensable to me for the next thirty years.

With their guidance, I was consistently ahead in the polls, not
overwhelmingly but by enough to win. But even the best-managed
campaigns are subject to outside events they cannot control. Shaffer,
who seemed highly motivated by his personal dislike of me, spent
most of the primary on the attack, until late August, when he dropped
out and endorsed Clark. This was a very dangerous moment for our
campaign, because it left Clark alone on the conservative side, while
Mofenson still drew some liberal votes from me. This led to strong
pressure on Mofenson, who wanted to continue his political career in
Newton, to emulate Shaffer. In September he announced he hoped
people would vote for me instead of him.

That was hardly the end of our difficulties, however. In early
September, the archbishop of Boston, Cardinal Humberto Medeiros,
suddenly issued a strong plea for Catholic voters to repudiate my
candidacy and that of James Shannon, a liberal first-term congressman from an adjoining district, because of our support for legal
abortion.

Medeiros issued the statement five days before the primary,
plunging our campaign into a state I had heard of but never fully
experienced—total disarray. Fortunately, I had some time to think
through our response because the cardinal had spoken on Rosh
Hashanah. When asked for a reaction, my campaign replied that I
was at temple—which was true—and would answer the next day.

After consulting with each other, Shannon and I calmly reiterated our positions, while expressing more respect for the cardinal
than I, at least, genuinely felt. I prepared emotionally for defeat. But
as it turned out, the power of Boston's once mighty cardinal archbish-
ops had waned significantly. Fewer Catholics than anticipated obeyed
the cardinal's instruction, and some Catholics and most Jewish and
Protestant voters resented it. Some commenters—I was conspicuously not among them—contrasted the pope's edict against Drinan
with the archbishop's message to voters. "Is the Church in politics or
not?" they asked.

On the Friday before the primary, we held a rally at a country club in Newton, featuring Ted Kennedy. Until the cardinal spoke, he had been formally neutral in my primary, as I expected him to be. But the archbishop's statement was a direct challenge to the pro-choice Kennedy, and there was the added factor that I had been a strong backer of his unsuccessful presidential effort. He was joined on the dais by another liberal Catholic political figure, Congressman Ed Markey, and together they helped reassure voters that supporting me was consistent with their religious views. To my great relief, I won the primary with 52 percent of the vote against Clark's 46. After Shannon and I both won, a Massachusetts newspaper ran the head-line "Kennedy 2; Cardinal 0."

Because Shaffer and Mofenson had dropped out so late, their names remained on the ballot. They each drew less than 1 percent in the actual tally, canceling each other out while serving to reflect pop-ular dissatisfaction with the choice between me and Clark. Frankly, I was surprised the dissatisfaction wasn't greater.

•

On primary night, almost everyone in my campaign was confident that victory in November was a certainty. I was the exception. Con-servatism was on the rise, and the primary had given the impression that I was even farther to the left than I was.

The Republican candidate was ideally suited to exploit these advantages. Richard Jones was a recently retired army dentist with an amiable personality. He was extremely conservative—he had been an official of the John Birch Society—but his bland demeanor and lack of a public record put all of the attention on me.

I didn't bear up very well under it. I became excessively argu-mentative, even by my previous standards. I was bent on winning every disputed point, even when that meant losing voter support. I was also engaged in an increasingly angry debate with my staff about "negative campaigning." Jones's campaign consisted entirely of harsh attacks on my record. He built on my primary opponents' partial suc-cess in portraying me as a radical advocate of immorality, and mixed in some of his own nastiness. When I defended the Chrysler bailout with a reference to the auto industry's employment of African Americans, he distorted my words to make a blatant racist appeal.

As Election Day approached, I knew that as long as the race was a referendum on my liberalism, I was in trouble. So I decided to go on the offensive. I told my staff that I wanted to use Jones's work for the John Birch Society in our advertising. Overwhelmingly, they recoiled. This, they insisted, was negative campaigning, which they considered a form of demagoguery. Since they believed my victory was assured, they saw attacking Jones as gratuitous nastiness. But my experiences on the campaign trail were worrying me, and I wanted to tell the truth in my own self-defense.

Our internal debate illustrates a larger theme: As conservatives stepped up their attacks in Massachusetts and elsewhere, too many liberals remained passive. The right understood the public's anger at government much better than a still complacent left. Fortunately, one of my key campaign workers, media specialist Dan Payne, understood my point. He fashioned a very effective—and accurate— radio ad conjuring up the return of the John Birch Society in the person of Jones. Incredibly, Jones complained bitterly that I was assailing him.

Instead of trying to persuade voters of my virtue, I was now informing them of Jones's defects. This approach worked just well enough. I won my first congressional election by the narrowest margin of my twenty-term career: 52 percent to 48.

In my very chastened victory speech, I noted the defeat that day of Birch Bayh, Gaylord Nelson, George McGovern, Frank Church, and many other great liberal legislators. I had barely managed to swim upstream against a strong tide, I said. Now I hoped to get to Washington and spawn.

4

THE CONGRESSMAN

I arrived in Washington, D.C., along with Ronald Reagan and a Senate that would be controlled by Republicans—the first time the party had organized either chamber since 1954. In the House, a narrow Democratic majority included enough Southern conservatives to give the right effective control of the agenda.

My timing was terrible. I had reached a place I never dreamed I would get to, but at the worst time in thirty-five years for doing what I wanted to do there. In 1961 John F. Kennedy had passionately urged citizens to "ask what you can do for your country" and serve the public good. Then came four presidents who left office involuntarily, diminishing the reputation of collective public effort. And then, in his first inaugural, Reagan implicitly repudiated Kennedy's message by proclaiming that "Government is not the solution to our problem. Government *is* the problem." I had arrived at the party just when the curfew went into effect.

My ideological unhappiness was alleviated by two factors. Almost unbelievably, I was now a member of the U.S. Congress. And though I worried then about being outed, I was proud that I had made it to Congress despite the political handicap of my sexual orientation.

I have no more vivid memory than that of first walking onto the House floor as a member-elect. During a lame-duck session, I bumped into a man who had been one of my heroes and was now a colleague. "Excuse me," I said. Morris Udall replied, "Hi, Barney." My response was silent but profound: *Wow!* Years later, I related this story to Udall's son Mark when he entered the House. He flatteringly told me that he felt the same about meeting me. I responded that since I would not be having any children, the tradition would end there.

While the thrill of serving in Congress never wore off, I did start getting used to it. As I did, another recognition boosted my spirits: I had traded Speaker Tom McGee (the conservative leader of the Massachusetts House) for Speaker Tip O'Neill. I had a strong relationship with O'Neill. I had been his constituent for twelve years, and when a conservative Democrat had challenged him for not obstructing racially based school busing, I had organized my ward for him. He had campaigned for me after the 1980 primary. At one appearance, when I told a questioner that I hoped to serve on the Banking Committee, which dealt with housing, O'Neill in effect appointed me on the spot, setting me on course to become chairman twenty-six years later.

In my first term, I worked with the House minority—liberal and moderate Democrats—to oppose President Reagan's rollback of government programs that aided the poor and working class. In stark contrast to today's congressional practices, O'Neill allowed Reagan's program to come to the floor, while of course trying hard to defeat it. In his mind, this was a good electoral strategy as well as a requirement of democracy. He believed that Reagan's approach would be popular until people fully understood its implications, and he also understood that using parliamentary moves to block a newly elected president's initiatives would undermine confidence in the legitimacy of our system.

But the notion that O'Neill had warm personal feelings for the new president is wrong. In fact, the Speaker deeply resented what he saw as Reagan's indifference to economic unfairness, and he was also wholly unimpressed with his grasp of the issues. His cooperation came despite his low regard for Reagan as president.

Our effort to slow Reagan's momentum was largely unsuccessful. Bearing bipartisan names and support, the Gramm-Latta bill severely restrained spending on domestic programs while Hance-Conable sharply reduced taxes.

But we did win some victories, one of which gave me my first opportunity to see if my legislative skills transferred well from the state to the federal level. In addition to serving on the Banking Committee, I served on the Committee on Government Operations, which was a secondary panel in importance. This reflected the normal practice that members sat on one major committee and one nonmajor one—congressional ego ruled out calling any committee "minor." And I was drafted onto a third one as well: the Committee on the Judiciary. That entity had jurisdiction over the hot buttons: abortion, school busing, school prayer, affirmative action, gun control, and almost all the other wedge issues of the day. Although I usually find political metaphors misleading, "wedge" is an accurate depiction. When the bulk of voters in one party hold a view that is unpopular with the general public, the party on the popular side of the question can drive a wedge between their opponents and that general public.

In those days, the function of the House Judiciary Committee was to protect most Democrats from having to choose between their primary and general election constituents. Those of us who sat on it were chosen because we'd been elected from districts that would support us when we voted to keep the wedge issues off the floor. When O'Neill's chief policy aide, Ari Weiss, told me the Speaker had designated me as a wedge blocker, I protested, "That's tough territory. Serving there means pissing off the gun people, the antibusers, the right-to-lifers, and the religious zealots."

"Yeah," he replied, irritatingly but irrefutably, "but all those people already hate you, so you've got nothing to lose."

Happily for me, there was a consolation prize. Reagan was on the unpopular side of one issue within the committee's jurisdiction: the provision of legal services to the poor.

He and Attorney General Ed Meese had scores to settle with the Legal Services Corporation, which provides free legal services to those who cannot afford them. The scores stemmed from Reagan's (failed) attempt when governor of California to block funding for the LSC and its organizing work for the United Farm Workers. Now Reagan proposed abolishing the agency. I was assigned management of the fight on the House floor to defend it.

This was a twofer—a chance to accomplish something of real societal value while at the same time demonstrating my legislative skills. It was unusual for a freshman to be given a lead role on a significant—albeit not a first-rank—issue. My designation primarily reflected the fact that there were only four Democratic members on the subcommittee in charge of the issue; secondarily, it reflected approval of my early performance on the panel.

Fortunately for me and the poor, Reagan had seriously underestimated legal professionals' belief in the integrity of our system of justice, as well as their commitment to seeing that it was administered fairly. Senator Warren Rudman, the former Republican attorney general of New Hampshire, took the lead in the Senate in defending the LSC, and we worked well together.

In managing the floor debate in the House, I was able to draw on members from both parties, and we won the vote decisively, 245 to 137, with 59 Republicans joining the majority. This was the first defeat for the Reagan rollback agenda, and one of the few he suffered in that Congress.

As it happened, the legal services fight also included my first national effort on behalf of LGBT rights. Back in 1977, Larry McDonald—a nominal Democrat and fervent right-winger and John Bircher—had sponsored a successful amendment to ban the Legal Services Corporation from taking any cases on behalf of LGBT rights. It passed, 230 to 133. Republicans voted for it heavily, 110 to 17, but even a narrow majority of Democrats supported it, 120 to 116. Back in 1979, I'd arranged for O'Neill to discuss the issue with a delegation of his gay and lesbian constituents—at the time, I was one of those constituents myself. I was careful to pick a delegation conspicuously heavy with Irish names, and I enforced a dress code. To the surprise of many of the attendees—but not to me—O'Neill was wholly sympathetic. He explained that while he and many others thought the ban an unfair manifestation of prejudice, and McDonald a bigot and a fool, there was no way in the existing political climate to stop it. But he encouraged the group to keep up its political work and made the further suggestion—which did surprise me—that the best way to combat prejudice was for all LGBT people to come out—although he did not use the phrase. Referring specifically to the prohibition on security clearances for LGBT people, he said, "If all the homosexuals identified themselves, there wouldn't be any argument that they were subject to blackmail." It was at this meeting that I began to realize that O'Neill was not only a confirmed liberal but also a far more sophisticated and insightful one than was conveyed by his public image. A self-described "six-foot-two-inch, two-hundred-and-fifty-pound Irishman" (on his thinner days) with a "mop of white hair, a big red nose, and floppy ears," he was easily caricatured as an old-time meat-and-potatoes pol, and the liberties he regularly took with the English language reinforced the impression.

He was all of that, and he excelled at the singing, storytelling "Hi, how are ya, pal?" persona that went with it. In fact, he likely realized that this very partial view gave him the advantage of being underestimated. He was a very smart man, whose sharp political instincts were guided by considerable analytic ability.

Due to O'Neill's farsightedness, I could now defend LGBT rights in Congress without worrying about being marginalized. Just as remarkably, my two collaborators in the fight were also gay men. One was Steve Endean, who'd become the head of the newly formed Gay Rights National Lobby. The other was Dan Bradley, president of the Legal Services Corporation. Bradley had taken the position under the Carter administration and was not long for the job in the new regime. He was closeted, but his sexual orientation was well-known to the LGBT community. After leaving his job, he came out in a *New York Times* interview; several months later, he wrote an eloquent explanation of the process in *Harper's*. His death from AIDS in 1988 was a significant event in the public discussion of that tragedy.

Together, Endean, Bradley, and I discussed the remarkable fact that three gay men were formulating Democratic Party policy on an LGBT issue. And in truth, our pride in that accomplishment was only slightly diminished by our ultimate failure. We drafted language that did not eliminate the McDonald ban outright but would substantially diminish its practical effect. Even so, we lost by a vote of 151 to 245, with 116 Democrats and 35 Republicans supporting us and 102 Democrats and 143 Republicans opposed.

During the debate, I received an important preview of coming distractions when I solicited my colleague John Burton of San Francisco to vote with us on the amendment. "I can't support it," he told me. "It's got anti-gay language. Gays in my district don't want me doing that." I explained that our measure in fact substantially lessened the McDonald amendment's anti-LGBT impact, but to no avail. Burton plausibly responded that this legislative complexity could not be explained to his constituents in a way that would defuse their anger that he had voted for something that was still anti-gay.

This was the beginning of my recognition that as the LGBT movement grew to include millions of us, and as some of its leading organizations came to question conventional political methods, controversy about strategy and tactics would greatly complicate our work. While there was some overlap in our positions, the debate between those—like me—who were convinced that we would win our rights mostly through conventional political tactics and those who scorned "the system" and (mistakenly) invoked the civil rights movement as a model for relying mostly on direct action would go on, often angrily, for decades.

•

That year, we lost another battle. In 1981, the District of Columbia City Council voted to repeal its law criminalizing sodomy. Under the system that then prevailed, a change in the district's criminal law could be vetoed by a resolution of either house of Congress. In contrast to my earlier experience in Massachusetts, this time there was no need for me to take the leading role. The Democratic chairman of the House Committee on the District of Columbia was Ron Dellums, an African American from Berkeley, California. He is one of the most eloquent people ever to serve in the House, and also one of the strongest opponents of discrimination in our history. As committee chair, he had multiple reasons for passionately opposing the effort to maintain criminal penalties. Like the other African American members, he resented Congress's close supervision over the largely black population in D.C. His predecessors in his job had been racist Southerners. He also objected when his colleagues refused to show his committee the

customary types of deference—a sensitivity that was hardly unjustified. When he and Congresswoman Patricia Schroeder were appointed to the Armed Services Committee, the chairman, Edward
Hébert of Louisiana, provided only one additional chair for the two
new members on the committee rostrum. Determined not to appear
ruffled, Dellums and Schroeder shared the seat. When Dellums recounted this story years later at a retirement party, by which time he
was himself chair of the Armed Services Committee, I noted that
this was the only time in my association with these two outstanding
members that either of them had ever done anything half-assed.

In opposing the rollback of D.C.'s initiative, Dellums was angered most of all by the homophobia behind it, and his speech on the
issue was the most powerful attack on anti-LGBT bias yet delivered
in the U.S. Congress. Although we lost the vote, 119 to 281, the experience encouraged me in one way and instructed me in another. The
encouragement came from the vote total. Sodomy repeal had received only 7 percent of the votes in liberal Massachusetts in 1973,
but 30 percent in the U.S. House in 1981. This was a real improvement. My lobbying efforts instructed me. Most of the colleagues
I approached—admittedly, I concentrated on liberal and moderate
members—volunteered that they agreed with me on the merits but
saw no reason to take a political risk on a purely symbolic matter that
had no impact on real life.

To most policy makers, I realized, anti-LGBT prejudice was an
abstraction. Even though increasing numbers of them were coming
to disagree with it, the millions of real live human beings who experienced its damaging effects were hidden from them. If we were
prepared to accept second-class status, and pay the psychological price
extracted by a life of denial, the closet could have its benefits. But for
a movement determined to defeat prejudice, anonymity was toxic.

A few years later, after I had come out, I experienced a vivid example of anonymity's costs. C-SPAN covered a speech I'd given to a
gay-sponsored meeting at Georgetown Law School. The next day, a
congressman who strongly opposed discrimination asked me why so
few students had attended. There was actually a pretty good crowd, I
told him, and asked why he thought the opposite. "Well," he said, "I

watched it on TV and the camera stayed on you and didn't show the audience, so I figured they were sparing you the embarrassment of showing an empty hall." The actual explanation, which he appreciated my sharing with him, was that law students did not want to be seen at an LGBT event because of the negative impact it would have on their job seeking.

Our collective secrecy brought with it another harm: It perpetuated the stereotypical views that we were either lisping, mincing males or brutish, stomping females, which hindered our efforts for equality. Of course, I very much wished that apparently feminine characteristics in a man or masculine traits in a woman had no effect on how others judged them. But that wasn't the world we lived in, and the prevailing images were not helpful. The cause of LGBT equality did not require our most visible brothers and sisters to hide, but it did require the rest of us to reveal ourselves. The broader society needed to know that we were a fully representative cross section of that society, not incidentally including its daughters, sons, sisters, brothers, parents, aunts, uncles, teachers, students, customers, doctors, teammates, friends—and congressmen.

When I arrived in D.C. after the 1980 election, I decided to adopt a hybrid status. I would be out privately to other LGBT people but not publicly to my colleagues, the voters, or other heterosexuals—beyond the handful I had already told. Personal needs drove the first stance, political prudence the second.

At the start of my career, I had adopted a self-description that is often applied to presumably closeted political figures: "He is so wrapped up in his job that he doesn't need a private life." I have yet to meet anyone whom those words could justly describe. The strain of living in the closet takes a heavy toll on your personality. And it is hard to keep the anger that should be directed at your own self-denial from spilling over into dealings with others. When I think of the politicians I deem likely to be taking this approach, a disproportionate number share my reuptation for being too quick to give and take offense.

So I resolved to start a new life in D.C. I would be open about my sexuality with other LGBT people, secure in the knowledge that

they would keep my secret as I dated, socialized, and, as with Endean and Bradley, strategized. Publicly, while I had stopped dating
women, I allowed the presumption of heterosexuality to apply. I followed the ethical principle that has guided me in other aspects of my
public activity: I tell the truth, and nothing but the truth, but unless
under oath, I feel no obligation to volunteer the whole truth if it is
inconvenient.

I persuaded myself that this bifurcation of my life was working.
With the exceptions of the sodomy and Legal Services issues, I was
able to concentrate my energies on the central question confronting Congress: How far could the Republicans and their Southern
Democratic allies drive the public's increasing unhappiness with
government?

Most of us still believed that antigovernment feeling was more a
cyclical trend than a secular one. With Reagan in office, the economy
was still suffering, and though we didn't want the suffering to continue, we nonetheless stood to gain from it. We were also confident
that the majority of the American people still agreed that the programs we were defending were important to maintaining the quality
of our national life. This perception was reinforced by the fact that
Reagan's tax cuts passed by larger margins than his spending cuts.
Embracing the strategy of Boston state representative John Melia,
several dozen Democrats voted both to preserve programs and to cut
the revenues needed to pay for them.

As a freshman, I had no significant role in formulating these decisions. I did join the liberal Democratic Study Group, which sought to
pressure the leadership into a sharper response to the right, and I was
part of several delegations that met with O'Neill on the subject. It
was in these meetings that my appreciation of the Speaker's judgment deepened. More often than not, I agreed with his explanation
of why he would not adopt our approach.

I soon came to feel more useful in a different role: as a leader in
our rhetorical counterattack against the right. "Counterattack" is
very much the operative word here. While the Democrats had a nominal forty-five-seat majority in the House, the conservative coalition
usually had the actual advantage, and this, combined with Reagan's

skill and popularity, and Republican control of the Senate, gave them the initiative. Our part in the debates on the floor, in committee, and in the media was largely reactive—debunking their arguments and documenting the social harm their policies would inflict.

I was happy to learn that I had an aptitude for this work—I am at my best in debate as a counterpuncher, due to a combination of my strongest and weakest rhetorical traits. The weakness, which I have noted, is my laziness, born of a very low boredom threshold. If I am assigned the task of preparing opening remarks expounding a point of view, I am easily distracted. But I respond well to the stimulus of opposing arguments, so much so that even when I am the sole speaker at an event, I prefer to debate my absent antagonists. I am also lucky to have a very good memory. This is extremely helpful in debate because over time, most politicians will use a line of reasoning that is useful for their current objective but contradicts their tack on a previous issue.

My sense of humor, which I am glad to have, and which I cannot think of anything I did to earn, was also a great polemical weapon. The force of an argument is greatly magnified when it can be phrased as a quip, especially a snarky one that is easily remembered. When Reagan paired his opposition to abortion with a budget cut for funds for pregnant women and poor children, I jibed that he "apparently believes that from the standpoint of the federal government, life begins at conception and ends at birth." This line had an impact—a leader of the antiabortion drive in the House even cited it in support of better funding for mothers and children.

By the end of 1981, I should have been satisfied with my political career. I believed that the conservative effort to roll back our domestic achievements would go no further. And I was happy that I had found a useful role in the legislative process and a reasonable way to live as a partially closeted public figure. But there was a problem— the growing likelihood that I would be a one-term congressman.

•

It was payback time in Massachusetts. In the national reapportionment following the 1980 census, Massachusetts lost one seat in the

U.S. House; its delegation would shrink from twelve members to eleven. That delegation consisted of ten Democrats and two Republicans. Ordinarily, by the rules of American politics, this would have meant the loss of one of the Republicans, given that the state's Democratic leaders controlled the redistricting. But Massachusetts was not then an ordinary state, and I was not an ordinary congressman. Two of the three decision makers—Governor King and Senate president Bulger—were no more committed to my political welfare than I had been to theirs. The third, Speaker McGee, had tolerated me in the Statehouse but did not have to think hard about siding with his two governing partners over me. The big three were respectful of Tip O'Neill's aspirations to fortify his Democratic majority in the House, but in Massachusetts, avenging past wrongs in state politics has a long tradition and easily took precedence over advancing a national Democratic agenda—especially when all three of these men shared little of O'Neill's liberal ideology. (I had by then assimilated enough of the state's political culture to put a high value on getting even. When an amendment to the redistricting plan that was favorable to me failed in the Massachusetts House, I kept a copy of the roll call in my top desk drawer for several years. I took any subsequent opportunity to retard the careers of those who voted against me, and to help those who had been my allies.)

The result was a new congressional map that divided my district into five pieces. My only slim reason for hope was that one of those segments contained both of my strongest bases of support: Newton and Brookline. Unfortunately, that segment now belonged to a district that had been represented since 1967 by Margaret Heckler, a Republican who was one of the longest-serving women in the House. Seventy percent of the new configuration came from her existing district; 24 percent was from mine; and 6 percent from a third. She was one of the most liberal Republicans in Congress and enjoyed the support of unions, community action groups, and elderly organizations because of her commitment to their issues.

And so I decided not to run for reelection. I told myself that I had only one more year to be in Congress no matter what I did, so it would be better to concentrate all my energies on being a great member—"They'll miss me when I'm gone," I consoled myself. Why be diverted from legislating by a futile, time-consuming, ego-deflating, and no doubt unpleasant campaign?

The decision did not stand for long. When I asked Jim Segel how people would react if I bowed out, he calmly replied that most of them would think I was "a fucking asshole. You came into the district and won a seat that a lot of people who lived there thought should have been theirs," he pointed out, "and if you give it up now without a fight, they will be even angrier, and your supporters will feel betrayed." Joe DeNucci, a state legislator, former contender for the world middleweight title, and future state auditor, told me to stop whining about how unfair the world was and fight for what I wanted. "Most people never get to be a congressman," he said, "so why are they going to be sorry for you because you only got to do it once?"

More gently, my brother, David, asked me how I would feel if another prominent liberal from the Newton-Brookline area ran in my seat, and got, say, 47 percent of the vote. My colleague Ed Markey had a more practical but compelling point. "If you run and lose, but get a respectable vote," he explained, "liberals will feel indebted to you for trying, and when O'Neill retires in a few years"—as he was to do two terms later—"you can move back into his very liberal district and be the favorite."

Finally, and most persuasively, I took to heart the words of Nick Roussos, a tough, principled, and highly influential leader of the International Ladies' Garment Workers' Union in blue-collar Fall River, the largest city in my new constituency. He bawled me out. "I thought you were a guy who cares about working people," he barked. "If you really are, you'll get off your ass and fight for them instead of moping around asking them to feel sorry for you."

So I ran.

•

I recount these painful conversations to correct certain errors common to political analysis. One is the presumption that political decisions are more rational than they really are. My decisions—first to quit and then to run—were largely emotional. The second, related

mistake is imposing a false sense of inevitability on past events. Analysts impress their audiences when they explain why certain results
had to happen—not by reporting that chance played a decisive role.

As soon as I began to run, my pollsters confirmed what I already
knew: I had very little chance of winning. In our first poll, taken in
February 1982, Heckler led by a margin of 52 to 34 percent. More
ominously, we were both well-known, and her favorability rating was
higher than mine. It's much better when you are behind because few
people know you than when voters know who you are and aren't very
impressed.

Fortunately, I had an opening. Although the passage of Reagan's
tax cuts was not in doubt, the fate of his spending cuts was a closer
question—and this posed a big problem for Heckler. Party leaders
usually allow considerable leeway to members from swing districts
like Heckler's. But not always. Before any important vote, each party's
whip operation canvasses members to get a good sense of the final
tally. When the margin is close, reluctant members are pressured to
stick with their party. Afer all, their vote could make the difference
between victory and defeat.

In the old days, voting was conducted by an alphabetical oral roll
call. When a member's name was reached, he or she might not know
it would be necessary to take one for the team. But electronic voting reduced that uncertainty. Members now register their votes by
inserting a personal card into one of dozens of computer terminals
throughout the chamber. As they do so, a running total of yeas, nays,
and presents—the constitutionally prescribed language—appears on
scoreboards at both ends of the room. Representatives who want to
vote against their party can postpone voting until the very end of the
tally to determine if their votes will matter. In the final moments
before the voting ends—an elastic period of time defined by the
party in power—the whips can either release the members in question, or call in their pledges to stave off defeat. Interestingly, members who tell the whips that they oppose the party's position due to
personal conviction are generally received less sympathetically than
those who express substantive agreement with the bill in question
but plead electoral concerns as their reason for dissent. In a partisan

politcal system, pleas of political self-interest outrank a claim to know better than one's party colleagues what is best for the country.

The pressure to vote with the party varies in intensity from issue to issue, according to the political stakes involved. The vote to roll back domestic programs was seen as a make-or-break issue for Reagan's presidency in its first months. To Republicans across the country, Reagan was leading a crusade that promised to reverse nearly five decades of government expansion. A defeat would have shattered his momentum—and enabled O'Neill to regain the initiative.

And so if Heckler had bucked her party, she would have faced a Republican electorate angry at her apostasy—and very likely a primary opponent in 1982. My contemporary impression was confirmed more than twenty years later when I read Richard Reeves's biography of Reagan. He notes that although Reagan greatly reduced his workload while convalescing from John Hinckley's assassination attempt, he did call Heckler to plead for her vote on the spending cuts. According to Reeves, Reagan also told his aides that he sympathized with her over the abuse she was taking from me on the issue.

In the end, Heckler tried to appease both sides, which only hurt her. Heckler backed the Republican–Southern Democratic coalition on an arcane procedural vote, and then voted no on the substantive package of cuts. By citing quotes from Republican leaders, I was able to demonstrate that it was the procedural victory that really decided the outcome. And once it became clear that Heckler's vote was instrumental in the conservatives' victory, her support in the blue-collar areas of the district eroded sharply. The AFL-CIO shifted from endorsing her in 1980 to backing me in 1982. Equally important, Heckler's vote brought me the invaluable support of Mark Sullivan, a larger-than-life character who ran the community action program in Fall River. He combined the ideological zeal of other anti-poverty activists with the skills and instincts of the best of the old ward bosses. Fall River and its adjacent towns made up nearly a third of the new district's population, and his support signaled that the race could become competitive.

Heckler also did me a favor when she voted to cut taxes on the oil industry, which was then at the nadir of its popularity in the Northeast.

The spike in oil prices after the OPEC embargo of 1973–1974 had an especiallly strong impact on our oil-deprived area, and the arrogance of many in the oil patch—LET THE BASTARDS FREEZE IN THE DARK was a popular Texas-Oklahoma bumper sticker—fueled our anger, if not our homes. I staked out my own position as strongly as I could.

When Texas Republican congressman Jack Fields spoke in favor of the tax cuts, he finished by appealing to the Democrats from his state to join him—"The eyes of Texas are upon us today," he warned. Happily, I was next to speak. "I do not object to the eyes of Texas being upon me," I rejoined. "I object to the hands of Texas being in my pockets."

That year public television had launched a new weekly program on Congress, conducted by two women who were on the verge of becoming leading commentators: Cokie Roberts—my old friend, whose objectivity was uninfluenced by this—and Linda Wertheimer. They featured my dialogue with Fields on their program that week, and for the rest of the year they included the clip in their introduction to the show. I could not have received a better political boost in a race against an opponent who had voted with Fields, nor could he have picked a better exchange to be shown regularly in his native Houston.

As the campaign progressed, I readily took the offensive. For the only time in my career, campaigning was truly fun. Heckler's early debate performances were hindered by the contrast between her own prior record and the pro-Reagan votes she had cast. In liberal Newton, she legitimately cited her work to help the city secure a large federal housing grant—credit for which belonged in part to the administration's eagerness to defeat me. I thanked her, but then added that given her vote for a bill that decimated that very program, it would be hard for either of us to replicate her feat.

On the paid media side, Dan Payne's creative gifts dominated the discussion. One ad asked who supported large tax breaks for the oil industry, and named Heckler, illustrating the point by showing a woman's arm raised proudly in support. She complained angrily about that one. We also responded aggressively to her campaign's implicit suggestion that I was an alien elitist, with no appreciation for mainstream American culture. In one ad, I pumped gas while talking about working at my father's truck stop as a teenager. In another, I was shown sliding headfirst into home plate in a softball game. (It required several takes to get the timing right—I was out on the first couple of tries.)

These ads would not have turned the race around, however, were it not for one overriding development: the national recession. Heckler, like other Republicans, was held responsible—not entirely fairly—for a sharp drop in economic activity. With all of these factors adding up, by the spring of 1982 the race had tightened considerably, and the polls showed that I was in striking distance of winning. Heckler became increasingly frustrated that her impressive political career was in jeopardy and, like others I have engaged with politically, she also found my personality infuriating. So she went on the attack.

At first, she and her supporters were somewhat restrained, but there were hints of what was to come. For example, her husband, John, made a point of telling fund-raisers that he "would now do something Peg's opponent can't do: introduce our children." (My rebuttal was that I knew their names and could in fact introduce them if the occasion arose.) Sometimes the inuendo comically failed. One of my supporters told me about a private meeting with veterans at which Heckler had strangely tried to link me to the Mafia: She had told the group that I "liked the boys in Providence," which was the headquarters of organized crime in New England. My first response was to wonder if she had uncovered my father's associations from his truck stop days, but I quickly realized that she had actually said "Provincetown." Somewhat guiltily, I recognized that my supporter had misheard her because it never occurred to him that I was gay. My residual New Jersey accent, the fifty pounds I had gained eating my way through the campaign, my gas-pumping and softball ads, and what one journalist described as my ill-fitting suits so diverged from the gay stereotype that her subtlety was lost on him. (I answered the journalist's charge by insisting that my suits were in fact very well fitting, I just didn't happen to be the one they fit. This did cost me the votes of the couple who owned a store where I had bought some of them.)

As the campaign went on, we decided that we needed to counter this line of attack. Especially worrisome was the claim that I did not share family values, being the unmarried defender of people's right to view pornography. Fortunately, Dan Payne and my brother, David, came up with an effective antidote. They made an ad that featured an attractive, white-haired seventy-year-old woman sitting comfortably in her apartment assuring her fellow elderly that I would be a staunch defender of their interests. At the end, she asked, "How can I be so sure Barney will do the right thing by us older people?" and beamingly answered her own question: "Because he's my son." In addition to the powerful boost it gave me, this ad, which won national awards, launched my mother on a career as one of the most respected and admired elderly activists in the state.

As the polls continued to shift in my favor, Heckler doubled down on the offensive. Her strategic calculation was obvious. I was taking votes away from her in the blue-collar, predominantly Catholic areas that had supported her in past elections by stressing her conservative votes on domestic economic issues. She sought to stem this loss by documenting my radicalism on social issues—homosexuality, pornography, prostitution, marijuana, abortion, and crime.

Her strongest attack came in our final debate. She spoke last, and knowing that I could not respond, she denounced me for the first time that evening as a purveyor of sexual immorality in all of its many forms.

It backfired. She was harshly denounced, most notably by Anthony Lewis, one of America's most respected journalists, in *The New York Times*. He accused her of engaging in "gutter politics" and said that "the ghost of Joe McCarthy must be grinning." A widely respected Republican woman I had known in the legislature appeared in a commercial attesting to my moral qualities. The highly educated professionals in what was now the northern part of my district recoiled at Heckler's approach. And to my surprise and her dismay, the attack did nothing to weaken my support in the southern blue-collar areas.

Most people in greater Fall River felt competent to judge for themselves what they should read, hear, and see. They resented being told what was permissable. Regrettably, Heckler also suffered from a sexist double standard that infused our politics. Even today, women who go on the attack are vulnerable to accusations of shrillness that are rarely leveled at men.

Not only did Heckler fail to gain support in the blue-collar south, but she also lost backing in the more affluent north, and in the end I won by nearly twenty points. On election night, I said that the result might have differed if the national economy had differed. And while those gracious words did not reflect my true feelings, I did brood over a point I have made several times—so much of what happens in politics lies outside the politician's control. In 1980, I had beaten an inexperienced official of the John Birch Society by a narrow margin of 52 to 48. Two years later, I defeated an experienced, first-rate campaigner with a solid legislative record in a district that was originally hers 60 to 40. I had not by any means gotten that much better.

Of course, the role that good fortune played in my victory did not diminish my enjoyment of it. Returning to Congress, I was optimistic about my personal life, my political situation, and the outlook for public policy. I had survived an election in which the opposition was hinting at my sexuality—and I had done it handsomely. The very fact that Heckler had to so subtly hint at my homosexuality indicated that public attitudes were evolving. Being gay was still not politically acceptable—but neither was gay bashing. We had come at least part of the way from 1959, when *Advise and Consent* told a wholly plausible tale of how the threat of exposure destroyed not just a promising Senate career but the senator himself. In 1982, I believed I could continue to live below the public radar as a gay man, socializing discreetly with other LGBT people. In fact, my first postelection resolution was to pay myself the attention I had deferred over the previous two and a half years. I resolved to lose weight (I had soared to 270 pounds), I got contact lenses, and I began regular attendance at gyms and barber shops, institutions where I had been totally absent or only sporadically present, respectively.

When I saw Kevin Poirier, a Republican state rep I'd been friendly with, he said it must feel good to know that I'd be able to keep my congressional seat for as long as I wanted. My estimate at the time was that I would stay until I turned seventy-five, in 2015. This was

one of my better attempts at a personal prediction: I was only two
years off.

•

If 1982 was a good year for my political fortunes, it was also a good
year for my party and political philosophy. The Democrats won
twenty-six seats in the House—the electorate, it seemed, was unwilling to dismantle the legacy of the New Deal and its successors.
To the pleasant surprise of many of us, given the choice between Tip
O'Neill, the symbol of that tradition, and Ronald Reagan, its archenemy, the voters chose O'Neill.

There was one important danger signal I failed to notice sufficiently at the time. The administration claimed that its tax cuts would
stimulate the economy so much that overall government revenues
would increase. "Supply-side economics," as it was called, was economically controversial but politically appealing. The doctrine's
adherents could finesse the choice between lowering taxes and slash-
ing spending. It was a way to eat your cake and have it and add another layer. The main problem with the idea would later be articulated
by one of the leading conservative economists of the period, Alan
Greenspan. When he was asked at a hearing if it was possible to increase government revenue by cutting tax rates, he replied, "That is
theoretically true, Congressman, but it hasn't happened in my life-
time." He was then in his late seventies.

In 1981, David Stockman, Reagan's budget director, proposed an
alternative rationale for the tax cuts. He explained his position in an
unusually honest interview he gave to William Greider in *The Atlantic*
magazine, who summarized it thus: "Stockman was buoyant about
the political implications of the tax legislation: first, because it put a
tightening noose around the size of the government."

Stockman later explained why this was the only effective way to
restrain the growth of government in his book *The Triumph of Politics*:

> Lavish Social Security benefits, wasteful dairy subsidies, fu-
> tile UDAG [Urban Development Action] grants, and all the
> remainder of the federal subventions do not persist solely due

to weak-kneed politicians or the nefarious graspings of special-interest groups . . . Congressmen and senators ultimately deliver what their constituencies demand . . . *The Wall Street Journal* somehow . . . manages to divine a great unwashed mass of the citizenry demanding the opposite of the spending agendas presented by the Claude Peppers, the homebuilders' lobby, and the other hired guns of K Street . . . The actual electorate, however, . . . is interested in getting help from the government to compensate for a perceived disadvantage.

In other words, "starving the beast" was the best available way to curtail popular government programs.

Stockman's outburst of inconvenient truth telling discomfited the Reaganites, and the president did rebuke him—avuncularly, and in recognition of Stockman's great talent, with no diminution in his authority. More important, as skepticism about supply-side economics grew, conservatives implicitly adopted Stockman's rationale. Tax cuts, which were originally hailed in part because they could *increase* the government's revenues, were now fervently supported precisely because they would have the opposite effect.

Conservatives had discovered a potent strategy. They would not mount a frontal attack on the public sector; instead, they would use the public's aversion to taxation to trump its affection for spending. The approach was bolstered by two additional bipartisan beliefs— the assumptions that the American way of life was seriously threatened by large budget deficits and by hostile forces in the world. The first of these beliefs called for smaller federal budgets, the second demanded that a very large share of those budgets go to the military.

Taken together, these political currents severely constrained our capacity to work through government to improve the quality of domestic life. The social safety net, public safety, improvements to our infrastructure, well-funded education, environmental protection, health care and health research—all of these vital causes had to compete against the popularity of tax cuts, balanced budgets, and military expenditures.

This competition for resources would set the overarching terms of political debate in the country for thirty years, and it continues to do so today. Tax cutting won a major victory when Walter Mondale's call for more revenue to sustain our quality of life played a major role in his devastating defeat in 1984. The protax side did win a victory with the passage of the Clinton tax increases in 1993, but the rationale for those increases had more to do with deficit reduction than with increased government activism. The context for today's debate over government was decisively established by George W. Bush's massive tax cuts in 2001 and 2003—a major victory for "beast starving."

Ultimately, the success of the Stockman doctrine had a secondary effect that grew into a primary one. As a financially strapped government was forced to do less and less to meet the demand for improved services that Stockman acknowledged, public dissatisfaction with government's performance increased. The conservatives' effort to defund the public sector paid them a bonus. When voters encountered public policies that fell short of meeting society's needs and desires, they were likelier to blame the victim—our capacity to govern ourselves fairly—than to hold accountable those who caused the problem. My hope to break this vicious cycle would guide my future political efforts, and my prescription for doing so constitutes the final part of this book.

I believe I was one of the first liberals to understand that the right valued tax cuts not just as ends in themselves but also as bulwarks against policies it objected to on philosophical grounds. Indeed, I received credit for this recognition from two of the strategy's staunchest journalistic advocates, Rowland Evans and Robert Novak. Even so, I did not initially appreciate how effective the strategy would be. In the rosy glow of defeating Heckler and observing large Democratic gains in the 1982 midterms, I believed—mistakenly, it turned out—that voters faced with the possible loss of programs to which they were attached would reject the starving-the-beast ploy.

•

As a second-term member, I was not a major participant in formulating the Democrats' overall strategy. But I was better placed to advance my agenda. In 1983, I became the chairman of a Government Operations subcommittee that covered housing and labor issues. I was able to change its official name from Manpower and Housing to Employment and Housing. While some of my conservative colleagues derided this as a silly example of political correctness, when the Republicans took over the House in 1995, their semantic gymnastics outdid us by a large margin. The Committee on Labor became the Committee on the Workforce. The Subcommittee on Constitutional Rights became the Subcommittee on the Constitution, and "environment" disappeared from the name of the committee that dealt with that subject. From their ideological perspective, they were right to do so. Words not only reflect political preferences, they also reinforce them. And the right has done a much better job of labeling policies to their political advantage. They can vote for every possible war that comes along and still be "pro-life," while a levy that applies only to the vast fortunes left by the richest 1 percent of Americans when a spousal exemption is claimed is the "death tax."

My major concern was to avert an imminent danger to low-income people: the disappearance of affordable rental housing. In the 1960s, the government had given developers subsidized loans on the condition that they charge affordable rents. Unfortunately, that restriction expired after forty years, and in some cases, developers had the option to prepay their loans and raise rents after twenty years. By the early 1980s, the prospect of eviction loomed over tens of thousands of renters, with hundreds of thousands more at risk over the next two decades.

I didn't know why the drafters had included the time limit; it's possible they already foresaw the widespread gentrification that would come to many cities. In Boston, much of the subsidized housing was built in the racially mixed South End. A relatively poor neighborhood in the 1960s, it was rapidly becoming a very desirable place to live by the '80s. Once the rent limits expired, property owners could market their units to gentrifiers who were willing and able to pay much more than the poor to live so close to Boston's core.

We could not revoke the property owners' right to raise rents, but we could pay them to sign new agreements that extended the arrangement. Buying out their right to evict poorer tenants was clearly less costly than building new units from scratch. This proved to be a successful approach.

But it was not enough. Given the impossibiltiy of preserving all of the affordable units, and the growing need for decent homes, we also had to construct new ones. Fortunately, there was one form of government activism that conservatives could accept: tax incentives. A coalition of housing advocates and builders devised the Low-Income Housing Tax Credit program and sought its inclusion in the ambitious rewrite of the tax code that leaders of both parties had undertaken. I supported their efforts strongly, along with my colleague Charlie Rangel of the tax-writing committee. By lowering tax rates and eliminating loopholes, the 1986 Tax Reform Act was hailed for its bipartisan deal making.

Even so, when the tax reform bill came to the floor of the House the first time, I voted against it because I thought it lowered top income tax rates by too much. Although it passed without my vote, Committee chairman Dan Rostenkowski wanted the bill to be adopted by a large majority, with strong liberal support. When I was told that the chairman wanted my vote, I traded. I promised Rostenkowski I'd support the bill if the tax credit for affordable housing was beefed up. It was. I cite this as an example of how liberals can bargain effectively for better outcomes—despite the criticism of those on the left who disapprove of such tactics. William Greider, an astute critic of economic inequality, told me he was disappointed that I'd supported the bill despite its insufficiently progressive tax rates. But I was happy to sacrifice my ideological purity to improve legislation that was going to become law with or without me.

As a civil libertarian, I would make few exceptions to the right to free speech. But I admit I'd be tempted to ban the use of metaphors in the discussion of public policy. Metaphors more often distort discussion than improve it. For example, countries are not dominoes; they do not lurch into their neighbors and knock them over if their regime changes. The Reaganite claim that a "rising tide lifts all boats" was also very harmful. People are not boats, and increases in GDP are not a tide that rises uniformly. To fight the metaphor on its own simplistic terms, if you are too poor to afford a boat and are standing on tiptoes in the water, the rising tide can go up your nose. Or in real terms, the fact that some—even most—people become wealthier may have adverse consequences on those who do not share in the prosperity. In the case of housing, the economic advances that made downtowns more desirable places to live threatened to submerge the existing residents, not float them. It took the government to ensure that good news in the private sector—sharply improved property values—did not become very bad news for low-income people who would have been driven out of their homes.

•

Shortly after I reached Washington, Congress began coping with the greatest public health crisis of our time: the AIDS epidemic. From the start of the crisis in 1981, there was a great deal of fear that the identification of AIDS with gay men would cause a popular backlash. For the most part, it did not. Some of this was a matter of visibility. The need to confront AIDS led many gay men and women to decide it was time to leave the closet. (AIDS victims, of course, rarely had a choice—Rock Hudson's sexuality became public knowledge only when he was dying.)

In addition, gays and lesbians won admiration for their response to the illness. There are few comparable examples of private citizens mobilizing to meet the needs of the sick and suffering. In a fairly short period of time, AIDS support groups and action committees provided medical, financial, and emotional support. Even that sector of the population least likely to contract AIDS—lesbians—became deeply involved. The sight of so many people acting selflessly—an impression enhanced by the false belief that AIDS was contagious—burnished the gay community's reputation. Admiral James Watkins, the career military man who headed President Reagan's AIDS commission, acknowledged as much in the commission's final report. It praised "the spark of human spirit which rises high when faced with the gravest of human tragedies" and made clear references to LGBT-dominated groups: "hospice volunteers," "community-based organizations," and "other humanitarian groups."

There were two aspects to the fight in Congress over funding for AIDS research and treatment. Most important was the general level of funding. It was never sufficient, and with Reagan's lack of attention to the issue, it was especially inadequate in the early phases of the epidemic. But when the Democrats in Congress began to fight for higher expenditures, they soon encountered another issue. As the need for funding became undeniable to all but the most hardened bigots, the anti-LGBT forces tried to prevent effective action by a different means: offering amendments to the funding legislation that would have rendered the money largely unavailable to those who could make best use of it.

It was in this context that I saw how, under the right circumstances, elected officials would take risks to do what was morally right. Sodomy laws were rarely enforced, and while I believed their symbolic impact was harmful, risk-averse legislators had little interest in acting against a harm they perceived abstractly. But risk-averse does not mean unwilling ever to take risks. And the AIDS epidemic was so clearly a danger, not simply to gay men but also to others in the population, that a significant number of my colleagues acknowledged a moral duty to vote in ways that would be described—or caricatured—by their opponents as "pro-gay."

The anti-gay forces did not explicitly oppose AIDS-related research or helping individuals who were suffering from AIDS. Instead, they proposed a series of amendments that would have required organizations that received AIDS-related funding to adopt policies that were in effect anti-gay. If they accepted federal funds, these groups could do nothing to indicate that they regarded homosexuality as in any way acceptable or benign. Literally, the amendments required recipients to refrain from "promoting homosexuality." Groups that offered counseling services for troubled teenagers, or forums in which gay and lesbian life could be discussed in a positive way, would have been ineligible for the funds. Hospitals would find it harder to refrain from stigmatizing gay and lesbian patients. Collectively, the provisions were known as the "No Promo Homo" amendments.

I was a leader in the fight against these amendments, working closely with a task force that had been set up by the Democratic leadership under Tony Coelho and Steny Hoyer. We were very fearful that the amendments would pass and retard the ability of caregivers and researchers to use government funds effectively. After Jesse Helms scored one such victory in 1987, a coalition of most Democrats and some Republicans—notably, Senator Orrin Hatch—devised an effective counterstrategy. That was to amend the damaging language so that while it still expressed negative sentiments it had no legal effect.

While the anti-gay forces in Congress generally refrained from singling out AIDS sufferers, there was one exception to their indirect strategy. This was a House amendment to the Americans with Disabilities Act that had the clear effect of allowing restaurants and other food-related enterprises to refuse to assign anyone who was HIV positive to a food-handling job. That provision was dropped in its entirety by the Senate and, after a heavy lobbying effort by the House Democratic leadership, it was left out of the final bill. These victories made AIDS funding more effective and improved the gay rights movement's political fortunes. I knew of no case where any member was defeated because he or she helped block the "No Promo Homo" efforts.

Unfortunately, AIDS advocates did not always recognize how important it was that majorities in both the House and Senate had stood up for a bias-free response to the crisis. Flamboyantly homophobic statements made by certain politicians received, understandably, a great deal of media attention. Advocates who fought hard for what rightly seemed to them simple common sense resented that they had to fight at all. And Ronald Reagan's inattention understandably prompted outrage—even as it also diverted attention from Congress's successful efforts to combat bias.

•

While the AIDS funding debates went on, I worked especially hard on another LGBT-related issue: removing the blatantly homophobic provisions of American immigration law. As I mentioned, when I got to the House, people afflicted with "psychopathic personalities" and "sexual deviation" were flatly prohibited from coming to America, either as visitors or permanent residents.

This egregious example of bigotry did not stand alone. It was characteristic of the exclusionary laws that followed the anarchist Leon Czolgosz's assassination of President William McKinley in 1901. Along with a general aversion to Italians, Greeks, Jews, Poles, and Russians, there was a fear of other "undesirables," including anarchists, people with mental illnesses, and us. These bans were strengthened in the 1921 immigration law, which explicitly imposed national origin quotas to preserve the ethnic—and political—balance that existed at the time.

Given the House's overwhelming support for keeping D.C.'s sodomy law on the books, I had no reason to think that repealing the prohibition on allowing sodomites into the country could prevail on a stand-alone vote. Fortunately, there was no need to try that approach. The Judiciary Committee was attempting a complete rewrite of immigration law, and I was to be an active participant in that lengthy and ultimately successful effort. Because the exclusion rules would be rewritten from scratch, I did not need to pass an amendment ending the LGBT ban; instead, I could simply ensure that the ban was omitted from the new rules—a much easier task. My effort had the support of many liberals and of three Republicans with leadership roles: Hamilton Fish and Daniel Lungren in the House, and Alan Simpson in the Senate.

Nonetheless, the work proved long and difficult. Opposition to the full immigration overhaul came primarily from the right. But there was some resistance on the left as well: Hispanic groups and their allies feared that the adoption of sanctions on employers who hired illegal immigrants would erect employment barriers for Hispanic citizens, whom wary employers might hesitate to hire as well. In response, I took the lead in drafting language to minimize Hispanic concerns about job discrimination. But I also said I would not support reform unless the obnoxious exclusions on "undesirables" were removed.

When the leadership realized that passing one comprehensive bill would be too heavy a political lift, they divided it into two parts. The first bill offered amnesty for some illegal immigrants, and the second bill, which was to be taken up only after the first bill passed, dealt with legal immigration.

I was willing to follow this path, but there was a problem. The anti-gay exclusion I was determined to end pertained only to legal immigrants. After all, there was no point applying it to illegal immigrants, who were already excluded no matter what their situation. This meant that even if the first bill passed and some illegal immigrants were granted amnesty, the exclusion provisions, including the anti-gay provision, would remain in full effect. As a result, gay people, among others, would be denied the benefit of that amnesty.

Fortunately, my leverage was at its maximum on that first vote, since amnesty was controversial and the measure needed all the support it could get. I said that I could not vote for the illegal immigration bill without knowing that I would have reciprocal support when the legal immigration bill came up. I received that support from the three Republicans who had won my strongest confidence: Fish, Lungren, and Simpson.

There was still a problem: Until we passed the second bill, the anti-gay provisions would remain in place for amnesty applicants. I was able to resolve the issue with an amendment allowing the commissioner of immigration to waive the exclusion of gay and lesbian amnesty seekers pending comprehensive reform. Once again I relied on someone in whom I had the utmost confidence: Alan Nelson, the immigration commissioner. With Reagan's approval, he used his waiver authority to protect LGBT applicants for citizenship.

At the time, the ranks of amnesty seekers included a large number of Marielitos—the Cubans who'd been expelled by Fidel Castro a few years before. These were Castro's "undesirables." Given his homophobia—which his leftist admirers in the United States tried to overlook—it wasn't surprising that so many of them were gay men, expelled solely for that reason.

When the commissioner agreed to waive the exclusion, most of them were given legal status with little problem. But I did receive a call from an attorney representing a Cuban who had been denied papers yet could not return home. It turned out that the INS agent who'd interviewed the man had used an obsolete form that directly asked if the applicant was a homosexual. Through his translator, the man answered no. He was then asked if he had ever had sexual relations with another man. Here the language barrier loomed large. His response was recorded as "No; I fooled around some, but I never had a real relation." In the margin of the form, the agent recorded that the man, on advice of counsel, sought to withdraw that answer but was denied permission to do so. When I learned of this, I went directly to Commissioner Nelson. With a laugh, he agreed to overrule the denial of amnesty and reissue his earlier order that all efforts to ask "the question" come to an end.

When immigration reform came back to the committee in 1988, it needed every vote it could get. By then, I had come out of the closet, and I made it clear that I could not offer my support to any legislation that included a legally binding reaffirmation of my inherent undesirability. When the bill finally reached the floor of the House in 1990, it failed on its first vote for reasons unrelated to the repeal of the anti-gay provision. I reported this tearfully to my partner at the time, worried all my efforts had come to naught. But it was resuscitated with bipartisan support and passed the second time. Senators Kennedy and Simpson ensured Senate acquiescence, and in 1990, President Bush signed the bill that eliminated the worst anti-LGBT provision ever put into American law.

•

My growing engagement with LGBT issues was deeply intertwined with the significantly increased attention I was giving to my own situation. Bluntly stated, my publicly neuter, privately gay approach was becoming incompatible with my increasing public recognition. This had both a personal and political dimension.

On the personal side, I wanted a healthy relationship with another man, but this was not easy to find. At a time when many gay people were trying to reconcile their sexuality with the demands of their professional and family ties, the stress of helping me sort out my personal and official roles was more than other gay men wanted to deal with. For guys who had opted for openness, helping me avoid exposure was an unwelcome burden they had left behind. For those still closeted, the rumors of my orientation—by then fairly widespread among insiders—invited unwanted scrutiny. I was tired of having to desex my pronouns, ration my visits to places I wanted to be, and avoid dancing with another man anywhere I might be photographed. (This was pre-Internet, when discretion was easier.)

What I did not fully realize at the time was that my attendance at the 1984 Democratic convention in San Francisco was a turning point. I went there with Joel Farley—a gay friend, not a romantic interest—and we stayed at a hotel apart from the Massachusetts delegation so I would have some privacy. He and I attended a party at the Marin County home of my colleague Barbara Boxer, then and since a fervent defender of LGBT equality. On an impulse, I quietly told her that Joel and I were there on a platonic date. She reacted with no surprise and considerable warmth. We went on to an event at a gay club, where I did dance, knowing that there would be no photographers present. The next day I addressed the convention at the invitation of the Mondale campaign. My remarks were distinctly unmemorable. I abided by the rule that speakers were to stick to carefully vetted scripts. In subsequent convention speeches, I reverted to my preference for speaking mostly extemporaneously. I realized that all I had to do was submit some pages of text, have them approved by convention staffers—who rarely impressed me with their expertise in speech giving—and then stand on the platform and say what I wanted, secure in the knowledge that no trapdoor on the stage would open beneath me. I may have inadvertently set a bad example for Clint Eastwood, who would so embarrassingly lose a debate with an empty chair twenty years later.

The next evening I attended a private party at a gay bar, and met Todd Dickinson, a lawyer active in San Francisco's gay politics, and we began a two-year relationship. (We remained good friends after we stopped dating, and he later served as the head of the Patent and Trademark Office in the Clinton administration.) The emotional effect of all this was overwhelming—and positively so. For the first time in my life, I'd combined socializing with other gay men and important political activity. For that week, the two halves of my life—personal and political—came together, and I knew I could not return to keeping them in separate spheres.

The conflict between my crusade against homophobia in the country and my accommodating it in my own life was becoming unbearable. I had to resolve an agonizing problem: How could I pride myself on being a national advocate for achieving LGBT equality while refusing to take the one important step that was directly under my control? I could no longer urge other members to show political courage on our behalf while I opted for cowardice. So I decided at last to come out.

As I noted, the media still observed the custom of never disclosing anyone's homosexuality without permission unless some scandal precipitated it. Initially, this tradition had allowed me to hide; now that I decided to be honest, it enabled me to control the timing and circumstances of the revelation.

But not entirely. Politicians' careers are rarely under their control. When Harold Macmillan, the former British prime minister, was asked what factors had the strongest influence on political outcomes, he reportedly said, "Events, dear boy, events."

Before I could leave the closet, I had to deal with events. My close friend Gerry Studds represented the neighboring congressional district, which covered New Bedford and much of southeasern Massachusetts. For many years, he, too, had lived in the closet. But in 1983, he became entangled in a controversy involving his relationship to a male House page. In the past, when political figures were publicly linked to homosexual acts, they either implausibly denied they were gay or, even more implausibly, claimed they couldn't remember the alleged events because they were too drunk at the time. (I believe that whenever you are too drunk to remember what happened, it's likely that very little actually happened.) Studds took a different tack: He acknowledged his sexuality and became the first openly gay member of Congress. Studds was censured by the House after Newt Gingrich, in one of his intermittent poses as a paragon of virtue, substituted that harsher penalty for the committee's recommendation of reprimand. (I voted in the minority for the reprimand.)

Studds ran for reelection the following year, 1984, and drew serious opponents in both the Democratic primary and the final election. He won both races, though not by overwhelming margins, and his victories made two things clear for me. One, I no longer had any electoral excuse for not being publicly honest about my sexuality. If Studds could win despite the unhappy circumstances surrounding his coming out, there was no serious possibility that my purely voluntary declaration would cause my defeat.

Two, I had to wait. Asking the people of southeastern Massachusetts to host both of the only high-ranking openly gay elected officials in America was a chance I was willing to take, but only after giving them at least a few years to get used to the idea.

5

COMING OUT

I was ready to leave the closet at last—but how would I do so? I had lived too long with the burden of "the gay thing" to treat coming out as a political matter alone. For thirty-two years, I had been in hiding. For much of that time, I'd been ashamed to belong to a universally despised group. Then I'd been afraid of exposure, and angry at myself for my self-denial. Finally, I felt shame again as I watched younger gay men and lesbians confront the bigots openly with a courage that I lacked. After all those years, lying to people was much easier emotionally than finally admitting my lie.

By 1986, I was as ready as I would ever be. But the circumstances of my disclosure were complicated by another factor: I talk too much. Specifically, I shared my decision with more friends and allies than was prudent, and word was starting to get around. This led to an unusual interaction with several members of the media. They remained committed to the "rule" that prominent people should not be outed unless they had been enmeshed in a gay-related scandal, but they were understandably eager to break the story. So various journalists asked me from time to time if they could do so. I consistently said no—I didn't deny I was gay but invoked their own nondisclosure principle. This arrangement was tested in mid-1986 when a book was published that implicitly, but unmistakably, told the truth about me.

The author was Robert Bauman, who'd been a stridently right-wing Republican member of the House in the 1970s. His primary concern was outlawing abortion, but he had followed the conservative movement's anti-gay line as well. In 1980, before I arrived in the

House, he was charged with soliciting sex from an underage male prostitute. His denial of his homosexuality was universally—and accurately—disbelieved, and he was defeated for reelection that year.

In his memoir describing his own gay life, he cited my attendance at a gay pride rally in the company of a friend whom he inaccurately assumed was a romantic attachment. No one reading it could miss the clear import: I was a gay man who enjoyed a media silence that he had been denied.

I was scared. I was ready to come out, but not at his hands, not in that way, and not at that time. This led to two important conversations in the early summer of 1986. The first was with Speaker O'Neill. As a great admirer of his leadership, I felt obligated to let him know that there might be another sex-related controversy in our party that he'd have to handle. I approached him on the floor of the House, as we were watching a majority vote doom our effort to curtail Reagan's aid to the Nicaraguan contras. I knew this was an inauspicious moment, but I couldn't stand the suspense of not knowing what his reaction would be. "Tip," I said, "Bob Bauman has just written a book that says I'm gay."

"Aw, Barney," he consoled me, "don't pay any attention. People are always spreading shit about us."

"But, Tip," I said, "the problem is that it's true."

He looked stricken, though he immediately made clear it was not my sexuality that troubled him but the negative impact its disclosure would have on my career. "I'm sorry to hear it," he said. "I thought you might become the first Jewish Speaker."

As upset as I was at the prospect of a premature outing, the fact that a man I respected so much had said such a flattering thing made me feel better.

I felt even better when I confirmed he wasn't just trying to be kind. Shortly after, I encountered one of my closest friends and allies, Congresswoman Pat Schroeder, leaving the cloakroom. "Oh, good," she said. "You're okay. I just talked to Tip, who said, 'Pat, have you heard the sad news about Barney? It's too bad; he was so talented.'" She was relieved when I explained that he was referring to my political standing, not my physical health.

Meanwhile, O'Neill set about warning his press secretary, Chris

Matthews. "Chris," he said, "we might have an issue to deal with. I think Barney Frank is going to come out of the room." With his unerring ability to translate O'Neill's malapropisms, Matthews quickly made the necessary metaphoric adjustment.

When news of Bauman's book broke, *The Boston Globe*'s Bob Healy called and asked if he could come to D.C. to talk with me. As the man in charge of political coverage at *The Globe*, he faced a dilemma. He did not want to break the no-outing rule, especially as it applied to a politician in good standing with *The Globe*. But he could not allow his newspaper—by far the dominant source of news in New England—to be scooped on a national story in its own backyard. Healy hoped I would give *The Globe* the story, but Bauman's book was not getting much attention and I told him I was still not ready. When I was ready, I assured him I would give *The Globe* an exclusive—that is, I would let them publish the news first. And I promised that if any other media outlet got hold of the matter, I would call him right away, guaranteeing *The Globe* no worse than parity.

Throughout 1986 and 1987, I continued to speak with friends and colleagues about my impending declaration. The reaction in the LGBT community was unrestrained happiness. This itself was a sign of improvement. When I had asked Steve Endean to take me to a gay bar in 1980, during Congress's lame-duck session, he was chastised by a senior gay political leader for threatening my cover, thereby endangering an important LGBT political asset. By 1986, the movement's leaders unanimously believed my coming out would do little if any harm to me and a great deal of good for the cause.

Many of my straight political allies and supporters, by contrast, tried to talk me out of it. They said I was a valuable ally on a wide range of other issues—helping the poor, fighting racism, reducing military spending. Their fear was that my influence would diminish. Not surprisingly, perhaps, they signally failed to understand the anguish of life in the closet. "Of course we have no problem with your sexuality," many said, "but why can't you keep on the way you've been—leading your private life as you want to but without the political baggage of coming out?"

By the spring of 1987, I was ready, but still apprehensive. What followed was a peculiar pas de deux with *The Globe*. As I had promised, I called *The Globe*'s editors and told them that the time had come to go public. They happily replied that they would be glad to receive my statement and interview me about it. I then explained that I did not intend to announce anything, but that I would answer honestly if a reporter asked if I was gay.

I'd thought more carefully about this process than about any other decision I'd ever made. It seemed to me the best way to contain any political damage was to minimize the entire subject. I would do everything I could to downplay the significance of the revelation, and subsequently to insist that my sexuality was "no big deal." Executing this strategy obviously precluded my initiating the discussion. If being gay was no big deal, people would reasonably ask why I announced it. Politicians are not in the habit of issuing public statements about subjects that they prefer to be ignored.

This was a problem for *The Globe*. Asking if I was gay—even with my permission—would break the no-outing rule and require them to explain why I was a one-time exception. But failing to ask would risk losing a big scoop. And so once it became clear to them that I would not volunteer, they asked.

The reporter they sent was Kay Longcope. She was a lesbian and I believe the only out reporter on the paper at the time. I had met her back in the 1970s when she'd been Elaine Noble's partner. Neither of us being big on ceremony, she came into my D.C. office, turned on her tape recorder, and asked me, "Are you gay?"

I gave the most carefully considered answer I could: "Yeah. So what?"

There was an immediate glitch. I had agreed to answer the question on a Friday for a story that would appear the following Monday. But *The Globe*'s beat reporter who covered the House, John Robinson, was infuriated that his paper had sent Longcope to do the interview. He insisted—successfully—that he should break the news under his byline on Saturday. Robinson had two reasons for being so proprietary: It was his journalistic territory, and he was himself a closeted gay man whom I had met at social functions in D.C. (Inappropriately, *The Globe* later assigned him to the "society" beat, where he often commented from his closet in a snarky way about other gay people.)

That Saturday was a day to remember. It was Memorial Day weekend, and there were two parades taking place in the most politically conservative part of my district—the adjacent communities of North Attleborough and Attleboro [*sic*]. (I am not responsible for the peculiarities of Massachusetts's official orthography.) I could not think of a worse way to spend my first day out of the closet than parading myself for hours through that particular area. It started badly when an older, conservative Democrat confronted me, complaining that I had lied to him when he'd asked if I was gay during my race against Heckler. I did not remember the exchange, but given my state of mind that year, he was probably right. Fortunately, I soon received reassurance from an unexpected source: David Locke, the conservative Republican state senator from that district, approached me with a smile and asked me to march alongside him.

With Locke at my side, I began my normal parade routine, which I had learned from John Parker, the area's previous representative. Noting my awkwardness reacting to crowds, Parker gave me great advice: "Just do what I do: Take three steps and wave to the right, then take three steps and wave to the left." (I found this very helpful, even when it occasionally meant waving to trees and telephone poles along lightly attended parts of the route. Better to be nice to inanimate objects than to ignore live ones.)

From then on, the reactions I encountered were almost wholly positive. For the second, larger parade in Attleboro, I marched alongside a uniformed navy veteran, Gene Moore, who was married to my local office manager, Joanne. Things went from good to better as the weekend progressed. That Saturday evening I had been invited to a Cirque du Soleil performance in Boston. Christopher Reeve was in attendance and received a warm reception from the audience when he was introduced. Then my presence was announced. The response is best described in the language of the annotated transcripts that used to chronicle meetings of the old Soviet parliament: "prolonged stormy applause; all rose." It was the only time in my experience that an entertainment-oriented crowd gave a politician a greater ovation than a genuine star. For the first time, I relized that coming out could have political advantages as well as liabilities.

That impression was strongly reinforced Sunday morning, when I joined tens of thousands of people at a rally on Boston Common marking the start of the AIDS Walk. One of the first speakers was Ray Flynn, then Boston's mayor. He had come to political prominence as an antibusing leader, and was and still is one of the state's leading opponents of legalized abortion, although unlike most of his allies in this fight, he was always strongly supportive of well-funded social and health services for children born to poor mothers. In a bit of well-delivered pretense, he claimed that when he'd heard a TV announcer say just before a break, "We will return with big news about Congressman Barney Frank," he'd wondered which of my important achievements as a legislator would be described. He added that I was a great congressman who did so much to help people, and that this was still the most important thing to say about me.

When I was introduced, the outpouring of emotional support from the large crowd was tangible. I tried for a minute or so to respond without crying—unsuccessfully.

There was one slight discordant note. Michael Dukakis, in his third term as governor, greeted me warmly, but he made no reference in public or private to the news of the weekend. This was a reflection of his personality rather than of any opposition to our fight for legal equality. Though he was originally ambivalent about our cause and opposed our right to adopt, he would become a full supporter of legal equality, signing an antidiscrimination bill and naming the first openly gay judges in Massachusetts history. One of his aides later told me that Dukakis's silence at the rally was entirely intentional. When he'd been reminded that I had just come out, and that he should praise me for it, he'd said this was not the kind of thing he did and that I would understand. I did, to some extent, but I also wish he'd spoken up. With some embarrassment, I confess that his reticence led me to what I now acknowledge was an unbecomingly petty retaliation. When he called me in November 1988, a few days after he lost the presidential election to George H. W. Bush, I consciously omitted any reference to that event.

For the next few days in Massachusetts, and then when I returned to Washington, the responses continued to be overwhelmingly supportive. Two conversations in particular had a powerful emotional impact. Alan Simpson of Wyoming, the Republican senator who supported my efforts to remove the anti-gay immigration rule, called to apologize. "For what?" I asked him. "Well," he said, "knowing myself and my telling outrageous jokes about everything, I figured I might have made one in your presence, and I respect you way too much to want you to think that's how I feel." He added that he admired my courage. I was deeply moved.

A day or two later, as I entered Roland's, the fabled Capitol Hill late-night convenience store, Warren Rudman, the Republican senator from New Hampshire, was just leaving. (Greater awareness that members of Congress do their food shopping in the p.m. after a long day's work might correct the wildly inflated views of our lifestyles prevalent on the Internet.) Deliberately waiting at the door until I was in the back of the store, and then speaking loudly so that everyone could hear him, Rudman said, "Barney, my friend, I'm proud of you."

On the House floor, my Democratic colleagues literally embraced me. In so doing, they conveyed their willingness to protect me from any harm—political or other—that might threaten. And my first appearance before an LGBT gathering produced the greatest outpouring of emotion—from them and me—that I have ever experienced.

Shortly after the announcement, I went to lunch at a restaurant near the House with one of my oldest friends, Mark Furstenberg. It was crowded, with a long wait to be seated. As we stood there, the maître d' immediately escorted us to a table. Mark expressed pleasant surprise at our being singled out and wondered why. I explained that a lot of gay men worked in restaurants.

Media response was also largely favorable. The right-wing *Washington Times*, owned by the Reverend Sun Myung Moon, enthusiastically added gay bashing to its regular denunciations of me—in which I took considerable pride—but they were a minor exception. One story that portrayed my decision in a favorable light was not only very important for me politically but also became a footnote in the history of journalism. Linda Greenhouse of *The New York Times* published a piece on Wednesday, June 3, that gave me the chance to explain my decision, and contained generally favorable reactions from others. But there was a small fly in the very soothing ointment. The headline across the top of the page read "Public Man, Private Life: Why a Congressman Told of His Homosexuality." And the article described my "homosexual acquaintances" and my support for "homosexual rights." By then, "gay" was the adjective in general use. "Homosexual" was not explicitly derogatory, but it was the preferred term among those who wanted to maintain some semantic distance from our cause. In the phrasing of certain aptitude tests, you might say that "homosexual" was to "gay" as "Negro" was to "black." It wasn't exactly an insult, but it was a message to the minority in question that the majority would decide what to call us, rather than let us pick a name we liked.

In this case, the message was sent by the man who ran the paper, A. M. Rosenthal. (Incidentally, because *The Times* was sensitive about its Jewish appearance, reporters with identifiably Jewish first names for a long time used their initials—A. M. (Abe) Rosenthal, A. H. (Abe) Raskin, M. A. (Myron) Farber. In a related example of bowing to bias, women were also asked to use initials. Of course, those initials more effectively hid the writers' sex than Rosenthal's initials obscured his Judaism. Rosenthal was famously uneasy at best about LGBT rights and insisted on using "homosexual" instead of "gay." Coincidentally, Greenhouse's story appeared a week before Rosenthal's last day as editor, so I believe I am the last man in history to be described as "homosexual" in *The New York Times* as a matter of editorial policy.

The overwhelmingly positive reaction I was getting from my colleagues, the media, and the general public was good news politically. Even so, my advisers and I knew it was unwise to rely solely on my past success when it came to evaluating my prospects for reelection in 1988. So we polled. Our reading was that I would lose only a few points if I ran as an openly gay candidate. (We were right: I had won 74 percent of the vote in the presidential election year of 1984, and that fell to 70 percent in 1988.)

To my dismay—because I didn't want to know the answer—my pollster Tom Kiley also insisted on asking respondents if they were disappointed to learn that I was gay. The good news was that a majority were not, but the breakdown by gender—cross-tabs in polling language—deflated my ego. Men were on the whole unhappy to hear the news; women by contrast overwhelmingly said that they could not have cared less. From the standpoint of my hopes for a better social life, this was not encouraging. I did search the comments appended to the polling data to see if some men had expressed particular enthusiasm, or if a few women had expressed any disappointment at my unavailability. They had not.

The polling data had one more interesting element. Only 22 percent of voters said that my sexuality made them less likely to vote for me—but twice that number said they expected that it would make others less likely to vote for me. This result reminded me of the reaction LGBT people often received when they came out to family members. "Thank you for telling me," they were assured. "I don't know why you were ever worried that those of us who care for you would have any problem with you telling us who you are. Of course I still love you, and will always love you—but don't tell your father." Based on the frequency with which I had heard some variant of this story, I was coming to a tentative conclusion: The average American was not homophobic but still feared that he or she was supposed to be.

There was one more consequence of coming out. In the flood of mail I received—most of it welcoming and some very touching—I found a note from someone I did not know, Herb Moses. He told me he was an openly gay Jewish man who, given these traits, had the unlikely job of editing an economics journal for the Department of Agriculture. He suggested that we meet. I agreed, and we began a relationship in June that lasted eleven years. Now I was not just the first voluntarily out member of Congress; Herb and I were also the first openly gay congressional couple.

Of course, this meant the end to my short-lived "minimization" strategy. I was now accepted as a gay politician doing my public job. But would I also be accepted as a flesh-and-blood gay man involved in a physical relationship with another guy? Herb was a Washington veteran and he knew dating me would involve some inconvenience, but I could hardly expect him to accept being described as "no big deal" in my life.

For the first time in my career, I read a book not for intellectual stimulation or information but as a manual on how to perform a tricky job. It was Charles Hamilton's *Adam Clayton Powell, Jr.: The Political Biography of an American Dilemma*, which traced the life of the Harlem congressman.

Powell was only the fourth African American to serve in Congress in the twentieth century. (The other three represented the same heavily black district in Chicago.) I was shocked to learn from Hamilton's excellent work that when Powell arrived in D.C. in 1945, he was told he could not swim in the House pool, eat in the Members' Dining Room—in this case by the black headwaiter—or get his hair cut in the House barbershop. The three Chicagoans had apparently acquiesced in these exclusions, probably due to the racist national mood at the time and the docility they'd learned serving as cogs in Chicago's political machines.

Powell refused to accept this. After World War II, black resistance to segregation was gaining strength—the cause was enhanced by the gap between FDR's proclamation of "the four freedoms" and the denial of real freedom to part of our population, and by the need to use all of our available manpower in the war effort. But Powell's struggle also had a personal dimension. His insistence on being treated respectfully also extended to his wife, the jazz singer Hazel Scott. When she was not allowed to perform in a hall owned by the Daughters of the American Revolution, and Bess Truman subsequently attended one of the organization's functions, Powell criticized the first lady. He received in return a sharp rebuke from Harry Truman, who, in this case, unfortunately let his family loyalty outweigh his commitment to principle. I drew a clear lesson from Powell's experience. Herb and I would not do anything only to make a point, but neither would we stand for any second-class treatment just so some homophobe could make his or her point.

My rule was simple: Wherever congressional spouses were invited, so was Herb. I did not have to argue the matter with Tom Foley, who had just become Speaker. He was fully supportive of equality and authorized Herb to wear the same pin that was given to other spouses as a form of identification inside the Capitol.

We did exercise some prudence. At the first White House Christmas Ball we attended in 1987, we wanted to join the other couples who were dancing, but we were too timid. So I asked my two San Francisco colleagues, Barbara Boxer and Nancy Pelosi, to start us off. Nancy and Herb and Barbara and I gyrated for a couple of minutes, and then they discreetly—and very graciously—walked away, leaving Herb and me to dance facing each other.

•

With my private life in good shape, and my reelection assured, I was able to put all my energies into legislating. Until then, I hadn't realized the full effect on my personality of living in the closet, but several of my colleagues enlightened me. Simply put, I was now nicer.

Legislating is a personal business. In the executive branch, there is a hierarchy with the president at the top. The judiciary is similarly hierarchical, with even more strictly defined responsibilities. Legislating is very different—not just from other branches of government but also from almost any other organized human endeavor.

There is no true hierarchy in either the House or Senate. Each body is composed of individual—and usually individualistic—members. The Speaker of the House and the Senate majority leader have the most influence, but neither of them can order any of his or her colleagues to do anything. To add to the free-for-all, all members are able to vote on all issues.

All of this puts a high premium on certain gifts. A legislator must have persuasive powers and also a great tolerance for messiness and uncertainty—for bargaining with a large number of players simultaneously, in a process where all issues are on the table. Personality is a secondary factor, but still a critical one. It generally works in one direction: Not even the most popular member can charm colleagues into voting his or her way, but the obnoxious and unpleasant pay a price—sometimes in lost votes, more often by being excluded from the informal conversations that typically determine outcomes.

When I retired, I said that one of the benefits of no longer running for office was that I would no longer have to try to be nice to people I didn't like. Some people said they were surprised by the remark, since they'd never associated me with the practice. My quick response was that I had said only that I had *tried*. In any case, I concede that even in my new friendlier out-of-the-closet disposition, I remained less patient than almost everyone else.

This was a conscious choice. One of the most useful concepts I had learned from the study of economics was the notion of "opportunity cost": In this case, the price of politely tolerating conversational repetition was having less time to deal with pressing matters. I also benefited from reading the memoir of Sherman Adams, Eisenhower's very effective chief of staff. Every day he took part in more than a hundred phone conversations; he coped with the overwhelming time pressures by omitting to say hello and goodbye. I make a sharp distinction between speaking unpleasantly to people, for which I sometimes apologize, and telling them that they have said enough, for which I do not.

Whether or not I was easier to work with, I was happier. And so I was able to turn my full emotional attention to legislative matters, with satisfying results. In January 1987, I became chair of the Administrative Law Subcommittee. It was something of a grab bag, with no jurisdiction over the most contentious judiciary matters. But it did handle an issue I cared a great deal about: the outrageous decision by Franklin Roosevelt to force tens of thousands of Japanese Americans out of their homes in 1942 and imprison them in internment camps. (He was urged to commit this blatant violation of civil liberties by, among others, California attorney general Earl Warren, and he did it over the objection of FBI director J. Edgar Hoover. Go figure!) I had learned of this serious blot on America's record in a course on constitutional law, when I read the Supreme Court decision in *Korematsu v. United States* that upheld the constitutionality of Roosevelt's action. I decided then that if I ever had a chance to help atone for this, I would do so. Membership in the U.S. House obviously provided that chance—and chairing my new subcommittee an even better one.

Of course, there was no way to undo the terrible historical fact of the relocation. But I soon learned that the Japanese American community had been working on a bill to accomplish the next best thing: The government would officially apologize and provide some compensation to those who had been mistreated. The two Japanese American House members, Californians Norm Mineta and Bob Matsui, who had themselves been interned as children, introduced legislation calling for the apology and payment. I immediately became a cosponsor, working closely with Glenn Roberts, Mineta's key staff aide. Coincidentally, Roberts's brother was the journalist Steve Roberts, my old friend from Bayonne and now the husband of Cokie Roberts. This web of prior relationships allowed us to navigate a tricky parliamentary situation with complete mutual trust.

The situation was tricky because of an aspect of legislative life that is not widely understood. For liberals or Democrats to flout the views of conservatives or Republicans generally carries little political risk—people who are already going to vote against you can do it only once. Politicians who claim credit for standing up to their enemies deserve skepticism. As I've said, the usual result for them is increased fund-raising opportunities.

The true test of a politician's willingness to take risks for principle is when his or her usual supporters are on the other side of an issue. Standing up to your enemies is fun and often rewarding; standing up to your friends is stressful and often costly, and consequently very rare. When a member's supporters are divided, indecisiveness is the frequent response. Having to choose between ardent groups of constituents is an elected official's worst nightmare.

Mineta and Matsui were frustrated and puzzled by the Judiciary Committee's reluctance to act on the Redress bill, as it came to be named. That committee was dominated by liberals who were strongly committed to protecting minorities from mistreatment—but this effort to address one of the most flagrant cases of mistreatment in this country's history was going nowhere.

When I became the chair and started to move the bill, I found out why. Democratic leaders assumed that some veterans' organizations and voters with a rigid understanding of patriotism would oppose the legislation. But that alone would not have deterred them. The problem was that some senior Democrats believed the Japanese American community itself was divided on the issue. Some older people, including many who had lived through the physical and mental torment of relocation, did not want to relive that terrible time. Some also believed that anti-Japanese prejudice was still alive, and that demanding an official apology would kindle a backlash. I understood the reaction, because I had encountered similar feelings within the Jewish community. Many older Jews feared that a strong insistence on equal treatment would trigger a resurgence of anti-Semitism.

The problem was generational. Naturally, the older Democrats had closer associations with the older, more fearful Japanese Americans and saw no point in pushing a bill that might be strongly opposed by many of its intended beneficiaries. Just as I knew that the fears of some elderly Jews did not represent the sentiments of the larger group, Matsui and Mineta knew the same was true of their community. So they urged me to go forward. I did, using my authority as chairman to put the bill on the subcommittee agenda without asking for approval from either the committee chairman or the House leadership. I reasoned that while many members wished the legislation would not come up for a vote, they would have no choice but to support it if it did.

The legislative path turned out to be even easier than I had expected. Japanese American support was overwhelming, both in numbers and in enthusiasm. Opposition on patriotic grounds was far less than some had feared, although one inflamed Republican did lament on the House floor that if we passed the bill, she did not know how she could face her World War II veteran husband. (This was not the last time I was warned that my advocacy on an issue would jeopardize a heterosexual marriage, and the charge proved to be as unfounded then as it was later.)

In those pre–Tea Party days, I worked closely with Republicans to find consensus where we could—and to allow robust debate where we could not. Most Republicans supported the apology, and while many opposed compensation payments, those on my committee agreed not to obsruct the bill's passage so long as they could later offer an amendment to strike the payments. The amendment failed, 162 to 237; the bill passed, 243 to 141; and there was no further opposition from any senior members.

One last hurdle had to be overcome. President Reagan, who also opposed the payments, threatened a veto. This was in the election year of 1988, and Vice President George H. W. Bush was running to succeed his boss. We pointed out, forcefully, that the bill was important not just to Japanese Americans but to all Asian constituencies. If the administration killed the bill, it would surely hurt Bush's fortunes. Reagan's advisers—by then, he was heavily dependent on them—accepted political reality. When he signed the bill in a White House ceremony outside the West Wing, I did not even try to restrain myself from pointing out the administration's political calculation. As a result, I was informed, I was banned from the White House for the rest of Reagan's term. Six months without going somewhere I rarely went anyway was a negligible price to pay.

I am as proud of my work on this issue as of anything else I have done in my public life. Contrary to the hackneyed phrase, this good deed not only went unpunished, it was richly rewarded. Seven years later, the Japanese American Citizens League's board of directors unexpectedly recommended that the league endorse same-sex marriage at its annual convention.

For a nongay organization, representing a community not known for social radicalism, to take that position would be a major advance in our struggle. But opposition within the JACL membership was vocal and acceptance of the board's recommendation very much in doubt. Needless to say, members of Congress typically avoid getting involved in angry disputes that are not already on their docket. And yet when Norm Mineta addressed the meeting, his message was direct: A gay man played the leading role in winning the fight for the Redress bill; we can't walk away from helping him in the fight to win his rights. The conclusion of everyone involved was that Norm's speech propelled the resolution to victory.

•

In 1986, the Democrats won solid majorities in both houses. Under the active leadership of Jim Wright, who'd just succeeded O'Neill as Speaker, and with the concurrence of the newly Democratic Senate, we adopted legislation advancing our goals in trade policy, welfare, civil rights, and arms control. I began to hope that the nation's shift to the right was closely linked to Reagan's political popularity and that the antigovernment tide had been significantly slowed, if not reversed.

But then came the 1988 presidential election. The competent, uncharismatic George Bush defeated Michael Dukakis, and he did so by demonizing liberals and making his famous pledge, "Read my lips, no new taxes." Semantically, the phrase bothered me because it is illogical—you tell people to read your lips when they cannot hear you, and this does not apply when you are speaking to them through a microphone. But my ideological unhappiness was much greater. The pledge's effectiveness demonstrated that public aversion to expanding government was alive and well.

When Congress reconvened in 1989, the previous year's support for government expansion had dissipated. Democrats retained majorities in both Houses, but Bush's decisive victory over "the liberal" significantly strengthened the hand of those who argued for a move toward the center in intraparty debates. That same year, Speaker Jim Wright felt compelled to resign when he faced the threat of an Ethics Committee rebuke over subsidized sales of a small book he had put together. It was an early triumph for Newt Gingrich's campaign to substitute all-out partisan warfare for any notion of bipartisan cooperation.

Tom Foley of Washington was the House majority leader and thus in line to succeed Wright as Speaker. As the likelihood of Wright's resignation became clear, rumors spread that Foley was gay. Disgracefully, some of these rumors came from senior Democrats who supported Foley's rivals for the job. When I confronted two of them, John Murtha and Dan Rostenkowski, they vehemently denied it. I had no proof of their role, but none was necessary. In a pattern I'd first encountered with Boston police supervisors, the denial of guilt was followed by an end to the offending practice. Foley dealt indirectly with the matter by very conspicuously noting the presence of his wife in the gallery when he was sworn in as Speaker. Even so, the story did not die. It was taken seriously enough that one very respected journalist was tasked to verify a physical characteristic of Foley's penis that had supposedly been reported to the police by a male sex partner. She indignantly refused, on both ethical and practical grounds.

Neither Foley's anatomy nor any other evidence provided substantiation of the rumor, but that did not deter the Republican National Committee from a demagogic effort to exploit it. The RNC put out a leaflet titled "Tom Foley: Out of the Liberal Closet," documenting the similarity between his voting record and that of someone they claimed was a randomly chosen liberal—me. (I had come out of the closet two years before.) It was a tactic typical of Lee Atwater, the master of political viciousness, who then chaired the committee.

In my response, I took inspiration from the turn-of-the-century Tammany Hall political hack George Washington Plunkitt. When Plunkitt was accused of profiting from inside knowledge of government spending, he protested, "I seen my opportunities, and I took 'em." I saw the opportunity to call Atwater's bluff, highlighting both the homophobia and the dishonesty of the attack. I could also renew my brief that such scurrility needed to be strongly attacked and not high-mindedly ignored.

Most important, I was among the few who could counterattack on Foley's behalf without implicitly legitimizing the bigotry in question. People who are "accused" of membership in a minority group that is the target of prejudice face a dilemma. Indignant denial—How dare you say such a thing about me?—dissociates the accused from the bias while simultaneously reinforcing it. Saying nothing will lead many people to believe that you belong to the group but are ashamed to admit it—a stance that implies you think it is a bad thing to be. The inherent difficulty of the situation was best illustrated by the *Seinfeld* episode in which Jerry and George awkwardly add to the denial that they are gay the now-stock-comic phrase: "Not that there's anything wrong with that."

I did not need any disclaimer. Nor could I be accused of gratuitously injecting myself into a controversy that many of my colleagues wished would just go away. Atwater's hatchet job didn't only imply that Foley was guilty by association with homosexuality in general, it also impugned him for his closeness to me in particular.

The Speaker's Lobby is a large room that adjoins the House floor.

Admission is only for members, selected staff, and journalists accredited to cover Congress. I did not discover until my last term in office exactly how restricted it was. I tried to enter it with my husband, Jim, just after our marriage, and was stopped. My Adam Clayton Powell–conditioned reflex kicked in, and I started to object, but when I was told that no spouses were allowed, I apologized and Jim went to the cloakroom—where he had become a very popular figure with the staff of the snack bar. I was given to understand shortly afterward that members were not averse to the existence of at least one spouse-free zone in the building.

I realized that calling a formal press conference in response to Atwater's attack on Foley would be dignifying it more than it deserved. Instead, I simply said my piece to the assembled reporters in the Speaker's Lobby, addressing a few at first but gaining, as I knew I would, a larger audience as I spoke. My message was, in a word that is perhaps ironic in this context, straightforward. Obviously, I said, I did not consider being gay a defect in any way, shape, or form, but precisely for that reason I was very angry that the Republicans were treating it as if it were. Although I had no reason to believe that Foley was gay, I continued, I knew that there were closeted Republicans in the House. If the official voice of the national Republican Party continued to use the imputation of homosexuality as a political weapon, I would identify those members of the party who chose to benefit from this tactic while concealing their own sexual orientation. I would out them if I had to. It was big news.

I made my statement at the end of the week, and it was widely publicized over the weekend. The denouement came the following Monday night. When Herb and I returned home from a late dinner, the light on our message machine was blinking. Heather Foley had called and asked me to call back, no matter what time I got in. When I did, her husband told me that while attending an event that day, he'd been contacted by the White House switchboard and connected to Atwater, who had apologized for the leaflet. He'd unconvincingly denied any prior knowledge and promised it would be repudiated and never repeated. He then asked Foley if he knew how I was likely to respond to this information. Without Foley explicitly asking me, I immediately volunteered that I would consider the matter closed and would have nothing further to say about the sexuality of my colleagues. I was happy and relieved. Rarely had—or have—I taken a gamble that ended better. I had sucessfully articulated what became known as "the Frank rule" in discussions of sexual privacy: The right to privacy does not include the right to hypocrisy. But to this day I do not know what I would have done if the matter had escalated. I don't know whether or not I would have carried out my threat.

Ten years earlier, the campaign against Foley would have damaged him, and probably rattled some of the Democrats who were voting on the next Speaker. And it likely would have gone unanswered. But in 1989, Atwater's appeal to homophobia backfired emphatically, tarnishing him and greatly enhancing Foley's position. The AIDS epidemic was still raging, but the crisis, it seemed, had weakened, not strengthened, homophobia. Atwater's final act was an effort to appease the gods of political combat with a sacrifice—a hapless RNC employee, Mark Goodin, was fired for having allegedly acted on his own. The higher-ups' denial of responsibility was widely disbelieved.

My satisfaction with my handiwork was enhanced when Wes Pruden, editor of the right-wing *Washington Times*, mocked the Republicans for backing down, especially, as he said with his usual finesse, to "a Democrat in lavender drawers." Foley's victory was also a great vindication for our cause. Unfortunately, my satisfaction soon turned to unbearable shame. In August 1989, Pruden got his revenge by exposing my two-year relationship with a male prostitute, Steven Gobie.

6

THE TRUE STORY
OF DON'T ASK, DON'T TELL

One of my primary reasons for leaving the closet was my recognition that I'd been responding irresponsibly to its frustrations. My liaison with Gobie was Exhibit A. It began with pay for sex and evolved in my mind—but not his—into an ongoing nonsexual relationship. I knew this was inappropriate, but I lacked the emotional strength to bring the relationship to an end. It was only after I left the closet that I came at least partially to my senses and broke off relations with him. He reacted angrily and eventually took the story to *The Washington Times.*

The revelation of Gobie's role in my life devastated me. I was deeply ashamed and overcome by feelings of guilt. I deplored the damage I had done to the cause of LGBT equality; to Herb, who had known none of it when we began our relationship in 1987; to my family; and to my staff, as I knew that when a political figure messes up badly, those who work for him are automatically assigned much of the blame. I did have the presence of mind to state repeatedly that I'd taken great pains to conceal the relationship from the people in my office and none of them bore the slightest responsibility for my misbehavior.

But while I was depressed to the point of disfunctionality, and resolved not to run for reelection the following year, I refused without a second thought all calls to resign. I did this for one unshakable reason. As badly as I had acted, I was completely inaccurately being accused of much worse, and there was only one forum in which I could prove that—the House Ethics Committee. That body had jurisdiction only over sitting members. If I had quit, their inquiry would have ended—which of course is why many other members facing accusations do resign, precisely to stop any further investigation and judgment.

To this point in my narrative, I have tried my best to be wholly forthcoming about my weaknesses and failings. Given all the emotions involved, I do not know if I can fully meet that standard in addressing this set of events. Instead of trying myself to refute the more sensational, inaccurate accusations, I refer readers to the Committee on Standards of Official Conduct's report—which rebuts them, while recommending that I be reprimanded for what I did do.

After an intensive, lengthy investigation, in which Gobie and I both testified under oath, the panel found two specific grounds for rebuking me. One, I had used my congressional privileges to cancel parking tickets that I thought Gobie had received while using my car to do errands for me, though in fact he'd been using it for his personal purposes. Two, in a memo I had written to an attorney discussing Gobie's probation status, I had lied about how I had met him—this was part of a pattern of concealing my sexual orientation. I had sent the memo to an attorney in private practice, seeking his advice. But without my knowing it, he had passed it along to a prosecutor who would be making a recommendation on Gobie's probation. In the committee's judgment, this was negligence on my part, because I "should have known" that the memo might be passed on.

The House dispenses three main forms of punishment: expulsion; censure, which results in the loss of any chairmanship; and reprimand, which carries no further sanction. When the committee presented its report and proposed reprimand to the full House, one of the most right-wing, explicitly homophobic members, William Dannemeyer of California, moved to substitute expulsion. He lost by a vote of 38 to 390. More serious was the effort by Newt Gingrich, newly installed as Republican whip, to toughen the penalty to censure. He had done that successfully in 1983 in the case involving my Massachusetts colleague Gerry Studds and a House page.

Ethics Committee chair Julian Dixon vigorously and cogently

defended the committee's position—labeling Dannemeyer's presentation "garbage"—and Gingrich's motion failed. With the Democratic leadership urging support for the committee position, all but twelve of my party members voted against Gingrich. Because of my own profound guilt over my irresponsible behavior, and the political damage I had done my fellow Democrats, liberal causes, and especially LGBT equality, I refrained from asking anyone to vote against censure. Indeed, I urged several Democratic colleagues who held contested seats in conservative areas to vote for it. I did not want my conscience further burdened by responsibility for their defeat. I recall one response I received for its extraordinary generosity. Congresswoman Liz Patterson of South Carolina gently chided me for suggesting that she put electoral concerns ahead of being fair to someone she considered a friend. In the final vote, a much larger than expected Republican minority voted against censure: 46 to 129. In the end, I benefited from a widespread view in both parties that Gingrich's effort to politicize the process was inappropriate.

I believe I also benefited from my decision to be totally honest about what had happened from the moment I was publicly confronted. When Gobie first leveled his accusations, the well-meaning advice I received from friends and advisers was to say little if anything in response. In particular, I was counseled to admit nothing and let the accusers carry the burden of proving their case. This is generally good advice if you are facing criminal prosecution. But I was not. At no point did any prosecutor even suggest such an action. It was my political career and my reputation that were at stake. My goals were to salvage my career and confine any personal damage to what was justified by the facts.

Given these objectives, I knew I had to tell not just the truth, but the whole truth, and do so immediately. After all, there was no way I could deny Gobie's most demeaning—and wholly false—accusations without acknowledging those parts of his story that were true. Years later, when one of my colleagues was accused of both an extramarital affair and the commission of a terrible crime that was possibly related to it, he denied neither, though he was guilty only of the first. When I asked him why he had not made his innocence of the crime clear, he explained that he did not want to own up to what he had done. Even though I knew I could only partly discredit the lurid falsities spoken about me, letting them go unchallenged would have further harmed my reputation, especially among those closest to me whose continued approbation I sought.

If a transgressor has not seriously harmed other people, a full, credibly contrite confession is more often than not enough to preserve his job (the use of the male pronoun here is an accurate representation of reality), although it is equally often a bar to further advancement. People may hope for perfection in elected officials, but they do not have a high expectation of its prevalence. But such a confesson must be believable. An acknowledgment of past misdeeds that is promptly followed by new revelations renders any promise to behave better in the future unpersuasive. The fact that no second shoe dropped as the committee pursued its intensive inquiry was also a major factor in my survival.

As the Ethics Committee went forward, I reconsidered my initial decision to leave office at the end of my term. I'd made that decision when I was depressed and convinced that people would believe the worst about me. My sister Ann, who has always been a great source of strength, did me the service of passing along people's unvarnished reactions to my case, and what I heard was not encouraging.

But I soon became confident that the committee would separate damaging facts from poisonous fictions. For example, I knew that my landlady had written a letter stating that she had observed none of the illicit activity Gobie claimed to have presided over in my basement apartment. (She lived upstairs.) I was also receiving more support than I felt I deserved from my constituents. Journalists who traveled to my district to sample opinions were disappointed to encounter an unexpectedly strong tolerance for human frailty. I experienced that myself when I marched in a parade in Fall River, along with Herb and members of my family. In this largely blue-collar community, in 1989 as in 1987, most people said they were much more interested in what I was doing to improve their lives than in anything I was doing to my own.

At first it seemed as if the campaign might be tough. A moderate

Republican with an appealing family decided to run. But he turned out to have political defects. There were serious inconsistencies in his policy positions, and he was accused of trying to exploit the fact that his wife was Jewish, prompting a messy debate. Facing more criticism than he found bearable, he soon dropped out of the race. First-time candidates often expect running for office to be easier than it turns out to be.

That left one other Republican, a very conservative man with a penchant for saying outrageous things. On one occasion, he assumed I was younger than I really was and denounced me for dodging the draft during the Vietnam War, even though I'd been too old to qualify for universal conscription. This gave me the chance to welcome him to the ranks of those who believe that gay people should be allowed to serve in the military. He also took an AIDS test, and when he passed, demanded that I do the same. I congratulated him, noting that passing tests was probably not a common occurrence in his life. Widespread revulsion at his attempt to politicize that terrible plague further eroded his appeal.

There was some slight slippage in my own support. I received 66 percent of the vote—my smallest total between 1982 and my tough reelection fight in 2010. Even so, I was able to return to the House with my political standing nearly intact. That standing was enhanced when Leon Panetta invited me to join the House Budget Committee that he chaired. Membership on that committee is a mark of leadership confidence, and I accepted gratefully.

On Panetta's committee, I was able to work hard on a cause that remained of the utmost importance: maximizing spending on AIDS. There were still no effective courses of treatment for this killer in 1991. As a result, I faced the most agonizing choice I've ever had to make in politics. Was it more important to fund the search for a cure or to fund the gallant organizations that provided aid to those who were sick? To me, this called for a tough but morally correct decision to choose our heads over our hearts. We should do everything we could to reduce the number of people who'd die from this plague in the future even if it meant limiting the comfort we could provide to those already dying.

Of course, the real issue was not research versus care but the insufficient funds available for both, and indeed for other AIDS-related needs, such as housing. An adequate response to the AIDS crisis required higher taxes and a sharp reduction in military spending, reflecting the collapse of the Soviet Union and the reduced threat we currently faced.

Unfortunately, not only was the AIDS coalition absent from our push for more resources for domestic spending, but also much of their rhetoric made that job harder, particularly regarding taxation. Their frustration with the lack of resources for their emotionally draining, morally compelling work was understandable. But, regrettably, it led them not to an insistence on increasing the funds available to the federal government to meet our societal needs but to blame those in office for that inadequacy. Rather than point to society's unwillingness to commit the necessary resources, they sharply denounced the government for callous neglect and thus added to the antigovernment sentiment that was the real problem. In fairness to those fighting AIDS, I acknowledge that they were hardly the only group seeking greater federal support who ignored the need for a larger pie. But of all the constituencies whose real interest lay in enhancing progovernment attitudes, they were by far the most vehement in demonizing the institution.

At the time, militant groups like ACT UP did bravely and effectively press pharmaceutical companies to undertake AIDS research and assist patients. Challenging the private sector made sense. Corporations are not accustomed to angry words and well-publicized campaigns of civil disobedience. Their instinctive response to controversy is to end it. But those same militant tactics are not successful in the political arena. Public corporations find it upsetting when 40 percent of the public thinks ill of them. For us, getting 60 percent support is deeply comforting.

•

My presence on the Budget Committee also allowed me to launch a surprise attack on what would become a critical target—the military's gay ban. In the 1980s, leaders in the community had begun a campaign to win over public opinion on the issue. Current and former service members played a crucial role. One articulate victim of the policy, Leonard Matlovich, neatly conveyed its moral bankruptcy when he said, "When I was in the military they gave me a medal for killing two men and a discharge for loving one."

My neighbor, friend, and sole openly gay colleague, Gerry Studds, played an important role in furthering the debate. In 1989, he received a leaked internal Defense Department report that was critical of the ban, and he released it. I stayed out of the public discussion at first, fearing that my foolish behavior would make me a liability. But after my comfortable reelection and appointment to the Budget Committee, I felt sufficiently rehabilitated to join in.

The opportunity came when Defense Secretary Dick Cheney appeared before the Budget Committee in 1991. As a very junior member of the committee, I would be one of the last to speak. By the time I could ask Cheney a question, all of the most pertinent defense-spending matters would have been covered. So I decided to ask him about the military ban.

At that time, the Eisenhower executive order decreeing LGBT people too untrustworthy for a security clearance was still in effect, and its animus obviously lent support to our exclusion from the armed services. I knew that Cheney would have great difficulty invoking that order to defend the military's policy. He had appointed as assistant secretary of defense for public affairs—the Pentagon's chief press officer—his former congressional aide and fellow Wyoming resident, Pete Williams.

Williams was ideal for the job. He was good at it, and he had Cheney's complete confidence. But there was one problem—he was gay. Williams has since come out and is a respected NBC correspondent, but he was then a closeted gay man who in the course of his job was privy to the most sensitive national security information.

I knew that he was gay. Cheney knew that I knew. And in a phrase that I am glad I am writing, because only Danny Kaye could have spoken it, I knew that Cheney knew that I knew. This gave me the chance to ask one of the two most effective questions I ever asked in forty years of trying to trap witnesses. (For the second, wait for Clinton's impeachment.) "Is it the contention of the Defense Department that because somebody is a homosexual, he or she is inherently a security risk?"

Cheney responded by saying, "I think there have been times in the past when [the policy] has been generated on the notion that somehow there was a security risk involved, although I must say I think that is a bit of an old chestnut." Of course, if Cheney had said yes, he would have had to explain why he had put a putative security risk in such a sensitive position. Such a glaring violation of government policy would have stripped Williams of the cover of the press's no-outing rule.

In fairness to Cheney—a phrase I have rarely felt motivated to use—the fact that he had put Williams in that job reflected his own lack of anti-LGBT prejudice. This became clear in his very significant answer. He could have simply responded that the military ban was based on other considerations. But he did not. Under the annoying but necessary rule that a committee member has no more than five minutes to question a witness, I was not able to press Cheney further. But I was more than satisfied with the exchange. In six words, Cheney had weakened one of the government's two most damaging homophobic policies, and explicitly repudiated the other.

Our momentum was slowed a few days later when Colin Powell, the chairman of the Joint Chiefs of Staff, testified. I had taken Cheney by surprise with my question, but Powell was prepared. With security clearances off the table, I asked him if we were unfit for military service in some other way. No, he said, it had nothing to do with our ability or character. Of course gay people had been members of the military throughout our history, Powell acknowledged, and they had served—and were serving—with the same dedication and competence as their comrades. He then went on to make the argument that would prop up bigotry for the next twenty years: Allowing us to join the military openly would seriously undermine morale. Our presence in living quarters or on training grounds or even on battlefields would be so disruptively abhorrent to the heterosexual majority that their prejudices had to take precedence over any claim we could make for fairness, or, for that matter, any need our country might have for us—even when enlistments dropped to the point that entry standards had to be lowered.

At first, I was actually encouraged by Powell's words. There was nothing intrinsic to gay people that rendered us unfit for service. It seemed to me that the two highest Defense Department officials had just rebutted the only even arguably rational point against us.

Of course, ending the gay ban proved a far more difficult enterprise than I expected.

•

In 1991, I met Bill Clinton, who was seeking support for the presidency. Tom Downey, one of my closest friends in the House, had gotten to know Clinton while working on welfare policy, and in the early fall of 1991, he asked a small group of House liberals to meet with the candidate. During the conversation in Downey's office, I'd urged Clinton to join us on the military ban issue, telling him, in one of my greatest political miscalculations, that I thought the country was ready for a presidential order lifting the policy. Lulled perhaps by my confidence, and eager to win my support and that of other LGBT voters, Clinton said he agreed with me on both the merits of the issue and the politics.

Clinton's support for lifting the ban was only one reason that I endorsed him for the nomination and campaigned actively on his behalf. At the time, many on the left believed that he was "too moderate." I had decided by then that I needed to be more pragmatic in my approach to intraparty contests. I'd supported Edmund Muskie in 1972 and Morris Udall in 1976 because I'd thought they were the most electable liberals. But after that, my dismay at the country's rightward shift caused my judgment to go awry. I'd made the egregious error of opposing Dukakis in 1978, and I'd urged Ted Kennedy to run against Jimmy Carter in the mistaken belief that my unhappiness with Carter's moderate stance was widely shared among Democrats and the wider electorate. In 1984, I supported Walter Mondale over his "neoliberal" opponent Gary Hart because I was enthusiastic about Mondale's record and found Hart's critiques of traditional liberalism unfair and sometimes sanctimonious. Four years later, when George Bush forcefully assaulted Dukakis as a "liberal" and won a decisive come-from-behind victory, I recognized that the increased conservatism of the electorate demanded greater deference. (Gary Hart likely would have lost to Reagan, but the result would have been closer.)

It was at that point that I consciously adopted the strategic approach I would follow for the rest of my career and aggressively proselytize to my fellow liberals, often to their irritation. I resolved to always support the most electable liberal candidates, with an edge in close cases going to electability. And in those elections where that candidate was successful, I would do what I could to push, cajole, pressure, or otherwise persuade him to move further toward my preferred policy positions, without jeopardizing his political viability.

There was a corollary to this approach. My major self-appointed task was to argue as convincingly as I could against political conservatism, which had become the major obstacle to the advancement of my values. But in the firm belief that I understood the power of that constraint more than many of my ideological allies, I took on a second job. I would not only try to dissuade my ideological allies from nominating unelectable candidates but would also argue against undermining our candidates by insisting that they ignore inconvenient political realities, or by denouncing them as betrayers when they took those realities into account.

This aspect of my work was much less fun. As I noted, taking on your enemies is generally enjoyable and often rewarding. Nothing boosted my campaign account more than being able to reproduce vicious right-wing attacks in my fund-raising appeals, and nothing did more to elevate my standing on the left than the frequency with which I was cited by conservatives as a leading example of liberalism's defects. Especially after I survived coming out with no political damage and I became a frustrating symbol to the bigots of the waning of their dominance, I echoed—mostly to myself—the sentiment of Franklin Roosevelt when he said of his harshest critics, "They are unanimous in their hate for me—and I welcome their hatred."

Even when my debates were with reasonable conservatives, who eschewed prejudice, I enjoyed being able to engage in all-out rhetorical battles in which I could try not just to demolish their specific policy arguments but also cast general doubt on the validity of their overall ideologies—especially since I believed I was very good at it. (My attacks on my opponents' personal morality were very sparse, limited to instances where some hypocrite—like Newt Gingrich—ignored his own flaws while impugning the character of others.) Candidly, I think it is both legitimate and politically helpful to make my ideological opponents look not just wrong but also foolish, especially if I can use humor to do it. A rebuttal to a mistaken policy argument always has more initial impact and more lasting effect if it is funny as well as logically compelling. And in another aspect of legislating that resembles trying to enhance your social standing in high school, I realized that my talent for ridiculing the opposition made me more popular with my friends and more feared by my opponents.

Arguing with those whose policy values I share is much harder, intellectually and emotionally. In these instances, I try hard—not always successfully—to distinguish between my disagreement on a particular point—usually strategic or tactical—and my agreement on our broad goals and the value I put on our continuing joint efforts to achieve them. It was important to rebut allies far more gently, restraining my instinct to add the insult of mockery to the unavoidable injury of disagreement. This restraint gets harder when I am especially emotionally invested in the strategic or tactical dispute in question. (I confess that I am hazy on how to draw the line between these two, so I usually lump them together.)

I chose a political career—even when I assumed it meant forgoing a satisfactory personal life—because nothing was more important to me than doing all I could to reduce the suffering inflicted on vulnerable people by unfair societal arrangements. (I say "was" because now that I've fallen deeply in love with Jim, the personal comes first, although not to the exclusion of the political.)

Given this, when I am accused by people who share my goals of betraying them for some personal advantage, even though our differences are really over how best to advance those goals, I get angry—all the more when I am convinced that my critics, while well-intentioned, are doing our effort more harm than good.

It will come as no surprise that all of these feelings are greatly exacerbated when the accusations involve the cause to which I have devoted much of my life: the defense of LGBT people against the ravages of prejudice. There had been hints of these tensions in the differences I had had with some LGBT leaders in the fight against AIDS, but they did not fully erupt until the bitter debates over our unsuccessful effort to end the military ban.

·

My assignment in the Clinton campaign was to persuade other liberals to support him. In the course of this, I spent a good deal of time making the case to the LGBT community. Consequently, after he won, I was doubly motivated to press the president to take action. I wanted to show my community that I hadn't misled them and I wanted our cause to advance. The two items highest on our list were appointing openly gay and lesbian officials and allowing us to serve in the armed forces. Many of us worked on the first item, submitting names to the transition team. Clinton delivered, hiring gay staff members, and the first openly gay or lesbian presidential appointee, Roberta Achtenberg, who became assistant secretary of HUD. (An openly gay man, Frank Lilly, had been appointed during the Reagan administration to a part-time, non-Senate-confirmable, purely advisory commission.) She was confirmed over the unsurprisingly vile opposition of Jesse Helms, whose reason for voting no was that "she's a damned lesbian."

It soon became clear that repealing the military ban would encounter serious opposition. The first major setback came again from Colin Powell. No one was in a better position to thwart us. He was not only the highly respected chairman of the Joint Chiefs, he was also the most influential and prestigious African American ever to serve in the executive branch. We frequently drew analogies between Harry Truman's executive order ending official—albeit not actual— racial segregation in the military in 1948 and what we wanted Clinton to do for LGBT people in 1993. Politically, that line of argument collapsed when Powell specifically repudiated it. In a statement to the press, he said, "The military leaders in the armed forces of the United States—the Joint Chiefs of Staff and the senior commanders—

continue to believe strongly that the presence of homosexuals within the armed forces would be prejudicial to good order and discipline. And we continue to hold that view."

The cases were not the same, Powell said separately, because race (unlike homosexuality) was "a benign condition." He explained that he meant "benign" as opposed to active. These words were disappointing even if correctly understood, because they implicitly aligned him with those who believed LGBT people choose to be "that way." "Benign" is also the opposite of "malignant," and so the overtones of his word choice were wholly negative. It was clear we'd be in for a very tough fight.

There are two opposing views of what happened next, both critical of Clinton, and both wholly unfair to him. The first is that Clinton erred badly by plunging into this fight in his first few days, instead of giving priority to other, more popular matters, and winning more leverage for a difficult struggle. The second is that he moved too slowly. According to this view, he flinched, and instead of issuing a repeal order and directing Powell to follow his commander in chief, he yielded to political pressure and let Congress decide this issue—unfavorably to us.

The facts refute both accusations.

The option of delay disappeared on November 6, 1992, when federal judge Terry Hatter ruled that the existing policy was unconstitutional. This thrust the issue onto the front pages two months before Clinton's inauguration. It also meant that the new president would have to make a decision about the policy almost immediately after taking office, ready or not. Within sixty days of Hatter's ruling, the administration would be required either to appeal the decision, that is, defend the ban, or abolish it by executive order, rendering the case moot. There was no realistic third choice: Refusing to appeal would have meant letting a single district court judge invalidate a long-standing national policy.

There is one criticism of Clinton's timing that has some validity, but it should be leveled at me, not him. Though Clinton had to respond quickly to Judge Hatter's decision, it's true he might have waited one or two weeks. He could have used that time to highlight other items on his agenda. He also could have used it to consult with the Joint Chiefs so he would not be accused of ignoring their input. It was my fault that he wasn't able to do either of these.

The day after the inauguration, David Broder of *The Washington Post* wrote a prominent story in which I announced Clinton's intention to repeal the ban by executive order shortly after the inauguration. My announcement was an egregious mistake. Privately informing LGBT leaders that the repeal was a done deal, based on Clinton's assurances during the transition, should have assuaged the needs of my ego and my insecurity. And I should have known better than to brag about Clinton's pledge to one of the country's best political journalists at an inaugural party and then be surprised when it made national news. My partial defense is that after serving for twelve years in the House under Republican presidents, I had never before had such access to presidential decision making. I had made no news of this magnitude because I hadn't previously known any.

In any case, Broder's article forced Clinton's hand, and that was not helpful to our cause. Still, even without my indiscretion, he wouldn't have had much time to prepare the debate.

The opposite charge is that Clinton should have acted unilaterally—as Truman did. This view overlooks an important point: Clinton did not invite Congress into the fight—it inserted itself and in a manner that he could neither avoid nor neutralize. The organized women's groups that strongly backed Clinton were eager to see the Family and Medical Leave Act enacted into law. It was their highest priority. Since George Bush had vetoed the bill, Clinton's pledge to sign it into law was a very tangible sign of his victory's significance.

The Democratic leadership accordingly scheduled the bill for early passage. As the first act introduced in the new Congress, it automatically received the highly symbolic designation H.R. 1. But there was a problem. Unlike all other legislative bodies I know of, the Senate does not require that amendments be germane to the subject matter of the bill in question.

This time it was Republican Senate leader Bob Dole who, like Tammany Hall's George Washington Plunkitt, seen his opportunity and took it. He met with his conference, and they overwhelmingly agreed to back a nongermane amendment to the FMLA. This amendment would transform the military's LGBT prohibition from an executive branch policy that a president could abolish on his own into a binding statutory provision that he could not.

It soon became clear that we did not have the majority necessary to block this amendment. Dole had successfully turned LGBT rights into a partisan issue. Just as important, Senator Sam Nunn, the Democratic chairman of the Senate Armed Services Committee, was, we discovered, a strong opponent of LGBT equality. Several years earlier, I learned, he had fired two staff members when he found out that they were gay, on security clearance grounds—demonstrating that the 1954 executive order was more than symbolically damaging to us. A few years later, when Ted Kennedy forced a Senate vote on a bill protecting gays and lesbians from discrimination, Nunn was one of only five Democratic senators out of forty-six to vote no. And in a very revealing statistic, he was, at fifty-eight, the only one of the Democratic opponents of the bill who was under seventy. His homophobia was too deeply rooted to be weakened by his generation's changing views. To make matters worse, Nunn was a respected authority on military affairs and highly influential on his fellow Southern Democrats.

Nunn made it clear that if Clinton removed the military ban, he would support Dole's amendment to the FMLA reinstating it. Clinton was in a box: He could allow us to serve in the military only by vetoing the FMLA, depriving his allies in the women's movement of the achievement of their number-one goal.

In the end, Nunn did yield to the claims of party solidarity to some degree. He agreed to oppose Dole's ploy if Clinton promised to hold off on abolishing the ban for several months, and to consult with Nunn and the military leadership. At that point, White House counsel Bernie Nussbaum asked me my opinion about how Clinton should proceed. My answer was as obvious as it was painful. I told him that I agreed with postponing the repeal, assuming that the administration would work with us to build support for another try. Nussbaum assured me that they were committed to doing so.

Nunn helped defeat Dole's amendment in a partisan vote—and

the family leave bill was signed into law. It has since been a great benefit to working people, especially women.

Over the next several months, I was in continuous discussions with administration officials as they worked to win the support of military leaders. I also sought to change the political equation in Congress. I had good relations with Les Aspin, Clinton's secetary of defense. He'd been an important liberal House member and was totally committed to the success of our effort. I had less confidence in my allies in the LGBT community. They were getting the politics wrong.

Given the left's vision of itself as the tribune of the people, it's a bitter irony that conservatives have proved so much better at grass-roots advocacy. They are likelier to forcefully inform members of Congress of their policy preferences; liberals are more inclined to hold public demonstrations, in which like-minded people gather to reassure each other of their beliefs. Writing or calling your representatives and senators, and organizing others to do so as well, is not inherently exciting and relies on the implicit belief that representative government works as it should. Applauding speakers who denounce the unfairness of a particular situation and rail against the political system is more emotionally satisfying—but very much less effective. After years of pleading with allies to favor the first course over the second, I formulated a rule: If you care deeply about an issue, and are engaged in group activity on its behalf that is fun and inspiring and heightens your sense of solidarity with others, you are almost certainly not doing your cause any good.

While our side held rallies, our opponents were flooding Congress with messages. I hoped that this disparity would galvanize LGBT leaders into effective action, but it did not. "You've got to get your people to contact us," lamented one of our strongest allies, Senator Dick Durbin. He said this not because he was wavering in his support but because he knew how the absence of constituent pressure would affect many of our colleagues.

The unwillingness of the LGBT community to act effectively in its own interest manifested itself most dramatically in April 1993, when hundreds of thousands of us gathered in Washington for the community's third mass demonstration against homophobia. It was called "The March on Washington for Lesbian, Gay, and Bi Equal Rights and Liberation."

I was looking forward to the march. On the personal side, it was an opportunity to alleviate the deep regret I felt over letting my fear of exposure keep me away from the first march, in 1979. When I reminisced about that event to Gerry Studds, who was also closeted in 1979, he told me that he had changed the route of his daily jog that day so he could at least pass by the Mall, where the march was being held.

On the day before the 1993 March, Speaker Foley visited the house where Herb and I lived for a widely advertised reception kicking off the weekend. I was deeply grateful. Foley was courageously refusing to be intimidated by the rumor that had been spread about him in 1989. His political risk didn't end there. After he'd accepted my invitation, he learned that an event was scheduled in his district celebrating a major project he'd helped to fund. His attendance there was politically very important. I told him that I would be deeply disappointed—indeed, embarrassed—if he didn't attend my event, because I had made so much of the historic significance of his doing so. He agreed to stay in D.C., sending his wife to represent him in Spokane. I could not have been happier, especially when so many LGBT people showed up, and Foley spoke from our steps to a crowd that overflowed our home and filled a full block of the street outside. But this story had an unhappy ending, which still troubles me. Foley was defeated in the next election, ending an extremely valuable thirty-year career. He lost for several reasons: his brave support for a gun control bill, his lawsuit against his own state's term limits law, and the strong anti-Democratic tide that gave the Republicans their first House majority in forty-two years. Foley lost by a narrow margin, and I continue to regret pressing him to miss the event in his district—especially as my own ego was a factor. In all honesty, my demand that he attend my event was issued not only for the good of our cause. I also wanted to demonstrate my effectiveness to my critics on the left.

At the time of the march, the military ban still awaited congressional action. Seven hundred thousand marchers had come to town, but as Tim McFeeley, the executive director of the leading LGBT organization, the Human Rights Campaign, notes in *Creating Change*, "Only a few hundred of the marchers bothered to lobby their members of Congress." To my deep disappointment, the march confirmed my impression that many of my allies preferred undisciplined self-expression to serious participation in the political processs. There were eloquent appeals to allow us to serve our country. But their impact was substantially diluted, if not obliterated, by the antics of those McFeeley describes as "foulmouthed entertainers and bizarrely costumed revelers." One prominent lesbian comedian exulted that there was finally a first lady she would like to "fuck"—her remark was carried live by C-SPAN and widely cheered by the march audience. If Nunn and Dole were watching, they must have been grateful.

I take credit for preventing what would have been an even greater disaster. As I waited behind the stage to be introduced, I was horrified to see nine or ten of the gay soldiers who had been victimized by the ban standing shoulder to shoulder, beginning a rhythmic kick routine, with accompanying campy gestures. Nothing could have been more devastating to our argument that LGBT people would blend comfortably into the military than a photo—or worse, a video—of these guys lined up not to march but to emulate the Rockettes. The soldiers agreed to halt their routine, though not without expressing their anger at me. Not for the last time, I was told I was too culturally restrained to be a gay leader. (In 2011, when I disassociated myself from outrageous, abusive comments made about Senator Scott Brown's family by the comedian Kathy Griffin, she responded that I was obviously an inhibited straight man pretending to be gay.)

There were obvious parallels between the 1993 gathering and the civil rights movement's great March on Washington in 1963. But the differences were far greater, and entirely to our disadvantage. A. Philip Randolph, the patriarch of the antiracist movement, put Bayard Rustin in charge of organizing the march and supervising the speaking program. The result was a series of disciplined, powerful messages calculated to have the maximum beneficial effect. John Lewis reports that he had to submit multiple copies of his speech to Rustin for vetting. In one case he was told that he could not say "the people demand" equality because it would sound too radical. The contrast between that great sober, moving occasion and the antics at our march could not have been greater. If a black comedian had begun to joke about having sex with Jackie Kennedy, he would have been thrown in the Reflecting Pool, not cheered.

In addition to being disappointed in the march, I was disappointed in the ad hoc organization that the LGBT community created to manage our effort—the Campaign for Military Service. The leaders of this group, David Mixner and Tom Stoddard, were talented men with impressive track records. I admired their past work, but I differed sharply with their strategy in this case. (Candor requires a personal note here: Stoddard and I had dated for a few months, but when that ended, we remained friends, and there was no ill feeling on either side—until strategic and tactical differences inevitably took on a personal dimension.)

In the aftermath of the Family and Medical Leave duel, Nunn campaigned obsessively to build support for maintaining the ban. He used his chairmanship of the Armed Services Committee to conduct a series of hearings and in a notable instance even held a session aboard a submarine. The event yielded photos of senators in narrow sleeping quarters asking young men if they wanted a gay roommate, with the press avidly recording their answers. Most of them did not. In response, I correctly noted that Nunn was spending more of the committee's time on us than on more important military issues, such as NATO, and I unwisely accused him of being obsessed with sex. Asked about my comment days later on *Meet the Press*, he effectively thanked me for trying to make him seem more interesting than he was but deferred to me as the man more focused on sex—the Gobie incident had faded, but not disappeared, from memory.

While Nunn worked the press and the public, the Campaign for Military Service was doing very little that I could see to counter him. The CMS's fundamental error was to act as if they were trying to win an election rather than influence Congress. In electoral campaigns, they correctly noted, early leads in the polls often dissipate, and given limited resources, the best course is to make your major push close to Election Day. But the analogy did not work. Members of Congress are under great pressure to make up their minds early and are rarely able to change them due to prevailing political winds. Throughout the late winter and spring, representatives and senators were being asked to declare themselves, predominantly by constituents who strongly opposed our position.

Meanwhile, CMS was doing little to counter Nunn in Congress. In a decision that I found especially inexplicable, the CMS leaders requested that I ask Nunn's House committee counterpart, Ron Dellums, to cancel a hearing in which he planned to defend our position. I was appalled. We had no better ally than Dellums, a highly principled African American leader whose experience in the Marine Corps in the 1950s had deepened his own fierce opposition to bias. As a young recruit of considerable ability, Dellums told me, he had been approached by a superior who urged him to apply to become an officer. Dellums is light skinned, and with his Marine-regulation shaved head, there was no indication of his race. When he presented himself as ordered, the officer in charge looked at him closely and asked, "Private, what is your race?" Dellums responded, "Sir, Negro, sir." He heard no more about promotion.

As one of the leading authorities in the House on the needs of the armed services, and as a leader of the Congressional Black Caucus, Dellums was ideally positioned to offset both the damage Powell had done as well as Nunn's efforts. But when I objected to asking Dellums to cancel his hearing, Stoddard explained that his group had a carefully planned strategy in which a House hearing had no place. I conveyed the message to Dellums, who complied, though he was understandably offended. I soon came to regret this decision as much as any I have made in my career. I resolved that I would never again let myself be intimidated by the demands of movement solidarity when I thought them unwise.

As the debate proceeded to our disadvantage, the time for hard choices had come. By May, after the public relations failure of the march on Washington, it was clear that we would not have the votes we needed for repeal. At that point, I did what I could to avoid the full defeat I knew was coming.

Both Nunn and Powell defended the ban by insisting that morale would be harmed if the heterosexual majority knew there were gays in their midst. Given this, I argued, it should be entirely acceptable for lesbian, gay, bisexual, and transgender people to serve, as long as we refrained from conversation or activity that revealed our sexual orientation while we were on duty. According to the ban's own defenders, there was no good reason to restrict our freedom when we were not on military bases or in the field with other military personnel. And so I publicly proposed allowing LGBT people to serve in a sexually neutral way when performing their military duties, while remaining free to express their sexuality at other times.

Admittedly, this proposal had little application to that minority of the armed services who at any given time might be engaged in combat overseas—in that context, off duty has no meaning. But for those not in combat, whether stationed in the United States or a foreign country, there would be many opportunities to be themselves in a relaxed way without in any way involving their straight comrades. Gay men who were able to live off base could do so with male partners without fear that a passing neighbor might report them. Lesbians could go to bars or restaurants without fear that they might be photographed and subsequently penalized. People could march in gay pride parades—in civilian clothes—without worrying that a TV shot would end their military careers. As I saw it, refraining from discussing our sexuality with fellow members of the military was a restriction, but not an intolerable one. In fact, it did not greatly differ from how a majority of LGBT people behaved at the time in civilian occupations.

There were several reasons why I considered my compromise preferable to the status quo. First, it would constitute an official acknowledgment that LGBT people were valuable members of the military. Second, allowing LGBT people to socialize and enjoy intimate relationships with each other would clearly improve the quality of their lives. Finally, I believed that even if LGBT soldiers strove to maintain a bright line between on-base and off-base behavior, some of their comrades would learn who they really were. Getting to know their gay colleagues as individuals would gradually erode the prejudice that upheld the ban.

There were two very strong reactions to my proposal.

President Clinton was pleased. Congress was still threatening to attach the ban to a bill he would have to sign for other reasons. He did not want to participate in his own repudiation and was eager for a way out. The evening my proposal appeared in the newspaper, he called me at home to thank me and to promise to work as hard as he could to achieve the best possible result.

The LGBT community responded with outrage. I was taken aback. I had not expected my plan to be warmly welcomed, but I was troubled that many movement leaders seemed eager to blame me for a defeat that was already inevitable, thanks in large part to their own ineptitude. I was especially disappointed in my colleague Gerry Studds, with whom I had previously worked in complete harmony. Earlier that spring he had dejectedly told me it was obvious we had lost. At that time I told him I thought it was too soon to give up and that we should try to find some better approach. But when I publicly acknowledged we were not going to triumph, he joined those who blamed me for conceding prematurely.

I was even more disappointed in those leaders of LGBT organizations who knew as well as I did that we had lost the all-out fight. They were afraid to tell their most activist supporters the truth. As I frequently told them, I found this ironic: The very people who criticized elected officials for putting political expediency ahead of moral courage found it hard to stand up to their own constituents when they knew it was desirable to do so.

In the spring, I began working with the Clinton administration to see if a version of my proposal could be adopted. At Clinton's direction, Les Aspin spoke with generals and admirals about my idea. General Powell, Aspin told me, had expressed a willingness to support a version of it, but only if other members of the Joint Chiefs also supported a meaningful compromise. Unfortunately, the other chiefs flatly refused any such accommodation. Given the political situation, it was clear that Congress would not approve anything over the brass's objections. We had lost.

At President Clinton's urging, the military did then grudgingly agree to the face-saving proposal that came to be known as Don't

Ask, Don't Tell. It differed sharply from the provision I had advocated. Under the new proposal, LGBT service members would face dismissal if they were discovered in any activity that exposed their sexual orientation or gender identity, even if it had no connection to their military duties. Any expression of their true selves, anytime, anywhere, anyplace, could have harsh consequences.

To my disappointment, Clinton put the policy forward as if it were an advance. The harm was not only rhetorical. The fact that the president, who'd been our champion, was calling this discriminatory measure a good thing would make our efforts to get rid of it harder. And so we needed to counteract the impression his words created. Working in close agreement with LGBT leaders, I pushed for votes in both the House and Senate that would at least allow sympathetic members to register that the fight was not over. My Massachusetts colleague Marty Meehan introduced our amendment in the House, and Barbara Boxer did so in the Senate. We lost in both houses, but at least we received Democratic majorities. This allowed us to keep alive the argument that Don't Ask, Don't Tell was being adopted in opposition to our desires and legitimate needs.

Though it made no sense to say so at the time, DADT was not entirely meretricious on paper. Had it been properly applied, it could have been of some benefit to some service members. As the policy was articulated, service members who took great pains to conceal their sexual orientation should have been protected. But to their great discredit, many commanders interpreted our political defeat as a mandate to root out gay, lesbian, and bisexual members. Some were expelled after others read their private mail or looked into their computers. Others were victimized by former lovers who decided to inform on them. In none of these cases could it be said they had "told" their status. Sadly, Clinton allowed these witch hunts, as they were accurately called, to go forward unhindered.

Years later, I got a vivid glimpse of how the policy might actually have fostered some improvement. I was speaking with Steve Morin, a police officer in the town of Raynham, Massachusetts, who worked in his off-hours as my driver. Steve was a veteran of the first Iraq War and remained in the reserves as an MP. One night, someone saw him at a gay club in Providence, Rhode Island, and reported this to one of his superior officers. She summoned him and began to ask about the sighting. As he reported to me, she said it had come to her attention "that certain establishments that you have been seen entering and leaving are quite undesirable to our organization."

As a police officer, Morin was well aware of how to use his rights when he was being questioned—he had frequently been on the other side of the transaction. He told her he did not know "quite where you are going with this."

Her response was to ask, "Are you a homosexual?"

He said, "Ma'am, are you asking me if I am gay?"

Aware now that she was on dangerous ground, she replied, "No, no—that would be against the law for me to ask."

Morin then responded, "Ma'am, then you also know it would be against the law for me to answer that question, and I am not to lie to an officer."

He reports that there was then a long period of silence in which they stared at each other until he stood up and asked, "Ma'am, is there anything else?"

She said, "No, Master Sergeant, that will be all for now." That ended the matter.

•

Despite Don't Ask, Don't Tell's deleterious impact, I did not regard Clinton as an enemy who held out false promise but as a friend who had tried to help us and failed. I knew that Clinton was genuinely opposed to anti-LGBT bias and wanted very much to diminish its impact. The magnitude of our defeat on the military ban—which I believe he understood, despite his claim that Don't Ask, Don't Tell was a partial victory—greatly increased his incentive in this regard. This was due to an important political principle: compensation. No politician long survives without understanding it, instinctively if not explicitly. It governs an official's relations with both his elected colleagues and his constituents. There will inevitably be occasions when you disappoint people whose goodwill you need. Sometimes, as in Clinton's case, it's because of an inability to deliver. In other cases, you made a conscious choice, either due to policy differences or the stronger competing claims of another group.

There are two possible ways to repair the resulting breach. One is to explain yourself, as patiently and sympathetically as you can. On the basis of my own experience, I do not advise this approach. In 1985, the House was struggling with the results of a too-close-to-call election in Indiana, and Speaker O'Neill appointed a special committee to preside over the final count. I greatly admired the Democratic candidate, Frank McCloskey, but as the proceedings went on, I came to believe it was impossible to know who actually had won. I voted against the Republican bid to seat their candidate, but I also voted against the committee's recommendation to seat McCloskey.

Hoping to alleviate O'Neill's anger, I sought him out and began to tell him why I felt so deeply about the issue and had voted as I did. He exploded. As I later told a colleague, "Tip was mad at me until I explained myself, then he became furious." Deeply disappointing someone with your vote, and then taking pains to explain exactly why you were right and he or she was wrong, is a perfect example of adding insult to injury.

As Clinton knew, the more effective alternative is compensation. Immediately after both houses voted to enact Don't Ask, Don't Tell, I began an effort to educate the president and his aides about how we could jointly invoke the principle.

The biggest single item that we wanted from the federal government was still unachievable—a law banning job discrimination based on sexual orientation. But I knew there were several things the president could do without Congress that would improve the quality of our lives as well as repudiate the intellectual underpinnings of homophobia.

Our biggest target was the forty-year-old prohibition on security clearances for LGBT people. No federal policy had done us more damage. Symbolically, it was a declaration that we were inherently flawed. It said that simply because of who we were, absent any sign that we had misbehaved in any relevant way, our government—indeed, our society—could not trust us. While the fear that we were vulnerable to blackmail was one justification for the order, the policy plainly assumed that we were bad people who corrupted those around us. (The Senate report that preceded Eisenhower's order by a few years was titled "The Employment of Homosexuals and Other Sex Perverts in the Federal Government." I later posted a copy of the title page in my congressional office.)

From the time I came to Congress and became known as a strong defender of LGBT rights, I regularly received calls from frightened people who had been told by their employers that they would now be subject to a security clearance review because their company was seeking a government contract. It wasn't only the State and Defense Departments that required security clearances. Employees of Treasury and Justice, as well as engineers, architects, accountants, and others working for private companies seeking government contracts, often needed them as well.

These reviews were thorough and intrusive. People who had been living discreetly—or openly, as they had a right to do—with a same-sex partner suddenly faced the prospect that friends, neighbors, and relatives would be questioned in ways that would reveal their sexual orientation and cost them their jobs. When asked direct questions, their friends and neighbors were equally afraid of lying or telling the truth.

In fact, the pattern was so widespread that Frank Kameny, one of the great leaders—and characters—of the LGBT civil rights movement, made a reasonable living as a defender of people facing such inquiries. Kameny was not a lawyer. He was an astronomer who had been dismissed from federal service in the 1950s because he was "a homosexual," and who, unlike almost everybody else at the time, decided to fight back. Using his own experience and sharp analytical mind, he was able to defend many people successfully in these circumstances. But few people had assistance of that caliber.

On August 2, 1995, Clinton issued an executive order revoking the ban on security clearances. It was a historic moment. But even though the ban had been imposed and now rescinded by executive order, Congress could still codify it into law. And after Clinton acted, one right-wing homophobe, Congressman Robert Dornan of California, threatened to do just that. The situation paralleled that of the military ban, but this time the circumstances were more favorable to us. Colin Powell had rejected the traditional argument for the security clearance restriction. Even more helpful to us, so had Dick Cheney when he'd made his "old chestnut" remark to me. Not even Sam Nunn, who'd invoked the order in firing two of his own employees, was ready to make the case for it. When Dornan persisted with his bill, I got the chance to revive my I'll-out-the-Republicans ploy. This time my logic was irrefutable. If the House were to assert that gay men are security risks, I announced, I would consider it my patriotic duty to provide a list of gay members to the appropriate authorities. Dornan backed down, undoubtedly at the urging of his own party leadership, and denounced me for my threat.

Ironically, a year later, Dornan became the first member ever to out another when he lost his cool—of which he rarely had much—and berated his Republican colleague Steve Gunderson for going in and out of the closet. (Gunderson, to his credit, had provoked Dornan by criticizing another Republican, Mel Hancock of Missouri, who was offering a homophobic amendment to penalize schools that were supportive of LGBT students.)

While some in the gay media quibbled about the wording of Clinton's order, it has proved to be a strong barrier to any further harassment of LGBT individuals. In 2000, I remembered my part in this affair very proudly when I spoke at the first Gay Pride Day in the history of the CIA. As George W. Bush entered office the next year, it would also be the last CIA Gay Pride Day for eight years.

Clinton also delivered what I requested on two other important matters. At his urging, Attorney General Janet Reno promulgated a rule adding people who'd been persecuted for their sexual orientation or gender identity to the list of those eligible for refugee status. The most vocal opposition came from an anti-immigration organization that called itself FAIR. They were not homophobic, but they predicted that the rule would become a convenient dodge for the hordes seeking to come to the United States. This was, of course, entirely unfounded. The policy has worked well, providing safety to the endangered in very moderate numbers. Not even FAIR has claimed that we suffer from a glut of African, Asian, and Latin American lesbians.

Finally, Clinton and his director of the Office of Personnel

Management addressed the problem of employment discrimination in the government. They sent a letter to every federal agency emphasizing that under existing law, hiring was to be on the basis of merit, and that this excluded any discrimination based on other factors, including sexual orientation and gender identity.

To my enduring frustration, Clinton has received little credit for these steps. For me, at least, he honored the principle of compensation impressively.

•

There is a postscript to the fight over Don't Ask, Don't Tell that I promised Clinton I'd keep secret. But I now feel free to reveal it because Clinton himself brought it up in a conversation with Taylor Branch that would be published with Clinton's consent in Branch's book *The Clinton Tapes*. Branch, whose work on Martin Luther King, Jr., is brilliant journalism that I wish every activist would read, is a strong admirer of Sam Nunn and apparently asked Clinton why he had not appointed Nunn to a major national security post in his second term. Nunn had in fact hoped to become secretary of state. Clinton replied that it was my fault, referring to a memo I had sent him.

I am delighted to plead guilty as charged. After the 1996 election, one of Clinton's top aides called to warn me that the president was on the verge of making Nunn secretary of state. I started to complain, and the response I got was, "Don't complain to me. I agree with you, but I haven't been able to stop it and that's why I am calling you." I immediately composed a memo to Clinton in which I said that Nunn had a consistent record of homophobia. As noted, he had fired two men from his staff because they were "security risks" back at a time when the anti-gay order was still in effect. He had vigorously led the fight against allowing us to serve in the military, and in 1996 when Ted Kennedy cleverly forced a vote on the Employment Non-Discrimination Act in the Senate, Nunn was one of only five Democrats to vote against us. In other words, I wrote to Clinton, Nunn has been one of the most effective and dedicated opponents of fair treatment for LGBT people. I have defended you, I went on, against those who have unfairly, in my judgment, accused you of selling us out on the Don't Ask, Don't Tell issue. But if you appoint this man, who has done so much to harm us, to the most prestigious position you have to give, you will do more to validate those criticisms than I could do to rebut them. I passionately told Clinton that he should not do this to those of us who had been his strongest supporters.

I must acknowledge that I got some personal satisfaction from apparently frustrating Nunn's aspiration to be secretary of state. But I also thought that something crucial was at stake: Being a leading opponent of fair treatment for LGBT people should be considered a disqualification for high honor within the Democratic Party. No comparable opponent of fair treatment for African Americans, women, or any other group would have been considered for such a post. I am proud that I helped establish the principle that we should receive equal consideration.

7

WELCOME TO AN EARMARK

In the political climate of the times, I continued to believe that Bill Clinton was the most liberal electable president. And so my mission was clear: I would be his loyal ally where our beliefs converged—while also trying to push him further to the left, especially on economic issues.

While Clinton had criticized certain liberal approaches, I understood that sentiments of that sort were politically necessary. Democrats had lost every presidential race since 1964, except when Jimmy Carter was elected in the aftermath of Watergate, and even then his margin over Jerry Ford dwindled to a very low point as that campaign went on.

More important, Clinton's first two domestic policy initiatives were strongly consistent with traditional Democratic priorities. His tax proposal was the largest in our history in dollar terms (though not in percentage of the economy), and it reflected liberal values in its composition. It promoted energy efficiency, and it fell most heavily on high-end earners. In fact, after its passage, the Congressional Budget Office noted that for the first time in decades, the tax code had become more progressive. Clinton's proposal for universal health care similarly embodied a long-held liberal goal, although as with Obama's plan sixteen years later, it bowed to political reality by using convoluted means to achieve that goal. I was an eager supporter of both efforts. I joined in the strong Democratic lobbying effort that produced a two-vote majority in the House on taxes. Because the health care bill never made it to the floor, and I did not serve on the relevant committees, I was only a cheerleader on the issue, but I was an enthusiastic one.

But while I was encouraged by Clinton's strong support for raising taxes and extending health care, there were early indications that something in American politics was changing. In healthy capitalist democracies, there are usually two basic political tendencies. Each group recognizes the need for a public sector and a private sector, and political debate concerns where to draw the line between them. In America, it was evident after the 1930s that the Republican Party would resist intrusive regulation and higher taxes while accepting a significant amount of each. Meanwhile, the Democrats would put limits on the market while recognizing the importance of profit making. As the Clinton administration initiated its policies, I operated under the theory that this political balance was still in place.

But it soon became clear that my vision of American politics as a private sector–public sector tug-of-war was losing its validity. The major assault came from the right. Republicans who'd once sought to maintain proper limits on the scope of the public sector now denied that sector's very moral legitimacy. In 1990, when George H. W. Bush had called for a tax increase, he got more support from Democrats than Republicans. This led to the defeat of his first tax proposal. He was forced to draft a second proposal that hewed closer to Democratic values, and to rely on Democratic votes to pass it.

There was a sharp contrast between that bipartisan accomplishment and the unanimous Republican opposition to any tax increase when Clinton became president. The Republicans were clear that their opposition to Clinton's plan was not based on its excessive progressivity or its effort to alter the mix of energy use. It was wrong in principle: "It's not the government's money," their mantra went. "It's the people's."

In fact, this makes no sense. In a civilized society that needs a profit-driven private sector and a tax-funded public sector, it is *all* the people's money. The task facing sensible people is to distinguish between the personal or family needs and wants best fulfilled by individual spending choices and those societal goals that can be achieved only if we pool our resources to buy collective goods.

In fact, the conservatives' stark dichotomy of "government" and "people" represents the harshest possible judgment on America. It implies that we are not self-governing, that the government, far from being representative of the voters, is a hostile entity that stands apart from the citizenry. When such a claim is made by the official organs of the Iranian or Chinese governments, American conservatives indignantly refute it. But when the same argument is used to block increased public transportation, aid to community colleges, or more money to clean hazardous waste sites, they find it very comforting.

The Republicans' unanimous opposition to any tax increase in Clinton's first term—in the face, for example, of Alan Greenspan's assertion that it was economically necessary—marked the next stage of their effort to starve the beast. By keeping government revenues low, they would force the kind of program cuts they could not win on the merits. In their post-1992 right-wing posture, the GOP was on the way to perfecting a politically potent two-step—delegitimizing the government while defunding it in a mutually reinforcing cycle.

The death of Clinton's health care plan demonstrated the power of that strategy. I was convinced then and am even more convinced now that political opposition to both the Clinton and Obama health care bills stemmed above all from a lack of public revenue to fund the expansion of care. In both cases, this lack of funds dictated a roundabout method of extending care even though more direct, but publicly costly, alternatives were available. This meant that both proposals were harder to explain than to denounce and, most critically, that large numbers of middle- and working-class citizens were convinced that the expansion of care to those poorer than themselves would come at their expense. Had Clinton been able to put some of the revenue raised by his tax bill into paying for medical care for the uncovered, the plan would have been less complicated and easier to pass. But in an early indication of his determination to avoid being labeled a big-spending liberal, the added revenue all went to deficit reduction—leading James Carville to say that when he died, he wanted to return as the bond market, because everyone in politics was bowing down to its demands.

I did not blame Clinton for these facts—a switch of one vote in either house would have killed the tax bill, and it would surely have lost if it had also addressed health care. But I did differ with Clinton's response to his health care plan's demise. As with gays in the military, I did not blame him for our failure, but I was troubled by his willingness to accommodate defeat rather than plan to overturn it.

•

On questions of economic policy, my feelings about the administration grew mixed. Throughout Clinton's first term, I was greatly encouraged by the support HUD secretary Henry Cisneros gave to my highest legislative priority, affordable rental housing. But another domestic issue proved more divisive, engendering an important intraparty debate over how to diminish inequality. That issue was trade.

I'd entered Congress as a believer in the old liberal doctrine of free trade. Franklin Roosevelt had rescued us from the Smoot-Hawley Tariff, which good liberal economists blamed for aggravating the Great Depression. One of President Kennedy's few legislative triumphs was a bill renewing his power to reach trade agreements.

By 1983, however, I'd begun to entertain doubts. Candidly, politics played a role in my initial change of heart. When I ran against Margaret Heckler in 1982, the garment and textile workers of Fall River were among my strongest supporters in Heckler's own backyard. I knew it would be politically damaging to support a trade policy that accelerated the loss of their jobs.

Before long, however, my political reflex turned into a reasoned belief. I joined a bipartisan coalition that sought to restrain garment imports. If my calculations had been entirely political, I would have limited my antitrade position to the garment industry. After all, in the Boston suburbs I represented, the dominant industries—health care, high technology, higher education—were thought to benefit from increased trade. In fact, it was precisely the disparity between Fall River and those suburbs that prompted my conversion. I did not doubt that trade expanded the overall economy, but I was deeply troubled by its negative impact on the distribution of income through-out the country. It was also endangering an important route into the middle class—the automobile industry. I was an early, enthusiastic supporter of domestic content legislation, which required that a certain percentage of automobiles sold in the United States be manu-factured here in whole or substantial part. This bill passed the House twice, and although it never progressed in the Senate, it did scare the Japanese into significantly increasing their investment—and employment—in the United States.

In this instance too, my motivation was both ideological and political. Even though I represented no auto workers after the 1982 redistricting, the UAW had offered vital support in my first race when the AFL-CIO did not. By the rules of politics, I owed them. There is nothing wrong with such sentiments. Political effectiveness requires allies, and alliances require the mutual observance of obligations.

By the time Clinton came to office, it was clear that unhindered trade in textiles and automobiles was on the ascent. One of Clinton's highest priorities was to take the cause even further and pass the North American Free Trade Agreement. I strongly opposed him on this. I joined a coalition demanding that Mexico and Canada estab-lish acceptable minimum standards on workers' rights and environ-mental protections. (This demand was obviously aimed at Mexico more than Canada, which exceeded our standards in some areas.) We could not fully protect American workers from low-wage Mexican competition, but we did hope to ensure that manufacturers of Mexican goods would not rely on near slave labor or degrade the air and water.

The administration said they agreed with us in principle and then proposed enforcement measures that would have no serious ef-fect. This was frustrating, to say the least, though it did have its ben-efits: Clinton's verbal bow in our direction strengthened our effort to achieve binding rules in the future. Politicians are sometimes less careful than they should be about making concessions that might seem merely rhetorical or cosmetic but that can be used against them later on, when the balance of forces has shifted. I always paid close attention whenever a colleague uttered a remark whose sincerity I doubted and whose future utility I anticipated.

As the free-trade debate proceeded, I saw that the displacement of workers was merely a symptom of fundamental changes in the global economy that were increasing inequality. The failure to make any real progress toward reversing this trend has been the great frustration of my political career.

There was one realm where I could fight effectively, however. In 1993, I became chairman of the Banking Committee's Subcommittee on International Development, Finance, Trade and Monetary Policy, and I used that position to challenge the International Monetary Fund and the World Bank to better serve the people of developing countries. In return for the loans it provided, the IMF often imposed rigid free-market policies. I worried that those policies were economically flawed and had the particularly toxic effect of discrediting democracy in places where we should be encouraging it. Forcing elected governments to impose painful economic reforms only led unhappy citizens to associate democracy with misery.

The World Bank's problems were somewhat different. Major infrastructure projects—dams, roads, and such—were planned and implemented with too little concern for their impact on the environment and the poor. My experience with highway building in the United States made me immediately receptive to this point. I was also disturbed by the bank's Doing Business report, which rated all the countries in the world according to their openness to commercial enterprise. It read like an unpublished chapter of Ayn Rand's *Atlas Shrugged*.

I was determined to do what I could to correct both institutions. I soon learned that my subcommittee chairmanship gave me the de facto power to block the financing of both institutions—if we exercised that power aggressively. My talented staff director, the economist Sydney Key, proposed two specific amendments to the World Bank's rules. The first was to create an independent inspection panel to investigate complaints from aggrieved citizens of any country where the bank was implementing a project. The second was to make the bank's project deliberations open for public inspection.

The bank protested indignantly, and somewhat smugly pointed out to me that under its charter, individual legislatures could not command such policy changes. Treasury Department officials told me that they agreed with the bank: I had no authority to do what I was attempting.

I agreed. "I know that I cannot make you implement these policies," I told the bank and its supporters. "But it is also true that you cannot make me give the support you need to get the funding you need." I also made it clear that I would not assume that they would faithfully carry out any agreement we made. For that reason, I would support authorizing their funds one year at a time, rather than in three-year chunks as had been the practice.

"You can't do that," they said once again. "The funds have to be voted all at once" according to applicable law. My response was one I find surprisingly effective and too rarely used by others: *Show me where it says I can't do it that way.* They couldn't. So I did. And the results were as good as I could have hoped.

In 2013, I was invited by the World Bank to give the keynote speech at an event honoring the twentieth anniversary of the inspection panels, which have proved their worth. Never believe anyone who says, "I hate saying I told you so." Saying "I told you so" is always enjoyable and one of the few pleasures that becomes more enjoyable with age.

•

In 1994, the Republicans took control of Congress in a landslide victory that had sweeping consequences. When Newt Gingrich became Speaker of the House the next year, he was determined to change the rules to his benefit. Gingrich had begun his leadership drive some years before by disparaging Bob Michel, the mainstream conservative minority leader. Gingrich believed that the GOP would never take over the chamber as long as Michel treated Speaker O'Neill as a friend with whom he could disagree without rancor. He believed that Democrats should not be described as reasonable, patriotic, honest people who had incorrect policy views, but as immoral, corrupt, treasonous hacks who threatened the nation's future.

He was very successful. Few, if any, nonpresidents in our history have had such a powerful impact on the political system. His tactics

did not cause the Republican off-year landslide in 1994. Negative reactions to the Democrats' health care, tax increase, and gun control
legislation played a bigger role in the short term and, as I will argue at
greater length later, white working-class Americans' unhappiness at
government's failure to alleviate rising inequality was the broader
cause. But Gingrich's flamboyant attacks played a significant role, and
more important, other politicians believed that they did.

It took a while for Democrats to respond appropriately. Many of
my colleagues had never been in a legislative minority and were
stunned to find themselves the objects of what they correctly believed to be wholly unjustified vituperation.

After the hustler incident, I feared that the political advantages
I'd brought to the national debate were gone and that my irresponsibility had turned my "differentness" from an asset into a liability. My
concerns were largely dispelled when Richard Gephardt, the House
minority leader, and David Bonior, his whip, encouraged me to take
the lead in countering Gingrich and his proposed Contract with
America on the House floor. While none of my colleagues would be
coming to me for relationship advice, their confidence in my political
judgment, and in my standing with their constituents, had suffered
no permanent damage.

I was delighted to honor the request. Ever since I'd been a delegate to the National Student Association congress in the early 1960s,
I'd been an ardent student and practitioner of parliamentary procedures. I arrived in Congress knowing that Northerners, especially
liberals, had a reputation for ignorance of the House rules and for
being stymied by Southerners—usually described as "wily"—who
used those rules to block liberal measures.

Learning the House rules gave me a comparative advantage because the great majority of my colleagues did not study them—
apparently Southerners had become less "wily" over the years. In the
House, unlike the Senate, the rules do not give minority members
the ability to block legislation, but they do make it possible to slow
things down and to raise issues the majority prefers to muffle. Delay
and exposure allow the minority to make its political points more effectively than would otherwise be the case.

While I wanted to continue my work on international financial institutions, it was clear that I could be more successful in fighting Gingrich if I exercised my seniority to become ranking minority member of the Judiciary Committee's Constitution Subcommittee. From that position, I spent much of 1995 and 1996 waging parliamentary guerrilla warfare against provisions of the Republican Contract with America, especially the balanced budget amendment and congressional term limits.

As the lead Democrat on the subcommittee, my job was not simply to defeat the proposals but also to provide a way for Democrats to vote against them without suffering political damage. Both the balanced budget and term limits measures were very popular. Our response was to offer alternative versions of each amendment—and it was here that knowledge of the rules became essential. We used parliamentary tactics to force the Republicans to take a stand on whether the balanced budget amendment would apply to Social Security. If it did, cuts in benefits for seniors could be required by the amendment's enforcement mechanisms. This approach did not lead to Gingrich's defeat in the House, but it provided a politically defensible position for Democrats in tough districts who wanted to vote no. Most important, our framing of the issue helped ensure the amendment's failure to pass the Senate.

We had fun on the term limits issue. There was an honest difference of opinion among term limit advocates over how many terms House members should be allowed to serve. While most House Republicans thought a six-term limit for representatives was reasonable, a militant group of citizens insisted on a three-term tenure. We gleefully added to the confusion by announcing that if term limits were going to be instituted, they should be made retroactive—lest we be accused of putting into effect new rules from which we were exempting ourselves. We underlined the point by having John Dingell, a twenty-term veteran, sponsor the Republicans' original amendment. When he did so, he sarcastically thanked the GOP sponsors for supporting term limits that took effect only prospectively, meaning that his service could extend for twelve more years. (In 2014, he announced his retirement after his thirtieth term.) In the ensuing disarray, all of the term limit bills were defeated—indeed, term limits were the most prominent provision of the Contract with America that did not pass the House.

Before the battle with Gingrich, I had enjoyed my reputation as an articulate, impassioned liberal with a talent for belittling my opponents. But I privately regretted that my public image made me seem more interesting than serious—an entertaining, unconventional advocate, lacking the gravitas required for a true national leader. I hoped that my new efforts demonstrated that it was possible to be funny and serious at the same time.

•

Fighting Gingrich was gratifying, but quarreling with the Clinton administration was not. I was disappointed when the president reacted to the 1994 elections by renewing his efforts to distance himself from liberalism. His highest legislative priorities were to cut back one of our few income transfer programs for the very poor—Aid to Families with Dependent Children or, in the hated word, "welfare"—and to seek a balanced budget deal with the Republicans that would have mandated cutbacks in other domestic programs as well.

Just as troubling, Clinton became the presidential tiebreaker in a thirty-year-long debate between John F. Kennedy and Ronald Reagan. Kennedy's call to "ask what you can do for your country" affirmed the moral value of collective action to improve the quality of our lives. Reagan's assertion that "government is the problem" was the rallying cry for those who regarded the public sector as the thief of the people's money. In Clinton's first two years, he raised taxes, especially on the wealthy, mandated family and medical leave, invigorated environmental protection programs, and fought to expand health care. True, he argued that he would correct traditional liberalism's flaws by making the government more efficient. But while I did not subscribe to most of that critique, this was a debate within the progovernment camp about how—not whether—to advance collective action.

So I was wholly unprepared for Clinton's State of the Union address in January 1996, when he resolved the Kennedy-Reagan impasse and set the agenda for his reelection campaign and presumably his second term by declaring, "The era of big government is over." No presidential utterance has come to me as a more unpleasant surprise. Years later, when Republican congressman Joe Wilson shouted "You lie" at President Obama during one of his State of the Union speeches, the House voted to rebuke him for his breach of decorum. Even though I agreed that Wilson's outburst was inappropriate, I abstained on that vote because regulating speech, including that of my colleagues, is something I do not choose to do. Indeed, I have considerable affection for the British House of Commons, where heckling leaders is business as usual. If I'd been in the House of Commons when Clinton announced the end of big government, I would have done some heckling of my own. "What country are you describing?" I would have bellowed.

I did pose that question, belligerently, to some of his staffers immediately after the speech. "Did I sleep through the big-government years?" I asked. I recognized no period during my service in Congress that his words remotely described.

As I calmed down—not entirely, as this passage makes clear—I realized that the "New Democrats" allied to Clinton were pursuing a strategy that would not work. Their plan was to accommodate antigovernment sentiment in general while attempting to increase government in the particular. But there was a logical flaw: A whole cannot be smaller than the sum of its parts. This is true of the political world no less than the physical one.

If I'd been a graduate student, I could have set out to write a dissertation on the disconnect between people's distaste for government and their attraction to its manifestations. But there is one key difference between the profession I forsook and the one I pursued: If your job requires very large numbers of people to vote for you, triumphantly pointing out to them how confused they are is not the likeliest path to success.

The understandable but regrettable reluctance of even progovernment elected officials to confront the growing antigovernment trend in public opinion was decidedly counterproductive. It strengthened the hand of those who opposed government programs on ideological grounds by giving them a more appealing basis for their opposition. Conservatives in the 1990s and since have sometimes conceded that it would be a good thing if we could accomplish the goal of a particular piece of legislation—only to add that, unfortunately, the fact of government's inherent incompetence made this a false hope, almost certain to end up, as per Reagan, causing more problems than it alleviated.

I confronted the appeal of that strategy in 2009, when conservative public opinion expert Frank Luntz counseled Republicans on how to block our financial reform bill. In his thoughtful, comprehensive book on that bill, *Act of Congress*, Robert Kaiser quotes Luntz's formula for opposing any significant legislative changes: "Washington incompetence is the common ground on which you can build support." As Kaiser accurately summarizes it: "To defend this donothing position, Luntz wrote, Republicans could depend on voters' distrust of all government programs and officials." It is true that in this case we were able to defeat the do-nothing position, but only because America's worst economic crisis in eighty years, and the anger it stimulated against the financial sector, created a powerful demand for action.

When advocates of government action fail to make their case, the result is a frustrating negative feedback loop. The fact that major advances in public policy are so rare exacerbates the antigovernment attitudes that form the biggest barrier to such advances. The public's thwarted desire for increased government efforts in the particular reinforces the public's anger at government in general.

I dwell on this point because I firmly believe it explains why the "government stinks" attitude is so prevalent among two sectors of the population that should be influential supporters of a stronger public sector: advocates on the left, with an ideological commitment to a larger government role, and white middle- and working-class men, who have been the victims of the growing inequality in our economy over the last forty years.

The first group is numerically less significant but is important in shaping the national dialogue. Even though most of its members continue to vote in a progovernment fashion, their efforts often work against the results they seek. By angrily denouncing government's failures and inadequacies, they unintentionally but effectively reinforce the general public's hostility to government activity of any kind. Too often they fail to differentiate between a government that is hamstrung by its conservative critics and the actions of those critics themselves, which have created the problem.

For most of my career in the House, I regularly had mutually unsatisfactory meetings that followed the same general script. Representatives of groups seeking more money for medical research, or public transportation, or affordable housing, or education, or nutrition, or poverty programs, or aid to cities, or similar causes, all of which I supported, would ask me to help increase government spending on their particular priority items. My answer was almost always that I agreed with their goal but that little was likely to be accomplished unless they could help me increase the overall federal funds available for them *and* for others. Otherwise, I would note, more money for food stamps might impinge on funding for home health care; increased cancer research dollars could compete with more work combating Alzheimer's; increased resources for affordable housing might come at the expense of adequate support for the Women, Infants, and Children program.

When I asked these groups to support higher taxes (or a more reasonably sized military), I usually received one of two responses. The groups that proudly saw themselves as apolitical maintained that they could not threaten their group's solidarity by espousing such controversial causes. The more consciously ideological groups, which knew they had ideological opponents, told me that they were focused on their own—undeniably worthy—issue. They could not rally their like-minded members to push for more general increases in funding without assurances that they would get a large share of it—assurances that I was unable to give.

I had occasional successes—as when the Massachusetts Hospital Association voted to support higher taxes without the unachievable commitment that much of the new money would go into Medicare and Medicaid. More often I was met with stark disappointment, usually politely expressed, that I was complicating the conversation.

A baby in Bayonne

Bicycling with my father and my younger brother, David, 1953

At thirteen, I outed myself as Jewish with a bar mitzvah. I am flanked by my parents, Elsie and Sam, my grandmother, and my aunts and uncle.

RIGHT: Recreation at a Catskills summer camp. My brother, David, is watching. BELOW: A family meal at the legendary Brown's Hotel in the Catskills, 1957. From left, my sister Doris (standing), my father, myself, my sister Ann, my mother, and my brother, David

My mother and I, with Eleanor Roosevelt at an Israel bonds dinner, in Bayonne, 1958

The Massachusetts legislature softball team. Kneeling, fourth from left, is State Representative Andrew Card, who later became George W. Bush's chief of staff in the White House.

After deciding to run for Congress, I had just fifty-two hours to collect the two thousand signatures needed to qualify for the Democratic primary ballot. (Ted Dully / *The Boston Globe* / Getty Images)

Waiting for election returns
with my mother and my
niece Julie and nephew
Jeffrey, 1982 (Richard Sobol)

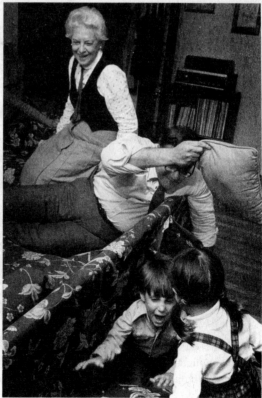

With Speaker Tip O'Neill, Senator Ted Kennedy, Congressman Ed Markey, and Nancy Korman, cochair of my finance committee, at the Sidney Hill Country Club, Newton, Massachusetts, October 3, 1980. After the archbishop of Boston, Cardinal Medeiros, warned voters not to support me, Kennedy broke his neutrality and endorsed my candidacy.

Talking immigration on the floor of the House, with Representatives Pete Rodino and Ron Mazzoli, 1987. I wrote in the margin: "Who says only Italians talk with their hands?"

With U.S. Marines
in Lebanon, 1984

Meeting with Egyptian president Hosni Mubarak, 1983

Meeting with Tip O'Neill and Congressmen Gillespie V. "Sonny" Montgomery and John Murtha, 1984

At the 1993 LGBT march on Washington, with my brother, David, and niece Madeline

After moving to Boston, my mother became a well-known advocate for the elderly.

With the unlikely trio of John Kerry, Ted Kennedy, and Mitt Romney, during a flood emergency in Taunton, Massachusetts, 2005. I was criticized for my casual attire, but I thought it was the proper clothing to wear to a flood.

Sharing a lighter moment with George W. Bush. Representative Jim McDermott stands behind Bush.

Before his state of the union speech in 2008, President Bush saw me talking on the phone and told me to say hi for him. After the speech, I told the president he had sent his regards to my boyfriend, Jim Ready. He replied, "See how broad-minded I am?" The exchange was caught by the Fox News boom mic.

Discussing health care with President Barack Obama in 2010 (Official White House Photo by Pete Souza)

With Bill Clinton at an award ceremony for my sister Ann Lewis, who served as his communications director (Jim Ready)

With Jim and President Obama

A rally at Boston City Hall, 2009 (Jim Ready)

We included a provision in the financial reform bill that Bono strongly advocated. It required American companies engaged in resource extraction to make public any money they paid to foreign officials. It was known as "publish what you pay."

President Obama signs an executive order significantly increasing same-sex spousal benefits for federal employees, 2011. I am flanked by Senator Joe Lieberman and Vice President Joe Biden. (Jim Ready)

The president autographed this photo: "To Jimmy— Showing you love for keeping Barney under control! Barack Obama."

With my successor, Joe Kennedy, and his former college roommate Jason Collins, the first NBA player to come out as gay, at a gay pride parade in 2013. Senator Elizabeth Warren is to my right. (Jim Ready)

With a doe on Fire Island. Contrary to some people's expectations, I did not yell at it, and it did not run away from me. (Jim Ready)

A well-earned trip to the beach (Jim Ready)

The pleasures of retirement (Richard Meseroll)

Jim is an avid surfer and snowboarder. (Richard Meseroll)

The leaders of the left also frustrate their own ambitions when they advance the self-fulfilling prophecy that our political process is so corrupted by the influence of wealth that the people's voice will never be heard. To be sure, this view would be easier to refute if it were less true. From the standpoint of democratic theory, money has had undue weight in our political system since the nineteenth century.

Representative government in a capitalist society involves the co-existence of two systems—an economic one, in which a person's influence necessarily increases with his or her wealth, and a political one, in which every citizen is supposed to have an equal say. If the mechanisms of the free market are going to work, that is, if they are going to increase productivity through incentives and allocate resources efficiently, money must drive decisions. For democracy to fulfill its moral promise, everyone's vote should have the same weight in making the rules by which we govern ourselves.

To the extent that money is allowed to buy political influence, the inequality principle dilutes the equality principle. Some of this is, of course, inevitable—the two systems can never be hermetically sealed from each other. And the very strong protections for freedom of expression that are fortunately embodied in our Constitution make it harder to restrict money's influence in the United States than in most other Western countries. When I was in France in the days leading up to the reelection of François Mitterrand, I was struck by the complete absence of campaigning on the day before the election—as was mandated by French law.

Especially after the Watergate scandals, our electoral rules sought to preserve some balance between the moral demands of democracy and the Constitution's prohibition of the tight controls imposed in other countries. But then came today's five-member activist right-wing Supreme Court majority, which has ruled against any significant effort to protect the equality principle from money.

I agree with those who regard the Court's campaign finance decisions as among its worst in recent years. I agree that we should do everything possible to overturn them, and until we can accomplish that, we should limit their impact to the extent possible—for example, by holding political donations to higher standards of transparency.

And I agree that the decisions' impact is wholly negative, tilting the scales of democracy heavily in favor of the wealthy.

But I strongly disagree that this impact is so great that it renders other forms of political activity useless. I deplore the extent to which many of my allies on the left preach this to people who should be hearing the opposite message—namely, that as influential as money has become, it can be countered by the effective mobilization of public opinion. I will provide some evidence for this claim when I discuss the passage of the financial reform bill (which I will not hereafter be calling Dodd-Frank, because the only person I have ever heard refer to himself in the third person without sounding both silly and pompous was Charles de Gaulle).

The claim that big money is politically invincible is especially self-defeating with regard to voter participation. It is now a truism that a critical factor in deciding whether the left or the right will do better on Election Day is turnout. Telling lower-income people and other supporters of liberal policy changes that their votes won't matter because big money has rigged the outcome is not as effective a means of voter suppression as the right wing's adoption of formal barriers to voting, but it does contribute to the same result.

The failure of the left's leaders to effectively support government activity is a persistent problem. But the even deeper quandary is why so many middle- and working-class white men, who would benefit from the enactment of liberal programs, vote so heavily for the conservatives who oppose them. The consensus answer is that their conservatism on social issues outweighs the appeal the left could make to them on economic ones. That is the thesis of Thomas Frank's *What's the Matter with Kansas?* It is embodied in the progressive lament that "God, guns, and gays" form the basis of the right wing's appeal to those we think should be voting for us; during the 2008 campaign, Barack Obama was caught on one of those ever-present digital recorders regretting the unbreakable attraction of religion and guns to many white guys.

If that analysis were true—and I acknowledge that I bought into it to a great degree at the time—then we did have a profound dilemma. We could soften our advocacy of these issues—same-sex marriage, limits on gun ownership, abortion rights—to increase our share of the white male vote. Or we could persist in our stances, while trying to persuade ourselves that we could talk our target voters out of their deeply held positions. "Gun control can be made popular if it is presented in the correct way," I was told by well-meaning people who generally avoided actual discussion with those whom they believed could be so easily converted. (Jim was exasperated by people who condescendingly explained to me how easy it would be to talk angry voters into supporting liberal stances. At a public meeting, he asked one of them why, if he knew how to get majority support for controversial progressive positions, he hadn't run for—and presumably easily won—high office.)

The good news is that the choice between dropping our support for social issues and redefining them is unnecessary. Those issues are not as salient as the "God, guns, and gays" argument implies. There are elements of truth in it—mostly regarding guns—but it is essentially the wrong explanation for the alienation of white men from the cause of activist government.

In my view, white men reject activist government not because they reject a major role for the public sector but precisely because they support one—implicitly, perhaps, but nonetheless strongly—and have been punishing government for its failure to fulfill that mission. In one very important respect, the 1992 Clinton campaign mantra, "It's the economy, stupid," was even truer than its chanters realized. Where middle- and working-class white males are concerned, the issue was not simply the importance of recovering from the recession of 1990–1991 but also the need to slow—and ultimately reverse—the steady erosion of their economic status that began in the mid-1970s and continues today.

I first began to doubt the argument that Democrats were losing the support of white males because of social issues when I attended a dinner in Washington that brought together a dozen or so House liberals with several national labor leaders. When some of my colleagues claimed that our recent losses in West Virginia and Pennsylvania were largely due to our pro-gun-control stance, and lamented the backwardness of those working-class whites who voted against their own economic interests because of it, one of the union men exploded. He angrily—almost threateningly—denounced those making that argument, insisting instead that working-class men were in fact voting to defend themselves economically—against Democrats who ignored the weakening economic position of people who worked with their hands in favor of environmental concerns, international trade, and the new economy.

My first reaction was to resent his anger, and his accusatory tone. And I still believe that he had unduly minimized the importance of gun control in the recent election results. But I have come to think that he was more right than wrong. The strongest piece of evidence against the "God, guns, and gays" explanation is that we—gays—have clearly played a negligible role in the decline of Democratic fortunes among the party's most traditional supporters. There is no evidence that any Democrat has lost his or her seat because of support for LGBT rights. Neither is there any evidence that we are being punished for being insufficiently religious. Abortion has been a factor in some Republican victories but has not been a dominant theme. The issue that has hit Democrats the hardest besides guns is the environment—and even that is primarily because of economic factors: Liberals are believed to support measures that would kill jobs. The same goes for the fraught politics of race. The chief political problem for Democrats is not anger at integration but the belief that the Democratic focus on "pleasing minorities" extends to giving them preference for scarce jobs. White working-class and middle-class men have not lost faith in government in general; they have lost faith in the willingness of Democrats to use the power of government to protect them from hurtful economic trends.

In short, a great many have high expectations of government's potential and then blame government when it does not live up to those expectations. The *Washington Post* columnist Robert Samuelson makes a similar point, albeit from a conservative perspective:

> Since World War II, American government has assumed more
> responsibilities than can reasonably be met . . . Government
> is, among other things, supposed to: control the business

cycle, combat poverty, cleanse the environment, provide health care, protect the elderly, subsidize college students, aid states and localities . . . Most are essentially postwar commitments . . . Government becomes almost "suicidal" by pervasively generating unrealistic expectations. The more people depend on it, the more they may be disappointed by it.

His answer to the confidence problem is to scale back people's expectations. My answer, as I will argue later, is to give government the resources to meet them. Politically, the burden of the disappointment with government—in fact, the sense of betrayal—falls almost exclusively on the Democrats because we are seen as the Party of Government. Democrats will regain a fighting chance to win majority support among working- and middle-class white men only when we demonstrate the will—and capacity—to respond to the economic distress inflicted on them.

In my own work, I did what I could to remind voters that government plays an indispensable role in their lives. Whenever I received public acknowledgment for a government benefit that I had helped bring to my constituents, I pointed out that the benefit was not the result of my personal largesse but rather an example of my success in seeing that tax dollars were being spent on their needs. In Ted Kennedy's posthumously published memoir, *True Compass*, he poignantly recounts the story of the last speech he gave before he was first stricken by his fatal illness. We were in New Bedford for the reopening of an important historic building that had burned down; he and I had secured the necessary funding for rebuilding it. Kennedy eloquently described the building's historic significance, situated as it was in the midst of the National Waterfront Park we had created, and noted its economic importance to the city. (As he noted, he left New Bedford for Cape Cod and was stricken the next morning.) When it was my turn, I began my speech with a phrase I used regularly— "Welcome to an earmark." I emphasized that we were able to do what we'd done for the city only because there was enough government money available.

These assertions worked well enough in my district to insulate me against attacks on my support of higher government spending. But too few of my colleagues advanced the same line of argument for it to resonate more broadly.

At the time, I could at least take some encouragement from the popular backlash against Newt Gingrich's shutdown of the federal government in November and December 1995. The shutdown was a logical extension of Gingrich's heretofore successful campaign not just to oppose the Democrats but also to delegitimize us—and the government with which we were identified. From our standpoint, the failure of Gingrich's shutdown had two very positive aspects. First, it broke the right's political momentum and invigorated Democrats who had become pessimistic about Clinton's reelection chances. Second, Gingrich suffered politically because it turned out that there was far more public support for government than he had believed. Many of my Republican colleagues confidently predicted that the shutdown would benefit them because people would not miss the nasty old government—in fact, they would cheer its repudiation. The opposite occurred: People reacted angrily to the denial of services they liked or needed. Representing a district with a lot of Portuguese Americans who had close ties with friends and relatives in the Azores, I heard several complaints about the unavailability of passport and visa services. This was the sort of government people took for granted—until it wasn't there. And that realization was important. The absence of government services led many to see that it wasn't just the specific program they wanted back—it was government as a whole that they missed, and they did not want it to disappear from their lives.

•

As the 1996 race took shape, I was determined to support Bill Clinton's reelection, despite my differences with many of his economic policies. The return of LGBT rights to the national stage dramatized what was at stake. Republicans were setting out to protect America from the terrifying threat of two people being inappropriately in love—that is, from same-sex marriage.

In the past, the party's right-wing fringe had driven its anti-gay activity. But this time, that activity came from the center. With the collapse of Gingrich's government shutdown, and the improving economy, Clinton's fortunes were improving and his opponent Bob Dole needed help.

It came out of the blue—almost literally, given the skies and ocean location—from Hawaii. In 1993, a narrow and tenuous majority of the Hawaii Supreme Court ordered the state's lower courts to examine whether the Hawaii Constitution dictated that same-sex marriage should be allowed, strongly suggesting that the answer should be yes. The vote was 3 to 1. This majority included only two of the five permanent supreme court justices because of temporary appointments, and so there was no clear supreme court majority even for this tentative decision. Early in 1996, a state trial court judge, after an evidentiary hearing, ruled in favor of same-sex marriage.

In the ordinary course of politics, no immediate congressional action would have followed this event. It was far from certain that Hawaii would make same-sex marriage legal—and in fact it didn't do so for eighteen years. But Dole saw a boost for his campaign. Forcing Clinton to choose between signing or vetoing a bill against same-sex marriage was a delicious prospect.

I set out to oppose Dole's efforts to send that bill to the White House. My preferred argument was that the Hawaii court decision was a remote matter: It would have little nationwide impact and did not merit a rapid congressional response. I didn't think we could win the debate, but at least this approach would maximize the number of dissenting votes. Unfortunately, our chances for success dropped from slim to none because of a serious strategic misjudgment by my LGBT allies: They hailed the tentative Hawaii decision as the harbinger of a nationwide right to marry for all LGBT people.

Their argument was legally wrong and politically disastrous. As the lawyers among them should have known, it was based on a wholly incorrect reading of the constitutional clause that says states must give "full faith and credit" to the laws of other states. Technical matters aside, the controlling fact was this: Throughout our history, states have been allowed to set their own rules for who can marry whom without having to defer to the rules of other states. By incorrectly

arguing that all states would have to honor Hawaiian marriages—
and that lesbian and gay people could therefore go to Hawaii, get
married, and return to Mississippi or Nebraska and live happily ever
after—the LGBT leadership validated the Republicans' claim that
this was an issue of immediate nationwide impact. This had more
than legal implications. The claim that same-sex marriage was an imminent reality in every state greatly raised the political stakes on the
issue. This made Dole's ambition to use us to his advantage much
easier.

For several reasons, I became the congressional leader in the
fight. My two openly gay colleagues—Gerry Studds and Steve
Gunderson—had both announced their retirements. More important, the so-called Defense of Marriage Act was in the jurisdiction of
my Subcommittee on the Constitution. There was, to reverse the old
saying, much less to the actual legislation than met the eye. The bill
claimed to establish the principle that no state was compelled by the
Constitution to recognize same-sex marriages performed in other
states. But no state could be required to recognize such marriages
anyway. Recognizing this, and eager to accomplish something concrete, House Republicans added a second section, denying federal
benefits to couples in same-sex marriages. If they couldn't stop us
from getting married, they could at least satisfy their political needs
by penalizing us if we did.

The Republicans provided our best line of attack when they
named their bill "the Defense of Marriage Act." In the military ban
debate, we were told we had to be excluded not because of our inherent shortcomings but because others didn't like us. In an application
of the old "let 'em down gently" breakup line, we were told, "It's not
you, it's them." By 1996, the leaders of the antimarriage effort were
even more explicit in their assurances that they meant no disrespect
to LGBT people. They said they believed we should be treated
fairly, and that their goal was not to penalize us but to protect "traditional" marriage.

In some cases their tone was apologetic. In 1995, the Republican
Sonny Bono had just been elected to the House. Our friendship began at one of those press-sponsored dinners where the media take

revenge on members of Congress by getting us to do short stand-up routines, usually to the member's embarrassment and the media's delight. Obviously, that did not happen to Sonny. He was funny and his routine was also very gratifying to me. He presented his early impressions of Congress by describing the modus operandi of two members, his very conservative fellow California Republican Bob Dornan and me. He skewered Dornan and then flatteringly described my parliamentary and rhetorical skills, noting that as a performer himself, he recognized a first-rate act when he saw one.

Our friendship included trading critiques of each other's performances. Unlike many other members, especially Republicans, he and his wife were perfectly at ease socializing with Herb and me. One night, we all went to dinner with John Waters, the famously outrageous movie director. He had given Sonny a part in his movie *Hairspray* when Sonny's career was limping after his breakup with Cher. In return, he later asked Sonny for an introduction to me. I was immensely flattered.

As the Defense of Marriage debate proceeded, our friendship resulted in one dramatic exchange. As the Judiciary Committee was taking its formal vote on the bill, Sonny ignored the custom of speaking only to the chair and dropped the aw, shucks pose he usually hid behind to disarm debate foes. Instead, he addressed me directly. "Barney," he pleaded in an anguished tone, "I just can't do it. You're my friend and I respect you, but I just can't tell Chesare [his young son] that it's okay for you to get married." Implicit in this eloquent plea for my forgiveness was the admission that I had a right to ask, and that there was no good reason to tell me no. It was just that instincts long bred into him stood in the way.

The culmination of my effort came when the bill reached the House floor. "How does my marrying another man damage any of your marriages?" I asked—loudly and emotionally—and offered to yield the floor to anyone who could answer the question. After an awkward— for them—pause, Republican Steve Largent, a former professional football player form Oklahoma, stood up and said that while I would not be hurting any particular couple's marriage, I would be hurting "the institution of marriage." In other words, he was repudiating one of the deeply held norms of his former career—he had to admit there was no harm, but he and his allies were still determined to call a foul. I cited his invocation of the "institution of marriage" and jibed that this argument could have been made only by someone who was himself *in* an institution. The response to my response was encouraging.

Of course, we lost the vote badly, but I believe our approach laid the groundwork for future victories. We forced the other side to claim that opposition to same-sex marriage was based on the real, negative social consequences it would have and not just on religious, moral, or philosophical disapproval of homosexuality. As a result, we would be in a very strong rhetorical position when those consequences failed to materialize. We also laid the groundwork of future success by keeping the issue of states' rights front and center. When I offered an unsuccessful amendment allowing federal benefits to flow to same-sex couples in states where their marriages were legal, twenty-nine Democrats who felt compelled to vote for the Defense of Marriage Act as a whole voted with me to strike the act's no-federal-benefits clause.

My role in the marriage debate enhanced my status as one of the national leaders of our movement. That fall, I drew on that status as best I could: I campaigned for many Democrats who were generally supportive of LGBT rights but who had been afraid to vote against DOMA. One of those Democrats was Minnesota Senator Paul Wellstone—and any reader surprised by this has plenty of company. He was one of the most principled liberals ever to serve in the Senate, and his defeat would have been a great loss for the causes I supported. With my own reelection in no doubt whatsoever, I traveled to Minneapolis at his request for an LGBT Halloween rally. Predictably, some Republicans sought to use my appearance against Wellstone, sneering that he'd had to send for help from a double outsider—I came from outside the state and outside what they defined as the political mainstream. I had an easy rebuttal. Wellstone's opponent, the former senator Rudy Boschwitz, employed Arthur Finkelstein, a political consultant who never let his own gayness interfere with his work on behalf of America's leading homophobes—like Jesse Helms. Since Finkelstein and I were both Jewish and shared a state of residence as well as a sexual orientation, I noted that according to the rules of the campaign, each candidate was allowed to send to Massachusetts for one gay Jew to help him. Since Wellstone was a much better candidate than Boschwitz, he needed me for only one day, while Finkelstein's involvement lasted months.

In defending Wellstone to LGBT voters, I was also defending Clinton. After all, I noted, if Wellstone felt that he had to vote for DOMA to survive in the progressive state of Minnesota, how could we blame Clinton for giving in to similar pressures in the larger and more conservative constituency of the whole country? It was disheartening that Clinton signed DOMA. But the choice that year involved a very clear application of the Henny Youngman principle: Compared to Dole, Clinton was a true LGBT champion.

My advocacy for Clinton did hit one bump in the road. In the fall, a disgusted caller informed me that the president's campaign had placed an ad on some Southern radio stations touting his signature on DOMA. At the time, my sister Ann was serving as the Clinton White House's communications director, a position that grew out of her close relationship with Hillary. While we had always been mutually supportive, we had refrained from pressuring each other. When I'd proposed a compromise on a bill to ban late-term abortions, she'd relayed the concerns of the pro-choice movement as an informational matter but made no effort to lobby me. But this ad called for an exception. I was infuriated by the damage it could do to my efforts to maximize the LGBT vote for Clinton. I'd been arguing that Clinton had signed the bill reluctantly and hadn't wanted to see it passed. Boasting that he had done what I had assured people he didn't want to do could not have been more harmful. I called Ann immediately, and the ad disappeared.

•

My own enthusiasm for Clinton's reelection was based on more than the comparison to Dole. Even though I had been troubled by the president's decision to compromise with the Republicans on budget matters, and I was unhappy with his role in passing a welfare reform bill that unduly restricted benefits for our poorest citizens, there was one significant legislative battle in 1996 where he had provided strong, effective leadership on a key issue of economic fairness: increasing the minimum wage. He organized a public campaign to win this fight, despite Republican control of both houses of Congress and the very vehement opposition of House majority leader Dick Armey.

The notion that presidents can use their bully pulpits to force a recalcitrant congressional majority to pass legislation is much more easily propounded by pundits than accomplished in reality. But it did work in this case—perhaps because the recent reductions in welfare benefits allowed Clinton to argue that rewarding hard work was a logical concomitant to penalizing sloth.

Even in the minimum wage debate, there were signs that the administration's progressive commitments were not as strong as they could have been. I was able to play an important role in raising the administration's tentatively proposed 75¢ increase to a slightly less inadequate 90¢. The best description of what happened is in former labor secretary Robert Reich's memoir, *Locked in the Cabinet*. I have never been happier to read a snarky description of my work in the House.

The crucial events occurred at a House Democratic caucus in February 1995. In the sneering tone of superiority with which he often discusses others, Reich sets the stage by describing the caucus as a zoo, and in an example of the fashionable cynicism that undermines support for an active government role, he implicitly dismisses the idea that any of us were seriously motivated by a commitment to good policy. "They're all entrepreneurs," he writes, "angling for credit with their constituents, favors for big donors, attention from the national media" (presumably in contrast to his own aversion to publicity).

He then describes how I took the lead in forcing him to commit the president to the higher number.

"Mr. Secretary!" yells Barney Frank of Massachusetts. Barney's political views lie to the left of the rest of the Massachusetts delegation, which puts him in the Twilight Zone.
    "Yes?"
    "You said that if Congress wants to go *higher* than seventy-five cents an hour the President will consider it. How high will he go?"

A trick question. I remember Leon [Panetta]'s admonition, so I hedge. "It depends on you guys coming to a consensus about what you want."

"I think I hear what you mean, Mr. Secretary." Barney normally speaks in a nasal yell. Today his volume is even higher than usual. *"You're saying that if we could get a con-sen-sus on a hike of a dollar an hour, the President would sign on?"*

The room is suddenly quieter.

"It's really up to all of *you*. We look forward to working with you on it."

"So your answer is *yes*! We agree among ourselves to raise the minimum wage by a *dollar* an hour, and the President *would support it*!"

"Yes, but only if—"

"That's *wonderful* news! *You made my day, Mr. Secretary.*"

The room erupts in cheers mixed with howls of protest.

I take considerable pride in Reich's account, both because the result was an important gain for poor people, and because it provides a good example of how I put my debating skills to use.

Reich never does say which of the selfish motives he ascribes to us drove my actions. I can declare that no big donors rewarded me for making them pay some of their workers more. As to getting constituent credit or national media attention, if I had sought either of these, I would surely have mentioned my exchange with him publicly. I did not.

There is one last point I cannot forbear mentioning. When the former secretary of labor in the Clinton administration complains that the Democrats' policies have been insufficiently liberal, I am reminded of the statement Oscar Levant made about Doris Day: "I knew her before she was a virgin." On the other hand, while Reich's description of my voice was unkind, I cannot claim it is inaccurate—I long ago realized that it would be unwise for me to try to make anonymous phone calls.

●

When the 1996 election essentially preserved the status quo—a second term for Clinton and a continued House Republican majority, though a smaller one—I entered a period of self-reflection. I had decided earlier that I would retire when I was seventy-five. I had seen too many representatives enjoy great congressional careers and then stay too long. Once figures of respect, they became objects of pity, and in some cases derision. I was approaching the midpoint of my career. What could I hope to accomplish?

Following the Republican victories of 1994, I had spent two years reacting to their initiatives. But in 1996, I believed—correctly—that they had been sufficiently chastened by their political and legislative difficulties to scale back the scope of their plans. As a result, I would be more able to decide where to focus my energies. Of course, this was a trade-off I would prefer to have avoided. I was gaining more freedom to choose the issues I would concentrate on, yet I was not gaining more ability to act on them.

My strategic-planning process began with an assessment of the state of public opinion on economic inequality, LGBT legal equality, and myself. I acknowledge that one of these things is not like the others. But a clear understanding of my personal appeal, both in the district I represented and in the broader political context, was a prerequisite for deciding what steps I could take to advance my substantive goals.

I prided myself on being much less easily intimidated electorally than most of my colleagues, but I enjoyed the job too much to be suicidal. My attitude toward electoral risk at the time was an adaptation of the old saying, "I may be courageous, but I'm not stupid." Since I expected to spend less time legislating and more time trying to influence the national debate, it was important to be clearheaded about the mix of credibility and liability I brought to such public work. The more I enjoyed of the former, and the less I suffered from the latter, the greater my influence would be on my colleagues and on the important sectors of public opinion I wanted to sway.

The conclusions I came to are easily summarized. LGBT issues and I were doing better than I had expected. But support for the battle against economic inequality was lagging badly.

•

Fortunately, my district remained a source of confidence for me, even though its borders had shifted yet again a few years before. In 1992, following the 1990 census, Massachusetts Senate president William Bulger asked if I would agree to add half the town of Easton to my new district. This was for the convenience of my colleague Joe Moakley, who was disturbed that a resident of that town intended to run against him. Joe did not fear losing, but he believed that after thirty years of public service, he was entitled to enjoy a summer on Cape Cod without the annoyance of an opponent.

Those following this narrative closely will note the contrast between Bulger's solicitude in 1992 and his vindictive effort to redistrict me back into private life in 1982. In other jurisdictions, the fact that ten years had passed might have been a sufficient explanation for this new cooperative attitude. But not in Massachusetts. I had learned early in my career that many of the state's politicians took pride in their definition of Irish Alzheimer's—"the disease in which you forget everything but your grudges." (Indeed, I would see the idea illustrated vividly at Joe Moakley's wake in 2001. One of my colleagues brought a retired congressman to the event. A younger former member came up to them and expressed his pleasure at meeting the older member again after many years. The latter responded effusively, "It's great to see you too, pal. How've you been?" When the younger man walked away, the older man asked his friend, "Who was that guy?" When he was told, he exploded, "That's who that was? I hate that son of a bitch!")

As it turned out, I didn't need the passage of time to heal my relationship with Bulger. I had my mother. After her star turn in my 1982 TV commercial, she had become the most influential advocate for elderly needs in the state. She also lived in Bulger's Senate district, and they bonded. My mother got the best possible ally for the legislation she supported. Bulger got enthusiastic praise from a woman who was well-known statewide and among the more prominent residents of the most liberal part of his Senate district, which was where he was weakest. Their marriage of convenience bloomed into a strong friendship—they were both highly intelligent, committed to improving the lives of the elderly and, not incidentally, great believers in the importance of family ties. In other words, my mommy made the bullies stop picking on me. (My siblings and I honored their relationship in 2005 when we asked Bulger to speak at her memorial service.)

When Bulger asked me to accommodate Moakley's request, I responded too flippantly. I said that as long as Newton, Brookline, and Fall River remained in my district, they could add Utah and I would be okay. When my words became public, I had wisecracker's remorse. As it turned out, my newly drawn district was not what I'd hoped for: It would contain only half of my beloved Fall River, and none of the adjacent towns that I had assumed would be part of the package. Instead I would now be running in New Bedford and its adjacent towns—meaning I would be seeking the vote of hundreds of thousands of people I had never previously represented, some of whom probably knew me primarily because of the unhappy events of 1989–1990. But the new district, it turned out, was as good for me as the previous one—so no harm was done by my mouthing off.

After I'd defeated Heckler in 1982, I'd had the good fortune to draw ineffective opponents. In 1986, for example, I faced only an Independent. An adherent of the fringe conspiracy theorist and perennial presidential candidate Lyndon LaRouche, he claimed, among other things, that Queen Elizabeth was a drug dealer. My only comment of note in that race was that I didn't think she was, because she didn't dress nearly well enough. In 1992, however, with my scandal still a recent memory, and a district that was 50 percent unfamiliar, I did draw a serious Republican challenger—a responsible, articulate lawyer who was a town selectman. Despite his endorsement by the *New Bedford Standard-Times*—which oddly explained that they were certain that Clinton would be elected and I would join the cabinet—the voters in the New Bedford area were as supportive as their Fall River neighbors had been, and I won by a comfortable margin. For reasons I do not understand, but for which I am grateful, no Republican filed for the seat in 1994. Perhaps regretting that they had not taken advantage of their landslide that year, the Republicans backed another very plausible candidate in 1996. But by this time, I had become solidly entrenched in the New Bedford area and again won by a large margin. This was to be the last time I had an opponent of any substance until 2010.

The absence of serious opposition meant, to my great pleasure, that I didn't need to engage in serious fund-raising. For most of my career, I was able to raise much of what I needed simply by sending letters to a well-established contributor list that I had built up. I did hold some fund-raisers in Washington, and I received support from several PACs. These PACs generally represented labor groups, gay rights organizations, or institutions interested in the construction of low-income housing, so I never felt guilty or at all corrupted by my association with any of them.

I tried to make fund-raising as enjoyable as possible by writing solicitation letters that I hoped were funny, and that I knew were at least whimsical. Knowing how many people were tired of semi-hysterical demands for immediate financial assistance lest disaster ensue, I once sent out a letter that said: "Dear Friend. Please send me money." It turned out to perform about as well as more elaborate requests.

•

Among my new district's distinguishing characteristics was that it had more residents of Portuguese heritage than any other legislative district in the world. (Of course, parliamentary districts in Portugal had a higher percentage of Portuguese people, but because those districts were very small, I represented a greater number.) These voters mainly hailed from the Azores, a chain of Atlantic islands one thousand miles from Portugal. When I first arrived in Fall River in 1982, I knew of the territory only from a line in a famous poem about Columbus—"behind him lay the gray Azores." Given the choice of traveling one thousand miles east to their home country, or two thousand miles west to America, hundreds of thousands over the years chose us. Like most immigrants, they were entrepreneurially minded, leaving home to better their economic position.

Portuguese Americans did not have a large number of politicians dedicated to their concerns. And they had a number of issues. With my Rhode Island colleague, Patrick Kennedy, I successfully won Portugal's inclusion in a visa waiver program for European nations. Reflecting the unusual ethnic composition of my district, and my general focus on domestic affairs, my visits to Israel and the Azores would outnumber all of my trips to other countries combined.

I worked especially hard to serve my new constituents in New Bedford. Like Fall River, it was a blue-collar fishing and manufacturing center that had a large Portuguese American population and had seen better days. To my considerable gratification, I began a twenty-year alliance with the fishing community. I fought to change the government's arbitrary, unreliable, and unfair enforcement of the rules against catching immature scallops—known inelegantly as "the meat count." More important, I pressured Secretary of Commerce William Daley to allow an increase in the scallop quota—an increase that was clearly justified by the science but angrily fought by the Conservation Law Foundation. This was not my first difference with the CLF, an organization I found to be rigid and openly contemptuous of any citizens who dared disagree with them. After Daley agreed to our recommendation, New Bedford became the country's leading scallop source and, contrary to the CLF's claims, scallops remained abundant in the ocean. I consider myself a committed supporter of protecting the environment. But my experience in southeastern Massachusetts left me severely disappointed with environmentalists who scorn anyone who would take other concerns into consideration.

I also worked with Ted Kennedy to establish the national park on the New Bedford waterfront that honors the history of the whaling industry. I was especially proud to see this park bestowed on a very Democratic area—and two outspoken liberal Democrats—by the Republican-controlled Congress at a time when there was strong resistance to the creation of new national parks due to budgetary constraints. It was an important legislative achievement, and an example of how Senator Kennedy and I were able to wage vigorous partisan battles on major ideological issues while preserving our ability to work with Republicans on less controversial matters. Kennedy drew on his friendship with Alaska Republican Ted Stevens to make a deal in the Senate, packaging the New Bedford park with some recognition for Alaska's whaling history. In the House, I worked closely with Massachusetts Republican Peter Blute, who had upset the Democratic incumbent Joe Early in 1992. Blute represented the town of Dartmouth, which was next to New Bedford, and many of his constituents were leaders in the drive for the park. Blute lost his seat in 1996, and no Massachusetts Republican has won a House election since.

Two buildings in the park are described by Herman Melville in the opening pages of *Moby-Dick*. There may be other ones as well. Now that I have retired, I can confess that I found the bulk of the book unreadable, although I did participate in public readings of it every year at the New Bedford Whaling Museum in the heart of the park. Fortunately, my part always came in the first half hour of the twenty-five-hour marathon.

My greatest hope for New Bedford and Fall River was to establish a rail connection between the two working-class cities and Boston. No matter how successfully we promoted employment in the southeastern part of the state, the greater Boston area would still be the place with more opportunity. This was made especially clear to me in 2005 when a group of Boston hotel owners told me that they were suffering from a shortage of workers. It was one of the rare times when I had what I thought was a perfect solution. I noted that there was a great pool of labor in the Fall River and New Bedford areas—people with a great work ethic, many of whom would be glad to take the jobs if they had an efficient, stable way to reach them. "Help us build a commuter rail from there to Boston," I said, "and it will be highly mutually beneficial."

The project was officially supported by the Massachusetts state government. But there were two obstacles. As always, one was money, and so I had another reason to press for increasing government revenue. To my shock, a determined group of environmentalists put up a strong fight against the rail line, and even though they were ultimately overruled by the relevant officials—after inflicting significant delays—the threat of their lawsuit still hangs over us. Their objection was that the rails would pass through a swamp, and they rejected any means of mitigation.

This dispute left me convinced that some amendment to environmental laws regarding wetlands and endangered species is necessary. It is important to note that the main victims of the environmental veto over much important economic activity are white working-class men, further embittering them toward liberals and increasing their frustration with government.

•

Since social liberalism was strongest on the East and West Coasts, I was often asked to campaign for other candidates within ten miles of an ocean. As I got invitations to Iowa, Colorado, Indiana, Michigan, western Pennsylvania, Ohio, and elsewhere in the interior, I became confident of two political facts: My colleagues believed they'd benefit if their LGBT constituents saw me with them, and they did not worry that the association would hurt them with other voters.

By the mid-1990s, our progress was not confined to poll numbers. Our legal position was better too. Starting with Wisconsin in 1982 and Massachusetts in 1989, states began including us in their antidiscrimination laws. Moreover, the Defense of Marriage Act did not prove to be a potent wedge. To my knowledge, no Democrat was defeated because of his or her opposition to the bill. The GOP would not initiate another anti-LGBT legislative effort until 2004.

Not for the first time, my political reading of the status of our struggle was more optimistic than that of many in our community. And once again I believe that subsequent events have validated my view. This was not merely a theoretical debate. It was directly relevant to deciding where we should put most of our energies. If I was correct, then we ought to step up our participation in the political process—we should register to vote, let our representatives know what we wanted them to do, and then, following the classic and still valid political maxim, reward our friends and punish our enemies with votes, contributions, and organizing.

The logic of the opposite opinion—that the "system" was stacked against us and in the control of those determined to keep us unequal— called for direct action instead of electioneering. "You want to play nice with the system," I was told scornfully. "We know that power never grants rights without struggle, without our making the establishment so uncomfortable that they have to give in."

Such a preference for demonstrative over electoral politics was often reinforced by a badly flawed reading of the careers of Mahatma Gandhi and Martin Luther King. They did rely on marches, sit-ins, and other forms of physical protest to put moral pressure on their opponents, who claimed to believe in the democratic principles Gandhi and King were invoking against them. And they sought to disturb the status quo so that it would be less socially disruptive for officials to accommodate them than to continue to repress them. But neither of these great leaders chose this route in preference to using the votes of their millions of followers to gain their ends. They engaged in direct action precisely because this was the only method available to them—Indians in the British Empire had no right to vote on their situation, and African Americans in the American South had that right in theory but hardly in practice. Once they gained full access to the ballot box, they sensibly made that their main focus.

When LGBT leaders cited Gandhi and King, I offered my own counterexample—the National Rifle Association's great success in dominating the policy debates about gun control, despite being in a minority on the issue in every national poll I have ever seen. As I enjoyed pointing out, especially to those LGBT activists who decried my lack of "militancy," I have never seen an NRA public demonstration. They do not have marches. There have been no NRA mock shoot-ins to rival the die-ins staged by AIDS activists. And those liberals who try to comfort themselves with the notion that the NRA wins legislative battles because of their vast campaign contributions are engaged in self-deceptive self-justification. The NRA wins at the ballot box, not in the streets and not by checkbook.

The NRA does what I have long begged my LGBT allies to do, at first with mixed results, and more recently with much greater success. They urge all of their adherents to get on the voting rolls. They are diligent to the point of obsession in making sure that elected officials hear from everyone in their constituencies who opposes any limits on guns, especially when a relevant measure is being considered, and they then do an extraordinary job of informing their supporters of how those officials cast their votes.

It was necessary for us to make our presence known publicly

when our fight started in the early 1970s, because our anonymity
was an obstacle to gaining support. It is impossible to generate sympathy for people who are largely invisible. To return to the comparison to race, African Americans never had to worry that white people
didn't know they were there or that discrimination existed. While
racism has done far more damage than homophobia, LGBT teenagers faced a problem that heterosexual African Americans did not:
breaking the truth to their parents. No teenager ever had to endure
the emotionally fraught task of informing her parents that she was
black. Once the public became aware of our existence, however, the
situation changed. The case for putting demonstrative politics first
became defunct.

•

Even as they refrained from assaulting LGBT rights, the Republicans did try to gain political capital out of racial resentment. In early
1996, they sought to repeal the federal mandate supporting affirmative action. As the senior Democrat on the Constitution Subcommittee, I was happy to take the lead in blocking the effort—with the
Clinton administration's full support.

At first, I was pessimistic. The Republicans needed only a majority vote to succeed. But they had one vulnerability. The man who
had turned the military ban debate against us now offered my side its
best chance—Colin Powell.

Powell was one of the most popular men in America, and he had
flatly stated that he would never have become a general were it not
for affirmative action. No quota bestowed his rank on him, Powell
made clear. Rather, he was able to win promotion on his merits only
because affirmative action had given him the chance. The military
officials who selected candidates for promotion to higher office were
required to cast a wide net for candidates. This was exactly how we
believed the process should work.

I wanted Powell to testify before the subcommittee. To our great
frustration, he refused—not in so many words, but by claiming one
scheduling conflict after another. Even so, he did issue a strong
statement reiterating his claim that he would never have achieved

high office if affirmative action were banned—as the Republican bill before the subcommittee planned to do. Committee and subcommittee proceedings are usually predictable, and occasionally all but scripted. But in this instance there was some real drama. One of our GOP members, Michael Patrick Flanagan, was an accidental congressman. To everyone's surprise, he'd defeated one of the most powerful representatives in history, Ways and Means chair Dan Rostenkowski, after Rostenkowski had been weakened by corruption allegations.

Henry Hyde, the chair of the Judiciary Committee, was eager to promote his fellow Irish Catholic Chicagoland Republican's career by putting him on the committee. In light of this relationship, Flanagan cast one of the most courageous, morally driven votes I have ever seen in the House. After assimilating Powell's description of how affirmative action affected him, and listening carefully to a thoughtful debate on the subject, Flanagan broke with the other Republicans—including a startled Hyde—and voted with all of the Democrats, creating a tie in subcommittee. At that point I was convinced that we could block the effort, because other Republicans would also refuse to disregard Powell's strong statement. To avoid further parliamentary moves that might revive the bill in subcommittee, I consented to pass it along to the full committee with no recommendation. The fact that the bill did not pass in the subcommittee, combined with the powerful example of Colin Powell, amounted to a death notice. Hyde took no further action that year and instead allowed the bill's most ardent defenders to try again the next year, when it was tabled on a bipartisan vote. In that situation, tabling the bill meant killing it.

Defending affirmative action gave me the chance to reaffirm my deep commitment to the second of the three questions famously articulated by Rabbi Hillel. My work for LGBT equality represented my answer to his first question: "If I am not for myself, who will be for me?" Combating racial prejudice and its lasting effects was my fervent response to his second question: "If I am only for myself, what am I?"

But even justly revered sages do not get everything right. Hillel's third question—"If not now, when?"—can be misleading. The proper reply is "It depends." That is, it depends on how likely you are to succeed; on whether it will be more helpful to your cause to try and fail, or to hold off for more propitious circumstances; on the impact of settling temporarily for partial success; and on what you can do to improve your chances of ultimate success. The hard truth is that correctly answering these subordinate questions will sometimes mean that "now" is not the right time at all. From the founders of the NAACP to A. Philip Randolph and Bayard Rustin and Thurgood Marshall, African American leaders consistently resisted the temptation to try to do it all at once.

•

I was delighted to cooperate with the Clinton administration on protecting affirmative action. In other realms, however, our relationship was suffering. Any hope that Clinton's assault on "big government" was mostly a reelection impulse faded quickly as he began negotiations with the Republicans over the budget, with the announced goal of deficit reduction. Since Republicans were no more supportive of raising taxes now than they'd been when they unanimously opposed the increases of 1993, I assumed this meant that cutbacks in already inadequately funded programs were on the table. My assumption turned out to be wrong—it was overly optimistic. Clinton proceeded to agree to a fiscal package that, as *The New York Times* reported, contained "some of the largest tax breaks in decades," including inequality-expanding reductions in the capital gains and inheritance taxes. To keep the bill weighted toward budget balance, these were offset by a large drop in Medicare funding—$115 billion over the life of the bill. In truth, subsequent events would mitigate the effects of those cuts, making them more of a nuisance than a serious problem. The bill required an annual calculation of what was called the "sustainable growth rate" for Medicare providers, with the fees they received being cut back each year accordingly. In a strong demonstration that my colleagues' appetite for cuts is far greater in the anticipation than in the reality, those reductions have never been implemented. In every year since 1997, my colleagues have either passed a bill to reduce the cuts severely, or to forgo them altogether.

While the budget negotiations were still going on, I drafted a letter to Clinton imploring him not to abandon his party's principles, and solicited signatures from my fellow liberals. As it became clear that we were having no impact on the process, we held a press conference to complain. When a reporter asked what response we had received to our letter, I answered that we had not gotten any because we had sent it to "The Democratic President of the United States" and the post office classified it as "addressee unknown."

When the package was completed, I charged that paying for inheritance tax cuts by reducing Medicare spending effectively elevated the claims of rich dead old people over those of sick, living middle-class ones. Other Democrats, most notably House minority leader Dick Gephardt, also opposed the bill. But as I knew would be the case, we had no effect on the outcome. The bill passed by large majorities in both houses. Even so, I was not merely venting. I hoped that by criticizing Clinton in the most wounding and attention-getting way I could, I would maximize my influence over his future moves. Ballplayers do not argue with the umpire so that he'll change the decision in question. They want to be on his mind when he makes the next one.

When the Asian financial crisis hit in 1997, I found myself at odds with the administration again. With Indonesia, South Korea, and other allies on the brink of collapse, the administration had to ask Congress to approve a renewed American commitment of funds for the IMF. As a result, House minority whip Dave Bonior—a longtime IMF critic—and I were in a good position to advance our goals.

First, we wanted the IMF to stop working as the enforcer of what had become known as "the Washington consensus." This was the prevailing doctrine that developing countries should follow rigidly orthodox fiscal policies. The Clinton administration Treasury Department typically advised crisis-prone countries to reduce government spending, raise taxes—usually in a regressive manner—and protect capital investment from any obstacles, such as regulations.

In addition to taking on "the Washington consensus," we also wanted Indonesia to curb its human rights abuses. Very specifically, we demanded that the Indonesians end their violent repression of their labor movement and release their most prominent union advocate, Muchtar Pakpahan, from prison. Along with my two colleagues who also represented large numbers of Portuguese Americans, Patrick Kennedy of Rhode Island and Dennis Cardoza of California (himself of Portuguese ethnicity), I further insisted that our government do everything we could to end Indonesia's oppressive and increasingly brutal rule over the people of East Timor.

East Timor had been a Portuguese colony for three centuries, and in 1975 when Portugal finally relinquished control, the Indonesians took over by force. To my pleasant surprise, the Portuguese Americans in southeastern Massachusetts regularly included this issue among the concerns they wanted me to pursue. Adding support for East Timorese independence to my conditions for supporting the IMF bill allowed me to achieve every legislator's dream—taking a moral stand that was also a deeply appreciated constituent service.

Even though the administration disagreed with our concerns, its need for a bill ultimately outweighed its objections. Meanwhile, the Indonesians found that their need for IMF funds outweighed their insistence on continuing to rule East Timor. The ultimate result was that pressure from the American government, and from many others, persuaded the Indonesians to grant full independence—and we gave the bill funding the IMF the support it needed to pass.

That legislation also included a binding requirement that our representative to the IMF board support the establishment of "core labor standards." The Clinton administration was not happy with our meddling. But we never contemplated intruding in other countries' affairs to the extent that "the Washington consensus" did.

By mid-1998 I was concerned that my relations with the Clinton administration might become less cordial than I wished. I did not want to weaken the president politically, especially with Vice President Gore likely to be running on his record in the 2000 election. After twelve years of dealing with Republican administrations, I also found it politically helpful and personally pleasant to have friends in the executive branch. I had never felt penalized by the administration for my differences. But I did not want to cross a line that I knew had to exist somewhere.

Fortunately, any concerns about a falling-out came to an abrupt end in the second half of 1998. This was when it became clear that Newt Gingrich and his accomplices Dick Armey and Tom DeLay seriously intended to impeach the president.

8

DEFENDING CLINTON

Ever since 1993, I'd been defending both Clintons from Republican attacks on their integrity. Serving on the Financial Services Committee, I observed the investigation into the Clintons' Whitewater investments firsthand. At first, the Democratic majority easily defused the assault. When Clinton's aide George Stephanopoulos testified before our committee in 1994, I noted how nervous he seemed. As Stephanopoulos recalls in his memoir, I sent him a note from the rostrum saying, "Relax George. We're kicking the shit out of them." And we were.

Consequently, when the Republicans took over the House the next year, they were determined to turn the tables. They convened two full weeks of hearings, to be followed by a report that they were certain would expose the Clintons' bad behavior.

They fell embarrassingly short. Their first obstacle was that there was nothing there. Their second was the Republican chair of the Financial Services Committee. If Diogenes had come to Washington searching for his honest man, I would have sent him Jim Leach.

No one who tries to be effective in Congress can be entirely free of partisan considerations, not even those few who assert their independence. As a liberal Republican in the House—a category that is no longer an endangered species but an extinct one—Leach may have welcomed the opportunity to demonstrate his party loyalty by reopening the investigation. And he did appear to be genuinely put off by what he saw as the first couple's unseemly willingness to use political influence in the pursuit of private gain—a feeling not mitigated by the fact that they had done so ineptly and had actually lost money on the deal. But as the hearing proceeded, and it became clear that there was much less to the accusations than met the eye, his integrity overpowered his partisan instincts. The two-week hearing ended after one week. More significantly, the committee never issued a report on the matter. This reflected common political sense: If you don't have anything bad to say about your opponents, shut up.

The Republicans were not ready to give up, but to the Clintons' good fortune, the next congressional investigator was one of the House's least credible members, Dan Burton of Indiana, who chaired the Committee on Government Reform. I had experienced his penchant for silliness before. When I'd announced that I was gay, he'd announced that he would no longer use the House gym, lest I'd infected the place with AIDS. He got over it after a while.

This was not the only time my sanitary habits came up in a discussion with an Indiana Republican. During the gays in the military debate, Senator Dan Coats, who had volunteered to lead his party's effort to maintain the ban, said in one of our joint TV appearances that it was entirely legitimate for straight members of the armed forces to object to being nude in our presence. Borrowing a line from Alfred Hitchcock, I told Coats that I regularly worked out in the House gym and had not been having myself dry-cleaned. As far as I could tell, none of my straight colleagues had been traumatized by sharing the shower room with me.

Burton found Whitewater too tame—and unpromising—a subject for his inquisition, and so he tried to make political capital out of the terrible tragedy of the suicide of the White House aide Vince Foster. To make the case that Foster could not have killed himself given the disposition of his body, Burton shot a watermelon in his backyard. The "murder" of Vince Foster, allegedly at the behest of the Clintons, became a popular theme on the Clinton-hating right-wing fringe. Less bizarrely, but with equal futility, Burton and his allies sought to prove that the Clintons had rummaged through FBI files for partisan gains and had unfairly fired employees of the White House Travel Office, possibly to cover up abuse. Independent counsel

Kenneth Starr continued his investigations, but absent convincing evidence, the anti-Clinton case seemed to be withering away—until reports of a former White House intern named Monica Lewinsky appeared in January 1998.

When I first heard of Lewinsky's supposed affair with the president, my concern that it might be true was tempered by my assumptions that it could be neither proved nor disproved and that it would be politically irrelevant. The accusation was more plausible than the others against Clinton, given his personal history (which I reference nonjudgmentally, given my own record). But it was also far less serious, alleging neither criminal activity nor abuse of government power. For a Bill Clinton running for reelection, it would have been a problem. For a president who would never again be a candidate, it was a family issue, not an official or a political one.

When asked to comment on *l'affaire* Lewinsky, I minimized it on precisely these grounds. Then we heard about Lewinsky's blue dress, and I realized that this business could get very serious. The vehemence of Clinton's apparently categorical denial of "sexual relations" had clearly raised the stakes. In delivering a public statement from the White House, he elevated a possible sexual indiscretion—obviously not the first by a sitting president (or one in any other position)—into a head of state's possible breach of trust with his country.

That summer, impeachment transformed from the far-fetched wish of the far-fetched right into a real possibility. Democrats began to talk about it among ourselves—involuntarily, in my case. I received a call from a close friend who was also close to Al Gore, soliciting my position and predicting that Clinton would be forced to vacate his office.

I had no difficulty deciding where I stood. Ousting Clinton would be a grave error on several counts. It would vindicate the right-wing's tactics; it would endorse the notion that divergence from conventional sexual mores was, in electoral terms, a capital offense; and most seriously, it would undermine not just the Democratic Party but also the core principle of democracy.

The Republican Party's right-wing ideologues refused to accept Clinton's legitimacy as president. They believed he had been elected in 1992 only because Ross Perot had split the antigovernment vote, and their crusade to overturn the election results began almost immediately. When Whitewater proved inadequate, their leadership shifted toward shutting down the government, and when that didn't work, they tried to exploit same-sex marriage and abortion. When Clinton was reelected and the Democrats gained congressional seats, the Republicans temporarily shelved the delegitimization campaign, a decision made easier by the president's postelection willingness to work with them to diminish "big government." But the right-wing dream of ousting a man they considered a pretender to the throne had not disappeared.

Taken together, the work of Starr, DeLay, and the network of Clinton haters called Pirandello to mind: They were a lot of characters in search of an impeachment.

I soon became a leader in the fight against what Hillary Clinton accurately described as a "vast right-wing conspiracy." Once again I benefited from the process of elimination. Impeachments are referred to the Committee on the Judiciary, where I was the second ranking Democrat behind John Conyers—the only committee member who had sat on the panel during the Nixon impeachment. My relative seniority was not the only reason for my prominence in defending Clinton. There were very few other applicants for the position.

Today, it's hard to believe that something as trivial as the Clinton-Lewinsky affair could have driven a popular president from office. But in the late summer of 1998, that result seemed highly likely. Most Democratic members of Congress, especially those facing an election in November, were convinced that vocally supporting Clinton was politically risky—until he admitted to the grand jury that Lewinsky had been telling the truth. Then they decided it was toxic.

As the summer progressed, the ranks of Clinton supporters dwindled, a phenomenon he and I discussed in the several phone conversations we had on the subject at his initiation. (I can report that even at fifty-eight, after twenty-six years in elected office, being paged in a public place and told to call the White House operator to be connected to the president was a very big deal, even if it was to discuss that unpleasant subject.) I hadn't fully realized how little company I had until August 17, the day Clinton admitted his relationship with Monica Lewinsky to the grand jury and taped a short statement apologizing for it, though not as profusely as he should have from a political standpoint.

When the White House declined to elaborate on Clinton's recording and refused to supply an administration spokesperson to appear on the air, the networks followed protocol and asked for a list of surrogates. I do not know how many names were on the administration's list of favored supporters. I do know that I was apparently the only one who agreed to the part. My basis for this is that even though the networks usually try to avoid duplicating each other, I promptly received requests to appear live that night from NBC, CBS, CNN, and ABC, plus two local Boston stations.

I was happy to reaffirm my defense of Clinton, but accommodating the TV requests did pose a logistical problem. Herb Moses and I had ended our relationship earlier that summer—an event chronicled to my discomfort in a front-page *Boston Globe* story ominously headlined "Frank Breakup Ends an Era in Gay Politics." (Fortunately, the implication that our breakup would discourage other gay men from romantic attachments was unfounded.) Newly single, I had gone to Provincetown for the congressional recess, and on the night of Clinton's testimony, I was looking forward to a dinner at the home of some friends. In any other circumstance I would have had to choose between going to a TV studio and attending the dinner. But in this case, I realized I had considerable logistical leverage. For once, they would have to come to me. Harry Harkins, my host for the dinner party, turned his house into a temporary studio.

The TV interviews went mostly as I had anticipated. I argued that Clinton's behavior was irresponsible, and his dishonesty regrettable, but that none of this justified undoing the results of a presidential election. Dan Rather did surprise me with one question. He asked if I agreed with White House spokesperson Ann Lewis that the interaction in question could not be described as "sexual relations." Not wanting to give my own opinion on the subject, and knowing that Rather would not have time for a follow-up, I did what I usually warn people against in tense situations—I got cute. "If you think you're going to get me into a debate with my big sister about sex on national TV," I told him, "you're mistaken."

Making the case against impeachment to a large national audience exhilarated me. When asked if I had entered risky political territory, I responded that I did not think defending oral sex in Provincetown was particularly controversial. After I returned from the Cape, I received more praise than criticism in my district. In some quarters, I was a hero. When I had lunch with Charlie Halpern, my college roommate, in Manhattan, he said he now knew what it was like to hang out with a rock star.

If Manhattan accurately reflected the national mood, I might have been president myself, rather than trying to save Clinton. When I got back to Washington after Labor Day, I came down from my ego trip. I'd seen myself as Horatius at the bridge, defending democracy against the hordes. Then I remembered how Horatius ended up.

On September 9, 1998, Kenneth Starr sent Congress a damning 445-page report, formally stating, "There is substantial and credible information supporting the following eleven possible grounds for impeachment." The question before the House now was whether the report should be released immediately or withheld until the administration had a chance to respond.

This was a critical vote. Substantively, releasing the report would give the pro-impeachment forces a big head start in framing the national debate. Politically, the vote would show the relative strength of the two sides, which was in turn a good indicator of how the members read public opinion on the subject.

From my standpoint, the results could not have been worse. The motion to release the report without delay passed by an overwhelming margin, 363 to 63. Ominously for Clinton, Democrats opposed his position by a vote of 138 to 63. Nearly half of Clinton's supporters on this vote were African American. Seven of Massachusetts's ten representatives voted with him, as did six of the San Francisco Bay Area's ten. He won majority support nowhere else. Even Jewish members, the most liberal white group, were against him, albeit by a relatively narrow margin of 12 to 8.

It was clear that my colleagues saw very strong public support for impeachment. I do not contend that electoral considerations were the only reason for the large Democratic vote. Some of the members in both parties were genuinely offended by Clinton's behavior. (Clearly not all—among those voting to release the report were several who were later embroiled in their own sex-related difficulties: Mark Sanford of South Carolina, Gary Condit of California, Mark Foley of Florida, and most notably Speaker Gingrich, who was then, during his second marriage, carrying on an affair with his soon-to-be third wife.) But this was a high-profile issue, and the political element was unavoidable. Insisting that elected officials ignore deep public feelings on such a subject may have theoretical justification but has no predictive value. Of all the rules I have drawn from my experience in elected office, one is unchallengeable: If you want an issue to be decided on wholly nonpolitical grounds, you should not ask 435 politicians to decide it.

After the vote, I spent a good deal of time thinking about my predicament. What would it mean to be a leading figure on the Judiciary Committee trying to derail a highly popular impeachment? Politicians hoping to benefit from innocence by association often cite well-known and well-liked role models. In my career, I also have tried to keep negative role models in mind—people who screwed up badly dealing with tough problems, especially when they did so in part because of personality traits I share. Charles Sandman was a Republican from a solidly Republican New Jersey district who undertook an aggressive, even belligerent, defense of Richard Nixon as a Judiciary Committee member in 1974. He debated Nixon's prosecutors vigorously, often sarcastically. He did not simply try to refute the charges against Nixon. He belittled the charges and derided those who pressed them.

As the case against Nixon grew stronger, Sandman's position became weaker. Indeed, he barely outlasted the departing president in public office. After winning his seat by a 30 percent margin of victory in 1972, he lost it by 16 percent two years later. In certain ways, my debating style was uncomfortably close to Sandman's. And while I had never seen him in person, my recollection was that we had roughly similar body types, making for a combination of temperament and appearance that could seem overbearing on television. Backing away from my anti-impeachment role was unthinkable, morally and politically. But I did begin to think about how to approach it more carefully. I would show verbal restraint and take pains not to denigrate those who found Clinton's behavior deeply offensive. That last point was of special relevance. Others could argue that mutually consenting sexual activity was no big deal. For me to make this case would be to invite a politically effective response—"It takes one to defend one." Standing out as one of the country's most aggressive advocates of ignoring marital infidelity could result in a very big hit to my credibility.

It was in that apprehensive state of mind that I awaited the broadcast of Clinton's grand jury confession on September 21. I was at home in D.C. because it was Rosh Hashanah. I had long since stopped observing the High Holy Days at temple, but I abstained from doing anything in public lest anyone use my example to criticize other Jews who missed work because of their observance.

I do not remember a time when I was either intellectually persuaded or emotionally gripped by religious feelings. By my sophomore year in college, I'd stopped attending services when I realized they were more of a cultural than a spiritual practice for me. I did continue to feel very Jewish, reflecting the fact that being Jewish in America—and undoubtedly in other places as well—is a mix of religious, ethnic, cultural, and social elements. But even when I no longer professed religious views, I was determined never to do or say anything that would in any way suggest that I was trying to separate myself from other Jews. To the contrary, I often made reference to my Jewishness in various ways. Given the history of persecution, and the anti-Semitic influences that persisted in America, I believed and still do that giving any other impression would be contemptible.

For that reason, I never felt an inclination to publicly profess agnosticism. The issue of religion arose for me only in public policy debates. I consistently took the position that people's rights to their own religious beliefs and practices should be respected, but that they should not be in any way allowed to impose those practices on people who believe differently, or who do not, in the theological sense, believe at all.

Of course, being Jewish was inevitably an element in my career. When I ran for Congress, the Jewish voters in Newton, Brookline, and later in Sharon and elsewhere made up a significant part of my strongest bases of support. (I was struck, however, by a poll taken back at the start of my career in national politics, in 1980. It noted that while my standing among Jewish voters was high, my standing was higher still among those who either declined to answer the religious question, or said they had no religion at all.) As the state's first Jewish member of Congress in nearly one hundred years, and this in a state that had up until then elected only one Jewish statewide official—a Republican, George Fingold—I felt an obligation to other Jews to show some solidarity. Flagrantly not attending High Holy Day services would have detracted from that.

Still, as time went on, I believed I had done enough to demonstrate my Jewish solidarity. I concluded that participating in ceremonies that had no meaning for me was no longer necessary. Without making any announcement of the fact, I simply stopped going. In fact, over the past twenty years, my attendance at religious services has taken two forms: weddings and bar mitzvahs for other Jews, and funeral masses for people in the district I represented. (I made a particular point of trying to attend every funeral service I possibly could for anyone who was killed in war.) I did remember my bar mitzvah teachings, and at the various bar and bat mitzvahs of my nieces, nephews, and great-nephews, I very competently said the appropriate prayers. My Hebrew pronunciation is not perfect, but on the other hand it is probably as good as my English.

Subsequently, after leaving office, I half jokingly objected when Bill Maher, one of my favorite TV hosts, asked if I felt uncomfortable sitting next to a pot-smoking atheist on the set of his show. I replied that there were two of us on that stage who fit those categories. The media reached the conclusion that I had come out as an atheist. In fact, I am not an atheist. I don't know enough to have any firm view on the subject, and it has never seemed important to me. I have had a life-long aversion to wrestling with questions that I know I can never answer. My tolerance for intellectual uncertainty is very low.

As a member of the House, when I was administered the oath of office, I consistently said that I "affirmed" rather than "swore," and never added the words "so help me God." But because we were inducted en masse, no one ever noticed. In 2013, when I sought an appointment to the U.S. Senate, I decided that if I were selected, I would break with custom: I would not take the oath by placing my hand on a Bible. Instead, I would warn Vice President Biden that I intended to join the Senate by having my husband, Jim, hold a copy of the Constitution, on which I would place my hand as I affirmed that I would do my duty. As it turned out, the idea was moot.

•

To return to Clinton's impeachment, as the footage of the president's grand jury testimony rolled on Rosh Hashanah, I was sporadically monitoring it rather than taking in every word. I am too impatient and easily agitated to watch or listen to anything that will affect me politically or officially. Meanwhile, I checked in regularly with my offices in D.C. and Massachusetts. To my surprise and relief, they did not receive a deluge of calls opposing my stand. The volume of calls was limited, and a large percentage of the callers opposed throwing out the president based on his admission.

Public reaction in the following days was similarly reassuring. After watching the prosecutors grill Clinton for four hours, viewers learned just how weak the special counsel's case was. They understood that Starr had presented Congress not with eleven separate instances of wrongdoing but with eleven variations on the theme of oral sex.

On October 8, the House took up the subject again. This time the issue was more sharply drawn: The motion directed "the Committee on the Judiciary to investigate whether sufficient grounds exist for . . . impeachment," and the result reflected a very different reading of public opinion. Republicans remained unanimously in favor, but more than 100 Democrats who had voted for the earlier resolution voted against this one, joined by 5 Democrats who had missed the first vote. A broad bipartisan coalition had been replaced by a partisan split, both in the country and in the House. In fact, as the debate played out, and it became clear that prevailing public opinion opposed ending Clinton's presidency, the politics of the situation flipped. Virtually all Democrats felt free to vote against impeachment, while for some Republicans it became a wedge issue that we could use against them: They were forced to choose between party pressure to vote yes and an electorate that wanted them to vote no.

Unwisely for them, and fortunately for us, the Republicans ignored this development in public opinion. Chairman Hyde moved forward with his plan for the proceedings, with no input from Democrats as to how to structure them. This was the first clear sign that this impeachment would not resemble Nixon's. In 1974, Democratic chairman Peter Rodino worked closely with the ranking committee Republican, J. Edward Hutchinson, to adopt rules and schedules. In the Senate, Democrat Sam Ervin and Republican Howard Baker had done the same.

Hyde compounded his mistake by insisting, contrary to the facts, that he was emulating Rodino's bipartisan approach. I received wide attention for my comment that if the committee's actions were bipartisan, then the Taliban was a model of religious tolerance.

By the time the committee formally took up the matter, the midterm elections had taken place. Gingrich and DeLay had been counting on impeachment to produce Republican gains. Instead, House Republicans suffered an unusual loss of five seats—the opposition party almost always makes gains in the sixth year of a presidency. Among the casualties was Michael Pappas of New Jersey. His Democratic challenger, Rush Holt, had aired a commercial featuring Pappas's paean to the prosecutor on the House floor, "Twinkle, twinkle, Kenneth Starr."

In this unpromising environment for Republicans, the hearings started on November 19, and things only got worse for them. One weekend I turned on *Saturday Night Live* to see our committee conducting a hearing on oral sex, with a scantily clad Richard Simmons imitator as a main witness. In the sketch, the actor playing my colleague Maxine Waters complained that the Republicans were demonstrating their sexism by focusing only on male recipients of oral ministrations to the exclusion of females. I admired the wit but not the visuals, although I did enjoy being able to tell Waters that while I was disappointed that the guy playing me was so fat, at least he was better looking than the guy who portrayed her.

Personally, I was at a career high point. In the late summer, I'd done the right thing in an unfavorable political situation. And now, my good deed was rewarded. The Republicans had frightened much of the public with their obsessive crusade, and I was often thanked for standing against them. Indeed, I became so confident of their defeat that I misread the situation. I assumed the Republicans would accept the face-saving solution we offered: a vote to censure Clinton, not oust him.

Our offer was not motivated by any sympathy for their plight—we deemed the Republicans fully responsible for their own woes and we knew that forcing them to drop the impeachment effort would reverberate to our benefit. At the same time, most of us believed that the process was doing serious civic damage and had to end.

The Republicans surprised us by rejecting our offer. To the dismay of many, including Henry Hyde, the party leadership was determined to press ahead. We had underestimated the importance of hating the Clintons to the Republican right. DeLay and other House leaders knew that if they seemed to be letting their archenemy off the hook, they would sow confusion in their own ranks. Driving Clinton out of office was the best they could do; second best would be to go down fighting, blaming weak-kneed moderates and a biased media for the president's survival.

Our counterattack combined principled indignation and ridicule. Starr had accused the president of committing perjury when he gave the wrong date for the beginning of his intimacies with Lewinsky. This gave me the chance to comment from my seat on the dais that Starr was exemplifying Marx's insight that "history repeats itself; the first time as tragedy, the second time as farce." During Watergate, Senate Republican leader Howard Baker had famously asked, "What did the president know, and when did he know it?" Now, I noted, Starr's central question amounted to, "What did the president touch, and when did he touch it?"

If Charles Sandman had been alive in 1998, he would have had every right to be jealous of me. He scoffed, ridiculed, and belittled his way into losing his seat. My similar behavior served me well.

•

Before the committee voted on the impeachment counts against the president, both Democrats and Republicans internally debated whether to call witnesses. After much discussion, both sides agreed that there would be only one witness in that phase: Kenneth Starr. As Jeffrey Toobin noted in his insightful book *A Vast Conspiracy*, Democrats hoped to force the Republicans to rally publicly behind "a physical embodiment of the most unpopular man in American politics." But Starr proved to be skillful in his testimony.

At the risk of off-putting immodesty, I will quote Toobin's account of what happened next.

As usual, though, Barney Frank was operating a few steps ahead of everyone else. Listening to Starr's opening presentation, Frank noticed that, in passing, the prosecutor had conceded that he had found no evidence of impeachable offenses in the Travelgate and Filegate areas within his jurisdiction. This admission dashed the Republicans' central hope in summoning Starr—that he had some new bombshell to drop. But Frank, characteristically, was thinking of a further implication of this disclosure by Starr. Frank noted that Starr had said he sent the information about impeachable offenses to Congress "as soon as it became clear." But when, the congressman asked, had he decided that there was no information incriminating to the president in Travelgate?

"Some months ago," Starr conceded.

"Let me just say, here is what disturbs me greatly," Frank replied. Starr had filed his report about Lewinsky before the election, but his office had actually been studying the Filegate and Travelgate affairs for much longer than they had been scrutinizing Lewinsky, "yet now, several weeks after the election, is the first time you are saying that.

"Why did you withhold that before the election when

you were sending us a referral with a lot of negative stuff about the President and only now . . . you give us this exoneration of the president several weeks after the election?"

Starr mumbled a meager answer that began, "Well, again, there is a process question"—but it was more than a process question. Starr and his team had worked to exhaustion to get their Lewinsky allegations in front of Congress and the public at the most politically perilous moment for Clinton's party. But they felt no rush to reveal their exoneration of the Clintons on Filegate and Travelgate. Again, there was nothing illegal about Starr's priorities, but they did reveal a great deal about the "process" that was under way in his suite on Pennsylvania Avenue.

Asking Dick Cheney to defend the security clearance ban was my first great success in trapping a witness. This was my second. I take continuing pride in the fact that both Bill and Hillary Clinton cite the exchange in their memoirs as a highlight of the proceedings.

As Hyde had feared, an impeachment based solely on the Lewinsky matter was doomed to fail and cause further difficulty for the Republicans in the House. After the case left our committee and went to the floor of the House, I did not play a major role in that process. My relations with Minority Leader Gephardt had cooled—I'm still not sure why—and I was not included in top-level Democratic strategy sessions. I didn't mind. The preceding months had been a time of very intense activity on a matter of high national importance, and I was emotionally spent. And unlike the committee proceedings, where we had a chance to shape public opinion, the House debate was tedious. It was conducted under a procedure in which every member received five minutes to talk on a prearranged schedule, with no provision for any interaction. Four hundred or so entirely predictable set pieces later, we voted.

In the end, Starr's eleven charges against Clinton were reduced to four by the Judiciary Committee, and only two of those charges won a majority on the floor of the House. One of them passed only because the vote was held in a lame-duck Congress—the critical margin of support came from members who'd been defeated in November by Democrats who would have voted no. I thought of this years later when Republicans charged that the repeal of Don't Ask, Don't Tell by the lame-duck Congress in 2010 was a repudiation of democracy.

As the drama in the House came to an end, I seemed to be the only person who noticed my relative silence. I recalled the day in 1974 that the veteran Massachusetts politician Frank Bellotti had seen me grimacing over a newspaper. "Stop worrying so much," he told me when I complained about a negative reference, "you are paying a hell of a lot more attention to you than anybody else is." Indeed, I had no basis at all to quibble about the reaction I was getting to my impeachment work. In 1999, when Clinton addressed a Democratic fund-raising dinner and performed the ritual of mentioning politicians in the audience, he was interrupted by an enthusiastic response to my name. He proceeded to say that there was no one he would rather have on his side in an all-out fight. *Boston* magazine followed this with a cartoon depicting me as a knight in shining armor, wielding my lance to save the damsel in distress (Clinton, not Lewinsky).

As pleasing as this was in purely personal terms, there was a broader significance—homophobia had diminished to the point where an openly gay man could be one of the most effective defenders of a president accused of heterosexual misdeeds. Apparently, even anti-LGBT politicians were able to put aside their feelings in their evaluation of my work. The late senator Robert Byrd had many good qualities, but freedom from prejudice against us was not one of them. He was one of the small minority of Senate Democrats who voted against the Employment Non-Discrimination Act in 1996. He was also held in high esteem as Congress's staunchest upholder of procedural regularity. I was therefore very happy when one of the best journalists ever to cover Congress, David Rogers, told me about Byrd's reaction to one of my passionate anti-impeachment speeches— I'd cited my continuing shame over being reprimanded to argue that censuring Clinton would have a real impact. According to Rogers, Byrd had said that I had done an excellent job, although he hastened to add that he did not approve—whether of me in general or of my "lifestyle" wasn't entirely clear.

On some days, I could even make light of my sexuality in defending the president. At one point, when an exasperated Hyde was trying to sort out competing demands for recognition during a heated debate, he announced that he would soon swing to me. I began my remarks by saying, "Mr. Chairman, I appreciate your swinging my way," provoking loud tension-breaking laugher, and a mock-indignant cry of "regular order" from him. (That is the parliamentary phrase invoked when norms are transgressed.)

•

The next developments in my life were more strictly personal. Late in 1998, I had begun a new relationship with Sergio Pombo, a Colombian citizen working for an arm of the World Bank. When I told him we would be attending the White House Christmas ball, he was at first taken aback and later impressed with the Clintons' warm reception. Less happily, in July 1999, after experiencing chest pains, I went to the Capitol physician, who administered a few tests and insisted that I go immediately to Bethesda's Naval Hospital for what became a successful quintuple bypass. I have had no heart problems since then.

Five days after my bypass, I returned to work. The timing was good. Hyde had agreed to hold a committee hearing on a long-time LGBT goal: adding sexual orientation and gender identity to the hate crimes law. With several recent gory, hate-filled murders prominent in the news, most graphically the homophobic murder of Matthew Shepard in Laramie, Wyoming, the issue seemed urgent. My work helped me avoid the depression that men in very late middle age can succumb to after an operation for a life-threatening condition.

The hearing was especially good for my mental health because we so clearly won the debate. The Republicans' main witness against us testified that he opposed our effort on free speech grounds: He believed no government penalties should ever attach because of the accused's opinions, no matter how obnoxious. In response, I asked if his objection to penalizing expression in any form applied to banning flag burning every bit as much as to our proposed hate crimes amendment. He was obviously surprised, not having thought of this point, and his honest, if reluctant, answer was that both impinged on free expression. Since the Republican committee members were prominent advocates of banning flag burning, this comment made it harder for them to portray their position as a defense of free speech, unrelated to any anti-LGBT sentiment.

The legislative fate of the hate crimes bill provides an interesting example of how what I like to call legislative razzle-dazzle can allow congressional leaders to eat their cake and have it too. Republican members who sought to appeal to moderate voters felt the need—and, to be fair, in most cases, the desire—to support us. But the Republican leadership would have faced considerable grief from the right if they'd allowed our bill to actually become law. So they devised a clever stratagem that reveals something about how Congress really works, or doesn't.

In the Senate, Democrats had added our hate crimes provision—very nongermanely—to the annual authorization of Defense Department activities, and it had passed. In the House, Republican leaders blocked a vote on a freestanding hate crimes bill, then objected to the measure's inclusion in a defense bill to which it was not related. Our only parliamentary option was a motion to "instruct" the House-Senate conferees to adopt the Senate's hate crimes provision. But under congressional rules, "instructions" are suggestions—they are not binding. So despite the fact that we carried that motion by a vote of 232 to 192, with 90 percent of Democrats and 19 percent of Republicans supporting us, the Republican leadership of the conference dropped the provision.

The result was a leadership dream: Republican members who wanted a chance to vote yes were satisfied, and so were the much larger number who wanted the bill killed. We were finally able to get the measure passed in 2009, when we had a Democratic president, House, and Senate for the first time since 1994.

•

In 2000, Al Gore and George W. Bush waged their fateful campaign. The battle took on both political and personal significance for me. Its outcome would have a decisive impact on my public policy goals. It also allowed me to complete atoning for one of the bigger mistakes of my career—opposing Michael Dukakis's reelection in 1978 because I thought him insufficiently liberal.

Ralph Nader's presence on the ballot alarmed me. He had the potential to win enough left-wing votes to throw the election to Bush. My first move was to send a memo to the top levels of the Gore campaign, proposing that they set up a group to ward off the threat. I suggested that Ron Dellums, Pat Schroeder, and I—an African American, a woman, and a gay man—become core members. The campaign's first reaction was not to have one. My memo was ignored—possibly because in the intensely turf-conscious political world, it was seen as my bid to gain personal influence, and probably because they did not realize at first how much of a threat Nader represented.

My fervor in this effort was stoked by more than my fears of a Bush victory. Throughout my career, I'd been troubled by my allies' tendency to choose emotional gratification over tangible, albeit insufficient, progress. The fact that Nader appeared eager to help the right regain the presidency because he found the Democrats imperfect perfectly illustrated what was wrong with this approach.

I had worked with Nader on several issues during my time in Congress, and I admired much of what he had done. But I also regretted the extreme negativism with which he approached almost any political situation. I believed that like many self-styled tough negotiators, he'd adopted the flawed understanding of game theory I described earlier. This was the view that you should never let the other side think you're satisfied; you should always be asking for more; and you best maximize your gains in fact by minimizing them in characterization, until and unless you are 100 percent successful.

Those who behave this way run two risks. When you tell your supporters that nothing has gotten better, and that any concessions you've received are mere tokenism, you take away their incentive to stay mobilized. As for those you're negotiating with, if you denigrate anything they concede as worthless, they will soon realize they can obtain the same response by giving nothing at all.

In the 2000 campaign, I made my case against Nader's candidacy as strongly as I could. I believe I got under his skin. When I cited his claim that there were no differences between Gore and Bush on the issues, he responded with indignation: What he had actually said, he angrily noted, was that "there were no significant differences."

On LGBT rights, of course, Bush and Gore had diametrically opposed views. Since not even Nader could deny that these differences were significant, I further argued, he must consider the issues themselves to be trivial. Nader not only confirmed this, but also doubled down, sneeringly explaining that he'd ignored abortion and LGBT rights because he did not choose to get involved in what he'd called "gonadal politics." With those words, he added the insult of ridicule to the injury of urging voters to disregard our concerns.

The Gore people did become worried about the Nader effect by the late summer. I was given a speaking slot at the Democratic convention and used it to make my anti-Nader point. But while our effort did help drive Nader's support down, it wasn't enough. After the election, I was surprised to hear Nader complain that he was being unfairly blamed for Bush's victory. This was puzzling, since he had previously argued that it would make no difference who won. A more intellectually honest response would have been: "Yeah, I did it. So what?"

Of course, assigning Nader his share of blame does not absolve everyone else who was responsible for the least democratically valid presidential election since the Hayes-Tilden race of 1876. These include the designers of the Florida ballot, whose work gave us the unlikeliest political alliance in our history: thousands of Jews opting for Pat Buchanan on the confusing butterfly ballot; the Republican mob that intimidated election workers into ending a recount; statewide Florida election officials; and a Republican Supreme Court issuing a partisan opinion tailored to apply to only one election.

While I worked hard to counter Nader's appeal from the left, I was also concerned about one appeal from the right—the wholly baseless assertion of the gay GOPers who called themselves Log Cabin Republicans that they could make a substantial contribution to our cause by persuading more LGBT people to vote Republican.

The Log Cabineers' pitch was based on two equally invalid grounds. First, they pointed out that Clinton had signed DADT and DOMA. In making this argument, they were trying to ignore the elephants in the room—specifically the hundreds of Republicans in both the House and Senate who took the lead on both of these anti-LGBT laws, holding the Family and Medical Leave bill hostage to make Clinton agree to the first, and manufacturing an issue just before the 1996 election to get him to sign the second. By then, there was no issue in Americans politics where the party divide in Congress was greater.

The Log Cabin Republicans' second argument was an appeal to the ideal of bipartisanship. Wouldn't it be better, they reasonably asked, if there were strong supporters of LGBT equality in both parties? Some of them went on to accuse me of not wanting to see such support.

My answer, which they persistently pretended I hadn't given, was that I would very much welcome it and I was pleased that they were working to provide it, but that I objected strenuously to their penchant for make-believe. In asking LGBT voters to support Republicans who were antiequality in the hope that someday they might change their views, they were succumbing to fantasy. I added that in any election where the Republican was better than the Democrat on our issue, those most concerned with LGBT advancement should vote for the Republican. At the congressional level, in all my service, I found exactly one such case—in Fairfield County, Connecticut, after Stu McKinney died in 1987, and I urged people to vote for the pro-LGBT Republican who succeeded him, Chris Shays.

Year after year, the Log Cabineers continued to support a party that was hostile to us. In 1996, they remained loyal to Dole—the man most responsible for DADT and DOMA—even after his campaign showed its disrespect by refusing their contributions. As their efforts yielded no gains, I became increasingly angry at their attempts to persuade LGBT voters to support our enemies. Of course, I understand why they were so indignant when I explained their choice of name by saying that their role model was Uncle Tom.

•

The election of George W. Bush was a disaster for a vigorous public sector, but it was not as harmful as it might have been for LGBT rights. The trend lines of these two concerns were beginning to cross on the graph of public approval.

With control of the presidency, the House, and the Senate for the first time since 1954, the Republicans realized the cherished goal of the antigovernment purists: They starved the beast to a subsistence level. Their formula was elegantly simple and brutally effective. They killed two liberal birds with one package, enacting tax cuts that significantly reduced government revenues while also making the tax code substantially less progressive than it had been after the 1993 increases. Incredibly, when the administration responded to the 9/11 attacks by launching two wars, the tax cuts continued. Never before had our country coupled sudden, massive increases in military expenditures with a very large reduction in our ability to pay for them. What made this all the more galling was its accidental provenance. Gore and Nader received three million more votes than Bush and Pat Buchanan combined, meaning that a healthy majority of the electorate had voted for candidates committed to increasing the government's economic role.

Bush himself offered a tantalizing glimpse of what a Gore presidency could have accomplished when he pushed a prescription drug benefit for Medicare recipients through Congress. Democrats opposed it because it deferred to pharmaceutical industry demands and therefore made pills for seniors cost more than they otherwise would have. Most egregiously, it banned the import of drugs from Canada and prohibited the government from using its purchasing power to bargain for lower prices. The argument against imports from Canada was the insincere claim that they might endanger old people's health—it was advanced by those who more often accused drug safety regulators of overreaching. I will drop my charge of insincerity the first time I read about defective drugs producing a lot of dead Canadians.

Throughout this debate, Republicans stressed the importance of harnessing the profit motive even though their bill truly rested on a progovernment basis. If a Gore administration had passed such a program, it would have stressed that the public sector was meeting an important societal need—which would in turn have helped strengthen belief in government.

The basis for my wishful—wistful?—thinking is an indisputable economic fact. When Clinton left office, the nation's fiscal outlook was so favorable that Alan Greenspan warned that the national debt should not be fully paid off, since some level of debt was necessary to the conduct of monetary policy. If Gore had taken office, he would have been able to enact a tax cut, smaller than Bush's but still popular, while expanding government programs in several areas.

I do not write this only to remind myself of the phrase I'd always attributed to the great sportswriter Grantland Rice—but that my research assistant tells me stems from John Greenleaf Whittier: "For all sad words of tongue or pen, the saddest are these: 'It might have been.'" I also seek to buttress one of my central arguments: The anti-government feelings that followed the pattern-setting events of 2001–2003 reflected not a conscious decision by the majority of voters to repudiate the notion of collective action but rather the successful Republican effort to widen the gap between the demands made on government and its capacity to respond to them.

•

Substantively speaking, I might as well not have been a member for Bush's first two years. As the administration prepared to invade Iraq, I agreed that Saddam Hussein was a terrible ruler. But I also argued that there were a number of other very bad rulers in the world, some worse than Saddam in my judgment, and that it was neither possible nor desirable for the United States to go to war to overthrow all of them. I was wholly skeptical of the administration's claim that Iraq had weapons of mass destruction, and equally skeptical of the claim that it might have been involved in 9/11. The notion of an alliance between the murderous religious fanatic Osama bin Laden and the equally murderous secular tyrant Saddam Hussein had no basis. I did support action against terrorists when we knew where they were—as in Afghanistan.

I also believed that the War on Terror required significant efforts to build up internal security, although some of those efforts would end up going much further than necessary. As a member of the Judiciary Committee, I helped to write an early version of the Patriot Act.

This was one of the best nonpartisan collaborations on a major bill of my career. The effort was led by Judiciary Committee chair Jim Sensenbrenner, a mainstream conservative Republican with a stronger respect for civil liberties than is usually found in that faction. Despite a temperament that could make me look like Little Mary Sunshine, he worked well with our very liberal ranking Democrat, John Conyers, and others. We fashioned a draft that balanced the competing claims of national security and individual rights so well that it was unanimously supported by our ideologically divided committee. But the Bush administration was in no mood for balance. At the urging of John Ashcroft's Justice Department, the Republican House leadership rejected our bill and used the House Rules Committee to substitute a harsher, unbalanced one. (To take one example of the differences: Our approach put much better controls on the government's ability to engage in unrestricted and secretive surveillance of Americans.) There was little we could do except protest.

With many of my Democratic colleagues reluctant to oppose deep tax cuts, and even more of them eager to support the administration's response to terrorism, whatever it was, I had little sway. On the dominant issues, I was more isolated than at any other time in my tenure.

•

In 2003, the Massachusetts Supreme Judicial Court delivered a historic decision: It ruled that same-sex couples had a right to marry. Chief Justice Margaret Marshall's eloquent opinion in *Goodridge v. Department of Public Health* was based on the state constitution and could be reversed only by the actions of two successive elected legislatures, and then a referendum. I responded very positively. As Marc Solomon points out in his book *Winning Marriage*, I was one of the few elected officials to defend not just the court's right to make the decision but also the substantive decision itself and the value of same-sex marriage.

As we expected, the state legislature did not greet the court's decision with equanimity. By a vote of 105 to 92, it took the first step toward authorizing a referendum to overturn it. This meant that the legislature to be elected in 2004 would decide whether or not our right to marry would be on the 2006 ballot.

As a candidate for the next available Republican presidential nomination, Mitt Romney, Massachusetts governor at the time, saw a chance to turn a potential liability into an asset. Instead of being the governor on whose watch same-sex marriage was established, he could act to repel the menace by campaigning aggressively for Republican legislative candidates. He could stop men from marrying men and women marrying women and boost Republican strength in Democratic Massachusetts at the same time. (Though he had never expressed support for same-sex marriages, he had said in 1994 that he would support LGBT rights more strongly than his opponent at the time, Ted Kennedy—as perfectly inaccurate a description of Romney's subsequent career as the boundaries of the English language permit.)

As the 2004 campaign heated up, I turned my schedule over to a disciplined and effective organization, MassEquality, and became a featured attraction at events for besieged Democrats in various parts of the state. I was now spending the bulk of my time campaigning for legislators who'd been targeted for defeat because they had supported my right to marry. This earned me the respect not just of the liberals in the party but also of Democrats across the board. I was not only the gay defender of gay rights. I was one of the frontline Democrats in an all-out partisan war.

In the end, we won almost all the fights Romney picked. As it became clear there was no popular demand to overturn the court's decision, the antimarriage forces were left with only thirty-nine legislative supporters in 2005. There would be no referendum in 2006. Our rights had been first affirmed by the judiciary but, crucially, we used that affirmation as a foothold to win over public opinion.

As the Democratic nominee for president, John Kerry expressed his opposition to same-sex marriage while also expressing respect for the Massachusetts court. I agreed with this approach. Public opinion in the country was still strongly antimarriage, and with DOMA already federal law, his support for gay marriage would have made Bush's reelection more likely, while doing nothing for us substantively.

Kerry's position was also easy to defend before LGBT audiences because he had been one of the fourteen senators who had voted against the Defense of Marriage Act.

I did differ with Kerry over the best way to present his position. As we drove to a crucial meeting in Washington cosponsored by the Human Rights Campaign, he told me how he planned to explain his stand. My advice was that he simply state his view and not elaborate.

As I've reflected before, it's bad enough to tell people you disagree with them. It's far more aggravating when you tell them they're wrong on the merits, especially if you go on to validate some of the arguments that are commonly used against them. Given his commitment to reasoned political dialogue, Kerry not surprisingly objected to my advice, saying that voters would want to know why he took his stand. I replied that on this issue, the electorate was divided into two groups. Those who agreed that same-sex marriages should be banned would not ask for a longer answer. Since I'd entered public life in 1967, no group had ever demanded that I elaborate on my reasons for agreeing with them. Those who disagreed with him might demand a longer answer, but they'd only become angrier when they received one.

Exasperated, Kerry pointed out that if all he did was state his opposition, LGBT people would think he had taken his stand on purely political grounds. That, I told him, was exactly what I hoped they would think: Here was a potential ally who wasn't yet ready to join us, but he had no fundamental intellectual or philosophical objection to doing so later when the political climate had improved. Morally, I admire a politician who differs with me on principle more than one whose opposition is based on public opinion. But pragmatically, if I had the power to decide which one should hold office, I would pick the latter.

•

As the campaign went on, the Republicans turned their opposition to LGBT rights into a national issue. They hadn't done this since the Defense of Marriage Act debate eight years earlier. This time, they sought to pass a constitutional amendment that would prohibit the recognition of same-sex marriages by the federal government or any state. The amendment would snuff out the Massachusetts experiment and any others. Gallingly, one of its major advocates was Bush's designated Republican National Committee chairman, Ken Mehlman, whose homosexuality was widely suspected within the LGBT community. I wrote a public letter to him snarkily hinting that it was hypocritical for him to play that role. He did not respond, but I nurse the hope that my jab was one of the straws that eventually led him to break down the closet door and come out publicly in 2010. (I take my disrespect for metaphors as a license to mix them.)

In Massachusetts and elsewhere, the LGBT community turned its strong emotions into disciplined political action. I was confident that we had the support of enough Democrats to block Bush's anti-same-sex marriage amendment in Congress, where it would need to pass each chamber with a two-thirds majority. But an unexpected problem arose—elected officials whose eagerness to win our support swamped their understanding of how to help us.

Exhibit A was Gavin Newsom, the mayor of San Francisco. In February 2004, not long after the Massachusetts court ruling, Nancy Pelosi asked me to give him a call. He told me that he was thinking of using his authority as mayor to declare same-sex marriages legal in the city, and to authorize officials, including himself, to perform them. I told him this would be a well-intentioned mistake. Our discussion confirmed my understanding that in California, as elsewhere in the United States, marriage was governed by state law, and municipally authorized marriages would have no legal validity. If Newsom did have the power to confer binding marital status on men and women who loved a same-sex partner, that would have trumped any strategic or tactical consideration. But he did not.

Newsom's drastic move, and similar actions by a handful of local officials around the country, regrettably bolstered the GOP argument that an antimarriage amendment was needed. I knew from my constant lobbying on the subject that our margin of support in Congress depended on colleagues in moderate and conservative contested districts being able to explain to their constituents that the vote was all about Massachusetts and not their own states. Even without the amendment, they could say, we Pennsylvanians or Ohioans would retain total control over whether or not we allow women or men to marry each other. I hoped that this argument, combined with the popularity of states' rights and the view that our great Constitution should not be altered lightly, would hold enough Democrats for us to win.

This is why the let-a-hundred-marriage-jurisdictions-bloom movement that Newsom was spearheading posed a serious threat. With his action, that of a small-town mayor in New York State, and local officials in two or three other states, same-sex marriage was no longer a reality only in Massachusetts. If any local official could simply wave a municipal wand and legitimize same-sex marriages, then no members of Congress were insulated from the demand that they protect their states from such a possibility. I was sure that if Newsom's gambit were repeated in fifteen or twenty states, the amendment would pass, wiping out our gains and preventing future ones. (Bush's proposal, it should be stressed, would have prohibited same-sex marriage in any state even if a majority of the state's residents voted for it.)

This situation created a quandary for me. If I publicly expressed my opposition to Newsom's initiative, it would be misrepresented by some as opposition to all same-sex marriages, not just to the pretend ones. Getting across the proper distinction would be hard. Fortunately for our long-term success, local courts in New York and elsewhere quickly clarified the matter by laying down the law against the marriages. And I was relieved of having to decide if I should go public with my views when Newsom himself or someone close to him apparently did so for me. I had given Newsom the advice he solicited in confidence and did not plan to say anything about having tendered it. I was therefore surprised when a San Francisco publication called shortly after we spoke and asked me why I had tried to dissuade the mayor from taking his pro-LGBT step. My unhappy guess—I don't know for certain—is he believed that if people knew he had taken a bold step despite my urging caution, it would elevate his standing as our champion even more.

My conviction that Newsom's actions, and those of his imitators, would hurt us politically is supported by one of the best subsequent studies of the same-sex marriage issue. As the Harvard law professor Michael J. Klarman notes in his book *From the Closet to the Altar*:

> The gay marriage ceremonies conducted (mainly) in San Francisco and Portland early in 2004 generated at least as much backlash against gay marriage as had *Goodridge* itself . . . Given strong support for gay marriage among their constituents, the decisions of local officials such as Mayor Newsom . . . to issue marriage licenses to same-sex couples were politically shrewd. The political repercussions of their actions elsewhere, however, were rather different . . . Images of same-sex couples celebrating their marriages outside of city hall in San Francisco were quickly broadcast by national media across the country and enabled conservatives to mobilize grassroots campaigns for state constitutional amendments to bar gay marriage . . . The West Coast marriages, more than the *Goodridge* decision that inspired them, ignited the powerful political backlash of 2004 . . . Karl Rove had to stifle a grin when asked after the election whether he was indebted to Mayor Newsom for opening city hall to same-sex marriages.

In the right circumstances, of course, there is a strong case to be made for partial steps toward a cherished goal. It was a great accomplishment when the Vermont legislature enacted civil unions in 2000. This was the first statewide recognition of our right to love each other, and it conferred significant legal and economic benefits on same-sex couples. Despite this, some members of our community at the time opposed anything short of marriage. When Governor Howard Dean sought out my views before signing the bill, I was happy to tell him that I thought the anti-civil-union arguments lacked both moral validity and anything close to majority support among us. His signature on the bill was politically courageous—and vindicated when the state's positive experience with civil unions led years later to full marriage rights.

In arguing for the pursuit of LGBT equality through compromise, I frequently encountered the objection that the African American civil rights movement did not settle for partial victories. I often elicited shock when I responded that the NAACP's first victories in segregation cases after World War II did not involve direct challenges to the constitutionality of "separate but equal." Instead, the NAACP made a more limited claim: The segregated state-run law schools in Texas and Oklahoma were unequal in fact. The Supreme Court agreed—it required the whites-only state-run schools to admit black applicants, but it did not repudiate segregation in principle. These decisions offered benefits to some of the victims of discrimination, and served as political and legal stepping-stones toward ultimate victory. The NAACP lawyers were not acquiescing to the constitutionality of separate but equal—they were pursuing a thoughtful, tough-minded strategy to overthrow it. Incrementalism is not the enemy of militancy; it is often the only effective means of expressing it.

In Newsom's case, however, such lessons in the value of partial steps did not apply. He was not taking a step toward marriage. His actions made no substantive progress at all. To the contrary, many of the San Francisco couples who "benefited" when Newsom authorized their marriages in February were bitterly disappointed when the California Supreme Court pronounced these marriages invalid in August—as the state's constitution inarguably compelled them to do. The speed with which the court acted underlined how clear-cut the issue was. And this was a court sympathetic to our rights. Four years later, responding to a lawsuit brought in the appropriate, slower manner Newsom eschewed, that same court ruled that the California constitution conferred a right to same-sex marriage.

A month before the election, the Republicans brought their anti-marriage amendment to the floor. The quality of their debating points had not improved, and I felt sufficiently confident—and angry—to make my disrespect for them very clear. In one widely quoted exchange, when a former judge, Representative John Carter, lamented that he had presided over the dissolution of twenty thousand marriages, and with perfect illogic cited this as justification for not allowing us to form any, I "barked" (according to one published account) in response, "I'm a gay man and I presided over the dissolution of none," adding that "I'm sorry Rush Limbaugh's been divorced three times, but it ain't my fault."

The debate also featured one of the stupidest arguments I ever heard in the House. As *The New York Times* reported, "Representative Phil Gingrey said support for traditional marriage 'is perhaps the best message we can give to the Middle East and all the trouble they're having over there right now.'" Given the limits on speaking time, I never got the chance to ask Gingrey why he believed an amendment restricting marriage to one man and one woman would be so appealing to a region where polygamy was legally and religiously sanctioned.

With overwhelming Democratic solidarity, the amendment fell forty-six votes short of the two-thirds vote it needed. And no Democrats lost their seats because of their stands. The Massachusetts court decision survived and became the vital beachhead for same-sex marriage across the country.

•

Kerry's defeat in November was a great disappointment. Bush's presidency continued, with further disastrous consequences. On the personal plane, there was fallout as well. If Kerry had gone to the White House, I had planned to run for his Senate seat, and polls showed that I was a likely victor. That was not to be. Even so, I returned to the House with a new zest for debate.

The opportunity soon arose. I was at home in Newton on the morning of Sunday, March 20, 2005, when I received notification that the House would convene later that same day to consider the case of a Florida woman named Terri Schiavo. Fifteen years earlier, she had fallen into a comatose state. Once it became clear her condition would not improve, her husband asked the hospital to remove her feeding tube. This was in accordance with a wish he said she had expressed to him before she was stricken.

Schiavo's parents objected, and since the law as it stood gave her husband the right to decide, Florida Republicans, led by a passionately committed Governor Jeb Bush, rushed to change that law and nullify the husband's directive. When their effort was overruled by the Florida courts—with very little judicial disagreement—the president took over from his brother, and with the enthusiastic backing of the Republican leadership, asked Congress to accomplish what Florida legislators could not.

The Republican bill was debated but could not be enacted before Congress's spring recess began. With Congress not due to reconvene for eighteen days, this meant that Michael Schiavo's interpretation of his wife's wishes would prevail, the tube would be removed, and it would be too late for the returning Congress to do anything about it.

When the recess began, I made the same misjudgment that I had made during impeachment. I assumed that the Republicans would not push their ill-advised effort to a conclusion. I expected they would settle for claiming to have done their best. The summons to an extraordinary session—on Palm Sunday, with one day's notice— disabused me.

It's generally believed that the Republicans hoped for large political gain. In fairness to my colleagues, I do not think that was their major motivation. Jeb Bush, Tom DeLay, and other prominent Republicans genuinely and passionately believed that removing the feeding tube would contradict God's wishes, and that their moral responsibility to intervene overrode any other considerations. Hence the extraordinary session.

I did not want to go to Washington. My schedule for that day and the next included several events in the district that I looked forward to attending—the most significant being a dinner that evening sponsored by a congregation of orthodox Jews who were staunch supporters despite their religious views. The main organizer of the event in particular had been an unwavering friend. It was clear that there was nothing I or any other opponents of the bill could do to stop it, especially because everyone assumed it would have broad and deep public support.

Logically, staying home made more sense. But emotionally, I couldn't not go. When I first ran for office, I had promised myself that I would offset my cowardice on the subject of my sexual orientation by not ducking any other tough issue—and this looked like it would be one of the toughest. Moreover, I was as angered by the Republicans' effort as Jeb Bush and Tom DeLay were by Michael Schiavo's decision. The bill was an outrageous intrusion by the legislative branch into the proper domain of the judiciary. For Congress to reverse a specific court ruling, one that had clearly been made properly, meant an end to the rule of law. Politics, not the merits of the case, would become the arbiter of disputes whenever enough politicians got the urge.

Additionally, substituting Jeb Bush's personal religiously based view of what should happen when a person is brain-dead for her own wishes, and those of her husband, was a terrible violation of personal autonomy. No one was telling Bush, DeLay, or any other Republican what should be done if he were in an irreversible, totally insensate vegetative state. Their right to abide by what they believed God was telling them deserved full protection. Only in a theocracy did they have the further right to impose this position on people who disagreed with it. I stress this point for a reason. While the bill's most ardent supporters claimed to doubt that Terri Schiavo had instructed her husband to eschew life support, it became clear that they would have tried to prevent the removal of her feeding tube even if her wishes had been unmistakable.

There was one other aspect of the issue that was relevant to the broader public policy debate. Keeping Terri Schiavo on a feeding tube in a hospital bed for years was very expensive. This is not an argument for removing any device that sustains life. But it does demonstrate the hypocrisy of those who insist that unlimited amounts of money be spent in these cases while simultaneously trying to reduce funding for Medicare and Medicaid, the two programs that bear most of the resulting financial burden. The Republicans who had joined with Clinton in constraining those programs a few years earlier were in effect insisting that we spend large amounts of money providing care to people who did not want it and derived no benefit from it in preference to responding fully to the health needs of those who both wanted it and needed it.

I arrived in Washington expecting to speak against the bill at the behest of the Democratic floor manager and perhaps do a few TV interviews. Instead, I was met by two of my colleagues from Florida, Robert Wexler and Debbie Wasserman Schultz, who regretfully told me that the Democratic leadership had decided not to fight the bill. Nancy Pelosi had left the country on a congressional trip two days before and could not return. The rest of our leadership made it clear that it would be fine with them if we emulated our Senate colleagues and let the bill pass by voice vote.

We refused. Feeling as strongly as we did, we vowed to fight the bill as vocally and demonstratively as we could. I became the floor manager for several reasons. First, given the perceived unpopularity of our effort—bluntly, we wanted to let Schiavo's husband remove the feeding tube over the poignant objection of her parents—there weren't a lot of volunteers. Second, I was the most senior member committed to the fight and had by far the most experience in managing floor time—which is harder than it looks. Third, I wanted to do it. Why the hell disrupt my plans and rush down to Washington, I thought to myself, just to make one five-minute speech and then be frustrated by having to listen to a series of really offensive arguments without being able to answer them? (It is the debate manager's prerogative to inject comments throughout the debate.)

The exchange that followed was one of the best that I would ever see in Congress. Members did not have time to have their staffs write out their speeches for them. With no phone calls to make or answer, and no mail to read, there was not much for members to do in their offices, so floor attendance was far greater than the norm. We actually reacted to each other's words, correcting, amplifying, and contradicting, as in a real conversation.

I was very happy with how things went. They had the votes, but we had the arguments. As the vote took place in the floor, dozens of Democrats and a few Republicans made a point of telling me that they thought we had made a compelling case, but the politics of the issue were too strong for them to vote with us. We lost, 58 to 203, with Democrats dividing 53 to 47 and only 5 Republicans voting no. To block any preemptive action by Michael Schiavo, President Bush flew from Texas to Washington to sign the bill.

We had wanted a chance to vent. What we got was a chance to persuade—to engage the public more deeply. I was pleasantly surprised over the next few days to learn that an unusually large number had paid attention to this fight, and most of them were on our side. Average citizens were indignant that politicians would intrude into such an intensely personal decision. For the first time since impeachment, I was approached by people on the street, in restaurants, and in other public places who thanked me for my work.

I can remember no other situation where the political community—myself included—so badly misjudged public reaction. Voters hadn't previously urged politicians to stay out of end-of-life decisions because no one imagined that politicians would dare intrude into them. As soon as they did, voters told them to butt out. A month later, on a plane back to Massachusetts, Ted Kennedy told me that he had been eager to debate the bill in the Senate as we'd debated it in the House, but his leadership had begged him to spare his vulnerable Democratic colleagues the fallout they feared. "You really had fun with that, didn't you?" he commented wistfully.

The public reaction to this controversy had a broader political significance for Democrats. It was further confirmation—conclusive to me—that blaming the disaffection of white working- and middle-class males on social issues was a bad mistake, intellectually and politically. How could our problem with these voters be our disrespect for traditional sexual morality and our flouting of conservative religious principles if the Republicans lost support when they tried to impeach a president who had oral sex outside his marriage, lost even more support when they sternly insisted that life should end only by God's unaided will, and, in 2006, lost their House majority despite making Democrats vote—as we overwhelmingly did—against banning same-sex marriages?

The noneconomic explanation for our weakness with these voters was not totally invalidated, but only one-third of the alliterative trilogy could still be assigned a share of the blame. Guns remained an obstacle for us, but God and gays were off the hook. I became even more convinced that "It's the economy, stupid" was the best guide to what we should be advocating and to winning back the support of white men. It was time to stop seeing white working-class males' legitimate unhappiness about economic trends as a manifestation of excessive religiosity, a gun fetish, or homophobia.

9

THE UNNECESSARY CRISIS

I left the closet in 1987 in large part because I wanted to enjoy a personal life, and from that year on, I did. But even when I was in a relationship, my career came first. Then I met Jim Ready.

In fact, our initial meeting was wholly consistent with my career-first pattern. In the summer of 2005, I'd been asked by my House colleague Tom Allen to travel to Maine, where opponents of the state's LGBT antidiscrimination law were trying to repeal it in a referendum. After I agreed to attend an event in Portland, Tom asked if I would add a second one in Ogunquit. This meant driving eighty miles in one evening and then taking an early flight back to D.C. the next morning—more work than such visits usually entailed. I said yes, because it was for LGBT rights. This good deed would be more richly rewarded than anything else I've ever done.

At the time Jim was in a loving relationship with his partner, Robert Palmer. In the happiest coincidence I have ever experienced, Robert and I had known each other in the 1980s, when he was a leading adviser to Mike Dukakis on prison issues and a senior executive at Polaroid. This was before either of us had ever met Jim, and we were both closeted—including to each other.

After Robert retired, he moved to Maine and began a fourteen-year partnership with Jim. But by the fall of 2005, he was seriously ill. In an extraordinary example of love at its most generous, he began to think of Jim's future after his own death and mentioned me as a potential partner. With this in mind, he insisted—as Jim later told me—that they attend the Ogunquit fund-raiser at which I spoke.

Jim introduced himself and said that he remembered when I'd come out of the closet—he was living in Massachusetts at the time—and brought me over to say hello to Robert, whom I hadn't seen for years. I was very attracted to Jim, and struck by his unselfish commitment to doing everything possible to ease Robert's obvious pain. Jim and I stayed in touch throughout the next year. I visited Ogunquit several times, staying at the home of a mutual friend, and on one occasion visiting Robert, who was by then bedridden. He and I reminisced about our political joint ventures in Massachusetts, and I was gratified when Jim told me that during that conversation Robert was more animated than he had been in some time.

Robert Palmer died on January 4, 2007. Jim settled his estate and began his own healing process, in part by organizing memorial services in the two states where Robert had lived, Massachusetts and Maine. By the early spring, Robert's intuition became a reality, and Jim and I started dating, discreetly at first out of his respect for Robert's memory. By that summer, I was deeply in love, experiencing at sixty-seven more profound feelings than ever before. Even though I was much older than Jim, he was the emotionally mature one in our growing relationship. His love and understanding of what love entailed sustained me through the extraordinarily challenging and stressful years ahead, and has enriched my life ever since.

•

As the 2006 elections approached, Bush's popularity was at its nadir, and Democrats anticipated large gains. In an attempt to hold us off, some Republicans began using my advocacy of LGBT rights as an argument against a Democratic takeover of the House. I had recently become the Financial Services Committee's senior Democrat and was in line to become chairman. And so one of their fund-raising letters invoked the ominous prospect that three important House committees would soon be run by Charlie Rangel, John Conyers, and me. Apparently the impending committee leadership of tough, effective straight white liberals like George Miller, Henry Waxman, and David Obey lacked the pocketbook-opening power of two African Americans and a gay man. When I received a copy of the letter from someone who'd apparently received it by mistake, I proudly showed it to Rangel, whose immediate response was, "Gee, Barney, I didn't realize you were colored."

Some Republican candidates were more blatant. One Southern Democrat told me that thanks to his opponent, I was better known in his district than he was, and he thanked me for drawing so much of the Republicans' campaign fire that his own record went relatively uncriticized. My favorite foe was John Hostettler, an extreme right-winger from Indiana who had famously denounced the Democratic Party for warring on Christianity in a debate over the propriety of forcing Jewish and other non-Christian Air Force Academy students to attend Christian religious services. If you make Nancy Pelosi Speaker, Hostettler told his constituents, she will enact "her radical plan to advance the homosexual agenda, led by Barney Frank."

My feelings about Hostettler's charge were mixed. On the positive side, anyone wanting to know what gloating looks like should have seen me on election night. Thanks to Indiana's early poll closing time, Hostettler was the first incumbent to publicly lose his seat. In a year when many Republican incumbents were defeated, he lost his reelection bid by the widest margin in the country. On the other hand, I knew I could not live up to the billing. As I told the Greater Boston Chamber of Commerce the next morning, I felt a little inadequate. Apparently, I noted, at least one district in Indiana expected me to promote a radical homosexual agenda, but I didn't have one to offer. I hoped to secure our marriages, our jobs, our safety from hate-inspired violence, and our right to serve in the military. Any self-respecting radical would sneer at the incorrigibly bourgeois nature of my legislative goals. With profound apologies to those who had served in combat, I added that the Republican effort to make me a bogeyman called to mind Winston Churchill's comment after the Second Boer War: "Nothing in life is so exhilarating as to be shot at without result."

When the new Congress convened, we knew that President Bush would veto any important pro-LGBT legislation. But we decided to try anyway, for two reasons. Sometimes, the only way to pass breakthrough legislation is to put it out there and learn what you can about the reactions it elicits. Supporters can then tweak a bill to preserve its substance while curing some of its political problems and come back later with a new, improved, and more viable version.

Meanwhile, the LGBT community had become an invaluable part of that famed political animal—our base—and Democrats owed it our best effort. LGBT leaders were a major source of campaign funds—the best kind, because what the community wanted in return was legislation we could feel proud of. LGBT people were also, after African Americans and Jews, our most reliable bloc of votes.

The top two items on our nonradical agenda were bringing LGBT people under the protection of the hate crimes bill and the self-explanatory Employment Non-Discrimination Act (ENDA). On both bills, public opinion was clearly on our side. That had been true of hate crimes for some time, but banning employment discrimination was now also more popular than not. I received an unexpected confirmation of this at the press conference we held to announce the introduction of ENDA: One hostile reporter noted that we were obviously pushing for a vote just to gain political capital at the expense of the Republicans, forcing them to choose between the pro-ENDA general electorate and their anti-LGBT primary voters. We had come quite far.

But not far enough. In a series of floor votes, we demonstrated that we had majority support on both issues, yet to my considerable frustration, we were unable to send either bill to the president's desk and force a veto. I had badly underestimated the difficulty of getting the various factions on our side to reconcile their differences, given the reality that nothing we did was about to become law. "He's going to veto it anyway," was the response I got as I tried to forge agreements, "so why should I give in on a point that's important to me?"

At least the fate of the hate crimes provision was familiar. Once again, the House strongly supported a hate crimes provision while the Senate attached the language to the annual defense authorization, and having done that, declined to take it up as a separate item. Then, with a Bush veto threatened, and the Democratic committee leadership in the House fearing for the defense authorization, the conference committee dropped the language.

It was not a total loss. Once we had a Democratic president, we'd clearly have the votes to enact the law easily—which we did in 2009. And I made a speech of great personal importance. At a closed caucus of House Democrats, several African American members said they needed help responding to clergy in their districts. The ministers were concerned that the legislation would criminalize their religiously based denunciations of homosexuality. I was eager to respond, and not only so I could firm up votes for the bill. I was enormously grateful to my colleagues in the Congressional Black Caucus for their staunch support of our fight. I made a point of telling LGBT groups that members of the CBC voted for us more consistently than almost any other group in Congress, and even had a better voting record on our issues than the gay members—although they were not quite as good as the subset of us openly gay ones.

My answer for the clergy came easily. The original hate crimes law did not make anything criminal that was not already illegal behavior, and our amendment very explicitly reaffirmed that it did not criminalize any form of expression. What it did was enhance sentencing in cases where hate was the motive for acts of physical violence or property damage that harmed individuals. As I stressed this point, I added the personal element that's so important in persuading one's legislative colleagues.

"I'm a big shot now," I noted. "I'm chairman of the Financial Services Committee of the U.S. House, and a lot of very important people are now being very nice to me. But I used to be fifteen, desperately afraid that people could find out who I really was, and I know how important it is to vulnerable LGBT people all over this country for the Congress to offer them this protection." I closed by adding, "Even if this bill becomes law tomorrow, it will still be legal to call me a fag. I just wouldn't recommend it to anyone in the banking business."

The opportunity to use my elevated official position to fight the prejudice that still blighted the life of so many other fifteen-year-olds meant a great deal to me. And the raucous hilarity with which my colleagues greeted my last remark was powerful confirmation that we had the bigots on the run.

Our effort to pass ENDA was equally unsuccessful legislatively and, sadly, much more embittering. Providing job protections for gay, lesbian, and bisexual men and women was a popular cause. But majority opinion had not yet embraced the rights of transgender people—especially the large number who identified with the other gender but had not had surgery as part of their transition. By 2007, LGB groups had embraced their cause, evidenced by the addition of "T" to their names. The antidiscrimination bill we submitted that year was the first to be fully inclusive: It would contain the key words "gender identity."

Unfortunately, we were not at the point where rationality would govern the outcome. I had forgotten "the ick factor." Senator Nunn and the Republicans had once skillfully exploited the majority's anxieties about sharing showers and other intimate spaces with people of the same sex who might be attracted to them. In the case of transgender people, the problem was exacerbated by the worry that people who identified as female but retained male sex organs would gain the legal right to be naked in the presence of other women. Some men, it was feared, would even pretend to be transgender precisely for that purpose.

The bill fell within the jurisdiction of the Education and Labor Committee, whose chairman, George Miller, was a committed liberal and one of the best legislators in the House. Along with Miller, the leadership fell to me and Wisconsin Representative Tammy Baldwin.

In 1998, Tammy became the first out candidate to be elected to the House. That year, many Democrats had declared their intention to run in her district, and a well-founded concern arose among LGBT leaders, including Baldwin herself, that the House Democratic leadership feared an open lesbian would lose the race to a Republican. Learning of this, I spoke with the leaders of our House campaign committee and pointed out emphatically that it would be a terrible mistake to oppose her, morally and politically. As was often the case in lobbying my colleagues, I thought the pragmatic approach would be more persuasive than the moral one, so I noted that if our community believed the Democratic leadership had hurt the chances of a popular, successful out lesbian, it would be very angry. I believe I helped ensure their scrupulous neutrality in the race.

Nine years later, Baldwin, Miller, and I set out to pass ENDA. Unfortunately, we encountered strong resistance to the full inclusion of transgender people in the bill's scope. It became clear that when it came to the floor, there would be overwhelming Republican support for an amendment that would either remove the transgender protections entirely or, more dangerously, put serious restrictions on them. While House rules let the majority party block the minority's amendments, the minority still has the right to offer what is called the "motion to recommit." This is the last step before a bill is passed. At that stage, the minority can offer any provision it wishes, as long as it is germane. To the Democrats' envy, the Republicans have developed a strong ethic that this vote is a matter of basic party loyalty. While we hoped we could hold 90 percent of our side, we would still need at least fifteen Republicans to defeat the amendment. And we couldn't be sure of the 90 percent.

At this point, tensions arose between Miller and me on one side and Baldwin on the other. She and I had worked hard to maintain a friendly relationship, personally as well as officially. This was not something we could take for granted. Politics is a profession rife with jealousy. Jostling over status is, of course, a factor in most cases where human egos are involved, but the nature of legislating magnifies the effect. More than in most lines of work, our effectiveness is determined in substantial part by what people think of us—our colleagues, whose goodwill we need to accomplish anything; our constituents, without whose favorable opinion we would not survive; and not least potential contributors, who may prefer giving to our peers. As a result, we are strongly conditioned to worry about our reputations, not just absolutely but also relative to our colleagues.

Counterintuitively, the tensions among ideological allies can be especially strong. When people prefer to collaborate with, vote for, or give money to a conservative rather than me, I don't take it personally. When they favor someone else on the basis of individual merit, I do. This problem gets worse when the two competitors share a particular niche in the political world—geographic, ethnic, or, as with

Tammy and me, membership in a demographic minority. We worked hard to minimize all this, but our disagreement over ENDA strained our friendship.

As we approached the final vote, Tammy did her own informal whip count and concluded we would have enough Democratic votes. Speaker Pelosi, a strong supporter of the bill, asked Tammy for her count, checked it herself with the members, and decided that Tammy had been too optimistic—a conclusion that Miller and I, based on our own work, fully agreed with. We did not have the votes for the inclusive bill. It was sadly but unmistakably clear to Pelosi, Miller, and me that we could pass ENDA only in its earlier form, covering only lesbian, gay, and bisexual workers. The pro-ENDA community was divided, with many organizations (including many of the non-LGBT groups) opposed to any bill that did not cover transgender people. Others preferred something to nothing—especially given that, to us, it was a very significant "something" that represented a major advance in our fight.

With Miller's and my endorsement, Pelosi decided to proceed with the LGB-only version of the bill. Baldwin disagreed, but she still worked hard to support our work. We now faced the problem of a Republican motion to recommit, which would allow some Republicans to appear supportive of the bill while in fact voting to poison it. It was the availability of this maneuver that had convinced us in the first place that we could not pass a law that included protection for transgender people. A Republican motion to recommit might have added fraught language—for example, we heard that they might offer provisions saying that no teacher could transition from one gender to the other during the school year. My very intensive lobbying effort convinced me that there was no way we could defeat such a provision, and I believed it would be better not to bring a bill to the floor at all than to add to it terms like that.

As it turned out, the Republicans employed the motion to recommit to make a different kind of trouble. When we brought our LGB-only bill to the floor, they offered a recommit that affirmed that nothing in the antidiscrimination legislation created a right to marriage. Of course it did not. The amendment was wholly unnecessary. Indeed, we offered to agree to their recommit. But they insisted on using a parliamentary form that would cause the adoption of the recommit to delay the bill's passage until after Congress was due to adjourn. We therefore had to persuade members to reject the maneuver—we had to convince them that in voting for our bill, they were sufficiently protected against the charge that they were for same-sex marriage.

When I rose to speak, I spent too much of my five minutes trying to convince Democrats that there was no need to attach any anti-same-sex marriage language to the bill. But George Miller rescued me. From his place at the committee table, he somehow signaled I should be talking about the historic nature of the vote: For the first time, Congress was proactively protecting gays, lesbians, and bisexuals from discrimination.

The words I went on to speak are among the highlights not just of my career, but of my life. From the well of the House—as we call the spot just below the Speaker's rostrum—I gave a speech that had taken me fifty-three years to prepare:

> Mr. Speaker, we say here that we don't take things person-ally, and usually that is true. Members, Mr. Speaker, will have to forgive me. I take it a little personally.
>
> Thirty-five years ago, I filed a bill that tried to get rid of discrimination based on sexual orientation. As we sit here to-day, there are millions of Americans in states where this is not the law. By the way, nineteen states have such a law. In no case has it led to that decision [to adopt same-sex mar-riage]. The Massachusetts law passed in 1989, that did not lead to the decision in 2004. [In fact, it was 2003, a misstatement that indicated how emotional I was.] Unrelated.
>
> But here is the deal. I used to be someone subject to this prejudice, and, through luck, circumstance, I got to be a big shot. I am now above that prejudice. But I feel an obligation to fifteen-year-olds dreading to go to school because of the tor-ments, to people afraid they will lose their job in a gas station if someone finds out who they love. I feel an obligation to use the status I have been lucky enough to get to help them.

I want to ask my colleagues here, Mr. Speaker, on a personal basis, please, don't fall for this sham . . . Don't send me out of here having failed to help those people . . .

So I will close with this. Yes, this is personal. There are people who are your fellow citizens being discriminated against. We have a simple bill that says you can go to work and be judged on how you work and not be penalized. Please don't turn your back on them.

My Democratic colleagues rose and began clapping as I finished—choking up as I did. The applause and cheering got louder, as more members than I could count rushed down—the floor is on an incline—to embrace me. The orientation that had once threatened to make me a pariah was now the reason I was standing on the floor of the House of Representatives receiving the emotional support of two hundred members of Congress.

The bill passed the House by a vote of 235 to 184, with 200 Democrats and 35 Republicans voting yes. It then died in the Senate, where party leaders didn't have the 60 votes they needed and didn't want to force Democrats to vote on a controversial measure that had no chance of passing. We knew that would happen. Even so, we wanted to establish that there was majority support for the bill, with an eye toward passing it when we had a Democrat in the White House as well as a Democratic House and Senate.

Many transgender activists and some of their supporters bitterly complained that the Democratic leadership could have delivered an inclusive bill if we had really wanted to. They blamed our decision to exclude transgender people on a mixture of political cowardice and our own prejudice. To my sorrow and anger, the last accusation was most often aimed at me.

I was sad because the charge reflected a stubborn, enduring ignorance of the political process. I had begged transgender advocates to join in our lobbying effort. I told them that getting transgender voters to lobby their representatives—in person, if possible—would be very helpful. We tried to facilitate this by providing a list of members whose votes seemed to be in play and by noting that we could hold off on the roll call until this work was accomplished. While a few advocates may have attempted such work, I never heard any reports of it. Instead, my interlocutors seemed to think Pelosi and I could have passed the bill by willpower alone. To illustrate the political difficulty we faced, I pointed out that even among those states that had enacted their own versions of ENDA, more than a third covered only lesbian, gay, and bisexual victims. "Given that efforts to include transgender people have been unsuccessful to date in New York, Massachusetts, Maryland, and Wisconsin," I asked them, "why do you think it gets easier when you add Texas, South Carolina, Utah, and Nebraska to the political equation?"

I was angered by the accusation that I was selfishly acting to shelter my own group while abandoning transgender people, who were different from me. In 2000 I had stressed on the House floor that transgender men and women were the most frequent victims of hate-based violence. Moreover, ever since 1973, I had fought the unfair treatment of African Americans, Hispanics, Asians, noncitizens, women, the elderly, and those with disabilities. I have never been a member of any of these groups, except the elderly, whose ranks I entered long after the legislative struggles on their behalf were over. Through those years, I did not always put my own group first. When Massachusetts considered the Equal Rights Amendment in the 1970s, I vocally opposed including protections for gays and lesbians, lest the amendment lose favor. I repeated this argument to colleagues in the House twenty years later. Insisting that some people must suffer until we have the power to end all suffering is a recipe for embedding misery, not diminishing it. I have never agreed with the maxim "No one is free until everyone is free." If that were true, no one would be free today, and no one would ever have been free in the past.

An egregious example of inconsistent absolutism on the issue came from the LGBT activist Matthew Foreman. In 2002, as the head of the Empire State Pride Agenda, he had made a deal with the Republican governor George Pataki, then running for reelection, to support a state antidiscrimination bill that did not apply to transgender people. Foreman asked that I come to New York and defend him against attacks from activists angered by the deal, and I agreed to do so. Apparently my memory of this was much better than his. In his new position at the National Gay and Lesbian Task Force (as it was called), he was one of the most strident critics of our efforts to pass the same kind of bill in the House.

Once again, my debates with LGBT leaders hinged upon history, especially the history of the civil rights movement. In one version of the past, African American leaders eschewed morally flawed compromises, never accepted less than their full demands, and scorned halfway measures. "Rosa Parks never asked for the right to sit in the middle of the bus" is the mantra of those who argue this way. In fact, the NAACP Legal Defense Fund, A. Philip Randolph, Bayard Rustin, and Martin Luther King, Jr., did all of these things, not out of a lack of fervor or political timidity but because they infused their insistence on full equality with a shrewd, sophisticated understanding of how to achieve it within the existing political context. While many of the participants in the 1993 LGBT march on Washington competed with each other to see who could most offend Middle America, Randolph and Rustin tightly structured the 1963 March on Washington to maximize its broad political appeal.

The argument that a civil rights movement cannot in good conscience accept a law that goes only part of the way to equality comes from people who mistakenly attribute the sentiment to those who fought for racial equality. The 1964 Civil Rights Act did a great deal, but it left out vital areas of concern. Voting rights came a year later, and housing discrimination wasn't statutorily outlawed until after Martin Luther King was murdered in 1968. The assertion that passing a law that reduces inequality without totally abolishing it amounts to complicity with the bigots has no historical basis.

•

During my twenty-three years of service on the Judiciary Committee, I'd often imagined I might become its chairman one day. I was second in seniority to John Conyers, who was a decade older than me and one of the most senior members of the House. On the Financial Services Committee, there were two Democrats ahead of me on the seniority list who were about my age. But one of them, Bruce Vento, a dedicated advocate for the homeless, suddenly became ill with mesothelioma and died. And the other, John LaFalce, from Buffalo, lost his seat. After the 2000 census required New York to reduce its delegation, the legislature and governor agreed to eliminate the seats of one Democrat and one Republican and the Democrats settled on LaFalce. I was surprised, because finance is a key industry in New York, and a state rarely sacrifices a member of the congressional leadership who deals with such an industry. I count the 2002 New York state legislature second in importance to Pope John Paul II as an enabler of my career.

When I became the ranking member of Financial Services, party rules forced me to step down from my Judiciary post. I appealed to Pelosi for a waiver, but she wisely turned me down.

As ranking member, I had a large role to play. But first, I had to become more discreet, as opinions I expressed took on more weight in the minds of my audiences. This was especially so in the area of the financial markets. I had not thought a great deal about them previously, but I soon came to the conclusion that the various stock markets have a dual personality—they are reasonably good predictors over the longer term of our economic health, and they are nervous hysterics in the short term.

The summer before I took on my new position, I made my second trip to the Republic of Cape Verde, an island nation formerly colonized by Portugal and the ancestral home of many of my constituents. I brought with me *Master of the Senate*, the third volume of Robert Caro's biography of Lyndon Johnson, which covered Johnson's work as Democratic minority leader in 1953 and 1954 as well as his later efforts to advance civil rights as majority leader. It would become the second instruction manual on my bookshelf, after Charles Hamilton's biography of the African American trailblazer Adam Clayton Powell.

Reading Caro, I decided to emulate Johnson's practice of making himself as useful and important to other members as could be. Recognizing that he had no power over his caucus, no authority to order them to do anything, Johnson needed to exercise power by other means. His method was to convince his colleagues that they had as strong an interest in having good relations with him as he did with them. My role did not compare to Johnson's in the scope of authority, but as ranking member, I could allocate certain privileges—the right to hold hearings, or select witnesses, or manage bills on the floor. I made it my job to know as much as I could about the members on my side of the aisle, so I could grasp which privileges were important to which members. There is a mistaken notion that legislators often trade specific favors with each other. That is very rarely the case. I do not remember ever telling a member that if he or she voted with me in a particular way, I would confer this or that benefit. Rather, I tried to do as many favors as I could and to respond to requests. Then, when I did have to ask colleagues to cast a vote that might be politically difficult, I hoped they would at least think about it in the context of their interest in maintaining their ongoing rapport with me.

In my new Financial Services role, I enjoyed the only productive private meeting I ever had with Alan Greenspan. When I became the ranking member, he dutifully invited me to have lunch with him at the Federal Reserve, since I was the leading Democratic member of the committee that had the most to say about his agency—although, in his mind, even that should be very little. At our lunch, I did not find him wholly enthralled with my conversation—until I brought up the subject of the presidency of the World Bank. James Wolfensohn, who had successfully moved the bank in the right direction, was due to leave. Under the informal rules that govern the bank, the United States gets to name its chief executive, subject to a veto in the rare case that the rest of the world finds our pick offensive. I suggested to Greenspan that he recommend to President Bush the appointment of Jim Leach, my Iowa colleague with whom I had worked closely on debt relief for foreign countries. Leach was a liberal Republican and had taken an especially enlightened approach to international financial institutions. As the immediate past chairman of the Financial Services Committee—the Republicans had a six-year limit on chairmanships— Leach had a better chance of maintaining waning Republican support for the institution than any other individual. When I mentioned Leach's name, Greenspan perked up and blurted out more than he probably wished to say. "That's a wonderful idea," he enthused. "That suggestion makes this lunch worthwhile."

I was disappointed when Bush selected Paul Wolfowitz, not only because he was not Jim Leach, but also because he was Paul Wolfowitz. Wolfowitz was the neoconservative who had been one of Dick Cheney's closest collaborators in leading us into the Iraq War. I'd been particularly outraged by one of his maneuvers. After the democratically elected Turkish parliament rejected our request to march into Iraq through its territory, Wolfowitz suggested that the Turkish military should pressure the government to change its mind.

I did learn later that the idea I'd given to Greenspan had some force. Leach told me one day as we talked on the floor of the House that with Greenspan's advocacy, the World Bank decision had come down to a very close one between Wolfowitz and himself. The deciding factor, Leach said he had been told, and it was entirely plausible, was that if he had taken the job and resigned his House seat, it would certainly have gone to a Democrat. Leach had long represented a district that supported Democrats for almost every other office. Indeed, Leach himself would be defeated when the Democrats took control of the House in 2006.

That same election repudiated the Bush administration, elevated Nancy Pelosi to Speaker of the House, and made me the chair of the Financial Services Committee. It was an exciting job—in some respects too exciting. As I took office, the economy was on the brink of the giant meltdown that occurred the following year.

As chairman, I would be closely involved in managing the crisis itself and in devising far-reaching reforms to avert any repetition of the terrible event. I would also find myself in the right wing's crosshairs as never before. Misunderstanding my years of work on housing issues, some conservatives even held me personally responsible for the cataclysmic collapse of the housing market. Because of the all-important issues at stake; because as a leader in the drive to enact comprehensive financial reform I became a lightning rod for the right wing's counterattack; and, candidly, because the facts of the case are both highly favorable to my side of the argument and, to my frustration, not nearly as well understood as we should have made them, I go into them in some detail here.

•

After the crash, the most conservative elements in American politics went to great lengths to absolve the private sector of significant responsibility for the crisis that devastated the economy. They did not blame the financial industry for its bundling of loans into securities that relieved lenders of any need to worry about repayment. Or for wildly overleveraged derivatives that were sold by entities—like AIG— that did not come remotely close to having the funds needed to meet their obligations. Or for complex, opaque securities given overly optimistic scores from the rating agencies. Or for heavy liabilities owed by banks that had concealed them on their balance sheets. To the contrary, in conservatives' version, the private financial sector was more than merely innocent; it had been taken hostage by an oppressive government that forced it to lend money to the undeserving poor so that they could buy homes.

In the conservative narrative, liberals did this by establishing two sets of policies. The first is the combination of statutes and regulatory pressures that allegedly forced private institutions to lend money to people who did not have the economic wherewithal to meet their mortgage obligations. They cite the Community Reinvestment Act as the primary statutory villain.

The second conservative accusation is most authoritatively repeated by President Bush and Vice President Cheney in their memoirs. This charge is that Democrats—with me almost single-handedly in the lead—prevented any reform of Fannie Mae and Freddie Mac, the government-sponsored enterprises (GSEs) that help subsidize homeownership by buying mortgages. In this ideologically convenient history, we were responsible for keeping the bad loans flowing.

Two of the pillars of the right-wing case—that liberals pushed lenders into making mortgage loans that were highly unlikely to be repaid, and that Democrats blocked Republican efforts to rein in Fannie Mae and Freddie Mac—are more than simply wrong. They stand the historical record on its head. The third—that the crusade to increase homeownership beyond the boundaries of financial sustainability was a liberal creation—is a half-truth with regard to the political community in general, but another example of truth turned upside down as it applies to me.

The right-wing effort to rewrite the record on these issues is driven by more than the urge to score particular points against liberals. Taken together, their blatant misrepresentations form the basis for a larger argument—that our worst economic crisis in eighty years was caused by too much government rather than too little. Ideological necessity has prevented conservatives from being honest about the role of Republican congresses in leaving Fannie Mae and Freddie Mac unreformed, *The Wall Street Journal*'s strong defense of subprime loans, and George W. Bush's initiatives in support of low-income home ownership. Once the right began to misplace responsibility for the crash, it was hard to stop. They could not put all the blame for the crisis on government policies without having to pretend they had been strongly opposed to those policies but had been overruled by liberals—despite the inconvenient fact that Republicans were in power for the most critical years.

•

The relevant history begins in the 1990s. Thirty years earlier, people borrowed money to buy their homes mostly from banks. These were regulated institutions that held the loans until they were paid off. Lenders had strong incentives to be careful about their borrowers. Too many unpaid loans brought intervention by bank regulators, and also hit the institutions in their bottom lines.

Two developments drastically changed this business model. One was the availability of money. As funds became available for mortgages from sources outside the banking system, including oil-producing countries and Asian nations with large balance-of-payment surpluses, institutions flourished that did not need depositors and could keep free of existing regulatory arrangements.

The second factor liberating mortgage lenders from the need to pay careful attention to their borrowers' finances was the revolution in information technology. Securitization is the process of bundling vast numbers of individual loans into "securities," which can then be marketed to a wide range of investors. When this became technologically possible, both banks and nonbanks soon saw the advantages of making large numbers of loans and selling them to securitizers, in effect being repaid up front for the loan they'd made. At this point, a borrower's failure to repay was no longer a problem for the originators, who had passed along the risk to investors. Banks and nonbanks alike had little incentive to screen prospective homebuyers.

In 1994, Democrats responded to these developments by passing the Home Ownership and Equity Protection Act (HOEPA). Bill Clinton signed it enthusiastically. The purpose of HOEPA was to empower the Federal Reserve Board to substitute its supervisory powers for the due diligence bankers were no longer providing. By 2000, it was especially clear that imprudent mortgage lending had reached the point where the Fed's intervention was needed. But Alan Greenspan refused to use the authority he had been granted by the law. There was little to be done about that. His prestige, and that of the deregulatory philosophy he espoused, was at a very high point, leaving him largely invulnerable to congressional pressure.

With conservative control of the federal government firmly in place, advocates who saw the need to combat predatory lending turned to the states. Liberals took the lead, but there was broad support wherever the abuses prevailed. One of the first states to regulate irresponsible mortgage practices was Georgia, and several others were joining the effort. The financial industry responded in two ways. First, they threatened to drop mortgage loans in states that interfered with their freedom. When that seemed unlikely to succeed completely, they turned to their allies in the Bush administration, who responded enthusiastically. In fairness to Bush, it should be noted that their chief savior was a Clinton appointee, Comptroller of the Currency John Hawke. In 2004, he issued a sweeping new policy that denied states the authority to regulate any aspect of a national bank's activities except in areas like zoning, building safety, or employment practices. States could no longer prohibit mortgage loans that left borrowers burdened beyond what they could repay. It was one of the boldest examples of the federal preemption of state policy-making discretion in our history.

As the ranking Democrat on the Financial Services Committee, I organized a letter strongly objecting to Hawke's decree, and in this case, some Republican members were also opposed to the administration's actions. But with Republican control of Congress, the best we could do was hold one hearing chaired by an antipreemption Republican, Sue Kelly of New York. As with Greenspan's decision to ignore HOEPA, Republican control of Congress meant that one more avenue for curtailing irresponsible lending was shut down.

There was one remaining course of action: pass legislation to curb damaging mortgage practices. The initiative for such an approach came from North Carolina, where an effective advocacy group called the Center for Responsible Lending was active. Working with them, North Carolina Democrat Brad Miller introduced a subprime bill, with his colleague Mel Watt as the main cosponsor. Miller and Watt lined up sixty-five other Democratic sponsors, including a majority of those on our committee. Encouragingly, the Republican who chaired the relevant subcommittee, Spencer Bachus of Alabama, told us that he shared the belief that some legislation to reform existing practices was necessary. I knew that Bachus's views on this subject were somewhat more populist than those of most of his colleagues, and I thought we might be able to agree on something.

Regrettably, the discussions dragged on until the late summer of 2006 with no conclusion. The central problem was that Tom DeLay and the Republicans were ideologically opposed. As Sheila Bair, Bush's appointee to head the FDIC, affirms in her memoir, *Bull by the Horns*:

In 2005, Congressmen Barney Frank and Spencer Bachus (R-Ala.) tried to put together a bipartisan effort to establish national lending standards. However, the effort met stiff opposition from the industry, which complained to the Republican leadership. Bachus was forced to stop negotiating with Frank under pressure from the House GOP leadership.

In summary, liberals made three separate efforts to cut back on loans to people who should not have been getting them: granting the Federal Reserve regulatory authority over mortgages, using state laws and regulations, and adopting a federal subprime statute. Conservative believers in an unregulated market thwarted us every time.

The charge that the Community Reinvestment Act played a key role in the crisis is also an ideological invention. Most relevantly, the CRA applies only to a subset of mortgage lenders—deposit-taking, federally insured banks—and the bad loans were mostly made by entities not covered by the law. As the highly respected British financial journalist Martin Wolf notes in his book *The Shifts and the Shocks*, the U.S. Financial Crisis Inquiry Commission concluded that "only 6 percent of high-cost loans—a proxy for subprime loans—had any connection to the law. Loans made by CRA-regulated lenders in the neighborhoods in which they were required to lend were half as likely to default as similar loans made in the same neighborhoods by independent mortgage originators not subject to the law." Three of the four Republican appointees to that commission explicitly repudiated the argument that the CRA has been a cause of the problem.

•

The story of Fannie Mae and Freddie Mac is less clear-cut, but it also refutes the conservative notion that reckless liberal efforts to expand homeownership destroyed the economy. To begin with, the goal of homeownership for the poor was not a liberal Democratic pipe dream but a widely shared, incessantly voiced bipartisan goal. To quote the economist Mark Zandi's excellent book *Financial Shock*, "President Bush readily took up the homeownership baton at the start of his administration in 2001." Second, while some Republicans called for cutting back the role of the GSEs, many of these same officials, led by the president, were simultaneously pushing them to do more for homeownership for low-income people. To quote Zandi again, "To reinforce this effort, the Bush administration put substantial pressure on Fannie Mae and Freddie Mac to increase their funding of mortgage loans to lower-income groups." And one indisputable fact stands out: Having overwhelmingly voted to revise Fannie and Freddie's structure in 1992, the Republicans did literally nothing in their twelve years of congressional control from 1995 through 2006 to change it.

I was reminded again of the gap between historical reality and the Republican mythmaking on this subject when I gave a Washington read to Dick Cheney's memoir while waiting to be interviewed at the *Huffington Post*. I turned to the one reference to me in the index and was bemused to realize that I had something in common with Iraqi weapons of mass destruction: Cheney had lied about what each of us was doing in 2003. In my case, it was his statement that

> in 2003, the administration had put forward legislation, which was blocked by Barney Frank, Democratic chairman of the House Banking Committee, that would have reformed these institutions and strengthened governmental regulations of their activities. We put forward similar legislation again in 2005, and again it was blocked by Fannie Mae and Freddie Mac lobbyists and supporters, particularly in the Democratic caucus on Capitol Hill.
>
> Finally, in July 2008, with the financial crisis looming, legislation that provided for regulation was passed, and it brought about a careful examination of Fannie's and Freddie's books.

I was opposed to that legislation in 2003, but the partisan motivation for this passage is to transfer blame for the defeat of the administration's GSE legislation from the Republicans who were in the majority to those of us in the minority—entirely contrary to the way Republicans ran the House during their twelve-year reign. Most glaringly, I was not the chairman of the committee in 2003. Cheney's fellow Republicans were in control that year—and for four years thereafter. I call this a lie because there is no possibility that Cheney had gotten confused about which party was running the House that year. There is no chance that while he was sitting behind the president during the State of the Union address, he mistook Dennis Hastert for Nancy Pelosi as his neighbor. No matter what my status, I had no opportunity to kill the bill because the Republicans who controlled the committee agenda never put it forward. If I had the power over the Republican agenda attributed to me, we would not have gone to war in Iraq, we would not have passed two very large tax cuts for the very wealthy, and DeLay would not have appeared on *Dancing with the Stars*.

By 2004, I realized that I had been too optimistic about the GSEs. I was particularly concerned when Bush forced them to buy up more mortgages that had been taken out by people below the median income. I objected publicly that this further step to extend the economic boundaries of homeownership would be dangerous for the institutions and problematic for many of the newly empowered borrowers.

At that time, I told Michael Oxley, the Republican chair of the committee, that I was ready to work with him on a Fannie and Freddie bill he'd decided to introduce. The bill would increase the restraints on Fannie and Freddie, and expand the power of their regulator to impose rules necessary to protect their fiscal soundness. While I agreed with Oxley's provisions, I had another high priority: the establishment of a trust fund to finance the construction, acquisition, and maintenance of housing for low-income people. The fund I had in mind would subsidize rental units, with the possibility that some small percentage of the money would support ownership. My preference would have been to put all the financing into rentals, but I recognized that I needed to make some accommodations to win Republican acceptance.

The idea of a permanent fund to support affordable rentals was brought to me by Sheila Crowley, director of the National Low Income Housing Coalition. Sheila is a passionate, creative advocate, and our decades-long collaboration is notable for two things: periodic angry shouting matches over strategy and tactics, and valuable public policy outcomes for the poorest of our fellow citizens. The housing trust fund we had in mind would not be part of Fannie and Freddie except in one way—we proposed to designate a small part of their annual profits as the necessary revenue source. (It was a mark of my excessive optimism that I envisioned the two entities remaining profitable indefinitely into the future.) Since Fannie and Freddie effectively subsidized the financing costs for all home buyers, we believed it was entirely fair to put some of their revenue toward helping those too poor to own—the renters.

My preference for renting over owning was long-standing. Indeed, over thirty-two years, my work to promote rental units for people with limited incomes had taken more of my time and energy than any other issue, including LGBT rights. Throughout my career, I gave the highest priority to increasing the availability of *rental* housing for low-income people, frequently and explicitly arguing that "almost by definition, the large majority of poor people are going to need rental housing." Lawrence Lindsey, the former director of George W. Bush's National Economic Council, said this himself in *The Wall Street Journal*: "In fact, Rep. Barney Frank is the only politician I know who has argued that we needed tighter rules that intentionally produce fewer homeowners and more renters. Politicians usually believe that homeownership rates should—must—go ever higher."

In my work with Fannie Mae and Freddie Mac, my constant focus was on increasing their financing of multifamily buildings for middle- and lower-middle-income residents. (To build multifamily units affordable for the poor, bigger subsidies were required than those provided by Fannie and Freddie's regular operation, which is why I pushed for a separate low-income housing trust fund.) Indeed, it was in the course of this advocacy that I made a poorly worded statement that became the basis for the gross distortion of my legislative record by right-wing mythmakers.

At a hearing in 2003 on the regulation of Fannie and Freddie, I said that "I want to roll the dice a little bit more in this situation toward *subsidized* housing." It is true that I was overly optimistic about Fannie and Freddie's financial status at the time. That was because I thought we could protect their solvency by tougher regulation of subprime loans, and I did not foresee the coming collapse of home prices in general. But the dice roll I called for had nothing to do with homeownership.

It was not until the debate over who killed the economy broke out several years later that I realized that conservative critics of my "roll the dice" comment had skillfully taken advantage of a semantic

confusion. They had the opportunity because those of us engaged
in the details of housing policy were using phrases that had very
specific meaning to us but were not sufficiently differentiated in
the public dialogue. I used one of two adjectives that advocates
employ interchangeably to refer to rental housing built by private
entities with some public financial aid—"subsidized" or "affordable" housing. In our conversations, these efforts were always dis-
tinct from policies seeking to promote low-income homeownership,
which was less obscurely referred to as exactly that—"low-income
homeownership."

In 2005, Oxley got the Committee on Financial Services to approve reining in Fannie and Freddie and establishing the housing
trust fund with my support. There was significant opposition, however. Most of it came from a large minority of Oxley's fellow Republicans, led by the free-market purists who thought his approach to
the GSEs too weak. They wanted to restrict Fannie and Freddie's
activities more tightly, or even abolish them outright. Some of the opposition came from Democrats on the opposite ideological wing, who
opposed any restrictions at all on the agencies.

Unfortunately, the balance of power shifted to my disadvantage
after the bill passed the committee. The House leadership, with De-
Lay in the forefront, was much less willing to accommodate the trust
fund than Oxley had been. Using the power of the House Rules
Committee, they substantially weakened the fund. As a result, I
voted against the bill on the final vote even as the leadership's efforts
persuaded enough of the conservatives to vote for it, and it passed comfortably. To Oxley's frustration, the Bush administration did not then
support his bill. It lobbied the Republican-controlled Senate Banking
Committee to replace it with a much more restrictive version. The
chambers could not agree, and one more Republican-controlled
Congress adjourned without passing any version of GSE reform.

Oxley did make one last effort to revive the matter in 2006, his
last year as chairman. He enlisted me to join him in a letter seeking
to persuade his fellow Republicans in the Senate and the administration that agreement on a good reform bill was achievable. Bush refused. The stated reason for this response—a "one-finger salute" in

Oxley's phrase—was that nothing short of the administration's precise bill would do any good.

•

When the Democratic majority took office in 2007, and I replaced Oxley as Financial Services chairman, I made our GSE legislation the first item on the committee's agenda. I was eager to highlight the contrast between Democratic action and congressional Republicans' paralysis on this tough issue—which they had been accusing us of evading. In his memoir, Bush's secretary of the treasury, Hank Paulson, recounts our collaboration:

> Fortunately, I had been forging relationships on both sides of the aisle. One was with longtime Democratic congressman Barney Frank of Massachusetts . . . [Barney's] a pragmatic, disciplined, completely honorable politician: he never once violated a confidence of mine. Secure in his seat, he pushes for what he thinks is right. To get things done, he's willing to deal, to take half a loaf.
>
> Right from the start, he indicated that he was willing to work with me on GSE reform, hashing out the issues of portfolio limits and regulation . . . We didn't get a bill passed in the lame-duck session, but Barney made good on his promise to honor the agreements we'd reached after the new Congress came in the following year. By the end of our negotiations in late May, we had pushed a far-from-perfect bill through the House.

Reflecting the accelerating deterioration of the housing market, our new bill was tougher than the House version of 2005 in its regulation of Fannie Mae and Freddie Mac. I also dropped the requirement that at least 10 percent of the low-income housing trust fund money go for homeownership and replaced it with a prohibition on more than 10 percent of the funds going for that purpose. In a new provision, 75 percent of the rental fund had to support housing that was affordable to extremely low-income families.

While neither the administration nor many of the committee Republicans were fond of these last provisions, their recognition of the need for reform outweighed any objections. Then we sent the bill to the Senate, which refused to act on it for more than a year.

With the reform of Fannie and Freddie no longer immediately pending, I turned the committee's attention to the very serious problem of irresponsible subprime lending. We moved on two fronts. We summoned Federal Reserve officials and insisted that they finally invoke the authority they'd been given to regulate mortgages. Simultaneously, Brad Miller and Mel Watt conducted a series of meetings with interested parties to help revive their bill directly restraining subprime lending.

While Treasury Secretary Paulson was not focused on this part of the problem, we did have a strong Bush administration partner in the subprime reform field. Federal Deposit Insurance Corporation chair Sheila Bair was one of the happiest accidents I have encountered in the federal government. In 2004, Bush made it clear that he was appointing a woman to head that important agency—a relevant fact since few women had served as financial regulators. His choice was Diana Taylor, the highly respected superintendent of banks under Republican governor George Pataki in New York. But after submitting her name, Bush suddenly asked the Senate committee to return it before taking any action on her confirmation. No official explanation was given, but I learned from various sources the bizarre story behind Bush's reversal.

Taylor is the partner of former mayor Michael Bloomberg, then and now one of America's staunchest advocates of sensible restrictions on guns. When Taylor's appointment was made known, the National Rifle Association complained to the White House that it was wrong for Bush to confer such a desirable benefit on someone so close to their number-one enemy, and the president caved in. This left the administration with a gap to be filled—they needed to find an experienced female Republican bank regulator. Given the sexism in the financial industry, there were not many available. Sheila Bair, who had worked on financial regulation under the first President Bush, was one, and she received the job. I do not know how strongly she was vetted, but it could not have been very thoroughly. She soon became one of the toughest, most socially conscious regulators I have worked with in thirty-two years, and I am dubious that the Bush people knew what—or who—they were getting when they named her. My guess is that she ranks with Justice David Souter on the list of high appointments by presidents named Bush who turned out to be much more liberal than expected.

We were hopeful that we could replicate the bipartisanship of our efforts on the GSE bill, especially because Spencer Bachus was now the Republican leader on the committee. But the opposition was both larger and fiercer than it had been before. For one thing, Bair was relatively isolated as a supporter of tough regulation in the Bush administration. Paulson was not opposed to us, but the issue was not on his very crowded radar screen. More important, the most conservative Republicans wanted to rein in or even abolish the GSEs, but they saw regulating subprimes as an affront to their basic ideology. We were committing the gravest sin in their economic worldview: We were interfering with the free market, telling willing lenders and willing borrowers that they could not make their deals.

An intellectual leader of the Republicans' fundamentalist bloc, Scott Garrett of New Jersey, put it this way:

> This increasing availability and affordability of subprime mortgage credit is and has been an important factor leading to the increase in homeownership in recent years. This bill may well limit now the products available to subprime borrowers, particularly minority borrowers, and will deprive many of those consumers from owning or maintaining a home . . . What we need to do is ensure that it does absolutely nothing to homeownership, particularly among minority communities who have benefited from the innovations that have occurred in the marketplace.

The very next day, *The Wall Street Journal* also celebrated subprime loans for expanding homeownership. Noting that "80% . . . are being repaid on time, and another 10% are only 30 days behind," the paper angrily complained that "Mr. Frank's legislation will ensure that far fewer of these loans are issued in the future." (After the crisis, *The Journal*'s passion for "marginal borrowers" cooled rapidly, decisively, and strategically. Its statements were airbrushed out of history.)

Resisting such arguments, Bachus stuck by his position and worked with us to successfully pass the bill. After he did so, the right-wing members of our committee went to the House leadership, not just to complain of Bachus's treasonous cooperation with us in increasing regulation but also to seek his replacement as ranking member. He survived, but only by accepting close supervision by his party's leadership. It became obvious to us over the next three years that he had been required to bring "minders" onto the minority staff who reported as much if not more to the Republican leadership than to him.

With this bill, unlike the GSE bill, we had little expectation of Senate approval. That would require sixty votes—and there was little chance that enough Republicans would defy *The Wall Street Journal*'s pronouncement of conservative orthodoxy to accomplish this. But the bill's House passage did have an effect. In 2008, the Federal Reserve, under Ben Bernanke's management, did some—not all—of what we were asking it to do. We would also include our subprime restrictions in the financial reform bill we passed after the crisis.

In the face of this record, I confess to some frustration that the "it was all the government's fault" line retains any credibility at all. Much of the reason it does is the prevailing deep skepticism about the public sector. Many people are eager to believe a story in which a government effort to help the poor is the source of the problem. The best example of this phenomenon at work is the book *Reckless Endangerment*, by Gretchen Morgenson and Joshua Rosner, which places particular emphasis on my own supposed misdeeds as a supporter of the GSEs. While they do express some criticism of the private sector, it is the government and the Democratic Party that emerge as the main villains in their telling.

Their account is highly partisan. While they do mention that Newt Gingrich, as Speaker, was somewhat supportive of Freddie Mac, incredibly, they make no reference to the $750,000 Freddie later paid him to lobby. The distortions continue when they state that "it wasn't until 2010, when Frank found himself in a relatively spirited contest for his congressional seat, that he spoke out with regret about his support for Fannie Mae. In August, Frank conceded that not every American should be a homeowner." Of course I expressed regret for my excessive optimism and my lateness in seeing the need for reform—but the fact is I'd been supporting efforts to rein in the GSEs since 2005. As to homeownership, the idea that I had previously been an advocate for universal homeownership reflects an impressive ability to ignore decades of history.

In their afterword, Morgenson and Rosner muddle the record further when they fault the Obama administration for failing to pass new legislation addressing Fannie and Freddie in 2011. The fact that the Republicans were by then in control of the House of Representatives never gets mentioned. In all of these instances, we can see how ideological necessity becomes the mother of historical invention.

Most important, when they argue that Fannie Mae and Freddie Mac were at the center of the crisis, and were in fact its most important cause, Morgenson and Rosner are advancing a minority view. Peter Wallison, a Republican member of the Financial Crisis Inquiry Commission, did conclude that "I believe that the sine qua non of the financial crisis was U.S. government housing policy." But three of his four fellow Republican members of the Commission disagreed. So did the widely respected bipartisan analyst Mark Zandi. Alan Blinder, who though a noted Democrat is also widely respected for his objectivity, writes, "Many other financial experts with whom I have discussed this matter see Fannie and Freddie as supporting actors, far from the star of the show. So do I." In *The Shifts and the Shocks*, Martin Wolf echoes Blinder when he writes, "It is certainly possible to accept that enthusiastic government promotion of home ownership, and in particular, the GSEs, played some role. But the view that this was the principal cause is entirely unconvincing . . . The view that the GSEs played a central role in encouraging the private sector to enter into the subprime housing mania is false." Wolf concludes that "the role of regulation was principally one of omission: policymakers assumed the system was far more stable, responsible, indeed honest, than it was."

The most important reason it makes no sense to blame Fannie Mae and Freddie Mac for causing the crisis is that neither institution ever made a bad loan. Their role was to securitize the loans that had been made by others. If they are at fault, it must be because they were somehow able to coerce lenders into making bad loans that they could then securitize. But in fact, they had no power over the loan originators. More important, they were neither the earliest entities to engage in large-scale securitization, nor were they the ones who securitized the worst of the loans. Of course, Fannie Mae and Freddie Mac did end up contributing to the problem—as many of us recognized early on in the crisis. That is why we made clamping down on the GSEs the Financial Services Committee's first item of business under my chairmanship.

If the GSEs were truly the key cause of the crash, then once they were put into conservatorship, the problem should have been solved. But in fact, every relevant official in even the Bush administration believed that further financial reform was needed. Only a right-wing fringe persists in thinking otherwise.

•

At the same time as we tried to curtail the GSEs, we were also engaged in two other important legislative efforts. Preventing abuses by credit card companies was one of the highest priorities of consumer advocacy organizations. Contrary to the fashionable view that it makes no difference which party controls what, they knew that a Democratic majority was a prerequisite for progress on this issue, and I was determined to live up to their expectations. Carolyn Maloney, a senior committee member, had kept that fight alive during Republican rule. Passing a tough credit card bill in 2009 was a gratifying example of how one member's persistence can pay off.

While opposition to the bill came from the Republicans, there was one important issue on which Democrats disagreed. Some of the most liberal members, both on and off the committee, wanted to impose caps on the interest rates that card issuers could charge. I opposed these caps, successfully.

Conservatives are typically mistaken when they portray liberals as opponents of capitalism and equate our support for reasonable regulation with opposition to the free market. But I acknowledge that some of my ideological allies fall into the trap of using rhetoric that seems to validate that accusation. Those on the left who decry private individuals or businesses on the grounds that they do things "just to make a profit" are as mistaken as conservatives who insist that "government is the problem." Our system requires recognition of the contribution each of these sectors makes to our society. Our private wealth is generated by the incentive to increase one's prosperity. Our job as liberals is not to obliterate that healthy motivation, but to contain it, by reasonable rules and by modifying its tendency, if totally unrestrained, to produce excessive, dysfunctional inequality.

Imposing rate caps on credit card companies seemed to me an unnecessary intrusion into the workings of the market. But we did ban one practice of the card issuers. That was the so-called universal default, according to which companies *retroactively* raised interest rates on debt that consumers had already incurred, not because they were in arrears on their payments but because they had been involved in a dispute over debt with a third party. No free-market principle justified forcing consumers who had never missed a payment to the card issuers to pay higher rates for purchases.

At the same time, our bill did not prevent issuers from raising rates *prospectively*. We did require that customers receive forty-five days' notice before such increases took effect. But that measure was a recognition of the role of the market, not a rejection of it, since it would enable consumers to shop for better rates.

The credit card bill went nowhere in the Senate due to the narrowness of the Democratic majority there. But it did become law after the 2008 election brought more Democrats to that body. The most authoritative study of its impact, by the Pew Charitable Trust, reports that it created a "new equilibrium," where rates flattened, penalties declined, and certain deceptive practices disappeared.

•

Our other major effort was less successful and would mark the beginning of my greatest legislative frustration. By 2007, foreclosures on home mortgages were exploding. Home prices were dropping rapidly. It was not only people who had received inappropriate mortgages who were losing their homes. Like many others, I had failed to anticipate the collapse of inflated home prices across the country.

We drafted a proposal to facilitate foreclosure relief. But there was one central problem we could not solve: Reducing foreclosures required reducing mortgage payments, but who would bear the cost of that? The easiest answer—public funds—was politically impossible. After all, even at the peak of the foreclosure wave, most homeowners were meeting their mortgage obligations, and many of them were vocally opposed to seeing their tax dollars go to reduce other people's mortgage payments. There was some validity to their objection. It is true that many of those who faced the loss of their homes had been victims of unscrupulous lenders, but others had willingly paid very high prices for conventional mortgages. In an undeniable number of cases, they had cashed in on the price spiral, taking out second mortgages to increase their own cash while adding to their indebtedness.

There was one possible solution that would avoid the need for public money. Before I got to the House, Congress had amended bankruptcy law to exclude primary residences from bankruptcy protections. Oddly, it was possible to discharge debts owed on your second and third homes, but you could not safeguard the home in which you lived. House Democrats did pass a bill to amend this by allowing homeowners to reduce their mortgage debts in exactly the same way bankruptcy proceedings allowed them to reduce other debts—but it lost in the Senate. Some of my liberal colleagues blamed the big banks for this loss. But their influence is exaggerated. As I knew from our tough battle to get the bill through the House, the most effective opposition came from the thousands of community bank and credit union presidents in constituencies all over the country.

Surveying government efforts to deal with the foreclosure problem is analogous in one way to surveying English history. Both feature one constant. The English at any given point can be seen mistreating the Irish. Our government can similarly be observed not doing much to reduce foreclosures. (This story is very well told by Alan Blinder, former vice chairman of the Federal Reserve, in his fine book *After the Music Stopped*.)

•

By the summer of 2008, the Senate was ready at last to act on the Fannie and Freddie reform bill we'd passed the previous year. A compromise package passed overwhelmingly, 72 to 13. The House margin was still comfortable, 272 to 152, but the no votes included most of the Republicans. Six years later, Mel Watt, who'd become the director of the Federal Housing Finance Agency with my strong support, recognized that Fannie and Freddie were sufficiently profitable at last to begin contributing to the low-income housing trust fund. As of January 1, 2015, the fund was operating—and I consider this to be one of the biggest achievements of my career.

The large vote against the reform bill in the House reflected the widening, increasingly angry gap between Paulson and the very conservative bloc that dominated the House Republican Conference. The House Republicans, especially on the Financial Services Committee, believed strongly in unrestricted free enterprise. They did not see the need for government to deal with the consequences of the failure of large financial institutions or to provide some means of protecting thirty-year fixed-rate mortgages. No lender will issue a thirty-year fixed-rate mortgage at a reasonable rate without some protection against future increases in interest rates. Paulson and I and others agreed that the structure of Fannie and Freddie needed replacing, but we didn't want to do it in a way that would jeopardize the thirty-year fixed-rate mortgage.

As a result, I became the primary congressional defender of George Bush's secretary of the treasury and the most prominent opponent of the House Republicans. (I share Paulson's appreciation of the full support he received from President Bush in the face of fierce Republican criticism.)

As the economy deteriorated, my friendly relationship with Paulson carried over to our increasingly frequent conversations about his efforts to put out fires in the financial sector. The biggest flare-up came in mid-March of that year, when he and Fed Chairman Bernanke orchestrated the purchase of the failing Bear Stearns by JPMorgan Chase. The free-market fundamentalists on our committee reacted with rage to what they saw as a complete abrogation of the basic principles of capitalism, and they launched a full-throated attack on its authors. They demanded that I immediately convene a public hearing at which they could excoriate Paulson and Bernanke.

I refused. Of course the administration's decision raised policy questions that were matters for our committee to consider—but not instantly, and not in isolation. With the financial world already unsettled by the collapse of a major institution, it was not the time for dozens of my colleagues to add to the turmoil. And I agreed with Paulson that the most relevant question for legislators to address now was not the specifics of that spectacular transaction but how we could establish procedures to handle such crises in the future. Pointing out that the hastily cobbled together ad hoc response to the Bear Stearns failure was hardly an ideal policy model was easy. Stoking public anger by unfairly impugning the motives of Paulson and Bernanke was damaging.

I had, I confess, a secondary, political motive for trying to tamp down the indignation. In the short term, Democrats would have benefited from a very public airing of this bitter Republican civil war. But I feared that in the longer perspective, the big loser would be the public's confidence in the fairness and competence of government. Given the circumstances we were in, there was no popular way for the government to stanch the economic bleeding. And I was certain the public would be more critical of the government's disturbing but necessary actions than of the private sector's irresponsibility that made them necessary. It would hardly do any good for our committee to stoke that fire. While right-wing Republicans would be most vehement, I knew that there were a few committee Democrats who would find the temptation to demagogue irresistible. Even the more responsible Democrats would be tempted to join in the criticism, albeit in a less ideologically sweeping fashion.

A large part of the problem was institutional. It is much easier for legislators to enhance their political standing by attacking executive branch actions than by defending them. When a president, or governor, or mayor does something, people who welcome the action understandably give credit to the official who undertook it. Media attention to a statement from Congressman X praising the president's decision is a rarity. Committee members who use their time in a hearing to express their support for Secretary Y do not show up on television. I am not a regular Internet browser, but I would be very surprised if a clip of a senator being nice to an executive branch official ever went viral. In my forty years of legislating, the only occasion I can remember when my defense of a chief executive made the news, generated supportive mail, or earned any thanks was the Clinton impeachment.

In many individual cases, of course, legislative criticism of the executive branch is fully justified. Nonetheless, the cumulative effect of the incentive for legislators to denounce, deplore, and disagree is to strengthen the prevailing antigovernment attitude. I had not found many reasons to help Ronald Reagan with his agenda, but I did find common ground several times with George W. Bush's appointees. As chairman, I had the right to decide when to hold hearings and how to structure them. This gave me a chance to counter my colleagues' attraction to the attack mode, and I made the most of it—to the benefit of the Bush and later the Obama administrations.

•

As a longtime critic of the Fed, I was especially pleased by Ben Bernanke. I had no reason to think Bernanke would be very different from his predecessor when he became chairman in 2006. He had been Bush's go-to guy for important economic appointments. But by 2010 he had joined Souter and Bair on my list of pleasant surprises from presidents named Bush.

In 2008, Bernanke departed from Greenspan's path when he pushed the Fed to invoke its HOEPA authority and promulgate rules restricting the subprime market. It was firm evidence that he did not share Greenspan's zealous antiregulatory stance and a welcome indication that he saw cooperation with Congress as important.

Turf battles are the occupational hazard of high executive officials, and treasury secretaries and Fed chairs have not always worked in perfect harmony. But Paulson and Bernanke came as close to that as is humanly possible. They combined a strong belief in the market with a recognition of the need for good regulation. My decision to work with them wholeheartedly was reinforced by their expressed commitment to work with Congress to establish a larger, more appropriate role for the public sector when things calmed down.

In the spring and summer of 2008, a pattern developed. Every other Friday afternoon or so, after the markets closed, Paulson would depress me with another phone call advising me of some looming disaster and seeking my reaction to his proposed response—which was usually supportive, sometimes a suggested tweak.

But one Friday he gave me good news. A constituent of mine, Yang Jianli, was a Chinese-born American citizen with a determination to bring democracy to China that made Don Quixote look faint-hearted. He had gone to China, been arrested and expelled, and banned from ever returning. Undaunted, he reentered, illegally, and was promptly rearrested. His strong point was bravery, not discretion. This time the Chinese sent him to prison for a very long time—it was not clear for how long, as is typically the case in that closed society. I had joined in a variety of efforts to cajole, pressure, embarrass, and otherwise persuade the Chinese to release him and let him rejoin his family. Nothing worked until I decided to ask Paulson to help.

As secretary of the treasury, he was the lead official in the ongoing Chinese-American economic dialogue and had developed very good ties with his counterpart. After holding a meeting in my office with him, his top aides, and members of my staff to discuss financial issues, I asked everyone but him to leave, which probably induced serious agita among both sets of assistants. The fear that two principals left alone might come to an arrangement that omits appropriate attention to some important point is common in Washington. But they soon were reassured. Knowing that Paulson was about to leave for China, I outlined the situation regarding Yang Jianli, stressed the great distress it was causing his children and wife, and asked him to intervene. Although neither he nor I needed any additional incentive, I did note that this would be politically helpful to me at a time when I was under some criticism for collaborating with the administration in a way that some of my supporters thought inappropriately kind to the financial elite.

Paulson's next phone call came while Jim and I were spending a weekend on Fire Island at the home of our friend Andy Tobias. He told me that he had succeeded, and that Yang Jianli was as we spoke on a plane to the United States. Chinese politics being what it was, he cautioned that he had no assurance that the decision to release him might not be overturned, and I should therefore say nothing until he had landed in San Francisco. Paulson himself had waited until the plane had left Chinese airspace to inform me. It proved to be of little use to me politically, because the human rights advocate who had been my interlocutor on the issue decided to announce the release himself, with no reference to me or Paulson. The good deed of which I was so proud went unpunished, but it also went largely unnoticed. Despite this political disappointment, the phone call I made to inform Yang's family stands as one of the emotional highlights of my public life.

Within a month, the bad news phone calls returned, and with a vengeance. Jim and I were in New York for a Democratic Congressional Campaign Committee fund-raiser when Paulson called to tell me that Lehman Brothers was on the verge of collapse, and that this would be the most serious blow yet to the financial system. Later that evening, he called again with more reassuring news—Barclays Bank in England was prepared to rescue Lehman, just as JPMorgan had stepped in to take over Bear Stearns. He expressed relief for this transatlantic help; he had been unable to find any American bank to take on the burden. I cite this to refute the view that Paulson was intimidated by the fear of right-wing Republican criticism into letting Lehman fail. The next morning I learned that the British authorities had vetoed the Barclays option. And so another important firm disappeared, this time into bankruptcy.

When Lehman failed, the free-market fundamentalists had gotten their wish, but not many of them were happy with the consequences. The global shutdown of credit markets spread fear of a worldwide economic collapse. It was clear the government had to do something. I could not resist—candidly, I did not even try to resist—a loud "I told you so." I noted that our experiment with the pure free market had lasted about twenty-four hours, and I announced that I would introduce a resolution declaring September 15 "Free Market Day."

I had to make the most of this chance to taunt my conservative colleagues because my job was about to become degrees of magnitude harder, and equally less enjoyable. The next day, I joined the other congressional leaders in answering a summons from Bernanke and Paulson to an emergency meeting. I was not to get my life back for more than two years.

10

REFORMING WALL STREET

On Tuesday, September 16, Bernanke and Paulson summoned us to Harry Reid's office to discuss the latest terrible news, and their response to it. Their plan came as a shock to us. With help from the Treasury, the Fed would advance $85 billion to the insurance giant AIG, in the hope of forestalling a general meltdown of the financial system.

AIG's great success in selling actual insurance had produced great profits—more, we discovered, than they knew what to do with in a sensible way. As a result, they'd gone into selling "credit default swaps"—a security that became the poster child for Warren Buffett's description of derivatives as "instruments of financial mass destruction." The result was cataclysmic. (It is relevant to note that this problem was entirely of AIG's doing. Not even the most devout free-market fundamentalist could think of a way to blame Fannie Mae and Freddie Mac for AIG's recklessness.)

Paulson and Bernanke were not asking Congress for any action when they met with us. Nonetheless, what they were spending was a great amount, even by federal government standards, and their words startled us greatly. I have found it generally to be the case that when I do not understand some complex, unfamiliar transaction, most others don't either, and I pride myself on being sufficiently self-assured to confess my ignorance. And so I asked Bernanke a simple question: "Where did you get 85 billion dollars?" Referring to a 1932 statute allowing the Fed to lend money, and to the total amount of money under its control, he replied in his usual calm manner: "I have *850* billion dollars."

But the very next day, it turned out that the Fed's largesse was not enough. The panic had become widespread, and even institutions that had been more careful than AIG about incurring debt would need some financial backstop to avoid collapse. Not even the wonderfully elastic Section 13(3) that Bernanke had cited could provide a deep enough money pot. "We are past the point of what the Feds and Treasury can do on their own," Bernanke told his fellow administration officials.

This is where Congress had to come in. We reconvened on Thursday evening in Pelosi's conference room to hear the bad news twins tell us that we had to appropriate hundreds of billions of dollars right away to prop up desperate firms—otherwise, there might not be a functioning economy by the next week. Paulson did not tell us exactly how many hundred billion he thought necessary, sensibly deciding to administer the terrible medicine in two doses. The next day he announced that his target was $700 billion. It was an admittedly arbitrary number, but it was of the approximate order of magnitude required while still being sufficiently short of $1 trillion to avoid complete political toxicity.

The response of the assembled congressional leadership was supportive, with the exception of the senior Senate Banking Committee Republican Richard Shelby. The economy was unmistakably in free fall, and no one—Shelby included—had any alternative plan to reverse it. Never in my career has Henny Youngman's "Compared to what?" answered itself so conclusively.

We accepted the need for quick action, but the members unanimously told the administration officials that there was no way we could write the necessary bill in only a few days. We correctly assumed that an immediate announcement of our intention to act would sufficiently reassure the country—and the world. Speaking for Democrats, I also stressed the need for restrictions on top executives' compensation. Their misjudgments had provoked the crisis. Why should they be the immediate beneficiaries of federal money to alleviate it? To my disappointment, Paulson resisted this request. His explanation for his opposition still stands as one of the worst things I have ever heard any responsible person say about the personal values of the leaders of the financial community.

Paulson did not defend the compensation levels of the industry's leaders, nor did he say, as many were, that Congress had no right "meddling" in the matter. His objection was entirely pragmatic. If government assistance came with restrictions on compensation, Paulson warned, the executives' resentment at this interference with their prerogatives would lead some of them to refuse to participate. And widespread participation was essential. If only the most troubled institutions took part, taking the money would become a self-fulfilling prophecy that the entity was on its last legs.

As the extraordinary Troubled Asset Relief Program took shape, Pelosi designated me the House Democrats' lead negotiator. I was flattered but also uneasy. Making decisions for yourself can be hard when conflicting values and complex realities are involved. But making them as the delegate of some greater authority is infinitely harder. The question is no longer just what is the best way to reconcile the competing considerations but whether your balancing act will seem appropriate to those on whose behalf you are acting.

My self-doubt was compounded by the recognition that I had not yet fully mastered the subject matter. I joined the Banking Committee because I wanted to work for rental housing for low-income people. I added to this agenda my interest in making the World Bank and the International Monetary Fund more socially responsible. But I had never focused on the workings of private financial institutions, except when Massachusetts banks asked for help in coping with some legal quirk that was a problem for them. Since Massachusetts banking laws predated those of the country, there were sometimes glitches that needed fixing.

By the time of our negotiations, I prided myself on having become very well informed, but I was still self-administering my crash course. I needed help, both in representing the Democratic membership and on the substance of the bill. Fortunately, one of my colleagues supplied both. Rahm Emanuel had worked in the financial industry and was a member of the House Democratic leadership. I asked Pelosi if I could call on him to work with me. He agreed, and we immediately became a very effective team.

The TARP bill that followed was an insufficiently understood bipartisan accomplishment. Indeed, there's no more compelling example in our peacetime history of one party in Congress putting aside any consideration of political advantage and extending complete cooperation to a president of the opposite party. The Bush administration's request for extraordinary legislative powers came at the most fraught time in America's political calendar—six weeks before a presidential election. Conventional wisdom about politics says that in that time frame, as things got worse for the country, the fortunes of Republican candidates should have been devastated. Despite this, Pelosi, Reid, Chris Dodd (chairman of the Senate Banking Committee), and I, with the full backing of the other Democratic leaders in both houses, did everything we could to ensure adoption of the administration's plan. At no point in any of the Democratic strategy sessions in which I participated—and I was part of all the important ones—did anyone even allude to the electoral benefits we would reap if we made a convincing show of being helpful but stopped short of the extraordinary effort that would be needed to guarantee success. To the extent we had any political motive for seeking to restrict executive compensation and protect taxpayers, it was to win votes in the House and Senate, not on Election Day.

•

Our role was critical because Democrats were not only supportive of the Bush position but also far more supportive than his fellow party members, who'd become so hostile to government action. In one of the most unexpected emotions I'd had since discovering at fourteen that I was sexually attracted to other males, I came to feel sympathy for Spencer Bachus, the Financial Services Committee's ranking Republican member. His obvious instinct to be helpful was overruled by the Republican leadership. This put him in the humiliating position of attending bipartisan meetings under the explicit instruction that he was neither to agree to anything nor to explain very clearly why not. The House Republican whip, Eric Cantor, did put forward a scheme for some form of insurance against failure that Paulson knew would do no good. The treasury secretary unsuccessfully tried to downplay his views of Cantor's approach in the interest of intraparty comity. Unable to fully observe our partisan monasticism, we Democrats needled Paulson into giving his real opinion of Cantor's proposal.

As negotiations over our financial rescue package accelerated, the presidential campaign pitting Barack Obama against John McCain intruded itself. On September 24, John McCain endorsed the House Republicans' refusal to support our efforts. He also insisted on delaying the upcoming presidential debate and suspending his campaign so that he could fly to D.C. and settle what he claimed was a serious enduring dispute over the bill. As I put it at the time, McCain's maneuver was "the longest Hail Mary pass in the history of either football or Marys."

Furious at being blindsided while I was doing everything I could to maximize Democratic votes for a politically unappealing bill, I called Paulson and vented. I do not remember everything I said, but I do recall beginning the conversation with the phrase "What the fuck." He did his best to mollify me and assured us that he and the president were doing everything they could to keep their copartisans on board. In fact I knew that this was true, but at that point in a very tension-filled week, I had to yell at somebody.

I'd previously had good relations with McCain. I had been his ally in passing the McCain-Feingold, Shays-Meehan campaign finance reform bill—in the good old days before five Supreme Court justices decreed that unlimited campaign spending was a constitutional necessity. But I did realize that when I analogized his intervention in the TARP talks to Mighty Mouse singing, "Here I come to save the day," I would weaken the bonds of our friendship.

At McCain's behest, President Bush convened a special White House meeting. I am told that the administration, probably with McCain's eager acquiescence, had sought to leave me off the list of attendees. But that would have required excluding Bachus, as well as Shelby and Chris Dodd, so I was included—a form of access by association. In any case, if the ensuing events had been portrayed on *The West Wing*, they would have been criticized as an outrageous departure from that show's sober, realistic depiction of national politics. (I will pass over the bizarrely scripted dark fantasy of *House of Cards*,

which too many uninformed viewers believe bears some remote re-
semblance to the facts.)

The meeting was ideal from our standpoint. Pelosi and Reid began the session by designating Senator Obama our spokesman. When
he finished agreeing with the Bush administration's stance, it was
obviously McCain's turn to speak. But he didn't—at least not substantively. He said that he was attending to make sure that House
Republicans were given a chance to present their view, and he declined to state his own preference. The other Democrats reiterated
our support for the president. We also repeated our request that Mc-
Cain tell us what he thought personally was the best way to proceed,
and he continued to refuse. I joined in pressing him, unaware, until I
was informed later, that I had violated protocol by speaking out in a
meeting with the president without having been called on. In my
defense I noted that the president had made no effort to run the
meeting and had in fact sat there throughout looking bemused. One
of my Republican colleagues whispered to me that he looked as if
he was already mentally back in Texas.

While I was not the only one seeking an answer from McCain, I
did take pride in learning from Paulson's later report that McCain
had called him the next day to explain that "the reason I didn't say
anything at the end was because it's pretty hard to say anything with
Barney Frank screaming at you." I do not think that my admittedly
emphatic tone qualified as screaming, and in any case that does not
explain why he hadn't said anything substantive at any other point in
the session. Any responsibility I might have felt for McCain's silence
dissolved when Jim pointed out that it seemed highly unlikely that a
man who had shown incredible bravery in resisting North Vietnam-
ese torture would be intimidated because I raised my voice in a
White House meeting.

After Bush dismissed us, with obvious relief, the Democratic participants caucused to help Obama decide what he would say to the
assembled media in the White House driveway. That caucus proved
memorable. Paulson joined us, got down on one knee before Pelosi,
and begged her not to react to his party's theatrics by moving away
from the deal. She didn't—although my recollection is that she did

move slightly away from the startling sight of a kneeling secretary of the treasury.

Pelosi was good to her word, as she has always been in my experience, and we went back to the House to prepare for the vote. With both parties in the Senate strongly supportive, it was clear that the outcome turned on the House, where Democrats would have to supply the bulk of the votes. The Democratic leadership launched a full-scale effort to muster support.

I became the bill's main presenter. Over the next two evenings, I spent hours explaining and defending it to our undecided members. Fortunately, we had more votes when these sessions concluded than we had at the start.

•

Through all the stress and strain that fall, Jim remained the most understanding partner. He had not signed up for a D.C.-based relationship. Herb and Sergio had lived in Washington; Jim did not. His business was in Maine, where he had put up a large share of the awnings on the businesses lining Main Street in Ogunquit. His house was a short distance from his favorite surfing sites, and he was also within a few hours' drive of good snowboarding locales. In the first months of 2007, I did not foresee any serious problem with our two homes. Being chairman does put more demands on your time, but offsetting that is the control you have over the committee's schedule. With somewhat more attention to time management than I was used to, I could give both my personal and official lives the time—and, more important, the emotional energy—required.

Then came the crisis. By 2008, Jim was sharing my Friday afternoon doses of bad news from Paulson and becoming one of Ogunquit's leading authorities on subprime mortgages, securitization, and failing financial institutions. The equanimity with which he made the transition from being a purely private citizen, practicing his craft in a small town, to immersion in a global financial crisis was one of the greatest gifts I have ever received.

The week Lehman collapsed, I was scheduled to attend a road race in memory of my mother, held by Kit Clark House, a leading social service group in Boston; the fall dinner of the Harvard LGBT organization; the Working Waterfront Festival in New Bedford; and a dinner for the prime minister of Cape Verde. These were no-stress, celebratory events with an interesting range of convivial people, none of whom would want to talk about financial gloom and doom. We never got to attend any of them. Instead, I called Jim from D.C. after the second grim meeting of that week to ask a big favor. I would be spending the weekend at the Capitol and I wanted him there to help me get through what I knew would be a very stressful time. He agreed to join me.

On Saturday morning, we were on the way from the Capitol subway to Pelosi's office when we were spotted by a crowd of journalists. They rushed toward us, cameras bobbing, mikes recording, and pads outthrust. Unused to even a peaceful horde rushing toward him, Jim was startled, and his wonderful protective instinct toward me kicked in. The result was a photo that went across the country showing Jim, with his eyes wide and his mouth open, holding his arm like a shield in front of me. It looked like an outtake from a cheesy Western when the heroes are surprised by the sudden appearance of a very large number of hostile Indians. Fortunately in this case, the charging crowd was unarmed, although not entirely unhostile.

Later that weekend, he joined the group of staffers and others who sat outside the conference room while we tried to reach a deal on the TARP legislation. At some point, Rahm Emanuel had been warned by his staff that accounts of our private session were being sent out electronically. Channeling Wyatt Earp, he stood up and demanded everybody's BlackBerry—not mine, since I don't like them. He put the devices in a wastebasket and then spread them out on a table in another room to be picked up after the meeting.

Jim wasn't in the midst of these proceedings because we wanted to make a point. He was there because I needed personal support. But the point was being made nevertheless. One of a handful of people engaged in the highest level of policy making in the American government at a time of crisis was a gay man accompanied by his partner. Major political players would recognize the significance of this in various ways. In his memoir of the crisis, Hank Paulson noted that when he wanted to speak privately with me at a time when the negotiators had temporarily taken a break and scattered to separate places, his aides found Barney Frank "on the third floor [of the Capitol] having dinner with his partner, Jim Ready, and asked him to meet with us." Given that Paulson's memoir was published in 2011, when same-sex marriage was still strongly opposed by most Republicans, this was an example of gratuitous niceness.

When I presented the bill to our caucus, I witnessed an expression of what by then was virtually unanimous Democratic support for same-sex marriage. The party leadership provided buffet dinners at these sessions. When one of my turns onstage ended up lasting more than an hour, I said that I hoped that we wouldn't run out of Chinese food before my colleagues ran out of questions. Jim had been watching from the side of the room where the staff assembles, holding a plate of food for me but refraining from delivering it to me onstage on the assumption that it would be a breach of decorum. Still unaccustomed to treating an important meeting of a hundred and fifty or so congresspeople as if it was his kitchen, he tried very hard to be inconspicuous. Within seconds, he was spotted as he cautiously came forward to hand me the plate and was greeted with a spontaneous, affectionate "aaw"—as in, "isn't that cute"—from the female members, followed by cheers from most of the room. This enthusiastic vocal affirmation of a gay relationship from members of Congress in the midst of these tense, high-stakes deliberations was incredibly moving. America—and I—had come a long way since 1954.

Democrats were not the only members who welcomed Jim's presence. He told me a few nights later that when he ran into a Republican member with whom I had regular, not always harmonious, dealings, he was told, "I figured you were in town. Barney was nicer to me today than is usual."

As the TARP vote approached, the Republican leadership was also lobbying their members, with Democratic majority leader Steny Hoyer and Republican whip Roy Blunt coordinating their efforts. When we believed we were as strong as we were going to be, Pelosi brought the compromise bill to the floor on Monday, September 29. To the world's shock, the bill failed. While Democrats voted 140 to

95 for the bill, Republicans voted heavily against it, 65 to 133, providing significantly fewer yes votes than everyone knew would be
needed for passage. It is fair to say that many members voted no
while praying yes, as an old legislative adage has it. Such an outcome
illustrates the fundamental mistake of applying Lord Acton's famous
dictum in all contexts. I agree that "absolute power corrupts absolutely" where it exists in authoritarian governments. But in the legislative bodies of representative governments, it is not power that
corrupts but impotence. Members of a parliamentary minority are
much more likely to vote no on a substantively necessary, politically
unpopular measure than the majority who know they will bear some
collective responsibility for failure. Anyone doubting this need only
look at the behavior of those many members—myself included—
who voted against raising the debt limit when in the minority but
proclaimed the need to be responsible and vote yes in the majority. (I
am hopeful that the debacle of 2013 has put a stop to this particular
form of gamesmanship.)

With the defeat on the first vote, and the entirely predictable
stock market crash that followed, our efforts went into higher gear.
Even before the final vote was tallied, I made one important intervention. When the scoreboard showed that the noes were going to
win, the leaders of both parties rushed to the well of the House to try
to get members to switch from no to yes. This is a common pattern
on close votes, although usually the party leaderships are working
against each other. I am ordinarily a supporter of my party's efforts in
such cases, and sometimes a participant. But this time I knew it
would be disastrous. Passing TARP through a very public display of
pressure on members would have added to the widespread view that
the establishment was rigging the game to favor their powerful
friends. Fortunately, several others shared my views, and we succeeded in persuading everyone involved to back off, accept defeat for
the day, and work in a calmer manner for passage.

A priceless rhetorical opportunity soon arose. After the vote, Eric
Cantor issued a very silly statement in which he tried to absolve his
party colleagues from responsibility. He explained that many of them
had changed their yes votes to no because they'd been deeply

offended by Nancy Pelosi's floor speech, in which she'd blamed Republican deregulatory policies for the crisis. He had obviously not thought this through, and I took advantage of his mistake. When a reporter asked Pelosi to defend herself against the charge, I stepped to the mike. "In other words," I said, "Mr. Cantor is telling us that some of his Republican colleagues who agreed that passing the bill that their president was strongly supporting was in the national interest, and would keep the economy from further damage, nevertheless voted to kill it because Nancy Pelosi hurt their feelings." Expressing my surprise at their sensitivity, and their sudden distaste for partisan remarks on the House floor, I made an offer with all the mock sincerity I could muster. "I am prepared," I continued, "in what I acknowledge is an uncharacteristic display of conciliation on my part, to apologize to all of those offended Republicans, in the hope that this will let them put the national interest ahead of any hurt feelings that remain." (Since no transcript exists, this is probably not verbatim, but it is everything I said and is very close to the exact form.) Neither Cantor nor any other Republican tried that defense again.

Later that evening, I called Paulson to commiserate, but also to assure him that we would win the next vote. I compared some of the TARP opponents to a young teenager who became so angry at his parents that he decided to leave home, only to get a few blocks away on a cold night and think better of the idea and come back.

I do not claim major credit for the vote switches that passed the bill on Friday, but I am convinced that I helped remove some of the obstacles to the bill's passage. It is noteworthy that even with a very angry business community pressing the case for the bill, a majority of House Republicans remained opposed. The final vote was 172 to 63 among Democrats, and 91 to 108 among the president's supposed supporters.

The passage of TARP and its subsequent prompt execution did not solve the crisis, but they did buy time for a series of other measures that collectively kept the meltdown from becoming the deep worldwide depression it had threatened to be.

As the 2008 election neared, my next concern was my reelection. My very able, astute chief of staff, Peter Kovar, had alerted me that opposition to TARP was audible in my district. With Dan Payne's great TV ads, and a Republican opponent who'd served time in prison after violating the probation sentence he'd received for hitting his teenage daughter, I won easily—too easily, because it left me overconfident when I faced a more serious challenge in a much tougher political climate two years later. That same day, Barack Obama defeated McCain, and a new era of Democratic control happily beckoned.

I had not worked closely with Obama before the crisis. I was a strong supporter of Hillary Clinton in the fight for the Democratic nomination, and had even made a radio commercial for her that played in Massachusetts, a state she won decisively. My first dealings with Obama had come when we coordinated our strategy for responding to the financial crisis and, particularly, the meeting at the White House. Things had gone well. As he took office, I did have some concerns that he was going to underestimate the difficulties of working with the Republicans. When he made a comment that seemed to me to put some blame on Bill and Hillary Clinton for the bitter partisan fighting that had marked the 1990s, I thought he was being unfair to them. Knowing as I did how deeply the right wing had entrenched itself on the Republican side, when the presidential nominee said that he intended to govern in a "postpartisan manner," I said publicly that this had given me postpartisan depression. It was not that I thought working with Republicans was a bad idea; I was simply convinced that it was impossible. In this case, I believe I've been fully vindicated.

My relationship with Obama and his administration deepened during the two years we spent writing and passing the financial reform bill. After the Republicans took over the House in 2010, I became concerned that his unjustified hope for "postpartisanship" would be a problem, and I was particularly troubled when he offered to restrain Social Security cost-of-living increases for moderate-income elderly people in the vain hope of getting a deal with the Republicans. Fortunately for good public policy, Republican intransigence took that deal off the table. On the whole, my relations with

Obama, and my approval of his approach to governing, were very strong throughout this first term.

In histories of the Great Depression, I had read about the long and fraught interregnum between the defeat of Herbert Hoover and the inauguration of Franklin D. Roosevelt. The result was a constitutional amendment that advanced the incoming president's Inauguration Day from March 4 to January 20.

But to my dismay, even a shorter transition period turned out to be too long in this crisis. For the first time since 1932, a handover of the presidency from one party to the other was occurring in the midst of a national emergency. And to my regret, our efforts to aid homeowners would be lost in the shuffle.

In the original TARP legislation, we had included strong instructions to the administration to reduce foreclosures. This would be done through the direct use of TARP funds and by using the leverage the program gave us over the banks. Paulson's refusal to carry out these instructions led to my one major disagreement with him, which I expressed vigorously in a hearing I called for that purpose in November. His response, which I know was entirely honest, was that the imminent threat of total financial collapse required him to focus single-mindedly on the immediate survival of financial institutions, no matter how worthy other goals were.

In what I took as a manifestation of our mutual respect, Paulson agreed to include homeowner relief in his upcoming request for a second tranche of TARP funding. But there was one condition: He would do it only if the president-elect asked him to.

That condition was rejected by Obama, who noted that we have only one president at a time. My frustrated response was that he had overstated the number of presidents currently on duty—a comment that, I was emphatically told, achieved full bipartisan status by irritating the incoming and outgoing chief executives equally. I understood Obama's unwillingness to take responsibility before he had the concomitant authority, but I believed that the situation justified an exception to that rule.

Throughout my efforts to achieve foreclosure relief, I found Sheila Bair a valuable counterweight to Paulson and Timothy Geithner, whose influence had grown as he went from being president of the New York Fed to secretary of the treasury–designate. I liked, respected, and trusted Paulson and Geithner, and agreed with their general approach. But my instinct was that they felt a greater need to show deference to the financial community than the federal government had to. Bair's independence was a powerful reinforcement for me, especially given her own intellectual credentials and status as a Bush appointee. When we learned that Paulson and Geithner were likely to ask her to leave the FDIC before her term expired, Chris Dodd and I intervened to object. I told Geithner that he and the other male regulators were coming across like ten-year-olds in the tree house who had posted a sign that said NO GIRLS ALLOWED. This did not, however, mean that I was permanently allied with Bair against Geithner. After the crisis, Bair, Geithner, and Paulson would all write generously about me. I know I am regarded in some quarters as a curmudgeon. I offer as strong evidence against this view the fact that I got along with Bair and Geithner much better than they did with each other.

•

Thankfully, I got to spend some relatively unharried time with Jim between the postelection dispute over mortgage relief and the first serious legislative business of the new Congress. Even so, we remained in the spotlight—with sometimes unforeseen consequences.

In December, Lesley Stahl profiled me for *60 Minutes*. For the program, her crew had taped my appearance at a Christmas telethon run by a community action organization in Fall River. As we sat on the couch watching the broadcast, we saw footage of Jim, in his usual protective fashion, doing some needed last-minute repairs to my hair and tie before I went on camera. "The man helping the congressman," Stahl noted when she reappeared, "was not a constituent. That was his boyfriend, Jim Ready." Jim had not hidden his sexuality from the people he had been associating with for the past fifteen years, but he hadn't had occasion to announce it to everyone he had ever known. As of that moment, he wouldn't have to.

Jim was surprised by the reference, as were others—for example, his teammates from his hockey-playing days and some of his fellow surfers and high school classmates. In fairness to Stahl, she had asked him if it was okay if she mentioned his name, and being new to television, he had said yes without realizing how prominent the "mention" would be. That prominence was elevated by the timing of the segment. It led off a program that came on right after a New England Patriots game, generating a huge audience in our area. Jim's instant, entirely understandable shock soon became bemused acceptance, and then, to my relief, the enjoyment of the surprised but very supportive reaction of people from his past. My only suggestion was that we immediately call his parents, so that in case they had not been watching, they wouldn't wonder why their friends were talking about me and Jim in the coming days.

Obama's inauguration followed soon after. As a committee chairman, I was seated prominently at the front of the platform. Jim was also onstage, seated with the spouses of the other chairs and ranking minority members. At the close of the ceremony, we went to the luncheon—as opposed to lunch—in the Capitol for all of the important people in our government, along with other prominent guests. It was not a first—my late colleague Gerry Studds had brought his partner to the Clinton inauguration when he chaired the House Merchant Marine and Fisheries Committee. But it drew the most public attention, given my post-TARP high profile, and the post-1993 role of social media.

Unleashing our inner tourist, we made sure to memorialize the day. Two photos in particular are prominently displayed in my office. Jim's seatmate at the ceremony obligingly took a picture of him standing in the aisle during the ceremony, with the new president giving his address in the background. ("Gee, Uncle Jimmy," his eight-year-old nephew Kyle rebuked him. "You weren't paying attention.") And in a reminder that partisanship in Congress is not always personal, the photographer was Congressman Paul Ryan's wife, Janna. The other picture was taken after Jim had asked Obama for a hug. The president inscribed it, "To Jimmy—showing you love for keeping Barney under control!

•

When the inauguration was over, so was my recess. If I had been able to choose the two-and-a-half-year stretch of my life in which I would work the hardest, with the most at stake, it would not have been as I was turning seventy. But it was what it was.

In the wake of the crisis, Chris Dodd and I agreed on the need for comprehensive regulation of the financial industry. I began the 2009 legislative session eager to get started on this momentous task. But it took a while. As Robert Kaiser correctly quotes me in his book on our bill, *Act of Congress*, we made slow progress because 2008 refused to end.

In March, the country learned that AIG was about to pay $165 million in employee bonuses. Just as I have sometimes found the use of metaphors unavoidable, in this case I can think of no adequate substitute for a cliché: all hell broke loose. Infuriatingly to the public, the beneficiaries of this largesse were the employees of its Financial Products unit, precisely the ones who had incurred the $170 billion debt that had precipitated the crisis. Even more infuriating, there was nothing we could legally do about it.

In his memoir *Stress Test*, Tim Geithner, who'd become treasury secretary by then, reports that he called Ed Liddy, the new post-bailout CEO of AIG, to remonstrate. Liddy's response, apparently and very regrettably true, was that the company had signed binding, unshakable contracts, and that if it reneged on them, the employees would sue and win. Liddy was right on the law, but that only made the situation worse on the political side. Voters had seen the executive and legislative branches come together in the recent past to do a lot of things that had no precedent—and that some commentators said were unconstitutional. A large majority of them were wholly unprepared to accept our explanation that we had suddenly become legally impotent. The more popular view was that the political establishment was demonstrating an outrageous double standard: Take extraordinary steps to aid large financial institutions but hide behind dusty legal rules to avoid penalizing their egregious misbehavior.

Never before or since have I seen vehement, universal public anger reach such a white-hot level. I feared that we were in danger of losing our capacity to govern—not just to enact a rational financial reform bill but also to pass any legislation that required public trust in elected officials. The depth of my concern is best illustrated by my response to the AIG flare-up, which included the single stupidest thing I have ever done in my official life.

When Paul Kanjorski, the second-ranking Democrat on our committee, learned of the bonuses, he too called Liddy and then called a hearing of the subcommittee he chaired, which had jurisdiction over AIG. I had the authority to supersede him with a full committee meeting, but he had taken the lead on this issue and was entitled to chair the session. I attended as a member, and when it was my turn to ask questions, I screwed up big time. I asked Liddy to give us the names of the bonus recipients and threatened to initiate a subpoena if he didn't. He reacted with as much horror as a dignified CEO could exhibit in a formal hearing. He quite rightly refused, pointing out that there had already been death threats leveled against those involved.

In my concededly inadequate defense, I was motivated only partially by my own indignation. As committee chairman, I bore considerable responsibility for the difficult political position of members who had voted for a TARP bill, which included funds for AIG. Even more important, I knew I would be asking them to cast further difficult votes. Those votes would be punitive enough to anger the financial firms whose support many coveted. But they would not be sufficiently punitive to suit the mood of an electorate which, at that point, reminded me of the villagers in a Frankenstein movie who march on the laboratory with pitchforks and torches. In demanding names, I sought to reassure committee members and their constituents that I shared their fury.

Fortunately, wiser heads prevailed, especially on the committee staff. I was never better served by having aides who'd known me long enough and well enough to tell me how badly mistaken I had been. Realizing my error, I wrote to federal and state law enforcement officials telling them that I would drop my demand for names unless I could be reassured that it would not endanger anyone. As I expected—and hoped—I got no such reassurances and used this to justify withdrawing my threat of a subpoena. It was an admittedly transparent ruse, and it did not save much face, but it did give me a way to save my butt.

Chris Dodd fared less well, in a classic reaffirmation that no good deed goes unpunished. With great foresight and political judgment, he had successfully added a provision to the Economic Recovery Act capping the bonuses that could be paid out by TARP recipients. His provision also authorized the Treasury to claw back bonuses that were already paid. When the Treasury Department correctly commented that this last piece would be unconstitutional and could lead to litigation that would jeopardize the entire idea, he agreed to make the restrictions prospective only.

When the AIG bonuses became public, Dodd was blamed for enabling them. In fact, his amendment was an important safeguard against future abuses. Without it, there would have been no anti-bonus language at all. But in the irrationally angry atmosphere that prevailed, the accusation stuck and became a political problem as his reelection approached. (A word here about political semantics. Most people know the Recovery Act as the "stimulus bill." When we were considering it, our leadership consulted some public opinion research and deemed "Recovery" a more appealing title than "Stimulus." I found this counterintuitive, since everyone I know prefers being stimulated to recovering, but this was not in my committee's jurisdiction, so no one asked me.)

Feeling even more heat from fellow Democrats than I was, Pelosi acted promptly. She had the Ways and Means Committee put a bill on the floor levying a retroactive 90 percent tax on any high-level bonuses given out by TARP recipients—singling out AIG alone would have added a clearly unconstitutional bill of attainder to an already constitutionally dubious proposal. The proposed taxation of non-AIG employees made it easy for most Republicans to vote against the bill, but it did give Democrats a chance to show our constituents that our hearts (if not our minds) were in the right place. I didn't like the idea, but I knew that my voting no would attract a great deal of attention, seriously undermine the credibility of the effort, and diminish the political capital with my Democratic colleagues that I would need to get a financial reform bill adopted. A combination of the bill's over-reach and an abatement in public fury allowed the Senate leadership to ignore the tax proposal with little outcry.

But abatement is not disappearance. AIG's serial irresponsibility—running up enormous debts that it could not pay, then giving bonuses to the people responsible—inflicted serious political damage on our system immediately, and in the long run. I have not checked public opinion polls before and after March 2009, but I would be surprised if public confidence in government did not drop at that time. Even though most people do not recall the specifics of this fiasco today, the deep resentment it triggered remains embedded in their minds. I am convinced it is one of the reasons that TARP, which staved off total economic collapse and did not end up costing taxpayers, remains so reviled. Indeed, it is the most wildly unpopular highly successful major program in America's history.

Compounding the problem from my standpoint, the onus of public anger fell disproportionately and unfairly on the Democrats. Everything but the announcement of the bonuses happened while Bush was in power, and it was the Bush administration that resisted our effort to put stronger compensation restrictions in the original bill. But we were in power when the public learned of AIG's payments, and Chris Dodd was blamed for not preventing them, even though he'd tried the hardest to do just that. Additionally, and frustratingly, I came to realize that for much of the public, we are in power even when we aren't. The fact that we are the progovernment party merges in some voters' minds with the notion that we are the government—all of the time.

•

Once the AIG firestorm subsided, I was at last able to turn to comprehensive financial reform. The events of 2008 had made the need for a new system abundantly clear. It is true that the flood of imprudently granted mortgages was a major reason for the crisis, but our problems went far beyond that. The failure of Bear Stearns and the messy ad hoc response to it demonstrated that we needed rules to keep large banks and investment firms from incurring obligations they couldn't meet. If such firms failed nonetheless, we would also need a legal framework to keep that failure from destabilizing the entire system.

As I understood it, the financial industry's dramatically changed business model required equally far-reaching revisions in the way that industry was regulated. This recognition brought out my inner amateur economic historian. What we were experiencing, I concluded, was a third iteration of the need to reinvent regulation to fit a transformed private sector. In 1850, there were no large economic enterprises in the United States; our economy was essentially regional. By 1890, large nationwide businesses had been formed—steel, coal, oil, and railroad corporations became immensely powerful, and often colluded with each other. New regulation followed, first with the Sherman Antitrust Act of 1890, then after a lag during the conservative administrations of Grover Cleveland and William McKinley, in greater volume under Theodore Roosevelt, William Howard Taft, and Woodrow Wilson. By the end of that period, we had the Federal Trade Commission, the Interstate Commerce Commission, a national food and drug law, the Clayton Antitrust Act, the Federal Reserve System, and more. A new set of rules was created to govern the new national economy.

One set of innovations usually calls forth another. With large enterprises now dominating the economy, the stock market took on a new, greatly enhanced role. But there were no new rules for new forms of financing. Thus the New Deal set about establishing institutions to contain finance capitalism within reasonable bounds. Federal Deposit Insurance, administered by the new Federal Deposit Insurance Commission, the Securities and Exchange Commission, the Commodity Futures Trading Commission, and the Investment Company Act governing mutual funds were Franklin Delano Roosevelt's response.

This set of rules worked very well for fifty years. Then came the great changes that I described earlier: securitization, shadow banking, derivatives, the proliferation of financial engineering. This time, the ideology of deregulation had taken so strong a grip on our politics that the appropriate updated regulations were delayed for more than twenty-five years. Our great mistake was not deregulation but non-regulation. We waited too long to put new rules in place. In some cases, we even took pains to prevent new rules from being established. The Commodity Futures Modernization Act of 2000 exempted many derivatives from scrutiny.

My view of how to create a new regulatory framework had one central theme. The transformative innovations that began in the 1980s had weakened the linkage between risk and responsibility. Our job was to reestablish it. With very few exceptions, it was neither our intention, nor the effect of the legislation, to forbid the private sector from conducting transactions that had become part of the financial system. We did not want to inhibit institutions from making investments, placing bets, or engaging in speculation. We did want to ensure that when they carried out these activities they would remain responsible for at least a part of any losses and have the financial resources to meet that responsibility.

As we embarked on our effort, the Obama administration drew up an initial draft, reflecting the broad consensus that existed among those of us who had worked together since the financial crisis exploded. Given the concentration of expertise in the executive branch, and the existence of that consensus, we were happy to take it as a starting point. Dodd's Banking Committee and the Financial Services Committee I chaired would each mark it up, make changes, and proceed from there.

There were several major components of the bill. First, in tandem with the actions of international regulators who worked through the Basel Accords, it would raise capital requirements for banks and nonbanks alike. This additional capital would serve as a cushion against losses resulting from misjudgments or adverse economic conditions.

Second, and most important in my mind, we could require entities that packaged loans made by others and sold them as securities to retain some of the risk. They would keep "skin in the game." If the original loans defaulted, they would pay a price. This measure, we hoped, would correct the practices most directly responsible for the crisis.

Third, we would attempt to limit those "financial weapons of mass destruction" known as derivatives. We directed the regulators, particularly the Commodity Futures Trading Commission, to promulgate rules that would transform the $400 trillion derivatives market from one dominated by opaque individual deals between parties with prices known only to the participants into a much more open and transparent system.

The loud objections to our proposal reminded me that for many businesspeople in America, competition is a great spectator sport. They like to watch others engage in it, but they can readily produce reasons why it would be harmful in their own lines of work. When I met with two insurance company representatives, the younger of the two complained that if we made his company publish the price they planned to charge for a given deal, some other company could offer their counterparty a lower price. His older colleague quickly intervened to assure me that this explicitly anticompetitive argument was not their basis for opposing the rule. Further discussion made it clear that he objected to voicing the argument so openly, not its substance.

The reform bill also contained a Consumer Financial Protection Bureau—an idea that had been supported most prominently by Elizabeth Warren. The CFPB would take all the consumer protection functions away from all the various financial regulatory agencies and consolidate them into one independent bureau whose sole function would be to protect consumers in financial transactions. It would be lodged in the Federal Reserve for organizational purposes but granted complete independence from any Fed interference with its policies, its personnel, or its funding. Senator Dodd was the one who decided on this arrangement, and Elizabeth Warren and I agreed that it fully protected the CFPB's mission.

I am especially proud of one other provision—one I freely acknowledge had no connection to the crisis. It gratified me immensely when Bono, the U2 singer who has done so much to combat poverty, disease, and deprivation in the poorer parts of the world, publicly thanked me for including the section known as "publish what you pay." This part of the law requires any American company that is engaged in resource extraction in any country to make public all the money it has paid to any source, official or unofficial, in the country where the extraction takes place. The scandal of corrupt rulers profiting handsomely from such activities while their people get no benefit seemed to me an entirely legitimate subject for our attention.

●

Adopting a new framework for the operation of financial markets was one of the major tasks we faced in 2009. But what if the worst happened, and even under the new rules a major firm was in peril? Our other task was to find a better way of coping with financial institutions that could no longer operate. Federal officials should not have to choose between letting a major institution go bankrupt or propping it up—both terrible options. Bankruptcy meant letting the insolvent firm's unpaid debts course through the economy, leaving further financial damage in their wake. But bailouts also had serious defects. They created moral hazard, effectively protecting the institution's leaders and business partners from the consequences of its irresponsibility. The other problem with this approach was that it required using public—that is, taxpayer—money to protect the economy from reckless private sector behavior. This was rightly a very unpopular thing to do. Neither the abrupt, unbuffered bankruptcy of Lehman nor the $160 billion taxpayer lifeline to AIG was an acceptable precedent for the future.

And so the bill provided a third way, which was called the Orderly Liquidation Authority. Under its terms, if an institution's imminent failure threatens to destabilize the entire financial system, the institution is put into receivership, under the direction of the FDIC. The officers and directors are dismissed, and any funds available to the entity are used to reduce its indebtedness. If the institution's debts remain dangerous, the receiver can advance funds—the minimum required to prevent a crisis. The secretary of the treasury is then mandated to recover those funds by assessing a special tax on financial institutions with $50 billion or more in assets.

To be explicit, we were not offering anyone a bailout. In a case

like this, the institution fails. Unlike AIG, it is no longer a functioning private entity: Its officers are dismissed, its board is dissolved,
and the shareholders' equity is wiped out. Unlike Lehman, however,
the government could pay off some of the firm's debts to prevent its
failure from precipitating a chain reaction of other failures. Other
large financial institutions would then foot the bill for paying off
those debts. The rationale for this was clear. These institutions benefit from the increased assurances of a stable system and should bear
the cost of sustaining it.

The law makes this explicit in unusually straightforward statutory language:

SEC. 214. PROHIBITION ON TAXPAYER FUNDING.

(*a*) LIQUIDATION REQUIRED.—All financial companies put
into receivership under this title shall be liquidated. No taxpayer funds shall be used to prevent the liquidation of any
financial company under this title.

(*b*) RECOVERY OF FUNDS.—All funds expended in the liquidation of a financial company under this title shall be recov-
ered from the disposition of assets of such financial company,
or shall be the responsibility of the financial sector, through
assessments.

(*c*) NO LOSSES TO TAXPAYERS.—Taxpayers shall bear no
losses from the exercise of any authority under this title.

Despite the bill's very clear, legally binding directives, some critics
insisted that taxpayer-funded bailouts were permitted and "too big to
fail" was alive and well. Some of these critics simply ignored what the
law said. Others took a different, and an even less intelligent, tack.
According to them, even though the law specifically prohibits the
Treasury and Federal Reserve from advancing funds to keep an institution alive, if a major financial institution were to become insolvent,
there would be irresistible political pressure to violate federal law and
intervene. My question to those who make this case is a simple one:
"On what planet have you spent your time since 2008?" Certainly no
cogent—even coherent—observer of the backlash against TARP

could imagine voters insisting that one more big, failing bank receive a taxpayer bailout and a new lease on life.

In fact, a more realistic critique came from a few people on the opposite side of the issue, including Geithner, who feared that we'd shut the door on even temporary bailouts too tightly. Of course, there were also some who argued that the only way to end "too big to fail" was to keep institutions from getting too big. In this view, the only true safeguard is to break up the banks. Since the collapse of Lehman Brothers precipitated the crash, this must mean that no firm should be as large as Lehman was in 2008. This is an intellectually legitimate argument, but it needs much more fleshing out by its proponents. What would be the consequences of drastically reducing the size of ten or more major institutions within a short time frame? Should the federal government mandate these reductions? By what method? Will this put American institutions at a competitive disadvantage internationally? I have no objection in principle to the argument that smaller is better, but I have not seen any practical plan for downsizing.

•

As our committees marked up the bill, the legislative process went more smoothly than I had expected in both bodies. We knew we'd have to make modifications to the Obama administration's original draft, both for reasons of substance and to make sure we could get the legislation passed. Fortunately, the liberal organizations were unusually well organized and helpful with both the substance and the politics. A group called Americans for Financial Reform brought together a variety of experts with whom we worked closely throughout the process. On the creation of the Consumer Financial Protection Bureau, I formed a mutually trusting relationship with Elizabeth Warren, which gave us the best possible source of wisdom on the subject. Interestingly, there were large differences among the administration officials involved, and we often found one of those officials lobbying us against the administration's view.

Our task was also made easier by the unaccommodating posture of the House Republicans. Spencer Bachus's unhappy experience when he worked with us on subprime lending in 2007, and the House Republicans' angry response to the Bush administration's TARP effort, proved to be an accurate predictor of the Republican reaction to a reform bill. With very few exceptions—3 out of 178—they were against it.

This meant that the specifics of the legislation had to be hashed out entirely among Democrats. It also meant I would have to get a committee majority entirely from the same source. Fortunately for the bill, and my mental health, the 2008 elections had greatly increased the House Democratic majority. The committee now had forty-two Democrats to twenty-nine Republicans. For the next two years, I got to sleep by counting Democrats, relaxing only when I could get to thirty-six. Both sleep and passage would have come more easily if I could have substituted sheep.

•

With a large Democratic majority, the full support of the administration, and the widely perceived need to make the financial system much less risky, I was confident that we would send a very strong bill to the Senate by the end of the year. I had the benefit of a first-rate staff. Jeanne Roslanowick, whom I'd inherited from John LaFalce, had a perfect combination of substantive knowledge, political judgment, and parliamentary understanding. Recognizing the importance of people who knew me well enough to tell me when I was wrong, I added to the staff two near contemporaries: Dave Smith, an economist who'd worked for Ted Kennedy and the AFL-CIO, and Jim Segel, my old Massachusetts friend. They would both prove indispensable to the work ahead.

There was one immediate problem, however. Jurisdictional disputes between committees show Congress at its worst. Some commentators mistakenly attribute these disputes to members' hunger for the campaign contributions that come with shepherding significant bills. In the broad scheme of things, this is a much less important factor than institutional pride, ego, and the strong desire to influence policy outcomes. Cynicism to the contrary, job satisfaction is, for most members most of the time, as significant a motivation as job retention. At any given time, no more than 20 percent of House members face any serious reelection threat, and few issues, by themselves, have a measurable impact on members' chances of survival. Representatives who have chosen to join a committee with jurisdiction over a subject they care deeply about naturally resist moves that would substantially reduce that jurisdiction.

As we began work on our bill, the first big obstacle turned out to be the messy status of derivatives. Before the latest innovations in the financial system, they had been used to protect businesses from volatility in the prices of physical commodities like wheat or oil. They were regulated—lightly—by the Commodity Futures Trading Commission. Because many of these commodities were agricultural products, jurisdiction over the CFTC belonged to the Agriculture Committee. With the introduction of financial derivatives, the Securities and Exchange Commission, which is overseen by the Financial Services Committee, acquired an overlapping authority. The logical response to this would have been to merge the two commissions and create one combined entity to regulate all derivatives. Logic never had a chance. Agriculture is politically rooted in the Midwest, the South, and some of the mountain states. Financial activity is at its most influential in the Northeast, with an outpost in Chicago and some presence in California. Since the day of William Jennings Bryan's "Cross of Gold" speech, the country has made progress in healing the former regions' antagonism for the latter. But the divide remains strong. Given the greater size and scope of the SEC, joining the two commissions would have been greeted in agricultural areas with all the enthusiasm of Daniel entering the lions' den.

And so, as we began deliberating on the bill, my first task was to reach an agreement with the Agriculture Committee, particularly its chairman, Minnesota representative Collin Peterson. He is a very good legislator, well-informed on substance and skillful in dealing with colleagues. We also shared the conviction that constraining freewheeling derivatives trading was an essential part of financial reform.

Peterson is also one of the few Democrats who vote consistently against LGBT equality. Indeed, he would become the only Democrat to oppose us who comes from a state that voted in favor of marriage in a 2012 referendum. I regretted his views and made a point of ignoring them in the hundreds of conversations we had throughout 2009 and 2010. Our successful collaboration allowed rural Democrats and those representing financial centers to pass a bill. To those who would take that collaboration for granted, I note that in 2014, Trey Gowdy, a Tea Party Republican, explained that even though he and many of his colleagues agreed with Attorney General Holder on the desirability of reducing long sentences for drug users, they could not work with him on the issue—or, based on this logic, on any other issue—because of his support for same-sex marriage.

•

As it turned out, there would be many other intraparty squabbles ahead. I soon learned that opposition to the Consumer Financial Protection Bureau from moderate and conservative Democrats was stronger than I'd anticipated. I had hoped to nullify these objections when I rejected the proposed administration requirement that any business offering a financial product must include what was informally described as a "plain vanilla" version of that product. I did not see how you could insist on a plain vanilla version of a mortgage without prescribing interest rates and other sensitive terms that I did not want the government to prescribe. I believed then and still do that we should prevent bad things from happening—and having done that, leave the working out of other arrangements to the market.

The impatience with overly complex products and fine print was well-taken, but the idea was wholly unworkable. Unless we were willing to break our rule against fixing prices in the bill, there was no way to ensure that the mandatory offering was a real choice for consumers. In addition, deciding what was and was not unnecessary complexity would require intruding too far into the affairs of the affected businesses. (It was also unwisely named. I could not resist pointing out to administration advocates that highlighting the virtue of a product by labeling it "plain vanilla" was hardly the best way to promote it to a committee that had more African American and Hispanic members than any other in the House.)

The Chamber of Commerce and other opponents used their dislike of the plain vanilla proposal to camouflage their opposition to any significant improvement in consumer protection. Making clear that it would not be included was a prerequisite for holding on to the votes I needed to keep an independent CFPB in the bill. And I had to do this quickly. A simplistic view of the legislative process suggests that it's wise to load up an early version of a measure with provisions you are ready to bargain away. This ignores the dilemmas of legislating in the era of instant communication. On contentious high-profile issues, public pressure forms quickly, and representatives must take a stand soon. Even if a controversial provision is removed from a bill, members rightly worry that those to whom they've promised a no vote won't grasp the change.

My first step was to approach Elizabeth Warren to explain my position. I did so a little nervously, because I did not yet know her well, and I had encountered what seemed to me knee-jerk support for the idea from some other consumer advocates. Happily, I learned right away that her brain works much more quickly than her knee. She told me that she agreed with my reading, which meant that it would be hard for anyone else to accuse me of selling out the cause.

With this obstacle to creating the CFPB eliminated, another roadblock remained. Many community banks were complaining to their representatives that the new consumer bureau would add to administrative burdens that were already excessive. Here I believed a compromise was possible.

I asked Camden Fine, CEO of the Independent Community Bankers of America, to meet. It seemed to me that his membership's real concern was not with the substance of any new rules the consumer bureau might promulgate but with the need to submit to the bureau's regular examinations. "Examination" is a term of art in the banking world. It refers to regulators coming to a bank on a periodic basis and thoroughly inspecting all its activities. For small banks, with few executives, setting aside the time for this has real costs, reducing the attention they can give to their basic duties. The prospect of another set of these meetings every year was disturbing to small banks. But given the nature of their business, they had much less to fear from the new regulations themselves, which would almost certainly have more impact on large institutions engaging in complex transactions.

And so I suggested a compromise to Fine: We would write the laws so that the bureau's rules applied to all banks, but we would also exempt institutions with less than $10 billion in assets from its examination powers. Instead, the local banks would remain under the scrutiny of their regular examiners. Fine agreed that this made sense, and he persuaded his board to remain neutral in the fight over the agency.

An editorial note is in order here. This was not the only compromise—deal, to be less euphemistic—that I made to win the necessary votes. My general view is that the private conversations that enable such compromises are legitimately kept private. It is impossible to conduct serious negotiations between parties who are not independent actors but are representative of others in an open forum. I have long been a believer in half of Woodrow Wilson's doctrine— responsible, democratic governance consists of open covenants, worked out in private. I have discussed my negotiations with Fine here only because the ICBA has already disclosed the deal to Robert Kaiser, who included it in his book.

Even with the ICBA's neutrality, and the support of one big bank CEO (Brian Moynihan of Bank of America), the consumer bureau still faced opposition from some of the more conservative Democrats. Walt Minnick, an able, thoughtful member from a very conservative district of Idaho, was their leader. He agreed to delay his efforts to eliminate the bureau until we reached the floor with our bill. In return, I insisted that the Rules Committee give him the right to offer his antibureau amendment. He did, and the amendment failed 208 to 223, with a loss of only 33 Democrats.

I had less success when it came to the ever-complicated question of derivatives. The issue was relatively unfamiliar to me. It was also the most complicated, and the hardest to dramatize for the public, which gave Democratic opponents of strong regulation greater leverage. Reflecting this, my initial draft of the bill was weaker than it should have been, and the Treasury Department did not push us to strengthen it. But then Gary Gensler, the bold chair of the Commodity Futures Trading Commission, testified before the committee and argued that our derivative sections were too weak. I was persuaded. He has since noted that when I called him after that session, he anticipated that I would complain about his criticisms. Instead, as he recalled, I told him that he had convinced me and that we would be adopting some of his proposed amendments.

Our new stricter provisions made it through committee, but they were cut back on the House floor, although not in a way that did serious damage. To protect their risky business, the financial institutions successfully enlisted large manufacturers and other customers who bought their derivatives products. With public opinion unengaged, and nonfinancial institutions lobbying heavily, our rules were not as tough as I wanted them to be.

The outcome was disappointing, although not a major drawback. But the reason for it should not be misunderstood. It is widely believed that the biggest financial institutions contribute so much money to so many members of Congress that they can virtually dictate policy outcomes. It is also widely thought that our final bill favored them at the expense of the smaller institutions. (For example, Gretchen Morgenson made this argument explicitly in *The New York Times*.)

This is simply wrong. Campaign contributions can be influential in the legislative process if the point of view they support is unchallenged by any countervailing force. Their influence diminishes greatly when those opposing the contributors' viewpoint represent large numbers of voters. There was a clear example of this in 2013 when an impressive coalition of deep-pocketed businesses in the entertainment industry sought to pass a bill that would have severely restricted what consumers can see and hear without paying full—or any—price. The initial expectation was that their political and financial clout would carry the day. In fact, they were routed decisively—by a flood of angry communications to members of Congress from those very consumers, urged on by the Internet providers who had their own financial interest in defeating the bill. But the latter did not have to make contributions. This result was an affirmation of an enduring principle: Money is very helpful in a political vacuum, but when members are forced to choose between their voters and their contributors, votes kick money's ass.

In matters pertaining to finance, the real power to influence Congress rests not with the big banks but with a group of organized interests with genuine grassroots memberships throughout the country. These are the real estate agents, the independent insurance agents, the credit unions, and the community banks. They are present in every member's district. Their corporate culture is more outgoing than that of the megabanks and investment firms. It is their members who coach Little League, belong to civic clubs, and actively solicit business in their communities.

The one loss I suffered in our committee demonstrates this point. A large minority of Democrats joined all the Republicans to pass an amendment removing loans made by auto dealers from the consumer bureau's jurisdiction. Auto dealers are not only present in every member's district. With their ingratiating, slightly self-deprecating TV ads, they also epitomize the outgoing, socially active businessperson.

With the bureau and derivatives debate resolved, there was one last, unanticipated barrier to House passage. The committee members from the Congressional Black Caucus were under strong pressure from their districts—indeed, from the national black community—to help African Americans recover from the crash. African American homeowners were disproportionately victims of predatory mortgages, and inner-city neighborhoods were plagued by foreclosures and the neighborhood deterioration that followed. I arranged a private meeting with the caucus and top administration officials on the subject, but nothing concrete came of it, and the CBC's frustration level rose.

Seeking leverage, they told me not to count on their votes in committee. But there was some ambiguity. I did not know if they planned to vote no or to abstain. If the former, the bill died. But I could secure the bill's passage with their abstention if every other Democrat voted with me. Jim Segel helped persuade the more conservative Democrats to vote with me, allowing the CBC to abstain without killing the bill. With the support of the House leadership, Dodd, and the administration, I then worked with Maxine Waters and other CBC members to direct unspent TARP funds and other government resources toward foreclosure relief.

•

In December 2009, the House passed our bill by a vote of 223 to 202. Attention turned now to the Senate, where Dodd's committee was hard at work.

For the most part, the bill became tougher in the Senate. Admittedly, this came as a surprise. Along with many others, including lobbyists for the large institutions, I expected the Senate to soften our provisions to some degree. But then, as Harold Macmillan would not have been surprised to learn, events reshaped our political landscape. The most important was the final enactment of President Obama's health care bill by the House in March. Financial reform was now the focus of media interest. And the media had become especially interested in the story of how Goldman Sachs had sold a large mortgage-backed security while simultaneously betting that those who bought it would suffer a loss. With his customary skill, Senator Carl Levin used the Permanent Subcommittee on Investigations he chaired to shed light on practices that showed the financial industry at its worst.

Around the same time, the administration embraced former Fed chair Paul Volcker's proposal to prohibit FDIC-insured banks from engaging in risky deals when they were trading for their own profit. (He had originally faced opposition from Obama's key advisers on the subject and we had not included the idea in the House bill.)

Nothing in the bill as it became law was more obnoxious to the large banks than the "Volcker rule," and the ease with which it was adopted illustrates once again their lack of influence. Indeed, the more strenuously the banks opposed the rule, the more popular it became.

The Senate did weaken one key provision, to my continuing great regret. Senator Mary Landrieu insisted on loosening the requirement that packagers of mortgage loans retain some skin in the game. We believed that if the packagers retained some responsibility if their loans defaulted, they would be far more careful. Landrieu's action struck at what I believed to be the single best part of the bill, but I was up against the magic number. There were only fifty-nine Democrats in the Senate. And one of them, Russell Feingold, infuriatingly announced that he was too pure to vote for a less than ideal bill, even though he acknowledged that it was in every way an improvement over existing law. Not even Elizabeth Warren's pleas changed his mind. We had the support of three Republican senators at most, and we knew there were political pressures on all of them to become opponents. As Dodd noted ruefully, in this situation every senator gets a chance to be number sixty, and it was Landrieu's turn.

•

After the Senate passed the bill in May 2010, we proceeded toward reconciling the two versions in a House-Senate conference committee. From the start of our work, I had wanted the bill's passage to be a model of democracy in action. Even after the legislation passed our committee, I pressed the House Rules Committee to allow amendments. And without informing the Obama administration or the Senate, I unilaterally insisted that the House-Senate conference take place in full public view before the television cameras. I wanted to increase transparency and keep the influence of industry at bay.

The conference would become the site of three important battles. Blanche Lincoln, chair of the Senate Agriculture Committee, faced tough opposition from the left in her reelection primary and so she pushed through a sweeping requirement that banks stop their derivatives activity. It went much too far, even for Bair and Volcker, and had to be civilized in conference. It was, with the assistance of timing—Lincoln's primary was over (she won it but lost the final election). Gensler helped broker a deal that aided the banks somewhat but was still a major setback for them.

The big institutions did win on two other points, though again not because of their formidable power. When it came to the details of the Volcker rule, the Massachusetts Republican senator Scott Brown got to be the sixtieth senator. Several Massachusetts institutions wanted to relax it. Actually, they wanted to kill it, but they knew this was too much to ask Brown to do, given that he was up for reelection in 2012. Instead, he told the Senate leadership that he needed a change if he were to vote for the bill.

I learned of this when I received messages in the House gym from Chris Dodd, Harry Reid, and John Kerry asking me to talk with Brown. He told me he needed to relax the Volcker rule in a small way, allowing banks to exempt a small percentage of their assets from its provisions. We would have to devise an amendment that would satisfy Brown while being acceptable to Volcker. With crucial help from Dave Smith and Jim Segel, we did.

The big institutions did win one last victory, but I knew they considered it a meager consolation prize. The Congressional Budget Office ruled that the bill would cost a total of $22 billion, including the foreclosure relief measures we'd devised at the request of the Congressional Black Caucus. Dodd and I proposed raising the money by assessing the largest financial institutions, just as we'd proposed raising any funds that became necessary to liquidate large institutions. We adopted this approach in conference, over loud Republican objections, and thought we were finished with our work.

But three Republicans now got to play the role of Senator Sixty. Brown and Maine Republicans Olympia Snowe and Susan Collins had agreed to vote for the bill. We did not need all three of their votes, but we needed one or two, and they were intent on sticking together. We would get either three votes or none. They insisted that they could not support a bill that included a tax on financial institutions. My first reaction was that they had picked an odd place to take a stand, since billing the big banks had obvious popular appeal. But I'd misunderstood their predicament. Since they were already defying strong party pressures to vote against the bill, violating their party's no-higher-taxes mantra was more defiance than they were prepared to show.

We had no choice but to reconvene the conference and put the burden on the taxpayers. It did not get much attention at the time, but Brown's role in shifting the $22 billion cost from the big banks to the Treasury did hurt him in the races he lost to Elizabeth Warren in 2012 and Jeanne Shaheen in 2014. With this last accommodation to pick up the three Republicans, Dodd had the votes he needed. The conference signed off on the bill and it was adopted by both chambers of Congress.

On July 21, 2010, we signed the bill in a White House ceremony. I basked in the president's high praise of my legislative leadership. We had passed the most important financial reforms since the Great Depression.

11

TRIUMPHS, SETBACKS, AND LOVE

I cannot remember a greater mood swing. One moment, Chris Dodd and I were celebrating the passage of our financial reform bill at the White House. The next, I was an embattled candidate for reelection to Congress, fending off the accusation that I bore major responsibility for the entire financial crisis.

I fended badly despite the fact that I should have been warned. For years, I'd been saying that no one should serve in a prominent legislative leadership position who can't afford to lose 15 percent of the vote in the next election. Leadership in legislative bodies typically involves enhancing your influence over policy outcomes at the expense of your electoral appeal. A large part of your job as Speaker, Senate president, or majority leader is to take the political heat for passing worthy measures over the temporary—you hope—resistance of the voters. That is why so few top legislators become governors or presidents.

This phenomenon also extends to committee chairs. By 2010, most voters, including many in my district, thought of me as the powerful chairman of the Financial Services Committee—a committee that oversaw the most dysfunctional part of our economy. I was prepared for the political fallout from the despised TARP bill. What I did not comprehend was that voters' anger went far beyond that. They had an understandably vague sense of time and did not necessarily differentiate between the years when Democrats controlled the committee and the years when they did not—and the economy went off the rails.

As I stood on the platform in D.C., accepting congratulations for my work on the reform bill, I imagined myself campaigning as the cofather of the independent Consumer Financial Protection Bureau, the banisher of predatory subprime loans, and the tamer of Wild West derivatives trading. But reality could not have been more different. The general public was mad at anyone whom they even vaguely connected to the financial crisis and the subsequent bailouts. Those who followed events more closely often belonged to the financial industry, which was aggrieved by our bill and the justifications we'd given for it. Many Boston-area financial leaders were supportive. But my Republican opponent, Sean Bielat, received significant support from the financial industry elsewhere in the country. Bielat was a former marine and ex-Democrat from upstate New York who had worked for a business called iRobot, and then, according to his résumé, as a consultant, although it was never entirely clear to us how much consulting he did. Carl Icahn and David Einhorn, two of the most active participants in the unregulated financial world, gave Bielat the maximum campaign contributions allowed. The *Boston Herald* reported that when Bielat visited the New York Stock Exchange, he was mobbed by people eager to cheer him on—and contribute.

They were not the only nonresidents of the Fourth Congressional District with an active interest in the campaign. The most conservative elements in American politics smelled blood in the antigovernment atmosphere of 2010, and Bielat also benefited from large "independent expenditures." Immodestly enough, I was pretty sure his donors were more motivated by their feelings against me than for him.

I too went about doing fund-raising—this time of the sort I'd fortunately been able to avoid in the past. This meant holding a lot of events in Washington and my district, traveling to some other places where people were willing to give me money, and, gratifyingly, receiving help from colleagues who had surpluses in their own campaign accounts and no serious opposition. I was especially pleased when Virginia senator Mark Warner read that I was in a tight race and volunteered a contribution. I raised several million dollars—but the race was fairly even financially, because Bielat received support from both the financial community and the organized right wing.

Electorally, I was becoming a cliché—the long-serving politician who has not had a tough campaign for many years and is organizationally and emotionally unready to wage one. In my partial defense, I was heavily occupied until July with getting the bill passed. But when I did enter campaign mode, I did it badly. I waited too long to put an organization together, and when I did, I made some unwise choices. I had trouble keeping my focus, and I revived the tendency to self-pity that had marred my first congressional campaign and my reaction to the 1981 redistricting.

While my personal funk was a problem in our internal deliberations, I at least had learned not to let it show on the trail. This somewhat unusual exercise of emotional self-discipline enabled me to take full advantage of one of my campaign strengths—debating my opponent.

The conventional wisdom dictates that incumbents should avoid debates with challengers. From my first primary race, I rejected that principle as a violation of democratic norms. I accepted every debate offer from every opponent in all twenty of my campaigns. Of course, I also realized that debates played to my strength. I was good at political argument, I had a sense of humor, and I usually had the benefit of a wide knowledge gap.

That was certainly so with Bielat. He came to our debates prepared to utter nice phrases but had trouble when pressed on their implications. Repeating slogans about the need to control entitlements is easy. Declaring how much you will reduce Social Security benefits, how high you will raise the retirement age, and how you will actually cut medical costs is hard. Bielat's fumbles on these questions gave us material for broadcast ads and undercut his image as a man in control of the facts.

The debates proved especially valuable to me given the media's stance in the race. The right-wing outlets went all out in a bid to upset a liberal leader. Fox News, for example, repeatedly aired footage of a confrontation I'd had with a supporter of the fringe conspiracy theorist Lyndon LaRouche. At a public meeting, she'd displayed a picture of President Obama with Hitleresque touches and demanded that I admit to supporting Nazi policies. When she persisted in these accusations, I told her, "It is a tribute to the First Amendment that this kind of vile, contemptible nonsense is so freely propagated. Ma'am, trying to have a conversation with you would be like trying to argue with a dining room table. I have no interest in doing it." When reports of the exchange appeared in the press, they were cheered by liberals and demonized out of context by conservatives—a good example of how I was able to raise money for myself and my opponent simultaneously. I say "out of context" because in Fox News's presentation, my dining room table line was aired as if it had been unprovoked: They edited out all the ranting about Hitler and the Nazis.

Most outrageously, Fox and the *Boston Herald* decided to go after Jim. At one of our debates, Bielat had blurted out that we should consider raising the Social Security eligibility age to seventy-two—a comment he clearly regretted. After the debate, he interrupted his conversation with the press when he noticed Jim, who is an excellent photographer, taking pictures of him. "Aren't you with the Frank campaign?" he asked, seriously understating Jim's connection either from a lack of knowledge or an excess of delicacy. "You don't have to take photos," he continued, offering to supply Jim with some. Jim responded that he wanted to take his own, adding that it was a free country. Clearly irritated, Bielat answered, "not till we take back the country," echoing the Tea Party conceit that the Affordable Care Act and the financial reform bill represented the onset of tyranny. Jim's answer to this verbal excess was a recommendation. "Quit the jokes, dude," he said. "You're not funny at all." (Jim's advice was borne out two years later when Bielat belittled the Peace Corps service of his next opponent, Joe Kennedy, by joking, "I'll take the Marine Corps over the Peace Corps any day." After the predictable negative response, he had to try to explain it away.)

When Fox News broadcast Jim's riposte, it left out Bielat's earlier remarks, giving the false impression that Jim had heckled Bielat at a press conference. But the right wing's bloodlust was not my only media problem. A lot of reporters think I am not nice enough to them. In their view, it is their job to debunk, expose, and rebut elected officials, and our role is to be very polite in return. Reporters regularly accuse the people they're interviewing of not telling the truth. If the interviewee expressed equal skepticism about the reporter's words, the latter's reaction would be indignation, and possibly a lecture on the First Amendment. I have never encountered a more thin-skinned group.

Shortly after Bielat announced that America would be a free country only if the Republicans won, *The Boston Globe*'s Brian Mc-Grory called me about a column he was writing about Bielat's exchange with Jim. At that time, McGrory didn't know that Bielat had spoken first, but finding this out did not deter him from a nasty attack on Jim, which began by complaining that Jim had called Bielat "Dude." This, McGrory lamented, was disrespectful of a U.S. Marine: Jim should have addressed him by his title. I explained that Jim is a surfer and calls many people Dude, including me at times. I also could not recall the rule that said that political candidates who had been in the military, or were in the reserves and not on active duty, were supposed to be addressed as Lieutenant, Captain, Major, etc.

While the public mood was unfavorable, and journalists often unfriendly, I had a strong base of support through the constituency work I had done. Leaders of the fishing industry in the southern part of the district pitched in. A full-page newspaper ad from the mayors of Fall River, New Bedford, and Taunton also helped greatly. Bielat himself later explained that he would do better when I was not his opponent because many voters disagreed with my views but had received my help. (He didn't. He was defeated by a larger margin next time, running against Joe Kennedy III.)

In the end, my rule of thumb that congressional leaders should be ready to lose fifteen points turned out to be more precise than expected. I had won with 68 percent of the vote in 2008. That dropped to 54 percent in 2010. (Minor candidates received 7 percent in 2008 and 3 percent in 2010.) Democrats did terribly everywhere in 2010, and I did no worse than most. In fact, my results were comparable to those for Governor Deval Patrick, who was reelected. He ran slightly ahead of me in the more conservative areas, while I did a little better in the liberal ones.

On election night, my duel with the media continued. In accord with my ongoing conviction that a deep belief in the First Amendment does not preclude criticism of journalists, I said what I thought—and felt.

I had been the major target of the *Boston Herald*, but not their only one. They had run a multipronged attack on Democratic candidates and had campaigned vigorously for the conservative side of three referenda. In every case, they lost. "One of the things we can acknowledge tonight," I enthusiastically said, "is that Massachusetts has reaffirmed the complete political irrelevance of the *Boston Herald*." I was prepared for the *Herald*'s howl of outrage, but I was surprised when *The Globe* deemed my remarks improper as well.

When I retired, I was the subject of many stories in the press. Typically they were very generous, but they also reproached me for failing to show proper reverence for journalists and disregarding their feelings. The sensitivity of those who pride themselves on discomforting others continues to bemuse me.

•

In 2009 and 2010, my involuntary absorption in the world of derivatives, securitization, and bank leverage ratios was almost total. Even so, my promise to myself when I first ran for state rep was still binding. With a Democratic House, Senate, and president for the first time since 1994, and the favorable shift in public opinion, I was determined to advance LGBT equality.

Of all our goals in Obama's first years, expanding hate crimes protections was clearly the easiest to achieve, and Nancy Pelosi quickly put it on the 2009 House agenda. Reprising an old tactic, we attached the protections to the all-important annual military-spending bill. Since Democrats on the Armed Services Committee knew that President Obama, unlike President Bush, would not veto the bill because of a pro-LGBT provision, they did not fear its inclusion. The measure passed and was signed into law in October 2009—over the continued objections of most Republicans.

Our next priority was to pass the Employment Non-Discrimination Act, the vital bill that had failed so many times. This time we kept transgender people within its purview. The legislation was of great importance to me. In many states, it remained entirely legal to fire, demote, or refuse to hire us. And it is the LGBT residents of those states who most needed the help of those of us who lived in more protective jurisdictions. I was eager to do my part and also to rebut the lingering accusation from the 2007 fight that I was unsympathetic to the transgender community. Indeed, my newest legislative assistant, Diego Sanchez, brought both commitment and political sophistication to his job as the first transgender staff member on Capitol Hill.

But to my disappointment and frustration, I could not get the necessary cooperation from George Miller, who remained chair of the Education and Labor Committee, or the Speaker. The main reasons for this were entirely valid. Their highest priority, like President Obama's, was the passage of universal health care. The memory of our intramural quarrels over transgender inclusion in 2007 didn't help either.

Pelosi's position was also strongly influenced by a meeting she had with LGBT political leaders—a meeting to which I was not invited, I believe at their request. As she understood it, they argued that repealing Don't Ask, Don't Tell was the higher priority. Ending the military ban was a more visible issue as well as a less controversial one. I pushed for acting on all fronts, but I realized that many colleagues who supported LGBT rights worried that passing so many measures in the same session would be an overreach. It would risk the charge that we Democrats were elevating LGBT equality over other concerns. In the face of these realities, I accepted the fact that ENDA would have to wait and decided to focus all of my nonfinancial reform legislative efforts on ending the military ban.

•

My narrowed focus turned out to be necessary. While I was at first optimistic, by the fall of 2010 it was clear that the repeal of DADT was in trouble. Both houses included repeal in their versions of the annual defense authorization. It passed as an amendment on a very partisan vote in the House—229 Democrats voted for it; 26 were opposed. Republican opposition remained overwhelming: Only 5 supported repeal, while 168 voted no. The Republican opposition to allowing LGBT people to serve openly was essentially as strong as it had been in 1993, and yet the nature of that opposition had changed. In 1993 we heard over and over that the presence of LGBT people in the armed forces would destroy morale. Now we heard more about uncertainty—we don't know what effect this change will have, we should not be conducting social experiments in the military, and so on. Anyone who compares the debates of 1993 and 2010 will see that the case for LGBT legal equality had been firmly established in the intervening years—both intellectually and morally.

In the Senate, repeal won the support of the Armed Services Committee but was then stopped in its tracks by a Republican filibuster. Not a single Republican broke ranks. This was very bad news. The filibuster occurred on September 21, 2010, shortly before adjournment for the midterm elections. This meant that the issue would have to be decided in a lame-duck session, after an election in which Republicans were expected to do well.

I was very distressed, substantively and politically. Our success on hate crimes was a good thing but of limited practical impact. Failing to end discrimination in both the workplace and the military was morally unacceptable. And it would dash the LGBT community's assumption that Democratic control of government was worth its while.

I knew we would need the active support of the president as well. Senate Democrats had tried to end the Republican filibuster, and would try again. But if they did not succeed, the Senate leadership, especially the leaders of the Armed Services Committee, would tell us that DADT repeal was dead and it was now imperative to pass an important defense bill without it. Any suggestion that the Obama Defense Department was thinking that way would be fatal, and so I was determined to make the contrary case directly to the president. When he came to Massachusetts in October to campaign for the re-election of his close friend and ally, Governor Deval Patrick, Jim and I attended the event. I was then in the midst of my tough race against Bielat, and my time would have been better spent with voters in my district. But I could not let any chance to press our case go by. When Jim and I spoke to Obama during the backstage photo op, I annoyed some of his handlers by using the opportunity to impress on him how important it was that we do everything possible to repeal DADT when Congress reconvened. I was reassured by his promise, which I knew was sincere, to make it a priority.

Of course, Election Day turned out to be a calamity for the party, even as I held on to my seat. In January, Republicans would take control of the House with a forty-nine-seat majority, and so repealing the ban in the upcoming lame-duck session became an even more urgent matter. As soon as the election was over, I called every high-ranking Democratic decision maker in the Senate I could reach and several top White House aides. I insisted that from both the moral and political standpoint, no defense bill at all was far better than one that perpetuated bigotry.

The news got worse when we reconvened. Senate Republicans stood firm, and the effort to achieve cloture—ending the filibuster and sending the whole bill to the floor—failed again. But there was one ray of hope. Susan Collins of Maine became the first Republican senator to support bringing the defense bill to the floor with repeal attached. Even better, she and semi-Democrat Joe Lieberman of Connecticut began lobbying other Republicans to join her. Lieberman was especially valuable because his support for John McCain against Obama in the 2008 election gave him considerable credibility on the Republican side.

Unfortunately, a new obstacle arose. Entirely legitimately, the administration, with the ardent support of Senate Foreign Relations Committee chairman John Kerry, had another "must" on the lame-duck Senate agenda—ratification of its nuclear arms treaty with Russia. Substantively these two goals did not conflict in any way. But to my great disappointment, Senator Lindsey Graham hinted that he and a few other Republicans might reverse their support for the treaty if the Democrats did not abandon the DADT effort. Graham has intermittently sought to moderate his party's shift to the right. I had no expectation that he would vote for LGBT military service, but I was appalled that he would devote such extraordinary energy to defeating us. Threatening to put anti-LGBT prejudice ahead of a treaty he believed to be in the national security interest hardly became a would-be leader of the responsible Republican faction.

We did have a very powerful force on our side. In contrast to 1993, the LGBT community and our allies mobilized very effectively on the issue. The leading prorepeal organization, the Servicemembers Legal Defense Network, spearheaded a vigorous, sophisticated campaign. They made it clear to the president and congressional leadership that failing to win this fight would severely curtail the enthusiasm of LGBT voters. As a result, we had the political muscle to persuade supporters of the nuclear pact to reject Graham's proposed trade-off. Rather than try to defend his legislative extortion, Graham backed off in the most decisive way: He denied that he had ever said what he said.

On December 9, after the Senate failed to invoke cloture, Collins and Lieberman proposed removing repeal from the defense bill and passing it as a stand-alone measure. This gambit, they hoped, would break the political deadlock. Republicans had made opposition to Reid's handling of the defense bill a party issue, complaining that they had not been given a fair chance to amend it. With the exception of Collins, they did not feel that they could back down and give the Democrats cloture without some concession. This dynamic may be hard for people outside the institution to comprehend, but it was very strong inside the Senate. Putting a "clean"—that is, repeal-free—defense bill on the floor would allow the Republicans to claim a procedural victory. Prorepeal Senate Republicans would then be free to vote for both bills.

But one serious problem remained. Adjournment fever had reached the virulent stage. There was by now one week left for Senate business, and repeal was competing for time and political support with two other major administration-Democratic priorities—the nuclear treaty and the DREAM Act to protect immigrants who had been brought to the United States as children without legal status. Republican votes were needed for both of these as well, and it was far from clear that there were enough Republicans willing to break with their party on all three measures. (There weren't. The DREAM Act was defeated by a filibuster.)

The days that followed became a grueling legislative duel. If we moved first, could we count on the Senate's cooperation?

In order to realize the Collins-Lieberman plan for a separate repeal bill, the Senate expected us to put aside the defense authorization we had passed and instead pass two new bills—a stand-alone repeal and a "clean" repeal-free defense bill—and send them both on to the Senate.

I learned this on Monday of the session's last week, while recuperating from a cataract operation. Steny Hoyer, the House majority leader, had called me while I was in the outpatient center, just as my anesthesia was wearing off. Jim was with me for the operation and took the call. He was shielding me for the day from most business, but he knew how important this was, and I called Hoyer later that day from home. I told him I was still a little groggy and would get back to him the next morning—Tuesday—so we could decide on our strategic response.

A call from Pelosi soon woke me completely. She pointed out that if we sent the Senate both bills, it was entirely possible that they would pass the by now noncontroversial defense bill, try to obtain cloture on repealing the military ban, and if that failed for the third time in a year, call it a day and move on to the other two major legislative items—the nuclear treaty and the DREAM Act. If that happened, Democrats would be able to claim—accurately—that they strongly supported ending the ban and blame the Republicans for its survival.

In some circumstances, settling for such an outcome might have been a sound political approach. But we were determined to do better. Together, Pelosi and I devised a strategy to make sure that the Senate would act. We would send a repeal bill to the Senate immediately, using a procedural maneuver that made instant action possible. We would then wait for the Senate to pass the repeal, and only once they did would we send them the clean defense bill.

This was very high-stakes gamesmanship. House Democrats would be holding the bill that established America's defense posture for the year hostage to the "gay agenda." Our gambit also posed a problem for Hoyer. He had been doing great work on behalf of repeal, and the Senate's offer to break the logjam by separating the two bills represented a major success. The hostage-taking strategy Pelosi and I devised might undercut him. It didn't help that Pelosi and Hoyer had a recent history of tension. They had run against each other for House minority whip in 2002, and after angrily debating Democratic differences over the Iraq War, she had supported a candidate against him for the majority leader's position in 2007. To their great credit, they put all that behind them and worked smoothly as a team during our four years in the majority, with a very constructive division of labor. While there were no significant policy differences between them, Hoyer was the one who worked more closely with the moderate and conservative Democrats.

And now it was conservative Democrats who would complain that their defense bill was in jeopardy. Dissatisfaction would be exacerbated by the perception that Hoyer, their champion in the leadership, was being disrespected—especially, to acknowledge an unpleasant fact, by a woman. Old wounds could quickly reopen.

Even worse, our plan could have undermined the tentative agreement with the Senate. Intercameral relations are inherently fragile. Cokie Roberts often recalled that her father, Majority Leader Hale Boggs, liked to repeat an old Capitol Hill line: "House Republicans are not our enemy. They are our opposition. The Senate is our enemy." (The rise of the Tea Party has rendered this line moot, even as a joke.) Our allies in the Senate, who had pressed reluctant colleagues to accept the two-bill approach, wouldn't be happy to be told that they hadn't done enough. In the hypertense atmosphere of a lame-duck session's last week, that could be fatal.

Given all this, Hoyer was in a tight spot. But as Pelosi pointed out, there was a solution: I should be the heavy.

On Tuesday morning, I got back to Hoyer as promised and outlined the legislative dance that I described above. I told him I could not support sending the Senate a clean defense bill until they passed repeal. He fully supported our approach. Once again I cannot tell the whole story without sacrificing any pretense of modesty. I was ideally situated to be the lead hostage taker. Given the importance of the personal factor in legislating, the fact that I was gay gave me more license to push hard on the issue than any straight leader would have. Hoyer and Pelosi could not demand that the House Democratic leadership pass the defense bill over my vehement, public dissent.

There was expected resistance to our plan from the more conservative Democrats. On the Wednesday before adjournment, this came to a head in a confrontation I had with Congressman Ike Skelton, chairman of the House Armed Services Committee, as Hoyer played the moderator. (It was one of the many conversations that occur on the House floor, apart from formal proceedings, audible only to the direct participants.) The main business of the House that day, according to our plan, was the DADT repeal bill, which had just passed with Democrats voting 235 to 15 in favor, and the Republicans now opposing it 160 to 15. Skelton was deeply disappointed that we were not also voting to send the defense bill along to the Senate simultaneously. As the leadership's designated spokesman, I upheld our refusal to do so.

This was painful for me. I liked Skelton very much personally and admired him professionally. He was a man of great integrity. He had accommodated us on both the DADT repeal and the hate crimes bill, despite being one of the more conservative Democrats and coming from an even more conservative district—so conservative that he had been defeated that fall. I told him that I'd appreciated his efforts against LGBT prejudice and was saddened by his defeat, though I don't think those words softened the blow. He was very eager to see his crowning achievement—the defense bill—become law. For his sake, so was I. But not at the expense of repeal. As we jousted, Hoyer told Skelton as gently as he could that the leadership's new plan was not going to change. We genuinely believed that the Senate would pass both bills and do right by all of us.

And just in time it did. As Pelosi related to me, with only two days left in the session, Senate majority leader Harry Reid called her to ask that the House adopt the repeal-free defense bill. In response, she reiterated that we would do that in the House just as soon as the Senate passed the Don't Ask, Don't Tell repeal.

According to Pelosi, Reid asked her to wait and then put her on hold briefly. When he returned to the phone, he told her that he had just filed a cloture petition—the first step toward ending a filibuster—and that the petition would be up for a vote on Saturday (the technical language is that it would "ripen at that time").

This was less than we had insisted on, but Pelosi found Reid's plan sufficient and decided to go ahead and pass the general defense bill. Reid's commitment to hold a public vote on Saturday clearly meant that he and others interested in passing a defense bill would do all they could to win the necessary votes for our cause. Pelosi also knew that had we killed the defense bill after Reid's honest effort to break the filibuster, serious intra-Democratic conflict would have resulted. Her instincts, which are among the best in American politics, were correct, and I concurred with her decision.

On Friday, I had the pleasure of taking the House floor to urge my fellow liberals once again to deviate from our usual pattern and vote yes on the defense bill. I explicitly noted that in doing so, they would be participating in a deal that would end one of the last explicitly anti-LGBT laws on America's books.

On Saturday, the last day on which controversial action could be considered in the very eventful Congress of 2009–2010, five Senate Republicans voted with Collins for cloture, and DADT was DEAD.

•

The repeal of DADT was an exhilarating conclusion to an extraordinarily productive two years. Working to pass financial reform and DADT repeal in the same Congress had left me mentally and physically exhausted. When the term was over, Jim and I left for a restorative trip to St. John in the Virgin Islands. We had become close to another congressional couple, my colleague Chellie Pingree and her companion (and now husband), Donald Sussman. She had been elected in 2008 to represent the area of Maine where Jim lived and where I was spending much of what little leisure time I had. We saw her at events in her district, I sought her out from time to time on the House floor when I wanted a respite from my colleagues' entreaties regarding the reform bill, and we were frequent traveling companions on the plane home. But what really cemented our friendship was the strong bond that formed between Donald and Jim as members of the male spouse caucus. They were both amused by the congressional wives' club's sometimes awkward transition toward becoming more gender integrated.

For the second Christmastime in a row, we were their grateful guests at Donald's home on St. John. Over the 2010 holiday break, however, I found myself agonizing over a difficult decision: Should my next term in Congress be my last?

The previous spring, when it became clear the financial reform bill was going to pass, I was exhausted mentally, emotionally, and physically. And so I had resolved that I would not run again after my race that fall. Following my victory, I did not fear losing in 2012—any Democrat who survived the rout of 2010 was highly likely to do even better in a presidential year, when the pro-Democratic turnout is much higher. But my subpar management of my reelection effort undermined my self-confidence. I had also seen too many talented legislators end their careers in a physically and intellectually diminished state. I had long ago decided that I would leave office when I hit seventy-five, and leaving office in January 2013 would cut only two years off that target date.

But as I vacationed on St. John, I had good reasons to reconsider. With the Republicans in control of the House, I did not want it to look as if I was running away from a tough fight. I had fought Newt Gingrich's aggressive Republican majority in 1995, and I didn't want anyone to think I was too afraid of the Tea Party to do it again. Indeed, to some extent I looked forward to it. It is easier to criticize the excesses of the other side than it is to pass complex legislation.

Fortunately for my self-image as a mature adult, there was also a more substantive reason for staying on. I could defend our financial reform bill against the alliance of fundamentalist free-market Republicans and unrepentant financial industry leaders who were eager to undermine it.

•

Even on holiday, Jim was an invaluable interlocutor as I talked out the pros and cons of leaving office. His full support for putting off retirement until 2015 was vital to me. So I went back to Washington in January as the ranking minority member of the Financial Services Committee, committed to stay—for two more years.

In the first Congress under the influence of the Tea Party, the Republican majority accomplished nothing of any significance.

Sherlock Holmes's nonbarking dog became the inescapably appropriate metaphor for the work of the Financial Services Committee. Little important legislation made it to the Senate, because the committee sent few bills to the floor, and the House passed even fewer. The split between mainstream conservative Republicans and the ideological crusaders on their right was too strong for the committee to function well.

I had expected that playing defense would be less stressful and take up much less time. I hadn't anticipated that it would also sometimes be very enjoyable.

It was especially fun to taunt the House Republicans for failing to live up to all their bluster. Jeb Hensarling, leader of the committee's most conservative faction, had previously sought to abolish Fannie and Freddie outright. When we reconvened in January, I said that I assumed that his legislation would be an early item on the committee's agenda. During the Dodd-Frank conference committee, the Republicans had said that Hensarling's GSE proposal was ready to be enacted into law without any further change and had been very disappointed when we did not agree. Since they'd said they believed the issue required immediate attention and already had a piece of legislation ready to become law, I asked them when we could expect the committee to be considering it.

I was to have the pleasure of asking this same question over and over for two years without ever getting an answer. As in the previous years when they'd controlled the chamber, they put on a show that could be called "How to Succeed in Making Political Capital About the GSEs Without Doing Anything at All to Reform Them."

The Republicans were no more active when it came to the substance of the financial reform bill. The contrast between their repeated votes to repeal health care reform and their acceptance of financial reform was implicit proof that they knew financial reform was popular with the public. Sponsorship of a measure to repeal our entire bill was left to Michele Bachmann—who was, to be blunt, never taken seriously by her Republican colleagues on the committee. Her bill didn't even receive the pro forma gesture of a public hearing.

The committee did pass several narrower bills that sought to fray our reform at the edges. Those bills typically addressed matters that were unimportant, or were so complex that the public might not realize what was being done. The one that seemed to me most dangerous would have exempted American banks' overseas derivatives activity from the oversight of regulators. After passing our committee, it was en route to necessary action by the Agriculture Committee when the financial industry inadvertently sabotaged its own wishes. The huge reckless derivatives transactions of JPMorgan's infamous trader nicknamed the London Whale cost the bank billions. Even the most conservative members understood that letting the foreign subsidiaries of JPMorgan and others go free was poor politics, although they still thought it was excellent economics.

Despite all this, I would soon reverse my decision to delay my retirement. Yes, we were fighting to shape public opinion on the role of government in our society, and I was confident that we would win if we made our case correctly. I also liked the fight. When I was asked after my retirement announcement if the rancorous atmosphere in Congress had driven me out, I replied, "No. I'm good at rancor."

What I wasn't good at was trying to influence the leadership of the Massachusetts legislature. For thirty years I had represented a district which, in varying forms, extended from the western border of Boston to southeastern Massachusetts. Ironically, in the 2010 campaign, my opponent and his allies complained that the odd contours of the district were due to a gerrymander on my behalf. To the contrary, the basic contours of the district had been constructed in 1981 with the goal of defeating me. The district defied cartographic neatness, but so did many others.

In 2011, the Massachusetts legislature created a new district that was no less ragged in its outlines or diverse in its demography.

It also persuaded me to retire. There were two problems. First, the district would no longer include the New Bedford area, with its fishing community. I had spent twenty years working closely with the people in that industry, and my ties were deeply personal as well as political. It was inconceivable to me that I could remain in Congress and not continue to be their advocate. But it was also hard to figure out how I would be able to take on the job of representing an entire congressional district while spending significant attention on an important industry wholly outside my own constituency.

That might have been doable if I was losing only greater New Bedford. But I was actually losing half my former district. Since I had already made a firm commitment to retire at seventy-five, that meant I'd be asking 350,000 voters I was not currently representing to let me be their advocate for only two more years. My view of my congressional responsibilities had always included a commitment to effective constituent service. Some of that involves attention to one-off individual problems, but much of it involves working over a period of years with local governments and communities on more complex issues. To be fully candid, I also wasn't too happy about having to ask 350,000 new people for their votes under any circumstances. Two more years of minority service did not seem worth one full year of campaigning. Far better to spend more time with Jim, do some serious writing, and get paid for giving the speeches I'd been giving for free for decades. In November 2011, I announced that I would not run for reelection in 2012.

Within a few weeks I became very fond of something I could not remember ever having experienced—a life entirely free of career-related worries.

•

At the beginning of 2012, I was asked by one of the president's top aides if I thought Obama's reelection chances would be hurt if he came out strongly in favor of same-sex marriage. To the contrary, I said, I thought it would help him. There couldn't be that many Obama supporters who had no objection to his stances on other LGBT issues but would suddenly turn against him if he supported same-sex marriage. On the other side of the equation, LGBT voters would be enthused by his endorsement.

To my great satisfaction, this was one of those rare occasions where I was both optimistic and completely correct. Obama's announcement cost him nothing that anyone could see, and raised his LGBT support to peak levels in the 2012 presidential campaign. Election Day was very gratifying. Obama defeated Romney by a healthy margin, and my successor, Joe Kennedy, won my seat with 61 percent of the vote. And for the first time, same-sex marriage was endorsed by the voters—not just in one referendum but also in four states across the country: Washington, Minnesota, Maryland, and Maine.

To my disappointment, but not my surprise, the verdict on a stronger public sector was much less encouraging. Democrats did win the presidency by a solid margin, hold the Senate, and make gains in the House—in fact, Democratic candidates received more votes than Republicans in House races, and would have gained even more seats were it not for the gerrymandering that followed the 2010 census. But our successes owed more to Republican extremism than to explicit public enthusiasm for a bigger government role. The Democrats owed their Senate majority in particular to Republican candidates with a penchant for expressing the most right-wing sentiments in the most off-putting ways. Even in Massachusetts, where I happily worked hard for Elizabeth Warren's Senate campaign, the Democrats' victory was largely attributable to her record as a fierce critic of government-business collusion. She won because voters resented the financial community and its political allies, not because they admired the government. While she was a strong, effective supporter of expanded regulation, she was also the beneficiary of continuing anger over what was actually an example of effective government action: TARP. (She had not objected to its passage, but as head of the program's oversight panel, she had been one of the sharpest critics of its execution.)

Obama did not join in the government bashing. He defended his health care bill—and, less often, our financial reform bill. But he did not campaign for an expansion of government's role in general. Nor did he disavow his efforts to reach a "grand bargain" with the Republicans that would further restrain public sector spending. His strongest electoral asset was his opponent. Although not as self-immolating as Republican Senate candidates in Missouri and Indiana, Romney won the nomination by positioning himself farther to the right than electability required. His campaign was further hampered by the unusually explicit cynicism of his high-ranking campaign aide, Eric

Fehrnstrom, who won the prize for the worst use of a metaphor in our political history when he characterized Romney's rebirth as a moderate as an exercise in the use of the Etch A Sketch. (In fairness to Fehrnstrom, Romney's even more damaging denunciation of 47 percent of the electorate appears to have been his own bizarre contribution to the art of gaining votes.)

By the summer of 2012, it was clear to me that we were winning the election because of voters' disaffection with the right rather than their agreement with the progovernment stance of the left. I expressed that thought in a bumper sticker I had printed, which said VOTE DEMOCRATIC. WE'RE NOT PERFECT, BUT THEY'RE NUTS. It was very much in demand at the Democratic convention and throughout the rest of the campaign. I was proud of the slogan. But I regretted that such an accommodation to the electorate's sour mood was the best case we liberals could make.

•

Having stepped down from the House, I figured my political career was over at last. In fact, retirement would come with one more wrinkle.

Following Obama's reelection, it was widely believed that John Kerry would replace Hillary Clinton as secretary of state, and several liberal Massachusetts legislators urged me to seek Kerry's Senate seat if it was vacated. At the time, I was so satisfied by my life with Jim and without stress that I rejected those requests out of hand. Not only did I shudder at the thought of running a statewide campaign for the seat, but I also disclaimed any interest in serving as the interim appointed senator for the few months that would precede an election.

But when the Republicans began talking once again about shutting down the government, the prospect of serving as an interim senator became more appealing. It seemed highly possible that the first six months of 2013 would crucially shape taxing and spending for years ahead. I wanted very much to be a part of the tumult. An interim appointment offered the best of both worlds: I could play an important role promoting social fairness without having to worry about reelection. As an ardent reader of nineteenth-century British parliamentary history, I had sometimes thought that it must have been very pleasant to be an influential member of the House of Lords. Here was my chance to experience that pleasure without having to buy a robe or pick a lordly name. (Although that last prospect did have its charms. Discussing American insurance law with the chairman of Lloyd's of London at the Davos forum, I could not help thinking how surprised my immigrant grandmother would have been to learn that one of the most important business figures in England was Lord Levene.)

I proceeded to pursue the interim appointment in what seemed to me the appropriate way. I told Governor Deval Patrick that I wanted the job, and when asked on *Morning Joe* if I was interested, I said that I was.

I'd made four major career choices in my life: deciding to work for Mayor White and for Congressman Harrington, and deciding to run for the legislature and for Congress. In each case, the choice was prompted by other people's phone calls and the decision made quickly. This time, the decision was the product of careful deliberation about a job with which I was intimately familiar and that I knew I could perform well. It was also the one decision that backfired. My quest failed, completely and very publicly.

To my surprise, my expressions of interest in the appointment were regarded as highly inappropriate by a number of people, most important the governor himself. While he assured me that he was not unhappy that I had made my wishes public, I got a very different impression from people who claimed to know his true feelings. Apparently he regarded any effort to pressure him on this matter as an infringement on his executive prerogative. Had the position involved service in his administration, I would have agreed. But it did not seem to me that an appointment to the U.S. Senate should be left to any governor to dispose of privately, with no public input.

I was gratified by the large number of people and groups that lobbied the governor on my behalf, although I came to realize that these efforts probably added to his irritation with me. I also came to surmise that while I had thought that the Obama administration might welcome me as a temporary Senate ally, the opposite was probably the case. There was renewed talk at the time of a presidential deal with congressional Republicans that would achieve long-term deficit reduction and include some cuts in Social Security and Medicare benefits. My interest in the Senate seat was based in large part on my determination to protect those two programs—the most successful antipoverty efforts in American history—and to press for greater military reductions instead. I also learned later that the president had preferred a member of his staff for the job. Presumably, that figure would have been much more supportive of such a deal.

In the end, the governor appointed one of his top aides, Mo Cowan, as rumors had suggested he would. There were two ways to describe the failure of my Senate bid. I had lost by only one vote. But since that vote was the only one cast, the rejection was unanimous.

I was now a private citizen. My disappointment over the Senate seat was soon wiped away by a burst of exhilaration as I realized that I was no longer flinching when the phone rang. For forty-five years, that ring had regularly signaled the arrival of some new problem I was obliged to deal with.

My public life had been one long trade-off. I'd worked as effectively as I could on those matters I needed to address in order to stay in office, and on those that became my responsibility because of my committee positions. The better I was at these tasks, the more influence I had in advocating the changes I believed could make the world a better place—the reason I had entered political life in the first place.

As a private citizen, I was now free to concentrate entirely on advancing those latter causes. I was grateful to my constituents, and respectful of my colleagues, but the freedom to ignore those things that were important to them but of no direct interest to me was a great joy.

Because I was as passionate as ever about improving the world—making it conform more to my values—I remained convinced that pragmatism in the pursuit of my ideals was morally compelled. This meant that it remained essential to analyze the political context in which I would now be working.

•

My first full year of retirement was 2013. This was also a year when the progress of LGBT rights and regress of economic fairness were more evident than ever.

In June, the Supreme Court struck down the Defense of Marriage Act and allowed federal benefits for same-sex couples. It also upheld same-sex marriage in California, albeit on a technicality. Apart from the predictable anti-LGBT diatribe from the homophobic Justice Scalia, these pro-gay decisions elicited little public reaction. Less than a week later, I was able to add Jim to my federal retiree health plan.

The way ahead on LGBT rights was clear enough. With public opinion on our side, and same-sex marriage spreading from state to state, we could continue to press forward on all fronts: pursuing judicial victories secure in the knowledge that they were unlikely to be overturned by popular votes, and using the political process to make further advances at the state level. (Regrettably, it will still require a Democratic president, House, and Senate to put ENDA back on the national agenda.)

Gratifyingly, the progress we've made fighting prejudice at home has also increased our ability to fight prejudice abroad. We took a first step in 1994, when we allowed victims of homophobia in other countries to win asylum. Subsequently, Obama's State Department came to include anti-LGBT persecution as a ground for complaint in its human rights statements. We have not been as successful as I hoped in protecting the victims of brutal prejudice in Africa, and discrimination in Russia. But our government has at least put itself on record on the right side of these issues.

Overcoming public opposition to government will be harder and more complicated. The task for liberals is to find some way to bridge the large gap between public support for government programs in particular and majority disapproval of the idea of government in general.

At the very least, the response to the government shutdown in October 2013 proved encouraging. As in 1995, Republicans found that closing down the government was highly unpopular once voters recognized what it meant in practice, program by program. This led to an amusing spectacle. Legislators who had forced federal agencies to shut their doors were now denouncing those very entities because their work was not getting done. The party soon abandoned the shut-down tactic altogether.

The right's efforts to shut government down have failed. But is there any way to win public support for the more vigorous government we need? Obviously my ideas on this score will have no appeal to those who are philosophically against an expanded public role. Opposing the Bush administration's plan to avert economic collapse in 2008, Congressman Thaddeus McCotter conceded that it might very well work to end the immediate crisis. Even so, he warned, "As the free market is diminished your freedom itself is diminished." Invoking "the Bolshevik Revolution" in his closing remarks, he summarized the philosophical view of the antigovernment side: "It has always been the temptation in a crisis especially to sacrifice liberty for short-term promises of prosperity." Fortunately for the country's ability to survive the crash, most voters did not deem the right of financial institutions to engage in reckless derivatives transactions essential to their personal freedom. This does not guarantee that the reform will survive intact. But the near defeat of the 2014 omnibus appropriations bill because it included an amendment making a relatively small change in the regulation of derivatives demonstrates that opponents will face a very hard fight if they attempt a significant regulatory rollback.

I respect the intellectual consistency and moral integrity of those who oppose regulation on principle. I also take comfort in my conviction that they represent a fairly small minority of the electorate, and that there is potentially a strong majority composed of two other segments. First there are my fellow liberals who tend as strongly in the opposite position—given the complexity of our society, and the inevitable tendency of the free-market system to generate more inequality than is economically necessary or socially tolerable, maintaining a decent quality of life requires an expansion of the public sector along with private economic growth. The second group is open to the claims of both philosophical camps. These are the voters whose disillusionment with government is precisely that—the angry reaction of people who favor effective collective action in many areas of our common life but who have been so disappointed by government's inadequate performance that they have lost faith in it.

This critical bloc of voters is disaffected from government not because they don't believe it should play an active role, but because they are disappointed that it hasn't played an effective role. The biggest single reason for this is that conservatives have made sure that there is not enough government revenue for it to succeed. Compounding the problem for the progovernment position is the self-reinforcing nature of this situation. The angrier voters become with government for not meeting their expectations, the more they vote for politicians who are philosophically opposed to an extended public sector role and support cutting taxes. This obviously results in government becoming even less able to deliver, which leads to more antigovernment voting.

This dynamic helps to explain the conservatism of so many lower- and middle-income white men. These voters have seen their relative economic position seriously eroded by the global economic shifts of the past thirty-five years, and they hold the government largely responsible. They believe that given its levers for directing the economy, the government could have prevented their exclusion from the fruits of economic growth if the people running it really wanted to. Even worse, when government does intervene in the economy, it often seems to subordinate their economic interests to other goals. One of these goals is helping "others"—providing job preferences and subsidies to racial and ethnic minorities, illegal immigrants, and others they may deem suspect. The government is also faulted for elevating environmental concerns over the need for jobs that pay decent wages.

The white males who used to vote for Democrats have not become philosophical opponents of an active public sector. They dislike much of what they perceive that the government is doing, but they are even angrier at what it is refusing to do—adopt policies that will reverse the harm they have suffered from the economic shifts of the past decades.

•

Reversing these voters' antigovernment sentiments is the challenge for liberals. It requires adopting measures that will reduce inequality. This leads to a crucial first question: How is it possible to expand

popular programs without raising taxes on the middle class? Fortunately, there are two golden opportunities to do just that: reduce the
military budget and end criminal penalties for drug users. They are
both twofers—they save money not by cutting back on things we
should be doing, and from which society benefits, but by reducing
expensive government activity that often does more harm than good.

By the time I arrived in Congress, I agreed with those who believed we were spending more on defense than necessary. But our
differences concerned a billion here or a billon there, not the nation's basic strategic structure. With the collapse of the Soviet
Union in 1991, for the first time in fifty years we did not face any
hostile power that represented an existential threat to our survival
as a free society. Reacting to this, President Bush began a significant reduction in military expenditures that continued through the
Clinton administration. The rationale for this approach was ably
summarized in November 1991 by a man with unquestioned credibility on the issue:

> Perhaps the most important single issue we face in defense is
> how to provide the American people with a peace dividend,
> and still preserve our national security. I believe that this is
> possible if we double the present rate in cuts in our defense
> expenditure, and shift from a Europe and nuclear-oriented
> strategy to one based on power projection . . . It is my hope
> that this plan can be translated in FY1993 into reductions in
> the budget deficit and taxes that will be of direct benefit to
> the American taxpayer.

The author, Senator John McCain, then provided a specific set of
proposals for how to implement this and noted the significant cost
savings it would produce.

> To be specific, the end of the Cold War means it is possible
> to double the rate of cuts in real defense spending that the
> Bush Administration planned in early 1991, and to go from
> an average cut of 3 percent in annual defense spending dur-
> ing FY1991–FY1997 to a rate of 6 percent.

Neither Bush nor Clinton brought defense spending down to the levels my congressional allies and I—and indeed John McCain—wished for. Even so, the savings they achieved helped Clinton and the Republican Congress balance the budget in his second term, and even contemplate paying off the national debt entirely.

With little dissent, policy makers reversed the course of military spending after the mass murder of Americans on September 11, 2001. The virtually unanimous national resolve to cripple Al Qaeda meant full support for the war that became necessary when the Taliban regime announced it would continue to provide Osama bin Laden safe haven. Domestic spending on security also began a steep upward climb, with the establishment and generous funding of the Department of Homeland Security. But the administration's response to bin Laden's assault went far beyond formulating an effective response to this new threat. With Dick Cheney playing an unusually influential role for a vice president, the neoconservatives scored a great victory: They won public acceptance of the notion that terrorism poses as grave a danger to our national existence as we faced from Germany, Italy, and Japan in the 1940s, and from the thermonuclear-armed Soviet Union in subsequent decades.

It doesn't. The terrorists are no better morally than these earlier enemies of freedom. But they are not remotely equal to them in their capacity to harm us. The false equivalency between a network of murderous fanatics who have no ships, planes, heavy armaments, or secure home territory and alliances of heavily armed nations with populations in the hundreds of millions has been the source of a serious, damaging distortion in our national security policy.

The first great manifestation of this was the Iraq War. The invasion was the worst single policy decision any U.S. president has ever made, with its terrible cost in human lives—American and other—and its deleterious effect on our standing in the Middle East. By the later years of Bush's term, the military budget had swollen from $400 billion a year in 2001 to $700 billion—$200 billion allocated for the two wars, and an additional, greatly excessive $500 billion for the regular military budget. When Speaker John Boehner suggested that paying our country's debts was a favor he was doing for spendthrift Democrats, I responded that he had voted to put much more debt on the books than I had. (He had supported both the increased military spending and Bush's trillion dollars of tax cuts.)

Worst of all, most of the increased defense spending was irrelevant to the new threats at hand. If nuclear submarines carrying MIRVed missiles and similar weapons were useful against terrorists, our battle would probably be over. We have a lot of them and they don't have any.

As the wars in Afghanistan and Iraq dragged on for years, the national mood began to shift. In every post–World War II election but one, Democratic candidates were careful to reaffirm their commitment to a high level of defense spending. In 2004, John Kerry made his valiant combat record a major part of his presentation at the Democratic convention, but even that was not enough to insulate him from a vicious, demagogic, inaccurate but sadly effective assault on his record.

It was therefore a sharp reversal of recent history when Obama was elected president in 2008 while a war he had voted against was still being waged. His opposition to the Iraq War was a great political asset. It helped him win the nomination against Hillary Clinton, who had voted to authorize the invasion. It helped him again in November against John McCain, who had been one of the most vocal advocates of increasing our commitment in Iraq, and who differed sharply with Obama's pledge to end our participation. (A position he reaffirmed when Obama carried out his promise—belatedly, in my view—in 2011.)

By 2012, voters had become even more resistant to arguments for a larger military establishment and increased deployments to combat terrorism. When Mitt Romney asserted in a debate that the defense budget was dangerously small, citing a decrease in the number of combat vessels from World War I levels, Obama's response was ridicule: He equated his opponent's argument with a nostalgia for cavalry horses and bayonets. In a campaign in which Obama's debate performance was uneven, this was widely regarded as one of his best moments. That impression was reinforced on Election Day when the swing state of Virginia, where combat shipbuilding is a major economic activity, voted Democratic.

My last session in Congress gave me further evidence that curtailing military spending had become politically popular. In 2011, two amendments were offered to reduce the House Appropriations Committee's proposed defense budget. One was offered by me, the other by Mick Mulvaney, a freshman Tea Party member from South Carolina. Both of our amendments lost. After the votes, Mulvaney approached me and proposed that we collaborate on one amendment the next year. We did, with his name going first. Given the fast pace of action when votes are being tallied on the floor, some members decide what to do largely on the basis of who is the main sponsor—his or her name is indicated on the electronic scoreboards at the end of the chamber. With liberal Democrats already predisposed to support us, we knew that having Mulvaney's name rather than mine on that board would be helpful.

We won, 247 to 167, with 158 Democrats and 89 Republicans taking our side. The cut we endorsed was not as big as either of us would have liked, but it was still extremely significant. It was the first time in all my years in the House that a majority of members voted to lower the defense spending levels recommended by the Armed Services Committee. More important for the future, there was a large minority of conservative Republicans—including Tea Party members—whose commitment to deficit reduction and skepticism of intervention into the affairs of other countries made them supporters of a realistic—i.e., reduced—military budget. To the surprise of neither Mulvaney nor me, the Armed Service Committees of the House and Senate ultimately restored the funds we'd cut. But our win was an important indicator that ever-increasing military budgets would no longer be reflexively accepted. I believe our success helped persuade congressional hawks to abandon their plan to insulate the military from the pain of the 2013 budget sequester.

Looking ahead, the opportunities to cut the military budget are many. One way is to substantially curtail the far-flung network of bases we sustain throughout the world. A presence in South Korea is clearly required given the threat from a North Korea that is governed by a heavily armed lunatic. Reassuring friends in the Middle East who are confronted by a range of hostile fanatics justifies maintaining a presence there, especially a naval one. But the army should be prevented from expanding its mission in Africa. And while an American presence in Europe was needed to protect the poor, war-weakened nations of that continent from an aggressive, heavily armed Stalin, those states are now rich and fully capable of defending themselves— even from a Vladimir Putin.

We can also safely cut back on our capacity to engage in an all-out war with the Soviet Union's Russian successor. I am prepared to err here on the side of safety. We can currently launch thermonuclear attacks via three separate means, known as "the triad": intercontinental ballistic missiles, strategic bombers, or our fleet of nuclear submarines. I propose—seriously—that we instruct the Pentagon to pick two, thereby saving billions of dollars per year. We can also safely cut down—not eliminate—spending on new weapons. Here is where politics intrudes. Taking benefits away from people who have been enjoying them, and count on continuing to do so, is very hard. Never providing the benefit in the first place is much easier. Even if we have to maintain most existing contracts, a decision to scale back future expenditures will yield massive savings.

This program, which is entirely feasible substantively and politically, reduces currently projected spending by more than $1 trillion over the next ten years.

The fact that public opinion in America has moved away from supporting an aggressive military posture is only confirmed by its recent reaction to the savagery of the Islamic State in Iraq and Syria. The efforts by hawks such as McCain, Cheney, and Senator Lindsey Graham to push Obama into a muscular military intervention lacked any political appeal until the gruesome beheading of Americans, and the lack of effective resistance to the murderers as they advanced through Iraq. Even then the public supported air strikes but not ground troops. Tellingly, congressional leaders advised the president to act without any authorizing legislation—reflecting, I am certain, a reluctance among their members to vote for military action in the face of public skepticism. Most important for my argument, the scale of intervention in Syria and Iraq is well within the capability of the smaller military structure I support. It is entirely possible to combine vigorous antiterrorist activity with a substantially reduced military budget. Maintaining overwhelming superiority over barbarous fanatics who have no air force does not require expanding our capacities.

•

There are few comparable opportunities to free up money by making cuts in domestic spending. But there is one area where a change in policy could save billions of dollars a year on the federal, state, and local levels—and even create new revenue sources. It is time to recognize that the glaringly unsuccessful and disruptive battle we have waged in recent decades is not the War on Poverty, but the War on Drugs. Criminalizing a willing adult's decision to ingest substances that do no harm to anyone other than the drug user himself or herself has been ineffective and very expensive. It also leads to crime that harms nonusers.

My advocacy of decriminalizing most drugs stems in substantial part from my libertarian conviction that adults should not be subject to government coercion for choices that primarily affect themselves. But even those who think it is legitimate to prevent people from doing things the rest of us think are bad for them must acknowledge that this war has been a failure.

This case is most easily made with regard to marijuana. The idea that using marijuana is the first step toward substance abuse is true in one respect only: The law treats it that way. But this is beginning to alter. The parallels with same-sex marriage are notable: Growing acceptance of legal marijuana is driven by generational change, and by the fact that once a few jurisdictions removed criminal penalties, the predicted negative consequences of such "permissiveness" failed to materialize. Thus far, voters in Colorado and Washington show few signs of regretting their decisions to allow unrestricted adult use.

I acknowledge that legalizing heroin, cocaine, and other currently illegal substances has little such popular appeal. And I acknowledge further that the case I am making does not extend to all drugs. We must do what we can to stop people from swallowing or injecting substances that increase the likelihood that they will injure others. Of course, there is one substance that does clearly increase the incidence of antisocial behavior. But the prohibition of alcoholic beverages from 1920 to 1933 did more harm than good, and almost no one advocates trying it again.

While I generally disagree with colleagues on the left who believe that the mass of voters are in agreement with us, the evidence is strong that in this case they are. The fear of being considered "soft on drugs" has inhibited my former colleagues in government whose careers began in earlier decades. But the consistent support for relaxing marijuana prohibition in referenda and the accession to office of a newer generation are rapidly changing the political equation. It took too long for the Obama administration to accept legalization on the state level. But once it did acquiesce, there was little negative fallout—which is itself indicative of the changes under way.

In the case of heroin, cocaine, and other substances, there is little support for legalization. But there is growing support for reducing criminal penalties and for offering nonpenal treatment alternatives to those who wish to curtail their habits. Scaling back the War on Drugs in such ways could save as much as $40 billion per year according to the Cato Institute.

•

If government were more solvent, it would also be more successful—and more popular. We could do more to support children in poverty or working families unable to earn enough to live decently even with their best efforts. We could withstand the pressure to cut off benefits to the long-term unemployed, and we could fund rental-housing programs that keep lower-income people from being victimized by the upward pressure on housing costs or even becoming homeless. In addition, we can make a serious effort to provide genuine equality of opportunity for those who, forty years ago, would have gotten manufacturing jobs that paid a decent wage but whose prospects in today's economy are bleak, and whose inadequate income prevents them from enjoying anything close to equality of opportunity.

Two very different chairs of the Federal Reserve gave identical answers when I asked them a compound question: Has inequality in America gone beyond what is healthy for the economy, and if so, what can we do about it? Alan Greenspan and Benjamin Bernanke both told me that inequality was excessive, and both cited greatly increased access to community colleges as a partial remedy. These institutions provide their students with occupational skills that lead to jobs that can support families at a reasonable level, and are not susceptible to going offshore—for example, as technicians who repair television sets and heating systems and other machines.

Since community colleges are primarily funded by state budgets, as those budgets are squeezed, fewer students are able to attend. Meanwhile, those who do attend are more likely to incur unsustainable personal debt loads. Increasing federal aid to states in general and for community colleges in particular would help reduce tuition to an affordable level—and help strengthen the earning power of those in the lower economic sector. More Pell Grant funding for low-income students would also be beneficial, as would lower interest rates on student loans. In 2010, Democrats took a step in this direction when we passed a bill sharply reducing the subsidy that private banks receive when they offer federally guaranteed student loans at no risk to themselves. Unfortunately, a Republican filibuster in the Senate forced a substantial reduction in the program.

Liberals who are serious about spending money must also be serious about saving it. Properly deployed, the money that we can reclaim through sensible defense and drug policies gives us the chance to overcome antigovernment sentiment and redress growing inequality. Increased federal revenue would also relieve the pressure on the two most successful antipoverty, pro-middle-class programs America has ever enacted: Social Security and Medicare.

•

This represents the substance of what I'm advocating as I continue my engagement in policy debate. One postretirement question remains to be answered: What form will this involvement take?

The answer is easy: I will be an advocate, with no organizational affiliation. After devoting forty-five years to collegiality with colleagues, responsiveness to constituents, and figuring out how to maximize my individual input into collective decision making, I have no desire to check what I am doing or saying with anybody else. I am passionately committed to never again being responsible for anybody else's actions or opinions. (Except when it comes to Jim, and in this particular trade-off, I come out ahead. He is asked to explain or defend me much more often than the reverse.)

This means I will make my arguments using every medium of spoken and written communication in which I am proficient. I have made comparatively little use of social media, but I am working on that. I am not optimistic of complete success. (I have been engaged in a lifelong battle with inanimate objects, beginning with an exasperated elementary shop teacher who promised that he would pass me if I would stop touching the tools.) My determination to avoid organizational affiliations also complements my choice to live in two places—I divide my time between Ogunquit, Maine, Jim's longtime home, and Newton, Massachusetts, which has been mine for thirty-five years. (Fortunately, they are only about an hour and a half apart by car.) This arrangement accommodates my teaching and TV appearances and Jim's ongoing work for regular customers of his awning business. It also means he can accompany me on my political rounds—sometimes—and I can—sometimes—watch him surf and snowboard.

When I compare my life now to the life I expected to lead in 1954, I find significant similarities and differences. As in 1954, I plan to devote very little of my political energy to LGBT rights, and almost all of it to supporting a strong role for government in general. Of course, when I was fourteen, I expected to be arguing for more liberal policies within the framework of a broad societal acceptance of government's role. Now that role itself is at issue. Back then there seemed to be no serious chance of winning any battles on behalf of LGBT people like myself. Now many of those battles have been won. What was impossible in 1954—fighting for LGBT equality— became essential and then much less necessary. What was unnecessary then—building support for a strong government role—has now become essential.

Sixty years ago, when I began to think about how to maximize my participation in politics, I understood that it would require the repression of any private life. Today, I cite the emotional damage I inflicted on myself when I speak with younger LGBT people who ask my advice. It took me far too long to achieve a happy, fulfilling domestic existence. Even with my ongoing commitment to the public good, political activity now ranks a very distant second for me. Looking back, I think I was pretty good at my job. Now it is time to be good at life, and with Jim's help, I think I can be.

Appendix 1
Who Did What on Subprime Lending and Regulating Fannie Mae and Freddie Mac

SUBPRIMES

1994: A Democratic Congress passes and Bill Clinton signs the Home Ownership and Equity Protection Act, directing the Federal Reserve System to adopt rules to prevent irresponsible lending.

1994–2006: Fed chair Alan Greenspan explicitly refuses to use this authority, rejecting the urging of Fed governor Edward Gramlich that he do so to deal with an emerging pattern of lending abuses.

1995–2006: Members of the Democratic congressional minority also urge Greenspan to act. The Republican majority supports Greenspan's decision, refusing to allow Democrats to use official committee proceedings to make our case.

2000–2004: Troubled by an increase in imprudent lending practices, advocates persuade several states to adopt laws and rules restricting lending abuses.

2004: The Bush administration uses federal authority to preempt state rules restricting the activities of nationally chartered banks, and urges state-chartered banks to shift to federal charters to escape state regulation. This kills the state regulations on mortgages.

2004–2006: Led by Congressmen Brad Miller and Mel Watt, Democrats begin an effort to pass national subprime regulatory legislation. At first, Republican subcommittee chairman Spencer Bachus negotiates with us, with the Democrats favoring stronger rules. But the House Republican leadership directs the Financial Services Committee to drop these efforts, and no legislation can be produced. (Republicans are still in the majority.)

2007: Democrats are in the majority for the first time since 1994. In November, the House adopts a tough antipredatory lending bill. *The Wall Street Journal* and conservative Republicans on the committee angrily denounce it as an interference with the free market and praise subprime loans for helping poor people become homeowners.

2008: Prodded by House action, and not wanting to lose the initiative on the issue, Ben Bernanke leads the Fed to adopt rules under its HOEPA authority for the first time since the law passed fourteen years earlier.

2009: The House readopts the subprime bill and includes it in Wall Street Reform (aka the Dodd-Frank Act).

2010: The Senate agrees to accept the subprime bill in the conference committee on the Wall Street Reform bill, and it becomes law upon the president's signature.

2013: The Consumer Financial Protection Bureau adopts tough rules effectively prohibiting irresponsible mortgage lending.

FANNIE AND FREDDIE

1992: Large majorities of both parties in both houses adopt a bill that includes amendments to the charters of Fannie and Freddie, creating their structure for the next fifteen years. President George H. W. Bush signs it.

2003: President George W. Bush asks Congress to amend that law and tighten controls on Fannie and Freddie. The Republican-controlled House and Senate decline to act. Barney Frank expresses support for the institutions, especially their role in supporting multifamily rental housing. The Republican House committee chair does not schedule any action on the bill.

2005: The Republican-controlled House adopts a bill to tighten restrictions on Fannie and Freddie. It is supported by a majority of Republican votes in committee and on the floor. Barney Frank votes yes with the Republican majority in committee but votes no on the floor because the House leadership waters down a separate provision calling for a trust fund to build rental housing outside of Fannie Mae and Freddie Mac. The bill passes the House anyway over Frank's housing-based objection (rebutting the suggestion that he was secretly in control on this issue). Bush treasury secretary John Snow supports the bill.

2005–2006: At the urging of President Bush, the Republican Senate rejects the Fannie-Freddie bill passed by the Republican House as too weak. Senate Democrats support the House Republican bill. But the Republican split dooms the legislation.

2006: House and Senate Republicans drop the effort to enact GSE legislation. Republican House committee chair Mike Oxley later explains that GSE reform died because President Bush gave him "the one-finger salute."

2006: Hank Paulson becomes secretary of the treasury and persuades Bush to let him approach Congress again.

2006: Paulson asks Barney Frank to work with him on a new bill. Frank agrees.

2007: With Democrats now in the majority for the first time in twelve years, committee chairman Frank makes this bill an early item on the committee agenda.

2007: The Financial Services Committee passes a bill that Paulson supports, although he says it is less than perfect.

2007: The House passes the bill including the undiluted version of the trust fund to build low-income rental housing.

2008: The organization named FM Watch, formed to push for legislation to reform Fannie and Freddie, dissolves, noting that Frank and Paulson successfully collaborated to accomplish their goals.

2008: As the economy worsens, the House passes an additional bill to deal with foreclosures.

2008: Paulson, Senate Democrats, and House Democrats work out a comprehensive housing bill that includes the reforms Paulson seeks in the rules for Fannie and Freddie, including the power to put them into conservatorship.

2008: In September, Paulson decides to exercise that power. He fears Fannie and Freddie will use their congressional support to resist, so he calls Barney Frank and receives Frank's assurance that he will support the move.

2010: Republicans seek to include a provision leading to the complete abolition of Fannie and Freddie in the conference committee on the Wall Street Reform bill. Barney Frank rules it out of order. Republicans object strongly, insisting that there is an urgent need to act on the subject.

2011: Republicans regain control of the House and refuse to bring their 2010 amendment up for consideration by the Financial Services Committee.

2011: Republicans pass a dozen small amendments to the Fannie and Freddie rules in committee but take no further action.

2011–2013: The Republican-controlled House adjourns without having taken action on the Fannie-Freddie legislation that they argued for in 2010.

2013–2014: The Republican-controlled House continues to take no action on Fannie-Freddie legislation. It is now more than four years since they objected to the exclusion of their bill from the Wall Street Reform bill, insisting that action was urgently needed.

Appendix 2
Conservative Support for Subprime Loans to Minority and Very Low-Income People Before the Economic Crisis

June 2002: President Bush at a press conference announcing "America's Home-ownership Challenge" to the real estate and mortgage finance industries: "The goal is, everybody who wants to own a home has got a shot at doing so."

June 12, 2003: Bush appointee HUD secretary Mel Martinez, testimony before the Senate Committee on Banking, Housing and Urban Affairs:

> The administration wants every family to benefit from our emphasis on home ownership. However, because they face special obstacles on the road to owning their own homes, we're specifically reaching out to minority communities.
>
> The minority home ownership gap, Mr. Chairman, you pointed out during your comments, exists. We want to see what we can do to contract it, to reduce it, while at the same time improving the lives of so many more families.
>
> The barriers that we have found include the *inability to come up with enough cash* for a down payment, *a lack of credit history or a blemished credit record*, discrimination, and the unfamiliar terms and unreliable information that are often part of the homebuying process [emphasis added].
>
> President Bush and I consider removing these barriers and eliminating the home ownership gap to be a top priority for HUD, and one that is fundamental to our mission as the nation's housing agency.

Mark Zandi, *Financial Shock* (2008):

> Democrats in Congress were worried about increasing evidence of predatory lending. Some noted that the 2001 rule prohibiting such lending only applied to federally regulated lenders. North Carolina had passed a law banning predatory practices in 1999, and the Democrats wanted a federal

equivalent that would cover all lenders nationwide. The Bush administration and most Republicans in Congress were opposed, believing legislation would overly restrict lending and thus slow the march of home ownership; moreover, the Republicans argued, existing regulations were adequate to discourage the worst excesses. The last attempt to pass anti-predatory lending legislation occurred in 2005, but it was also stymied.

Alan Greenspan, *The Age of Turbulence* (2007):

I was aware that the loosening of mortgage credit terms for subprime borrowers increased financial risk, and that subsidized home ownership initiatives distort market outcomes. But I believed then, as now, that the benefits of broadened home ownership are worth the risk. Protection of property rights, so critical to a market economy, requires a critical mass of owners to sustain political support.

Alan Greenspan, in an interview with Greg Ip of *The Wall Street Journal*, June 9, 2007:

There is "a very large number of small institutions, some on the margin of scrupulousness and very hard to detect when they are doing something wrong," says Mr. Greenspan, who retired in February last year. "For us to go in and audit how they act on their mortgage applications would have been a huge effort, and it's not clear to me we would have found anything that would have been worthwhile without undermining the desired availability of subprime credits."

Representative Jeb Hensarling (R-TX), October 24, 2007, committee hearing, speaking in opposition to the Mortgage Reform and Anti-Predatory Lending Act of 2007:

We still have to remember that millions of people have homeownership opportunities due to a subprime market. I am very leery of any legislation that could undercut that market . . . We should also take note about what is happening in the marketplace now. The market has a wonderful ability to correct itself.

Representative Scott Garrett (R-NJ), November 6, 2007, committee markup, speaking in opposition to the Mortgage Reform and Anti-Predatory Lending Act of 2007:

The increasing availability and affordability of subprime mortgage credit is and has been an important factor leading to the increase in home ownership in recent years. This bill may well limit now the products available to subprime borrowers, particularly minority borrowers, and will deprive many of those consumers from owning or maintaining a home . . . What we need to do is ensure that it does absolutely nothing to home ownership, particularly among minority communities who have benefited from the innovations that have occurred in the marketplace.

Wall Street Journal editorial, "A Sarbox for Housing," November 6, 2007:

As early as today, Mr. Frank plans to hold a committee vote on his Mortgage Reform and Anti-Predatory Lending Act of 2007 . . . For the first time, banks that securitize mortgages would be made "explicitly liable for violations of lending laws." This is a version of secondary liability that holds the bundlers and resellers of mortgages responsible for the sins of the original lenders. The reselling of mortgages has been a boon both to housing liquidity and risk diversification. So to the extent the Frank bill adds a new risk element to securitizing subprime loans—and it surely will—the main losers will be subprime borrowers who will pay higher rates if they can get a loan at all . . . But for all the demonizing, about 80% of even subprime loans are being repaid on time and another 10% are only 30 days behind. Most of these new homeowners are low-income families, often minorities, who would otherwise not have qualified for a mortgage. In the name of consumer protection, Mr. Frank's legislation will ensure that far fewer of these loans are issued in the future.

Acknowledgments

I have tried in the book itself to note the great debt I owe to the talented, generous people who made my career possible. An appendix of a hundred pages would have been necessary to include all who are in that category. These formal acknowledgments are limited to those who had a direct role in helping me as I wrote this book.

My agent, Eric Lupfer, of William Morris Endeavor Entertainment, played a crucial role from the beginning in alternately advising and reassuring me. Alex Star, my editor at FSG, has been perfect from my perspective in understanding what I was trying to do, and helping me to do it better.

My friend of fifty years, Andy Tobias, made time in a very busy schedule to read the first hundred pages and urged me to keep on at a time when I was self-doubting.

Courtney Flynn, the personal assistant who has done a remarkable job replacing the several dozen staff aides I had while in office, has been an indispensable mediator between me and my computer. She is one of two people who translated the results of my two-fingered, clumsy typing into English.

The other translator is Geoffrey Browning, who also did an excellent job as my research assistant, drawing on his considerable computer skills and his own knowledge of how Congress works.

And then there's Jim. In this effort, as in every other part of my life since 2007, he has been indispensable. Writing this book was hard. Without Jim's constant advice, encouragement, and emotional support when I needed it—in sum, without his love—it would have been impossible.

Index